"*I dedicate this book, to the Glorification of God,*

for the service of humanity

and

for the furtherance of ***PURE LOVE.***"

A Mission of LOVE

by   ORISHUA

the
spiritual
messenger

Unity Books.

Published by		Unity Books
Address	:	P.O.Box 218
		East Ham
		London E6 4BG
		ENGLAND
Publication Date	:	1st July 2001
Copyright	:	© Dounne Alexander 2001
ISBN	**:**	**0 9519064 1 0**
Printers	:	Bath Press Ltd
		Bath, United Kingdom
Typesetting/Illustration	:	M. Moore
Design	:	M. Moore
Proof Readers	:	Rudolph Walker, Dee Moore
		Valerie Harmsworth,
Editors	:	Dounne Alexander, Patricia Bishop

ACKNOWLEDGMENTS.

It is true to say that we really do not make it on our own. Along the way there is usually an army of supporters, who increase our strength, reassure, support, raise our confidence and spur us on. Some we remember for specific reasons or special moment but many others... whose names we may have even forgotten, came into our lives just for a split second and touched us in a very special way.

I have been blessed to be touched by so many, that it is difficult to find the words to truly express my full thanks, gratitude and appreciation to everyone who has prayed, supported, motivated and assisted me throughout these trying years... my family, friends, customers, suppliers, the British media and stores. Individually and collectively you have all given me the 'will to survive' and the realisation that people need people. However, special acknowledgement goes to:-

- My daughters (Marsha and Dee), my mum and dad, (James and the late Beryl Alexander) and my husband (Rudolph Walker), for choosing me to be a part of their lives and filling me with so much joy, positive energy, unconditional love and endless support.

- My grandmother, (the late Wilhelmina Dallaway), for teaching me dedication, humanity, universal love, respect, dignity, humility and faith in God.

- My Ancestors, Spirit Masters and Guides, for all their teachings, wisdom and faithful guidance.

And above all else, I thank God, for giving me the talent, vision, faith, fighting spirit, courage, protection, blessings and eternal life.

"My personal and sincere THANKS to every one of you for keeping me sane, focussed and helping me to make it across the treacherous road called survival."

This is a mind blowing true story about a British Caribbean woman, Dounne Alexander, who in 1996, came face to face with God. She was told that HE wished to reveal HIS truths to the world through her. God warned her against fanaticism and told her not to form any churches, religions, cults, nor have followers. We should not be forced to believe but instead, encouraged to use our 'free-will,' follow our own minds and learn how to live in the 'consciousness of universal love.'

Dounne's mission included the writing of this book, which contains profound and prophetic messages for the 21st century. HE revealed her spirit name - ORISHUA - which means 'the power of the Seventh Star,' the spiritual messenger, communicator and teacher. HE also told her about the purpose for which she was sent to serve.

In addition, Dounne has to establish the 'first of July' as an annual day of love, to be observed as 'The Celebration of Life.' This amazing story thus shows her transformation from an enterprising business-woman, into a missionary working for love.

This is a powerful, extraordinary journey of self discovery; entwining real life experiences, showing the incredible ability of the human Spirit to triumph over adversity. It is a journey which takes you into the realms of spirituality and by this means, reveals your own divinity. It proves that spirituality is both natural and real and has nothing to do with indoctrinated religious beliefs and confirms God's existence. It looks at life uncompromisingly through pure spiritual eyes, which is pivotal for our existence and survival.

What makes this encounter even more fascinating, is that Dounne is just an ordinary person, who simply believes in God and considers herself 'a child of the universe.' She has no great knowledge or powers but noticed that for some unknown reason, the number '7' has always played an important role in her life. All the lessons and teachings were given by God, Spirit Masters and Guardian Angels... important lessons of life, which the world would be well advised to heed.

This is not a doomsday book. Instead, it is a 'ray of hope' for the future, offering you 'a torch light' to search within, whilst unveiling God's truth. It carefully places the challenges, controls and responsibilities into your own hands. The story eventually brings you to the realisation that if you desire change of any kind (whether personal or universal), it can only occur through conscious awareness, individual choice, commitment, motivation and positive actions. In other words, only YOU can change things for better or worse. Hence, although the book is about Dounne's life, it's ultimate focus is on YOU but without placing you under any obligations, conditions, impositions or demands. It simply suggest that you read it with an open-mind, then to

THINK & ACT accordingly.

ACCEPT Nothing

REJECT Nothing

but **CONSIDER** all Things

(God's words; August 1997).

A Mission of

Love

by **ORISHUA**

the
spiritual
messenger

CONTENTS.

A Mission of Love

BOOK 1

CHAPTER III.

For the Love of Zara... cancer recovery story 313

CHAPTER IV.

Health 2000 363

BOOK 2

BOOK 3

A Mission of LOVE

by ORISHUA

the
spiritual
messenger

BOOK ONE.

CHAPTER I.

Personal Background.

"I've come to realise why God is such a
forgiving & loving God, because He knows our

TRUE HEARTS.

When others may only see the **bad in us,**
God knows of the **good in us**."

A Natural Survivor

I made my unexpected entry into this world prematurely on 28th January 1949, the fourth of six children. My mother had a history of difficult pregnancies; many miscarriages and four stillbirths. I am the only premature survivor and even then, the doctors gave me just one month to live... but my grandmother's faith, herbal knowledge, tender loving care and my fighting spirit, formed a successful survival combination.

So I came into this world before my time, struggling and fighting for precious life and survived against the odds. It has taken over fifty years to realise that this is the way my life has always been and I now believe there was and still is, a meaningful purpose for every pain, agony, elation and continuous fight. In my short stay, I've experienced almost all of life's ups and downs but each new experience brought with it added inner strength and determination to fight on, whilst at the same time giving first-hand knowledge to enable me to understand others undergoing the same problems and providing some of the solutions to overcome them. It has given full meaning to the phrase:-

'She who feels it - knows it!'

So now that I am certain of my direction, I have learnt to accept life as a great adventure, each experience teaching me a valuable, enriching, worthwhile, triumphant lesson. Traumas or disappointments no longer distress and hurt me as much as before; mole-hills are no longer mountains and the scales of life are gradually balancing.

I have learnt to turn all my NEGATIVE oppositions, responses and rejections (timely minor set-backs) into POSITIVE thoughts and actions. Rather than allow them to serve their destructive purpose to deter, frustrate and make me give up, I use them to strive forward. I simply sort out other ways and means to achieve my goals without having to sell my soul. My priority has always been *'survival'* which simply goes to prove that:- **'POSITIVE against negative achieves RESULTS.'** For example; I'm not a professional writer, hence attempting to write this book has been a feat in itself, bringing both joyous and painful memories with floods of emotions. In the past, I've used writing as a form of therapy to defuse anger, which I found useful particularly during the early years of my business, as a method of grappling with the uncharted territories of racism within the British bureaucratic establishment. It resulted in the publication of my first book, 'The Black Cinderella' and I do believe that it was also my preparation for writing this second book. However, this time the negativities were deeply personal. You see, I don't like writing, not even as a hobby. I'm also a very private person and would have preferred not to expose the spiritual side of my life, especially as in the past, I use to be very critical of churches and disbelieved anyone who said they were called by God to do HIS work. So you can imagine my surprise, to find myself not only being CALLED but to also publicly expose how, when and why. I knew I would face the same judgement, proving the 'Laws of Karma.' So I had to fight my own demons to overcome and win this battle. The positive results were even more rewarding, as it helped me to confront, deal with, release and come to terms with many hidden problems, pain, insecurities, deep rooted fears and to appreciate life with all of its complications. In other words, it has freed me and I'm now ready and prepared to deal with whatever life dishes out, because I've learnt that 'SURVIVAL' means 'never giving up, as well as, the importance of sharing one's experience, in order to teach.' I later learnt that most autobiographies are not actually written by the authors themselves but by professional writers. Whereas, I've written, co-edited and published the entire book with the help of my own private 'ghost writers' (i.e. God and my Spirit-Helpers). Furthermore, having the ability to communicate spiritually, intuitively and physically, has not only given me the strength to overcome so many adversities but has also provided great comfort in times of depression; as well as positive guidance and the reassurance that *"all will be well - in the end."* I'm now just happy to be alive.

In this book, I've chronicled specific life changing episodes, which unfold a maze of experiences that brings you full circle to arrive at who you really are and for what purpose you are sent to serve.

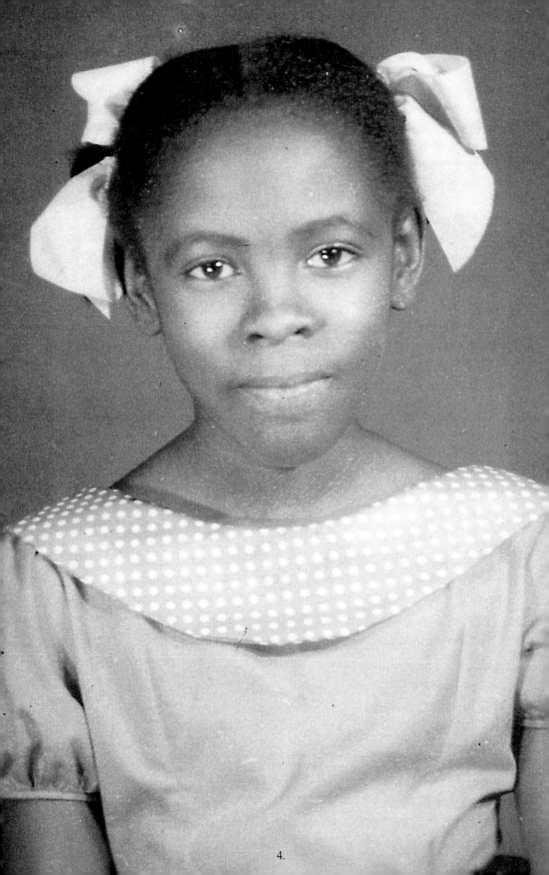

My Dual Up-Bringing

'In the Caribbean and Britain.'

It was my good fortune to have experienced a dual upbringing in the Caribbean and Britain. Two extreme cultures yet one and the same.

I was born on the twin Caribbean island of Trinidad & Tobago which was then part of the British Empire, so we were ruled, governed and schooled as British subjects. My teachers were mainly English, Scottish and Irish nuns, I even performed Scottish and Irish dancing in authentic costumes at school concerts. Every child was taught the British National Anthem which had to be sung weekly in Assembly. History lessons were more on British history and we were frequently reminded of our parents' and ancestors' patriotism, loyalty, pride, obedience and service to the Queen and our 'Mother Country' as Britain was commonly called. School days were great, as teachers took personal pride in all their children and encouraged us to excel in everything we did. This sense of pride did not only relate to exam results but covered all aspects of personal presentation and grooming... i.e. clean, washed and well moisturised bodies; combed hair; neat, clean, ironed uniforms; clean shoes and socks; neat legible hand-writing; good behaviour, manners and punctuality. In other words - well turned out and disciplined. They knew, that if we all took the time each morning to carefully prepare and present ourselves in the correct manner for school, this would instill both personal pride and discipline; which would remain with us throughout our lives. I'm proud to confirm that they were right, because to this day, I make sure that I'm always well prepared and properly groomed to face and meet anyone, which I later instilled in my own British born children, plus I always strive to achieve excellence and do my best.

However, the other beauty of Caribbean life was that everyone knew each other and watched out for one another. There was a strong sense of family; pride and community responsibility. Discipline and respect especially to adults, was paramount. Rudeness (as it was called) was never tolerated; we could not be insolent to any adult, including our parents, neighbours, teachers or strangers. Every child knew that if they were caught misbehaving in the street, they'd be chastised by whoever caught them, who in turn would certainly inform their parents and they'd be chastised again. This kept youngsters on the straight and narrow, because all eyes were on them and there was no getting away from punishment. Nevertheless, we still found inventive ways to be a little naughty and escape the consequences, by cleverly watching out for and protecting each other's butts. This created adventurous games, excitement and instilled trust by holding our little secrets. We used to whisper to each other, *"don't tell nobody you know!"* Many of our secrets were kept for life, many were forgotten altogether. So we had a great time with lots of fun and games. Our only responsibility was to work hard at school, be obedient, behave ourselves and make our parents proud.

Parents also took extreme pride in raising their children and would literally have died if any brought shame on the family. They set firm examples:- *"do as I do,"* which meant having to be mindful of their own actions, manners and words in the presence of children. For instance:- it was customary for adults to greet each other in the street with a loud and definite *"good morning, good evening or good night,"* accompanied with a pleasant smile. This greeting was also extended to children and strangers. So naturally, the children followed suit.

This warmth created an atmosphere of friendship and safety, to the extent that doors were often left unlocked and people could walk the streets at night, without fear of attack or crime. So you see, 'neighbourhood watch' was in vogue long before now and was far more effective, because adults set the examples and took direct responsibility for instilling the right sense of values, discipline and respect. Although these values were often reinforced with a great deal of fear and physical punishment, the majority of those children who are now adults and parents today, actually 'bless' their parents for their strictness, claiming that it did them more good than harm. Most never got involved or led a life of crime, because they never forgot the licks (i.e. flogging) they received for doing wrong. However, there is a fine line between corrective punishment and physical abuse. It is true that, *"it takes a village to raise a child."*

As a child, I was extremely quiet, thin, with thick long hair, an innocent face and was exceptionally obedient. I was raised in a strict Catholic household; where what the neighbours thought of us was more important to our parents, than what we really were on the inside... the false pretentious attitude, typical of affluent upper class folk. We lived in a very large house which my father designed and had built. It had huge living and dinning rooms with beautiful chandelier lights, fully fitted kitchen with a breakfast bar, four large bedrooms, separate bathrooms with bidets; on the ground floor there was a servants apartment, plus garage. Mum always had a lived in servant to help with the household chores.

Everything was lavish but false, because although our parents loved us; we could never be our true-selves, as everything was just for show. I became known as the quiet/shy/studious one, who kept to herself, hardly spoke and never quite fitted in. My timidness used to aggravate my sisters who frequently abused me. Yet because of my Spirit-Guides, I never felt lonely or unhappy as they'd show me the wickedness of their ways and the blessings of forgiveness. I longed to become a nun. My grandmother (my Mum's mother) would tell me all the beautiful biblical stories about God, love and angels. The Church also taught that we all had a Guardian Angel, sent by God to guide, protect and teach us 'right from wrong' and if we wanted to go to heaven, then we must obey our Guardian Angel. I was absolutely obedient, because I was determined to get into heaven. As far back as I can remember, I've always heard, listened to, learnt from and communicated with my Guardian Angels (or Spirit-Guides). I never spoke to anyone about it, because I believed it to be natural and thought that everyone else was also doing the same. Similar to the way we pray in private... no one would tell each other about their private thoughts to God. I looked upon it as the unspoken truth and accepted norm, simply because the Church, the Priest, the Bible or God would not tell lies. However, I considered myself as very lucky, because, whereas everyone only had just one Guardian Angel; I had lots. So I've been guided throughout my life, which doesn't make my life easier than anyone else's, because we all have to go through our own life experiences in order to learn and grow. Therefore, what some people might call unusual is perfectly natural to me. It is as simple as this:

Most people only use their **physical senses** but I use all of my senses, i.e. **physical and spiritual.** For instance, most only use their two physical eyes to see with, whereas I have learnt to use my three eyes; 'the third' one being my spiritual eye, which provides vision beyond this limited reality. Hence, I see visions when I pray, dream or meditate. So you see; *"there is more to life, than meets the eye."*

So under this strong religious and spiritual influence, plus my absolute love for God, I acquired this overwhelming desire to become a nun. I wanted to reject all material things; go into isolation and pray for world peace. In my innocent mind, I believed that this was the way God would want me to sacrifice all personal pleasures and devote myself to HIM in total prayer. I loved God and the world so much, that I really felt my prayers would make a difference. But as I grew up, I started to question the dictates of the Catholic Church. There were many things I had found uncomfortable including;-

- rumours of child molestation and abuse;

- secret love affairs between nuns and priests;

- drinking alcohol during church service;

- smoking cigarettes;

- instilling guilt, suffering, secrecy and extreme fear of God, instead of Love;

- confessing our innocent minor misdemeanours to priests, who made us believe that we had committed a grave sin;

- priests and nuns acting as if they were so 'Holy and Chaste' egotistically putting themselves above us ordinary mortal-beings and being treated like gods; instead of showing that they were just ordinary people who had chosen to serve God through the Priesthood and who were as susceptible to sin and other weaknesses like the rest of us;

- why didn't they marry and how could they advise or reconcile conflicts, having no experience or understanding of marital/parental pressures;

- the church's stance against contraception, encouraging poor people to have lots of children which they couldn't afford, whilst still having to keep the church and its priests (i.e. our weekly collection money);

- why weren't priests allowed to work in regular paid employment, instead of sponging off the poor;

- people with personal or financial problems, encouraged to beg their priest to 'pray to God on their behalf,' believing that the priests were closer to God.

- why were homosexuals persecuted? Would a *'God of love,'* abandon or ostracize any of HIS children?

It seemed as if priests were using people's poverty to instill a mind-set that misery, sacrifice, fear and belief in the church, as the only acceptable route to God which guaranteed entry into heaven. The more I questioned, the more quietly rebellious I became. I couldn't understand why, as a young child, I had so many doubts, yet the older folks never questioned and simply followed along like brain-washed dummies. They couldn't see that they were 'economical slaves' driven by fear. My understanding of a loving, forgiving God, was that HE created us with power and creative ability and wanted us to be happy. In comparison, I noticed that all in the clergy, including the Pope, appeared to be living in grandeur with all the necessary comforts - at poor people's expense. Did Christ need expensive buildings, designer clothes or jewellery to do his work? If there was truly only one GOD, why were there so many different religions and why couldn't we inter-marry? My youthful rebellion grew stronger as I got older but was horrified when I later learnt that there were priests who had molested untold numbers of innocent children and that the church had secretly paid out millions from our poor collection funds, to protect and harbour these criminals, plus many were also gay, yet preaching that homosexuality was against God...**living a lie in God's name.**

MANY are CALLED, but few are CHOSEN.

To add to these conflicts, I also had to deal with my parents and ancestors strong faith in God; their preparation to face and meet death as the ultimate glorious end of their miserable lives on earth; believing in 'life eternal,' they welcomed death and rejoiced over it; whilst mixing Western/Christian believes with ancient African spiritualism, mysticism, superstition and rituals. Coming from this dual religious/spiritual background, made me very sceptical and non-superstitious. I'd deliberately walk under a ladder, just for the hell of it, because my God is practical, considerate and realistic.

One day my grandmother said to me, *"Child, you must enjoy your youth to the full, because before long, you are old and its too late. You must also remember to allow your children to enjoy their youth."* I realised that she was quietly rebelling against her childhood, because in those days, girls had to work hard and grew up fast; becoming mothers from about the age of 14 years and because the Church was against contraception, they had lots of children; herself bearing 8 children. This meant they had little time for fun, no independence and before long they were old women. In their own simple way, they accepted their lot and enjoyed what life they had, which was mainly around their children and family. Hence, the extended family formed an essential part of their lives. But my grandmother also meant that 'at the stage of youth, you are at the peak of your glory; beautiful; full of zest, energy, firm and lively;' which is all lost through the weakening wear and tear of old age. What a wise old lady! She showed me that God did not intend for people to live in lonely, miserable isolation and steered me into the direction of going out and living life to the full. Fortunately, this was around the time when women were becoming independent and full-time professional careers were gaining acceptance. Whereas in my grandmother's time, 'a woman's place' was exclusively in the home; they were dependant on their husbands; open to physical and mental abuse. Divorce was an unacceptable sin to the church, so many women were forced to suffer in silence... yet they too survived.

However, I still religiously attended church; got married in the church, christened and baptised my children in the church, even though my husband was not a Catholic. It was not until 1979, (in Britain), whilst attending a church service that my youngest daughter Dee (who was then 5 years old) spotted a negro woman crying in despair, hugging and kissing the feet of the statue of St Anthony. Dee (being inquisitive) asked, *"Mum, what is that lady doing?"* When I looked, all my youthful anger surged, I then told my daughters,` *"take a good long look at that poor lady, never ever in your life bow down, pray or cry to any statue, because it is only a piece of stone, carved out and painted by some man; it is not God and cannot help you in anyway. This is the last time we are going to church. From now on I'll teach you about the God of love; who is the only one that can help you and the only one you are allowed to bow down to."* My children were not going to be brainwashed into believing in statues, no matter who it was and so from then on I taught them *"how to speak to God."* This does not mean that I believe churches do not have an important role to play in teaching and bringing people closer to God. I've simply chosen not to believe in any particular church. If on the off chance, I felt like going to church, then I'd go into any one which would allow me to enter it as a 'House of God' because my intention is simply to pray to God but not to belong to or believe in the church itself. Similarly, if a friend invites me to his/her church for a special occasion (like a wedding, baptism, festival or funeral), I'd go as a mark of respect to my friend.

In other words, *"I respect people's beliefs, as long as they believe in God or in which other divine name they choose to call HIM."*

❀ Spiritual Guidance.

I prefer to live a spiritual, rather than a religious life, as it has taught me to take full control and responsibility for all my actions. Spirituality also makes me aware of my own divinity and connects me to God. This does not mean that I receive spiritual guidance everyday or throughout the day. It only happens if and when my Guides want to talk or show me something. It occurred more frequently when I was a child, because I needed comfort, love and understanding (i.e. once or twice weekly, monthly or longer). I was allowed to live my life without focussing on my Guides all the time but I was aware that they were always there for me, when ever I needed them. With hindsight, most of the people around me were always unhappy or dissatisfied, whereas I generally felt happy, contented and at peace but concerned by the sadness I could see in others. I wore a constant smile which became my trademark but which also covered up my own inner pains. I've only been hurt by the people around me (i.e. family and friends) but never ever by my Guides, who compensated with so much love that I was able to endure much more than most. Their guidance and lessons made me strong, resilient and forever hopeful. To this day, everyone comments on my smile, which now radiates and reflects pure joy.

❀ Life With My Grandmother.

My grandmother's lifestyle was the complete opposite to my high society parents. She was poor country folk, had absolutely no luxuries; was unconfused and uncomplicated, whose simple ancient wisdom reigned supreme. It was here I spent many weekends and school holidays at her side, being nurtured and taught all the beauties of Love and Life; which has made me who and what I am today. The continuation of her lessons are the embodiment of GRAMMA'S (my business) initially named in her loving memory.

'Ma' (as we called her) and my grandfather 'Pa,' lived in a little mud/clay house which had three small bedrooms, a little living room and a tiny kitchen. Pa was the village baker and farmer. He had a huge mud/clay oven in the yard, with a large wooden platter to shove in and pull out the bread tins. You could smell his baking for miles. We used to gather around, (mouths dribbling) whilst anxiously waiting for him to hand us a hot loaf straight out of the oven. Nothing beats freshly baked hot bread, laced with salted butter. His sweet buns were simply the best.

The moment I arrived in the countryside, I used to feel free from all my parents trappings. I remember as a little girl jumping out of my father's car and before I could open the garden gate, my shoes and socks were in my hands; shouting *"Ma, Ma,"* before I reached the steps, I was pulling off the large ribbon bow from my Sunday best church dress, before long I was down to my vest and panty. Ma would come out smiling with arms stretched out, lift me up, kiss me and say *"my child."* I was home and in the arms that I belonged. She had acres of naturally fertilised land filled with every type of flower, fruit tree, herb and vegetable that one could find in the entire Caribbean, plus chickens, turkeys, pigs and ducks. She wanted for nothing. To me these were the real riches; wallowing in the midst of nature; running barefoot in the bush, smelling the sweet pure air, picking, eating fresh fruits and bathing in heavenly clean rain water. Meals were simple, tasty and freshly cooked every day; Ma was a great cook. Sometimes we'd pick cashew nuts and at night, sit round a bonfire in the yard, roasting and eating fresh hot cashew nuts, beneath a bright moon and twinkling stars. We'd sing songs and tell stories. At bedtime, I was the only one who slept with Ma. I'd watch her light a candle and she'd call me aside and we'd pray. Ma always had time for me and understood my simple, quiet ways. She also told me stories about Marcus Garvey and other black revolutionaries.

I was only 13 years when Ma died and I experienced for the first time the great pain of losing someone I loved dearly. I felt that a part of me had also died, because my closest friend and confidant was gone. Although I had a large family, I felt alone. I use to sit in her room and quietly sing her favourite songs 'Three coins in a fountain' and 'Sometimes I feel like a motherless child'. Shortly after her death, she started to visit me in dreams and continued to guide me. For example, months before my parents told us that we were going to live in Britain, I dreamt Ma, who took me (in Spirit) to England and showed me where we were going to live. She also showed me my first husband. Whilst at school in Britain, I was having problems with mathematics, in a dream Ma took me to my Uncle Simon who was a school Headmaster in Trinidad and he showed me how to solve it. Since then, she has always been there for me. Ma was and still is, the only 'true angel' I've ever met on this earth.

My father's parents died when I was very young, so I didn't know them well but I'm told that I resemble his mother (Emilda Alexander) who was a French/Creole and possess her gentle/stern ways.

A New Life In Britain

In 1963 my parents decided to immigrate to Britain. Mum, Dad, my younger sister, cousin and I, arrived in December (a month before my 16th birthday) on a freezing foggy day. We were going to stay with my mother's brother... Uncle Gus and his family, who lived in a little rural village called Ingatestone in the county of Essex. This was an upper/middle class 'white' area, where only a handful of black people lived. We were all very excited but on the journey I couldn't help noticing that all the trees had no leaves and everywhere looked a depressingly grey colour; in contrast to the bright Caribbean sunshine and vibrant flora. I soon realised that December was not the best month to arrive or to see Britain's rural beauty.

We experienced our first English Christmas and to our disappointment it did not snow. I thought Britain always had a 'White Christmas.' I also experienced the first quaint English custom of kissing under a mistletoe bush, which soon became a well practiced habit.

Within a few months, we moved several miles away to Goodmayes (still in Essex), rented the top floor of a house owned by a wonderful Jamaican couple, Mr and Mrs Cummings. In true Caribbean style as children, we called them Aunty and Uncle. They were middle aged and had no children, so we were instantly adopted as their own. Uncle was a true gentleman, very humourous, who reminded me of Bill Cosby (the American actor/comedian). Aunty was short, (just under 5 feet) and softly spoken. They were extremely kind, generous and frequently took us on outings to London's famous historical sites. Aunty's hair was very fine and was always at her wits end when it came to styling it. I quickly became her hairdresser and kept her fashionable. Although we only lived with them for about a year, our relationship became one of an extended family and we kept in touch throughout the years. Aunty and Uncle Cummings were one of the happiest couples I have ever met. They were truly loving, compatible soul-mates.

Within 18 months we'd bought our first house, just a few streets away. We were the only black family but our neighbours welcomed and treated us with absolute respect and accepted us as part of their community. Our Caribbean way of life was fully appreciated and of course! Mum and Dad soon befriended everyone.

I was enrolled in Canon Palmer Roman Catholic School. It took a little while to settle and to get used to their strange method of teaching. My teachers and friends went out of their way to make me feel welcome and comfortable. My only surprise and disappointment was that my proud, upright, loyal, obedient British indoctrination and patriotism was not taught in British schools, nor was there any traditional dancing; not once was the British National Anthem ever played or sung, plus the children were rude, untidy and ill-behaved. I knew more about British history and the Empire than the British children, who also didn't speak or write the Queen's English. In fact, there were so many English dialects that I collapsed in a fit of laughter, when I first heard cockney rhyming slang... dog & bone means phone, apples & pears means stairs, etc. In other regions their accents sounded more like a foreign language as the English was inaudible. I became even more confused to learn of the disharmony between the Irish, the Scottish and the Welsh, who all genuinely hated the English and wanted separate rule. *"A United Kingdom that was divided?"* To make matters worse there were anti-royalists among the British people. No way would you find an anti-Royalist amongst British Caribbeans:- *"We have been flying the flag long before we flew to Britain."* This was not the Great Britain I had learnt about in the Caribbean. However, I never experienced any personal difficulties from the ordinary British people; not in my neighbourhood, at school or later at work. I was always treated as the blue-eyed girl, never had promotional difficulties or forced into stereotypical roles.

I remember when I was almost ready to leave school at age 17. My Headmaster called me into his office to discuss my career options. I told him I wanted to become a nurse, not realising that this was the typical jobs offered to black people. He simply said, *"I don't think so! You are excellent at the Sciences (Chemistry, Biology & Physics) and should consider a career that would advance your natural talents."* But I insisted, mainly because I loved the story about Florence Nightingale and felt my role in life was to help, heal and give comfort to the sick... very romantic. He then decided that if I wanted to do nursing, I should become a Physiotherapist and arranged for me to have three days work experience in the local mental hospital, after which we'd discuss the matter again, if I was still adamant. My mother worked at the hospital and was not too happy with my career choice. To this day, I believe that both my mother and headmaster conspired to put me off.

On the first day, my mother accompanied me around the hospital, explaining in great depth the various patients, their conditions and treatments, leaving the worst for last. After experiencing the electrical shock treatment room; watching a young woman's head being wired up, hands and legs strapped to the chair for restraint, then the gruesome electric shocks administered - that was it! My nursing dreams were over. To add to this shock, I recognised one of the patients as a young girl who used to be in my school and questioned, *"how could such a young child be crazy?"* I couldn't handle the painful emotions. On our way home that evening, Mum quietly told me; *"if you ever have the misfortune of becoming mentally ill in this country, do not let them put you into a mental hospital, because you will go in SANE; but by the time they are done using experimental drugs and electric shocks to keep you quiet (zombified), you will certainly leave **insane**."* I looked at Mum and suddenly understood the sacrifices parents had to make for their children. The long unsociable hours, even having to work Christmas days. In contrast to her high society life-style in the Caribbean, where she ran her own small businesses as a hairdresser, beautician, clothes designer and poultry farmer. Britain certainly turned out to be well below the standards she was used to, even though we were living in an upper/middle class area. I began to appreciate why she used to be so tired and constantly worried about our future... but she was a true carer.

The next day, I returned to school and went straight into the headmasters office. He was surprised to see me because I was on a three day work experience, not one. I explained my change of heart. He smiled and said that he'd already arranged an interview for me to train as a Laboratory Technician, which meant working four days and going to college for one day and one night each week. I passed the interview and was on my way to becoming a fully fledged employee/student and young adult. My headmasters closing remarks on my school report said; -

"There is no doubt that Dounne has benefited greatly from her second year in the Fifth Form. She has worked quietly and steadily towards her goal of academic success. She is always of a friendly disposition and has never shown any sign of impatience or bad temper. She has been most eager to co-operate with her teachers. Loyalty and obedience are two important virtues and she has them in full measure. She is a young lady of whom her parents may well be proud. I am happy to endorse this warm tribute to a gentle lady"

Mr Murphy July 1966.

❀ My First Job.

Immediately upon leaving school, I went to work as a trainee Laboratory Technician for a large company that manufactured household detergents, bleach, disinfectants and toilet paper. I was the only black, the only female and the only person with an interest in Chemistry and Biology, hence I was the only trainee to be given the opportunity to work in both the chemical and bacteriological laboratories. I worked alone on the Bacteriological side with the head of department, (Mr Mitchell, an elderly gentleman). We connected immediately and got on extremely well. Suddenly one day, he started to tell me about his war time experiences. He wore a ring which was made from the metal fragments of a bomb, that had fallen on their house but didn't explode. He then went on to tell stories of his Spiritual experiences with his deceased mother, whom he said visited regularly and helped solve his problems. I was amazed and told him about the dreams I had of my deceased grandmother. He explained that she was my Spiritual Guide. That night

'Ma' visited me in a dream and I told her what he'd said and she confirmed it to be true. This was my first awareness that white people believed in Spiritualism. From then onwards, we had a very special relationship, which we kept secret and would speak for hours during and after work, exchanging experiences. He taught me a great deal and helped to allay some of my fears.

Within two years, there was a major cattle disease outbreak called 'foot and mouth' which threatened to wipe out Britain's cattle livestock. Chemical laboratories around the country were on red alert to find a cure. Our firm developed a powerful disinfectant which did the trick and we worked 24 hour shifts for months until the epidemic cleared. Shortly after, the firm decided to relocate to another area far away from our home. Essential employees were given the option to move with the company. I did not want to leave my parents just yet, so I resigned and moved into the fashion industry, working for a retail agency in London as an accounts assistant. This opened me up to a whole new world of financial control, which lasted a couple of years, only to find myself pregnant and motherhood looming at the age of 21. Thereby, taking me into the new arena of a working mother.

❈ Wonderful Neighbours.

One of our next door neighbours called Mr & Mrs Horn (an elderly English couple) simply adored the whole family and insisted that we kids called them Aunty and Uncle. They asked my parents if they could take care of us after school, until Mum and Dad returned from work, which was often quite late (7pm to 11pm) and refused to be paid for their kindness. I was 17, my sister 13, cousin 9. We looked forward to getting home after school, because Aunty would have our tea ready with delicious home-made cakes and helped with our homework. While they relaxed and watched television, I'd go home to clean up and prepare my parents dinner. My sisters would come home around 6pm, I'd get them ready for bed and then get on with my school work. Mum usually arrived about 9pm, I'd serve her dinner whilst we chatted about her day at work, my day at school and the children. Dad would arrive an hour or two later and I'd do the same. Being the eldest, I took full charge and responsibility for the home and the children. My parents attitude also changed a great deal, they became much more humble and less pretentious but still had to keep up with 'the Jones' to show that they had cultured class. They confided in me and we became very close. I began to appreciate the responsibilities of taking care of a family. This experience also taught me that many white people were genuinely loving, caring, supportive and unselfish. Aunt and Uncle gave us love but in return we brought joy and happiness into their lives. On my eighteenth birthday, they gave me a special book of good fortune, which I still have to this day. It lists the birth-signs; corresponding birthstones, flowers and their meanings; wedding anniversaries from year 1 to 60, plus a short character description for every day of the year. When a child in the family is born, I immediately look up the book to check its character and to date its been quite accurate. On the birth of my daughters, I recorded their names, weight, length, time and the date. I really treasure the little book, because it was given to me with real love.

In 1971, after I got married, my husband and I moved to East London (Forest Gate) and found an equally loving neighbour called Billy Gyp and his wife; (Gyp was his nickname for gypsy; although he wasn't a real gypsy; but believed in their way of life and herbal remedies). Bill came from Yorkshire; had little education and couldn't read or write but you couldn't cheat him out of a penny. He was in his seventies and had a rare love for animals. He immediately befriended us and would spend long hours telling us tales of his poor, harsh childhood. On the one hand he was kind, loving and gentle but on the other hand, if injustice of any kind raised its ugly head, he'd be as tough as old boots. My husband wouldn't dare ill-treat me in his presence. Bill was strong and could withstand the cold winter better than anyone I've ever known. He wore only a vest with an old wool jacket, which was kept wide open throughout the winter. He gave me his favourite gypsy cold remedy; sliced lemons (leave the skins on) with peeled sliced onions, boiled together until very soft; strain and sweeten with honey, then drink warm. He was the best animal medicine-man and said he learnt everything from the gypsies. When the vets failed, people would bring their sick animals to him and he'd heal them. He believed that animals instinctively knew which herbs to eat when they were sick. For instance; dogs would eat grass to vomit and clean out their stomachs.

Bill worked for a family business who owned a fruit and vegetable market stall. He drove the truck and left around 3am every morning for the wholesalers. For the 11 years I lived there, I never had to buy fruits and vegetables. Every Sunday morning he would leave two large crates on my doorstep and refused to take any money. When I became pregnant with my second daughter (Dee) he decided that it was going to be a boy and named it 'Georgie.' When Dee eventually arrived into the world, he refused to accept her name and called her Georgie. When they left for school in the morning, they'd both shout *"Bye Bill!"* He'd shout back, *"Bye Marsha, bye Georgie."* Every evening after school he'd walk down to the bottom of our road to wait and walk them back home. Even I had to be careful because if I scolded them, they'd say *"I'll tell Bill on you."* They adored each other. Through Bill, my girls formed a strong, loving, caring relationship for animals.

Years later, in 1986 when I decided to leave my husband and told Bill, he cried, because he was so attached to us, especially the girls and made a bigger fuss of them. They'd normally pop into his house every day but this time I noticed that he'd spend long hours alone with them. I knew he was heartbroken but accepted that leaving was for the best - he'd rather see us happy, than unhappy. He turned against my husband and refused to speak to him. To this day, we speak fondly of Bill and often cry in reminiscence. He died shortly after we left.

This experience made me realise that love, hatred or racism is born out of individual experiences, therefore, it is difficult for me to be racist or hateful. The fact is 'true love is blind' and you get back whatever you give in life.

My First Love

At 17 I met my first love at a cousin's wedding, where I was the chief-bridesmaid. It was love at first sight but my parents didn't like the sight of him. So for 18 months our courtship was sheer hell. At the end of the day, rather than continue to hurt my parents, I left him. Experiencing for the second time, the pains of leaving someone I really loved; who treated me very special and didn't sexually harass me because he respected my virginity. During the next couple of years I dated three other guys but always found myself comparing them with my first love. Of course none compared; I could not get him out of my mind. This was in the period of the swinging sixties, mini-skirts, hippies and parties. During the Summer months, there were regular coach tours to various seaside resorts, which ended with a big reggae dance-hall party, that finished in the wee hours of the morning. I'd go with a group of friends, have a great time and return home exhausted. One faithful day, my then boyfriend, (who was by now my fiancé), took me to one of these coach/party trips to a place called Luton. By the time we'd arrived at the dance-hall we were arguing, so in order to diffuse the situation a friend asked me to dance. In the middle of the dancing, I spun around and stopped, only to find myself face to face with my first love, who was standing with his mouth open in shock, looking at me. I too was in shock and could not move. As he walked towards me, my heart was beating so hard it felt like it would jump right out of my chest. I was shaking. My dancing partner asked *"what is wrong?,"* to which I replied, *"I'll explain later."* He came up to me and we danced a long, slow dance. I knew then that we were still in love. He then explained, that he and his friends were strolling round the dance-hall checking out the girls (as young men do). When his best friend said, *"now there's a girl I know you'd like"* and pointed at me dancing. Hence the shocked look on his face when I turned and he saw it was me. Well, I almost forgot about my fiancé. Our relationship went down hill after that and within a month, I broke off our engagement and was re-united with my first love. My parents were not pleased but this time I was not going to let him go again.

Our love blossomed and we made plans to marry. By the end of our first year together I became pregnant. In those days un-married mothers were still scorned, so I was petrified and didn't want to tell my parents; I thought Mum would kill me. I knew they'd be disappointed, as they had so much educational /professional plans for me. I decided to run away from home but he was against it and said we must confront our parents. I just couldn't do it and threatened if he did, I'd kill myself. However, being young and naive I didn't realise that mothers noticed changes in their children's behaviour. One Saturday morning whilst cleaning the living room, Mum came in and looked at me, for what seemed like ages. Then she said, *"Dounne, come over here."* I couldn't move and sensed she knew. She said, *"Dounne, you are pregnant aren't you?"* I dropped the hoover, ran upstairs and locked myself in my room all day. I'd never felt more ashamed in my entire life, I couldn't look my parents in the face. Mum was angry but Dad was hurt. However, neither of them could cope with the shame of neighbours and friends knowing that their precious Catholic daughter was going to have a bastard! 'Old habits die hard' and so their pretentious affluence and class-status was back in full force and I had to suffer the consequences. Mum insisted that we marry straight away but I refused. So she decided that I should go back to the Caribbean to have my baby, then leave it there to be raised by her sister and I again refused. Mum was used to my obedience but also knew that if I decided to go against her, I could be as bone headed or stubborn as she was. Although I was the quietest of her children, whenever I spoke, I meant what I said. This was the first time I'd gone against her wishes and she didn't know how to handle the situation. Mum cut me off, refused to speak to me and eventually told me to leave. I went to live with my brother and his wife.

Two months later, my best friend came to spend the day and when she was ready to leave, I decided to walk her back to the train station. On the way, I saw Mum walking towards me, with instant excitement I was about to run up to give her a big hug and kiss but when she spotted me her face became angry; she immediately turned away and crossed the street. I stood dismayed and just burst into tears. My Mum did not speak to me throughout my pregnancy, until the day I had Marsha. She turned up in the hospital and just said, *"I haven't come to see you, I've come to see my grandchild."* From then on we resumed our relationship and she showed me step-by-step, how to take care of my baby. This is an ancestral legacy; *"a child learns from and is taught by its mother."* I eventually returned to my parents home a few months later, because Mum could not cope with the housework.

————

Marriage

'the bitter/sweet joys and pains of love.'

My main reason for refusing to get married once I became pregnant, was because I didn't want to feel that I had to get married. Once my parents and everyone else knew, then there was no need to rush. My partner wanted to marry but I told him; he could wait until I was good and ready. Marsha was 18 months before I was good and ready. I wanted her to be my bridesmaid but my parents Catholic false pride/shame would not allow this, because it had to be a Catholic church wedding in virginal white. I loved my baby so much, I couldn't care less what anyone thought. She was the only thing that truly belonged to me, *"she was mine,"* nothing, not even her father was going to come between us. We finally got married on 24th July 1971 and although Mum made my wedding dress and cake, I had the worst wedding in the family but it didn't matter because I was in love and happy. My parents gave my sisters and brother lavish weddings but literally spent nothing on mine. I was the only one who had to pay for the drinks; Mum refused to cook or prepare any food, then at 12 midnight my Dad stopped the music and told everyone to leave his house. Fortunately, we had purchased a house and moved in on our wedding night. We had no money, so could not afford a honeymoon.

My parents never got to like my husband throughout our marriage and I continued to feel like an outcast. They'd take their other grandchildren on holidays abroad; mine were always left out. Dad and my husband argued constantly but I remained neutral defending neither, because I loved them both. It got so bad that one day, Mum recognising that I was close to a nervous breakdown shouted, *"don't you two realise what you are doing to my child; you'll send her crazy."* By this time I was crying and shaking like a leaf. From then on they tried to control their tempers but the arguments still continued because both men were too arrogant or egotistic to back down.

To make matters worse, we were both working for my father's Housing

Association and although I literally ran the association, his intense dislike for my husband meant that I was continuously passed over in favour of other staff members. Hence, I had to fight for everything I deserved, including promotions and salary increases. My father unwittingly punished me to get to my husband, yet I continued to work for him for 11 years, as I believed in what he was trying to achieve. This episode in my life is so painful that I would rather not record it, out of respect for my father.

However, other family complications and confusions were also affecting our marriage. The stress became unbearable and I eventually decided to disown them for 3 years. Our relationship resumed in 1986, after my marriage broke down and I'd left my husband. Unfortunately, it took years of heartache and stress for me to realise that my parents wanted the best for me and knew all along that my husband was not good enough and would not take good care of me. Unfortunately, they were right but they also wanted too much from me, which caused even greater pain and distress.

It is extremely difficult when the love for your parents and your husband is strong and both are forcing you to divide your loyalty, because each believe they have a claim to your ownership *(i.e. "it's my child - it's my wife")*. Such unfair, selfish divisions, can rip one's emotions to shreds and separation from both is essential to preserve one's own identity and sanity.

This experience taught me that some parents find it difficult to let go of their children and set them free to lead their own lives; and also of the bonded protectiveness of parents. As my mother use to say:- *"you'll always be my child, no matter how old you get and even after you die, you'll still be my child."* This was just one of the conflicting contrast between the Caribbean way of life and that of the British ways. I didn't make allowance for the fact that my parents were finding it difficult to understand or reconcile both cultures. But later on, as my own children matured, I realised that a parent's love, care, worry or concern, never fades and I then recognised the immense pain I had also put my parents through. This enabled me to come to terms; reconcile our differences; forgive, heal and make peace. Our lives were instantly transformed as we grew in true appreciative love and understanding. I no longer felt wronged and even learnt to respect and accept their pretentious ways. In 1994, I eventually returned to the Caribbean and was able to view it with open matured eyes. I blessed my parents decision for bringing me to England, which has broadened my horizon, increased my opportunities and enhanced my life.

Parenting

'Working Mum and Bonding.'

Although I've always wanted to become a parent, I also wanted to have a career and keep my independence, primarily because of what I'd seen in the Caribbean; where most women either got married or had children too young, mainly as a form of security to ensure that they had someone to take care of them throughout their lives and especially during old age. Unfortunately, many ended up either in abusive relationships or were widowed young and left with several children to raise. Having had no formal employment experience, the only work they could obtain was what they were used to... cooking, cleaning, ironing and washing. In other words; low paid, menial jobs. Nevertheless they managed and was able to raise well turned out children, many of whom went on to qualify in professional careers and took care of their sad, lonely, tired but proud mothers. This experience gave me an insight into the strength of a woman and her ability to cope and survive.

So, I made myself a promise not to become solely dependent on a man, for my children or my own existence and vowed to try and keep my independence. Therefore, it is not surprising that I've always been a full-time working mum and in career jobs, which stood me in good stead, firstly as a single parent when I had my first daughter and secondly - 16 years later, when I left my husband. I was able to take care of me and mine.

I thoroughly enjoyed both pregnancies right up until the actual birth. Each being particularly horrendous to the point of begging the Virgin Mary to end my life during Dee's birth. After this traumatic experience, I decided to have no more children, nor ever give up the ones I had. However, on each occasion I was back out to work within two months. My daughters were used to a part-time mum, childminders and nurseries, yet our love has an extremely strong bond, proving that working mums do not necessarily create a deterioration of family life but could improve it. However, it takes conscious daily effort and discipline, to make it work and also make you appreciate one another.

"Absence makes the heart grow fonder."

Furthermore, the children become independent and responsible earlier in life. In my case, my daughters always came first, every available moment was valuable time spent with them; which started from the first day they were born, using the natural bonding techniques learnt from my mother, as handed down by our ancestors. It ensured that we were well bonded before I returned to work and had to hand them over to childminders.

These techniques of 'loving touches' ensures that a baby recognises its mother almost instantly from birth and by continuing the process, creates a life time 'bond of love.' One of these valuable teachings is the art of full body massage, which I'd like to share.

Before bathing the baby, first prepare the mood... (i.e. the room should be warm, peaceful, calm; the only noise is either your voice singing a soothing song quietly or soothing music playing in the background). Then prepare the bath water to the right warm temperature; after which, prepare the baby. All the time your facial expression must be pleasant happy and smiling. Whilst bathing, gently clean the baby but also have a little fun, by teaching it how to play, splashing the water, as well as, give it gentle joint exercises in the warm water. Once bathing is completed, wrap the baby securely in a warm towel, place on the bed and gently wipe it dry. Using warm baby oil, gently oil it from head to toe and then give a complete 10-15 minute gentle full body massage, using upwards small circular strokes to stimulate circulation; gently exercise its limbs and joints, check its senses and reflex, (i.e. sight, hearing and grip);- then dress and place the baby on your lap onto its belly; gently massage its head for a few minutes and finally comb the hair, ending with gentle brushing. By this time, the baby should be sound asleep; put to bed and should continue sleeping for at least 2 to 3 hours, giving you time to get on with the housework and other things. This is done every day for the first 2 to 3 months and if you are not a working mum, then up to 6 months. Gradually reduce the massage routine to once a week but increase the duration to 20-30 minutes. Once the child becomes old enough to bathe and clean itself (say between 8 to 10 years), you should still personally bathe and massage it at least once a week. This massage routine is then transformed from baby bonding, into the vital process of relieving stress and tension during its maturing years. Additionally, massage has other extended benefits for long term health care; it relieves stiffness, aches and pains; manipulates muscles, bones and joints and stimulates circulation. Of course, most teenagers don't like their parents bathing them but surprisingly, if they are used to it, once in a while they'll beg for a bath and massage, as it is so comforting and relaxing, especially when stressed out. Furthermore, you should also teach your child to bathe and massage you, so that you too can be pampered once in a while. This also strengthens the bonding and removes inhibitions. Always remember, that as a mother you are the teacher who sets the example. So teach your child to be free in your presence, by being free, open and honest yourself. Occasionally, bathe together; dress and undress in its presence. Never be afraid or ashamed to show your nakedness; after all, you gave it **naked** birth and must not only teach but show that nakedness is natural. Together, neither of you should ever need to use clothing as a security blanket, because you would be secure within yourself and with each other. I believe children have enough problems to cope with from the external world, therefore you should try to make your home a place of freedom, security and love.

To this day Marsha, Dee and I, call on each other for massages, whenever we are under pressure and need to relax or sometimes, just scratch each others hair with a comb and give it a good brushing out. Either way, falling asleep is a certainty and leaves a mutual feeling of comfort, love and togetherness. This routine should also be extended to husbands or partners and vice versa, as it creates the same sense of uninhibited closeness. Try making a special day every month to pamper each other and you'll see how your relationship flourish and grow. Physical contact, through the 'art of gentle touch' is one of the major lessons of staying connected or well bonded.

❀ Conditioning and Indoctrination.

Dee was born on Friday 13th, traditionally known as black Friday, to those who are superstitious. Whilst she was still young, I managed to reverse this negative thought process, so much so that Dee sees it more as 'her lucky day.'

❀ Child Minders.

I was extremely careful when choosing child-minders, starting the search from about 4 months pregnant. I'd look for someone who didn't have a hoard of other children to mind and personally interview each to test their attitude, personality and temperament. Once chosen, we'd develop a Mum/Aunty relationship. The girls called them Aunty and knew they had complete responsibility; even to smack them if necessary. Aunty was in control by day, I was in control at nights and weekends. As their bonding grew, I'd watch the children's reaction every morning when getting them ready, by saying in a happy tone, *"you are going to Aunty's today."* I'd also watch their reaction on arrival and when collecting them. At every point they were happy, anxious and excited. Aunty did the same when she got them ready for my collection in the evening and they had the same reaction towards me. Each evening myself and Aunty would sit down, have a cup of tea and talk about each others' day and every detail of the children. Once the children began to speak, they always spoke lovingly about their Aunties, even when they were scolded, they accepted that they did wrong. I made a point never to undermine Aunty in any way in their presence. If there was something I was concerned about, we'd talk privately. I remembered an occasion with Dee's Aunty Kathy. When I arrived to collect her one evening, both Kathy and her husband (John) were acting strangely. I became suspicious and enquired what was the matter; noticing that Dee was not around - *"where is she, is she alright!"* I questioned anxiously. They both said, *"sit down, we have a little bit of bad news;"* thinking the worse, I immediately burst into tears. They reassured me that she was alright and in bed asleep, because she had spent the whole day out and was tired. It turned out that Aunty Kathy's father was a doctor, specialising in chest problems who ran a clinic miles away in Chelmsford. He had visited them that month and did a check on their young son (Christopher 3 years) and on Dee who was then 18 months. He said that something was not quite right and made arrangements for a detailed clinical examination. The results showed she had a heart murmur... a slight hole in her heart but confirmed that there was nothing to worry about, as it was very small; she was healthy, energetic and that it would eventually repair itself by the time she turned 18 to 21 years. The most she'd suffer was frequent bouts of colds. At the time I was devastated, Kathy and John reassured me that she'd be alright, then woke her up. She came charging at me with arms stretched out and a beaming smile, that reassured me more than ever. Kathy also had a 19 year old brother who loved motorbikes. He'd travel all the way from Chelmsford regularly to spend the day with Christopher and Dee. To this day, one of Dee's dreams is to own a motorbike and ride at great speed. By the way, Kathy's father's diagnosis was spot on. Marsha and Dee's childminders were both white.

On reflection, I believe that part of this mutual growing process was established from the role-playing games I developed with the girls from around the age of four. Every Saturday we'd swap roles with each other for half the day. I'd play the child and they'd play mum. They would boss and order me around, teach me lessons, scold etc, in the same way as I was parenting them. It's amazing what valuable lessons parents can learn from such role playing, if taken seriously. It taught me what I said; how I said it; my attitude towards them; what they liked and disliked; whether I was being fair or unfair; but it also exposed our depth of love, as well as, gave an insight into their individual personalities and how to deal with them accordingly. It allowed me to experience life through the eyes of a child and to adjust my treatment effectively. Each subsequent role-play showed the effects of my adjustment on them, the results of which also showed in our day to day relationship; with the additional benefits of mutual appreciation and respect, which made parenting much easier. It made me realise that people assume the role of parenthood without any prior formal training; leaving us to repeat the same mistakes our own parents made in trying to raise us, based on the 'hit & miss' theory. If we were lucky, some of our children would grow up to become responsible, independent, respectful, intelligent individuals and some would be the exact opposite. It is very rare for a parent to admit; *"my child is a direct result or mirror image of me and my training,"* simply because the majority are not sufficiently mature to take the blame for their mistakes. They are delighted to accept responsibility for the good ones... mothers would say, *"that's my child"* but quickly reject the bad ones... *"that's the father's child."*

Parenting should 'start with love; grow with love and develop through love.' All children (good or bad) should always be made to feel absolutely secure in their parents' love. Parenting takes tremendous patience and we need to acquire the skills of how to keep control by placing boundaries around the child... discipline. These boundaries are your laws, which they must obey. Disobedience means punishment but they must be told what they are being punished for, so that they don't repeat the same act. However, your laws and punishment must be persistent and constant to avoid confusion. In this way, they would learn their boundaries and stay within them. However, as they grow and show obedience and common sense, these boundaries should be widened (little by little) until they are eventually free, by which time they should have reached maturity and understand fully, right from wrong. They should also now be free to leave home and live their own lives. Hopefully, they should not then encounter too many problems living or working with others, because they'd know how to treat and respect people. In other words; they know their boundaries and value their space. At the end of the day, parents love and training remains with their children for life. The roots of any problems always starts from the beginning... i.e. childhood and up bringing.

This does not mean that I was the perfect parent; I too made lots of mistakes but I was also very lucky to have received children who had good minds. I also realised in time, that I was untrained and trying my best to be a good parent, which I explained, once I felt they'd reached the age of understanding (4/5 years old). I'd always immediately apologise to them when I made a mistake. This became such a regular routine that neither of us finds any difficulty in apologising to each other or to others; to the point that Marsha tends to apologise prior to making a mistake, which has become a house-hold joke. At the age of 12, Marsha said to me, *"You are the perfect Mum and when I grow up, I hope I could be as good as you."* Naturally the tears flowed but I thanked God that I was now a fully trained, experienced, qualified and bonafide Mum, because my child said so, (out of the mouths of babes cometh truth). So don't judge yourselves as parents, let your children judge you. Children are valuable, precious gifts, who deserve to be treasured.

"Once you've become a parent - you are a parent for LIFE."

"Some may choose to abandon this responsibility but their ownership remains absolute."

● This is me (age 7 months) in front of my grandmother's garden; Freeport, Trinidad.

● At 16 years in Kew Gardens, London.

● **1968:**
Mum and I in front of our home in
Seven Kings, Essex.

my special book of good fortune listing
birth-signs; corresponding birthstones,
flowers and their meanings.

● **1965:**
Mum and dad in our garden
(England)

● above:
Marsha at her first holy communion and with nursery school teacher.

● myself and Dee.

● Marsha and Dee.

- Returned to my school in England (Canon Palmer R.C.);
  Picture taken November 2000 sitting in my old history class.

Saint Gabriels R.C, (San Fernando, Trinidad); marvelling at changes made to the old school yard, since my attendance at age 11.

Picture taken February 2000.

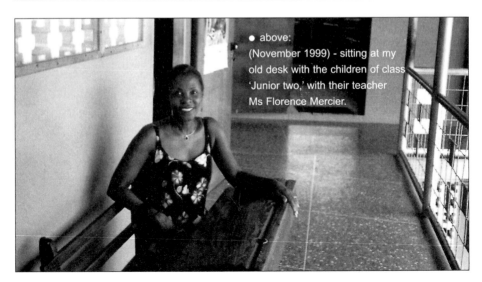

above:
(November 1999) - sitting at my old desk with the children of class 'Junior two,' with their teacher Ms Florence Mercier.

● These are just a few of my then regular customers modelling some of my own personal hairstyle creations, 1980's.

Marriage Breakdown

Being Catholic and Caribbean I believed not only in God but also in my marriage vows. I loved my husband so much that I'd do anything to keep my marriage and home together. I meant for better or for worse, therefore I was prepared to sacrifice my own personal happiness, even my life for him and our children. So although times were hard, it didn't feel like a punishment or abuse, it was more like a necessary sacrifice any loving mother or wife would make for her family. My love was so blind, that I could not see any wrong in him; all I focused on was what appeared to be his good side... his brilliant personality; the life and soul of any party; a good father, good disciplinarian and loving husband. But in truth, he was also immature, macho, domineering, manipulative, chauvinistic, insecure, irresponsible, intimidating, suppressive, non-supportive, aggressive, selfish, controlling and down right lazy. To the point that one year after Dee was born, he walked out on his job and did not work again until 8 years later, when I decided to leave him. Throughout, he never helped around the house, did the shopping, cooked or helped with the children. *"Slavery may have been abolished hundreds of years ago but it is still very active in many marriages today and many women are carrying both the physical and mental torturous scars."*

However, a marriage does not breakdown by one parent alone; 'it takes two to tango.' I played my fair share in that deterioration process. I was too soft, too timid, too loving, too caring, too forgiving and too afraid of loosing him, so I did everything in my power to please and keep him. I did not realise that many men, although they'd say they love and want to marry you, need to learn how to take on and accept the responsibilities that come with marriage and children. In other words, they need to grow up. I just assumed all the roles, believing that in time he'd learn. I also didn't want to become the nagging wife; I wanted to be too perfect... the perfect wife, lover, mother, housekeeper and provider and of course, the perfect marriage too and it almost killed me. One can love too much. I also didn't want my children exposed to continuous fighting or arguing, so I remained passive. Instead, I should have been stronger and make him play his part, which would have made him a better person, father and husband. Another part of this problem was also rooted in his upbringing and his mother's love. He was an only boy of a Caribbean mother who doted and waited on him hand and foot. Therefore he was extremely spoilt and used to getting his own way and doing nothing. Hence, in marriage he expected me to love him the same way his mother did... do everything for him. In his own logical mind, he could not see his faults but could see everyone else's. He did not understand that love goes beyond just being a good-lover and I was too young and naive to know better. Throughout our marriage, I kept him, working full-time by day and part-time by night and at weekends; which was never appreciated, but I still loved him... warts and all.

However, taking on all the marital responsibilities, coupled with regular mental abuse, eventually took its toll, which led to depression. At one point I suffered a severe bout of agoraphobia. How I managed to get to work or do the weekly shopping, God only knows, because being outside felt like a living a nightmare, struggling to breathe and walk. I do not remember how I recovered. At another point 'the abused became the abuser' and I began to beat Marsha and Dee (but especially Marsha) for no apparent reason. Thank God this did not last too long and they forgave me. I continued to suffer in silence, only confiding in my doctor, who would not prescribe any medication, because of its addictiveness and my frailty. His repeated advise was to leave my husband; saying *"he is slowly killing you."*

My husband used the most fearful form of control. He had a strong voice and used it with commanding authority. For instance, he would comment, *"I am the man in this house, so do as I say or else!"* leaving the *"or else"* to our imagination. He was also physically strong and used this to his advantage. Unlike most abusive men who would beat their wives to a pulp, my husband would strike only one hard blow generally to the upper arm, which was enough to keep me under control. Ensuring always that I never had any visible marks or bruises. Every evening, I had to serve his meals on a tray and personally hand it to him. Upon eating he would scrutinise the food with great detail. If the slightest thing displeased him (finding an eye-lash on the plate), he would throw the meal into the bin, followed promptly with harsh insults, before walking out of the house. On the other hand, if all was well, he would finish his meal, leaving the empty tray on the floor beside his chair and waited for one of us to quickly take it into the kitchen. On Sundays, we always had a proper family meal at the table. We could not serve ourselves before him, because he had to have first choice of anything. Naturally, take-away meals were out of the question, since his food had to be freshly cooked at home every day. He would refuse to eat leftovers. Every morning, he would stay in bed, whilst I organised the girls for school (breakfast, washing etc). If a cup of tea was not brought up to him within five minutes, he would hammer on the floor with a large stick which he kept by the bed. We had to make sure that he did not hammer twice, in fear of what he would do. So it became the norm that as soon as we woke up, we would run downstairs, put the kettle on and make his tea, taking enormous pains to make sure it was absolutely perfect, before running upstairs, taking great care not to spill it and then present it to him. All the while our hearts would be racing until his approval was met. His general attitude was, *"why should I have to do anything, when I have three women around me."* Of course! He was always right and should never be questioned. If I complained of tiredness or even illness, his response would be that I was a lazy, useless wife and that he would find another woman capable of meeting his needs. This re-confirmed his position of controller and I proceeded to do everything to please him, whilst continuing to keep my home together.

Being the sole breadwinner, providing for a demanding man who had to have everything he desired, also brought me close to imprisonment. Fortunately, my boss and doctor's testimonies vindicated my character but I lost my job. It was one of the most frightening experiences and even though he did not stand by me, I still hung onto him.

Another time, whilst at my wits end, in desperation to save my sanity and regain my strength, I went to my priest to seek refuge. I was hoping that the Church would have somewhere I could go and retreat for a month.

Unfortunately they could not help. I felt it was my last hope and slowly walked home in tears.

The turning point came when Marsha, then only 15 years had to undergo major spinal surgery to correct a 90° curvature called Scholiosis. She had reached the stage where she wanted to look normal and was getting tired of disguising her deformity by wearing baggy clothes. She could no longer stand or sit straight, suffered continuous back-pain and her shoulders showed a 5 to 6 inch imbalance, with one side sloping downwards. In other words, my child was deformed and needed help. My husband being afraid of doctors had previously instilled his fears into Marsha. He was adamant that she should not undergo any operation, because of the risk of becoming crippled or even die, if it went wrong. I'd never gone against his wishes before but this time, I could see her suffering both mentally and physically. I felt that if there was any chance of her leading a normal life, then she should take it. So for 4 years, I decided to strengthen her mentally and spiritually to make her own choices. This process took place behind his back, when he wasn't at home. It was then I began to question his love; see his faults and resentment started to seep in. I promised Marsha that I'd do everything in my power to ensure that she got the best possible treatment. I arranged an appointment with the best spinal specialist in the country (Dr Gardner) to discuss her options and the cost of Private treatment. Dr Gardner explained, that surgery could correct the defective spine and minimise the curative to $15\text{-}20^{\circ}$ increasing her height by 3-4 inches, which was almost straight. She'd need to spend at least one month in a private hospital. First, her head would be in traction for two weeks to stretch out and keep her spine straight. Afterwards the main operation would take place to open the entire length of her spine, remove and crush one rib which would be mixed with a special cement before repositioning her spine. This method minimised the risk of rejection. A long steel rod would be inserted; wired up to the spine and finally cemented into place. After two weeks, she'd be placed in a plaster-cast from neck to thigh for 6 months. The full cost for Private treatment was £8,000 or free under the National Health. It would take one year for full recovery, meaning that she'd lose a year of schooling. However, if the operation was not done before she turned 18 years, it would then be too late, as her bones would no longer be flexible.

Apart from my husband's personal fears, he also wanted to opt for the free operation. I was enraged and snapped. I remembered referring to his love of flashy cars and shouted, *"the operation would cost the same price as a new car, which was just a piece of old iron; I valued her life more than a car and if it meant I'd have to do three jobs to pay for it, then I'm prepared to do it."* In his anger, he replied that if the operation failed and she became crippled or died, then I'd have to carry the full guilt alone for the rest of my life, as he'd have nothing to do with it. It would be all my fault. This emotional blackmail was the final straw that drove the nail into our marriage. It also exposed his total lack of support and weaknesses, where as I'd always seen him as being strong. My love was slowly turning into hate.

It was at this point, I started to teach Marsha and Dee about placing their trust in God and how to hold onto HIM for strength. Together we prayed hard and cried a lot. Marsha's godmother told me about an English spiritualist church which held healing sessions. I was prepared to try anything; so hopefully I took her along. I too, tried to heal her but nothing worked. I also took her to weekly swimming classes with handicapped children, not only for physical exercise but to show her that there were others much worse off than she was and who were living happily with their deformities. To make her realise how lucky she was; as she had an opportunity of corrective surgery, whilst others were not so fortunate. However, it made me realise that it was easier to accept deformity if you were born that way. But Marsha was born perfect; her spine started to curve around the age of eight and progressively got worse as she grew older. So it was far more difficult for her to come to terms with it. In the end, Marsha knew that the choice was in her own hands.

One Saturday morning, she came to me and said, *"Mum I don't know what to do, I'm so afraid."* I sat her down, hugged her tight and explained that I understood her fears. We went over the options and the operation again and I allowed her to express all her fears. Then I told her to go to her bedroom alone and fight her fears. She must scream; shout, get angry; say what ever came into her mind, stamp and fight herself, until she reached a decision. Then come back to me with a firm decision. Whatever she decided, I'd support and be there for her. If she chose the operation, I'd act immediately to get her into hospital quickly and would take out a Bank Loan to pay for it. Marsha went to her room, whilst Dee and I sat downstairs hugging each other, listening to her tearing herself up for more than two hours. It was yet another extremely painful episode in my life. I cried and cried. She finally came downstairs, completely exhausted; threw her arms around me and said, *"Mum, I want the operation."* As promised, I got her into the hospital immediately; we trusted in God and HE repaid our faith and trust. The operation was a complete success in more ways than one. Marsha walked into the hospital as a shy, timid child but one month later, walked out as a confident, upright and matured young lady. This experience created a protective bond and strong attachment which has remained with us to this day.

However, during the two-stage operation, I stayed with her overnight in the hospital to pray, give her added strength and love. On the day of the first operation, I decided to go for a walk and wondered aimlessly around the area, feeling distraught, helpless and terrified of giving into my worst fears. Whilst walking I came upon a little old church, went inside and it was empty. I just sat there looking at Jesus's statue and from within myself, I quietly screamed out for help, pleading to God to save her and eventually cried myself to sleep. I woke up feeling exhausted, weak, in a daze and returned to the hospital. The operation lasted two hours, so I must have slept for at least one hour in the church. The doctor said on coming out of the anaesthetic, her first words were, *"I want my Mum."* The first stage went well and we waited anxiously for two weeks for the second operation, which was going to be the crucial one.

That morning we woke up early and prayed together. It was then I witnessed Marsha's strong will power. She said, *"Mum! before the operation, I'm going to will myself to sleep, please don't try to wake me."*

Marsha then put herself into a trance-like sleep, well before the nurses came to wheel her off to the operating theatre and stayed asleep even through the anaesthetic procedure. The five hour operation also went extremely well but this time I was not prepared for what I was going to see hours later in the recovery room. Dr Gardner explained, *"the next forty eight hours are crucial, we can only wait and hope that all is well."* Then he took us into the recovery room. There were various machines with wires and tubes connected all over her. To this day I don't know what kept me from collapsing. Although drowsy from the anaesthetic, she opened her eyes, looked at me and smiled, to confirm and reassure that she was alright. Forty eight hours passed and all was great! but she was in extreme pain, even though on a morphine drip and strong pain killers. However, due to terrible side-effects, she had to be taken off the morphine but remained on the pain killers. Marsha also began to suffer adverse side-effects from the pain killers, so decided that she would again use her will power and discontinued taking them three days after the operation. The nurses feared that the pain could become too acute and would be difficult to control but Marsha insisted and effectively controlled the pain for herself. Whenever the nurses wanted to turn, wash or move her; she would ask to be allowed five minutes to focus her mind on controlling the pain; which she did effectively every time to their amazement. One day I asked her, *"Marsha, are you praying daily,"* she replied, *"Mum what else do you think keeps me so strong but God and you."*

Marsha was also a vegetarian and didn't enjoy the bland hospital meals. So every morning at 5am I'd cook the family dinner, get Dee ready for school, get myself ready for work; return from work at 6pm; re-heat and pack the dinner. My husband would then drive us to the hospital, which was a few miles away and in her room we'd have our usual family meal together every night, plus at lunch-time on Saturdays and Sundays. However, oblivious to us all, Dee was suffering in silence, in the background. We were so stressed and focussed on Marsha's condition, neither of us paid attention or noticed that she too was pining and felt left out. We didn't take into consideration that it was the first time they'd ever been separated, so she was both frightened and missing her sister terribly.

Marsha was finally discharged a month later, still very weak, in pain and needed daily nursing care for another six weeks, by which time she'd be strong enough to support and help herself. But Marsha did not want a nurse to take care of her, she wanted me. However, I had to work full time to keep the family, as well as, to pay for her operation but some how, I managed to fit in all three routines. For two months I slept sitting at the foot of her bed, propped up against the wall with her legs on my lap, ready to massage when they involuntarily went into painful spasms, triggered by the severed nerve endings. Although my husband could see that I was tired and distressed, he refused to help but also consumed with guilt, he grew resentful and more reluctant. Over the years, his lack of support around the house and within the marriage; coupled with my constant over working, had previously taken its toll, causing two near nervous breakdowns and I was now close to my third. My doctor, knowing of our relationship had advised several times that I should leave before its too late. Throughout our marriage I weighed no more than 105 pounds but I was now down to 98 pounds. I didn't understand mental abuse. Finally, it took my children to convince me to leave him.

One Saturday morning, about two months after her operation, we sat watching an interesting television programme. My husband who was angry (for reasons only known to himself) came downstairs, looked at us; walked up and abruptly switched it off, then said in a rough manner, *"I'm going out, don't turn this television on again."* Although he rarely used physical violence, his tone was always so aggressively commanding that we would usually cower and obey, in fear of the worst. Marsha waited for him to leave, then hugged me and said, *"When I grow up, I will never let anyone treat me as if I have no value or worth. Dad treats you like a floor rag. He's using and abusing you. You love him too much and give your all but he gives back nothing because he doesn't care. I fear for you and don't think you'll live to see forty if you stay with him. I love him too but we must leave before its too late. Mum, I'm really afraid that you are working yourself into an early grave. If you don't leave now, then as soon as I'm 18 years I'll leave home, because he's too controlling. You have tried to prevent us from hearing your rows by putting us to bed early but Mum, 'walls have ears,' we know exactly what has been going on for years. Myself and Dee have discussed the situation and we both agree that we should all leave."*

She then reminded me of one of my grandmother's many teachings, *"Where ever you make your bed, you must lie on it but if it becomes too rough; turn it out."* This statement struck like an arrow straight into my heart and for the first time, I was being forced to choose between the love for my children and my husband. I knew how much Marsha and especially Dee loved their father and for them to tell me to leave, meant that our relationship had reached rock bottom and possibly beyond repair. The choice was easy because I was not ready to let go of either Marsha or Dee or prepared to prolong their suffering. However, I still wanted them to have a continuing relationship with their father and was hoping that we would be sufficiently mature to finally share the parenting... i.e. they would live with me during the week and with him at weekends. Even though we had previously discussed and mutually agreed on a trial separation, he rejected Marsha and Dee's decision to live with me and therefore, resented them. I never told him what Marsha had said, as I didn't want the children to become the scape-goats or the excuse for the breakdown of our relationship, because the true problem was between the both of us.

From then on my attitude began to change. I started standing up for myself and suddenly he began showing signs of serious physical aggression to regain control. One morning whilst preparing for work, he began to torment me about how I dressed up for work, that he thought my boss fancied me and that we were having an affair. I couldn't believe my ears and laughed. The torment continued until a row erupted. He then attacked me, pushed me on the floor, picked up both legs and was pulling me towards the top of the stairs, with the intention of dragging me down by my legs with my head bouncing down each step. I screamed in terror. Marsha ran out and screamed, *"Dad no!"* He let go and laughed, as a warning of what he was capable of doing. Realising my vulnerability, I immediately enrolled in a martial arts club (Ishinryu) which turned out to be one of the best in Britain. I wanted to learn how to defend and protect myself and my children in case he turned on us. As he was spending more time out of the house, I was able to practice for hours. For two months he remained unaware of my activities. He was so used to my habitual routine; I always came straight home from work everyday without fail. My karate classes were held Monday, Tuesday and Thursday from 7pm to 9pm. I told Marsha and Dee, if at any time he came home whilst I was at class and asked of my whereabouts, they must not tell him. Then one day during practice, I punched and shouted out as trained to do but this time the force which came out of me, gave me a fright. Something different had happened, so I did it again and the same powerful force came out. I was stunned; at that point I felt my inner-Spirit and for the first time I became aware of my real strength. With renewed confidence I told the girls, *"this time when he comes home and enquires, tell him I'm at the karate club."* My husband was in shock and immediately all his aggressive behaviour disappeared, as he was unsure of my ability and was to macho to ever allow or take the risk of his wife beating him in a physical fight. Martial arts had taught me the art of reverse psychology; the weakening effects of fear; how to combat aggression and release anger. At last, I'd come out from my shell and was in control and had to stay strong. Fourteen years of pent up anger from him, coupled with twenty four years of penned anger from my parents, equalled a whole heap of angry rage. I now had to do what I told Marsha to do several months earlier; 'bite the bullet, confront and fight my fears and get rid of my demons.' It eventually took seven years to finally release all my anger and frustrations.

In the meanwhile at home, Marsha was still in the plaster cast but also gaining strength. The staircase to the upstairs of the house was in serious need of repair, so she was confined to the ground floor. Once we had made the decision to leave, she secretly decided that whilst I was at work and the house was empty, she would attempt to go up the stairs and pack our clothing into large plastic bags and hide them away, so that her father would not suspect our actions. She did this everyday for a couple of weeks until I noticed that a lot of my clothes were missing. She then told me of her antics and showed where she had hidden them. I was petrified, realising the risk she had taken, because if at any time she had fallen, she would have damaged her spine beyond repair and crippled herself, plus I could not afford anymore private treatment. I shook all over and began to cry. I made her swear-to-God and promise never to go up the stairs again and to leave the rest of the work to me but that I appreciated her thoughtfulness, loving care, support and concern for my welfare.

On 25th March 1986, my local Council (Housing department) sent me the keys for a vacant 2 bedroom flat in East London. I took the day off work and raced down to view it. Getting there felt like ages. All I kept thinking about was how would Marsha and Dee find their way to school. But when I arrived at the flat and saw number 77 on the door, I was transfixed and knew intuitively that this was mine. That number told me, this was a God-send and the beginning of our new life . Whilst alone in the flat, my whole life flashed before me; I sat down and cried, then gathered myself, returned home, told the girls and my husband. It was only then I realised that he never believed I'd really leave him. He had taken my love for granted for so long; plus in the past, I always forgave him. He also had a fixation, that a woman would fight to the end to keep her home. So he felt secured; assured in the belief that I'd never leave the property. Whereas, I was not materialistic and considered a house 'old bricks' which was there before I came and would still be standing long after I die, so it's not worth the extra pain and misery. It had served its purpose and it was the right time to move on and find somewhere else which may bring us more happiness. So he was in shock when I left.

A year earlier, when we'd first discussed a possible trial separation, he had not worked for 8 years. Still trying to play 'Mr Macho' but like my mother, he too feared my determination. One day he suddenly broke down and confessed that he had lost his confidence and didn't know what job he could do to support himself. For once, he exposed the frightened little boy inside. I felt sorry for him and explained that he was an excellent driver, great with people and could become a brilliant driving instructor. I paid for him to go on a week's professional instructors course and he then started training with a reputable Driving School.

After nine months, once he regained his confidence, I encouraged him to set up his own driving school; personally saved up all my part-time earning (£600) to help him. However, he was also blacklisted and could not obtain credit or loans, so I signed the Bank's agreement to enable him to purchase his first car. Throughout that year I continued to pay all the bills and kept the family. Therefore, he thought that as he was now working and running his own business, I wouldn't leave him. What he did not realise was that he himself did not change. In fact, he became even more macho; less supportive around the house and had grown accustomed to not paying for anything; so he didn't. However, I knew that his enormous ego would never allow him to become a laughing stock amongst his friends. I knew that once I'd left, he'd work hard to prove that he did not need me. This way, he'd at last learn to take responsibility for something, if only just for himself. The night before I left, he pleaded with me to sleep with him, in the hope that sex would change my mind. It didn't and I laid awake all night, beside him in fear.

On the morning of 31st March 1986 the removal van arrived. I waited for him to leave for work and then packed. I took only our clothes, some cutlery, plates, cups and glasses, the girls old beds, Marsha's piano, a small black and white television, our dog (Zara) and 2 cats (Banjo and Zazu). I left the house, all the furniture and everything else for him. Once the van was packed, I gave the driver the spare keys to my flat to take our belongings. I then stayed in the house; cleaned it thoroughly, and even changed the bed sheets. Marsha and Dee were furious because they could not understand why I was doing this. Marsha said, *"you have spent all your life, spoon feeding him and doing everything. Why are you still making life so easy for him - let him go."* I explained, I was not leaving their father because I hated him but because I loved him; he'd have enough pain coming to terms with loosing us. It might be easier walking into a clean house; it would not be right to deliberately leave it in a mess or to strip him of everything. The least I could do is to let him keep his macho pride and dignity. They were also angry that I was leaving him with everything, which I had bought and was moving into an empty flat to start from scratch.

However, as we were moving Marsha's piano, some books fell out from a secret compartment. Whilst picking them up, it turned out to be his business books. Then Dee found two Building Society savings books, hidden in between them and asked what were they. I was shocked and opened them, only to find that my husband had savings of over £2,000. He had been sneakily saving up all his money, whilst telling me that he was not making enough to pay for anything, not even food. I replaced the books and didn't reveal our discovery until three months later. He kept nagging me to help him pay for the house-hold bills and especially for Marsha's operation but I had no extra money, because I'd lost most of my part-time clients. One day I just snapped and shouted that I'd paid every bill including the mortgage, right up to the day I'd left and revealed our discovery of his saving books. I then demanded my share of the house valuation, from which I could pay off for Marsha's operation and wipe the slate clean. I couldn't believe that he would stoop so low and no longer wanted to have anything to do with him.

I've focused the ending of our marriage on Marsha's operation, because it took this heart wrenching experience to open my eyes to fourteen years of accumulative mental abuse. It was the turning point which woke me up and gave me the strength to finally walk out. This was only one of many episodes of abuse, which occurred throughout our marriage. On the one hand he was extremely aggressive and controlling but on the other hand equally loving, tender and often cried for forgiveness, which is the most effective way of manipulating someone's emotions.

This experience taught me that abuse and manipulation can easily seep into a relationship and become the norm. One becomes blinded or even deaf to the sounds of abuse; accepting the unacceptable, especially when children are involved. Financial insecurities also adds to the fear, hence you stay in the hope that (one day) things would get better. I have seen many people who have stayed too long, only to find that at the end of the day, their lives continued to be absolutely miserable, unhappy, remaining loveless until old age. Whilst the 'abuser' carried on their lives, getting their own way, even enjoying long term affairs outside the marriage. Luckily for some, marital counselling has helped to restore and resume a loving relationship.

It often amazes me, that relationships starts out so loving and caring, yet somehow turns into so much hate and rage. I am glad that my departure was early. It goes to prove that we all have the power to take charge of our own lives and change it.

Starting Over

I recall, the 31st March 1986 was a bright sunny day. I'd finished cleaning the house around lunchtime, then with the girls and animals took a deep breath, walked out of the front door, closing it firmly behind us. My grandmother's words echoed in my ear, *"never look back."* We held hands and walked to the bus stop, feeling relieved, excited and anxious to get to our new home. When we arrived and I opened the front door, the animals ran inside as if they had been here before. We looked at them in amazement. They were equally happy and excited. The feeling of freedom was overwhelming and it showed on us. The aura was one of pure joy and elation and I could sense our Spirit-Guides rejoicing with us. There was no sorrow, pain or remorse, just a great feeling of looking forward to a happier future. We then said a quiet prayer of thanks. Although we had nothing; we had each other and made a pledge to always be there for one another. Then together we celebrated our new found freedom and courage, with a Chinese take-away and a bottle of wine.

Our only furniture were the two single beds, which doubled up as our table and chairs. Though I was working full-time, at the end of each month I only had ten pounds left after deducting expenses. Fortunately, I knew how to economise and could prepare a substantial healthy meal from next to nothing... valuable lessons learnt from my mother. Yet every day we looked forward to coming home from school and work. The girls used to throw themselves on the bed and say, *"Mum, its great to be home."* We were always laughing and kidding around, something which we had not done for years.

They did everything to break me out of my traditional motherhood routine and took on the responsibility of caring for me. Out went the traditional family meals. So we ate according to our individual needs and body clock. Dee took over most of the household chores and at last I was learning to relax.

Within a few months, I was able to get back some of my clients and continued to plait and weave their hair at nights and weekends to earn extra cash. We were poor but not starving. Rather than sit back feeling sorry for myself or wallow in self-pity, I decide to set about creating a beautiful home. I was determined to show Marsha and Dee the art of survival through faith. I drew additional strength from the life experiences of my parents and knew that love and togetherness conquers all. I also reflected on my grandmother's many teachings;-

> *"The Lord never gives you more than you can bear.*
>
> *Time is the greatest Healer.*
>
> *Seek and you will Find, knock and the doors will Open.*
>
> *Ask and you will Receive.*
>
> *Treat people as you expect to be treated.*
>
> *The more you give, the more you will receive.*
>
> *God is Love and know that HE loves you.*
>
> *Hard work doesn't kill but strengthens.*
>
> *Always put your own house in order first.*
>
> *One step at a time and you will Make it.*
>
> *A woman's work is never done."*

With such powerfully inspiring words, I sat down with the girls and explained my plans for our future together. We then committed to start rebuilding our lives by first laying down a strong foundation of love and support. Everything we did from then onwards, was by collective agreement; choosing wall paper, paint, colours, curtains, furniture, etc. As the girls could not decorate, the main task was left to me, as I had performed it many times whilst living with my parents. The entire flat had not been decorated for about 17 years, so it needed a complete overhaul. It took us four months to complete the job; working at it every night and on weekends, sometimes until three o'clock in the morning, yet I never felt tired. I was focused, positive and energised. Finally in July, it was ready for furnishing.

My mother use to say, *"you must always live within your means but when buying, don't go for the cheapest; but go for the best you can afford. Buy things that are beautiful, strong and long lasting."* However, I could not afford anything but as I was working full-time, I could obtain hire-purchase credit. We spent three exciting weeks carefully window shopping, calculating our budget and finally bought just the essential furniture required for each room.

My credit limit could not extend to carpets, so we went down on our knees and scrubbed the vinyl floor tiles clean. Our new furniture arrived and was put into place, dusted down and polished. I cooked a huge three course meal; served with wine. We sat down on our new dinning suite with our new dishes; prayed, toasted and celebrated our second big achievement. In the wee hours of the morning; light headed and full of laughter, we retired into our new bedrooms and slept peacefully. This is the way we've lived ever since;- discuss; argue a little; agree; commit; support; pray and achieve - *"one step at a time."*

Our wedding anniversary came two weeks later on 24th July and I decided to invite my husband to dinner. He had not returned since my angry outburst and was still convinced that I'd come back home. I spent every penny I had that day and prepared his favourite dishes, knowing that it was going to be the last meal I'd ever cook for him. The flat was spotless, we opened up every door, so he'd see that each room was completely furnished and that this was our new home. Before he arrived, we contemplated what we thought he'd say, with Marsha and Dee hilariously acting out his mannerisms. He arrived bang on time and could not believe his eyes... our contemplations were spot on. We were relaxed, comfortable, talked, laughed, trying hard to make him feel welcome but his smiles were forced. I could see he was uneasy and disturbed, realising that there was no turning back.

So, I was now ready to start afresh; our home was in order and we were happy. The time was right to start planning my future and on how to provide stability, security and protection. The protection part was solved by joining the girls into the same martial arts club, where they also learnt how to defend themselves. But Marsha went on to become a member of the British Women's Karate Squad, which took her to Europe fighting in competitions. It was also instrumental in releasing a great deal of pent-up frustration, anger, fear, boosted their confidence and set them on the road of self development, discovery and personal growth.

However, after a while, Dee (age 12) who was extremely close to her father, found that she could not handle the separation or his rejection, which eventually led to her becoming rebellious. She could not fight the intense love she had for him and feared that he no longer loved her. I tried in vain to reassure her that although he was acting strangely, it was his way of dealing with his own pain but in time they would both heal. She desperately needed his personal reassurance. No matter what I did or said made any difference. I could no longer get through to her. She started to blame me for everything and wanted to live with him. One night he visited and upon leaving, went to say goodbye to Dee who was asleep in my bed. To our surprise we found that she had a couple of old photos, one of herself with her Dad and the other with all of us together. Both photos were taken during happier times and it showed us smiling. Feeling her pain and despair I swallowed my pride and went to visit him the next morning. I begged him to take her back, even if it was just for weekends, which would have helped. But he wallowed in my pain and chose to use Dee to spite me. In my efforts to protect her feelings, I didn't reveal to her what I had asked her father, so she continued to believe I was the barrier. Feeling unloved, confused, hurt and angry, Dee began to lose respect and control. Unknown to me, she became aggressive in school and got involved with a bad crowd. She started to internalise her pain with self-loathing, smoking, drinking, became anorexic and eventually tried to destroy herself. Finally, one day she exploded and attempted to get violent with me. I knew as a mother, if at any time your child got the upper hand to the point of beating you, they have truly lost it. My karate training stood me in good stead, so the situation was easily controlled. This time Marsha and I packed her straight off to her father in the middle of the night. He had no choice but to reluctantly take her in. I knew she was in extreme pain which wasn't her fault, so I allowed her to come home at weekends. On the first weekend back, she had calmed down considerably, apologised and cried her heart out.

My husband eventually persuaded Dee to return home permanently. Although she was still rebellious, it was more controlled. Many times he promised to take her out and she would wait anxiously all day but he never showed up. I didn't have the heart to tell her that he has always been irresponsible and would not want the daily responsibility of a child on his hands; plus he too was still an adolescent and needed to prove his manhood and she'd only get in his way. She'd often voiced her hatred for him and I'd remind her, *"never hate your father, no matter what he does."*

Unfortunately, many times I would also lose my patience with Dee and angrily expressed, *"you are just like your father."* I didn't realise how emotionally devastating those few words could be, which definitely made matters worst and seriously affected our relationship. In my desire to make their lives secure and stable, I was more focused on building the business, believing that as long as I was at home every day, they would be alright. With hindsight, Dee needed more of my individual attention, just being there was not sufficient to make her feel secure in my love.

Our love/hate estranged relationship continued for 7 years, until 1993 when both herself and Marsha left home. To this day I thank God for Marsha because she has always been the balancing force and whom Dee could confide in. They have a sister/mother relationship, because Marsha made a promise before Dee was born to take care of her and has kept her word. Years later, Dee revealed some painful hidden secrets of life with her father and the many dangers she was exposed too. She drank heavily, often walked the streets with her school friends late at night and would sometimes arrive at his mother's home at 11pm, where he would collect her after finishing work. She didn't get on with her grandmother, who never told her father the times she was coming home from school. At one time, she was chased by a rival gang of violent boys and had to run for her life to avoid being beaten, stabbed and possibly killed. I was horrified with nightmare images flying through my mind, of my baby roaming in danger without our knowledge. The psychological scars of leaving her father remained deep and needed a great deal of guidance from myself and Marsha. We felt that she also needed independent counselling but she refused, so I used spiritual counselling, which was a tremendous help and she is now able to make that spiritual connection for herself.

During the course of the following four years, our relationship deepened, as she realised that I would never desert her. She had not confided in me for so long and tried to make up for lost time. More importantly, she recognised that I was always there, no matter what had happened. We still have our differences, which are more about our different personalities. Through patience, prayer, time, forgiveness and love, at long last, I've finally got my baby back. Even though she is still often 'a pain in the neck,' I can laugh it off, because she got this part from me. We are all still learning, growing and healing 'one day at a time.'

It finally took Dee ten years to overcome her pain and release her father but I know deep down inside that void would never be filled. She wrote me this beautiful poem on my 46th birthday, which summed up her inner most feelings.

❀ THE STRENGTH OF A MOTHER

The strength of my Mother,

has enabled me to recover a love that gives me pride,

no longer from you Ma do I want to hide.

THE STRENGTH OF A MOTHER .

At 21, I found you.

You had never gone anywhere

but in my mind you were never there.

I never looked for you - you see

because the last place I expected to find you

WAS IN ME.

We share a past

and now at last, I can see that

through all the pain, we both have so much to GAIN.

I've always loved you - though not enough.

MY God - how could I have been so rough.

For there you were trying your best

to lay both our pasts down to rest.

You instilled in me the goodness of your heart

but I always rejected you in favour of that stupid old fart.

Who instead of showing me the right way

he plotted to destroy my soul and send me back your way.

Maybe we were both fools to worship his every sound

but remember WHAT GOES AROUND COMES AROUND.

I'm sure your NEW LOVE won't stomp your heart into the ground.

I HAVE BEEN PRIVILEGED TO HAVE BEEN GIVEN TWO MOTHERS!

I have been truly blessed by finding YOU.

For YOU have helped to restore

My faith in YOU

My pride in YOU

My joy in YOU

My pain in YOU

My strength in YOU

And the LOVE in MY heart that continues to live on in YOU.

I have learnt from my FATHER - that it is possible to be surrounded by so much love and absorb it for one's own personal gain!

I have learnt from my MOTHER - that it is possible to be surrounded by so much love and to share that love with others!

Thank you for teaching me that life is not just about receiving and that the ultimate pleasure is GIVING.

Thank you for GIVING me the PLEASURE of life and a reason to continue living, by setting me FREE.

Dee Moore (1995).

Marsha on the other hand, being five years older than Dee, was more mature and coped well with the separation, mainly because she encouraged it and was convinced that it was the right decision. Her father never enquired or showed any interest in her. After a few years had past, Marsha finally confided her feelings and revealed that he had tried emotional blackmail before we left. He privately gave them an ultimatum stating, *"if you both choose to live with me, you will never see your mother again, or if one of you chooses me and the other your mother, you will never see each other again."* Aware of my love for the children, he knew that I would never leave if they were split up. He then asked her, *"do you realise if your mother leaves, she'd find another man who'd become your new father? Are you prepared to accept another man as your father?"* She replied, *"I'd accept anyone who would make my mother happy."* From that day, she knew that she'd lost her father for good because he knew she meant it. Marsha has an exceptionally strong will but her love is even greater. Her poem on the next page sums up our relationship.

Both girls have tried hard to protect my feelings, believing that I have suffered enough and do not want to add to my pain. But my pain will never cease until I know that they are both pain-free. However, I'm happy knowing that they too are survivors.

Remembering

I remember myself as a child,
quiet but inquisitive.
I remember a woman
who took care of me
who taught me
who nursed me
who protected me
who defended me
who corrected and disciplined me
who provided for me
who loved me.

This woman
who was also once a child
a teenager
an adult
a mother
a wife.
She was all these things when I was young.

Now I am grown, she is a person
who has dreams
who has aspirations
who laughs
who strives for whatever she wants or needs
who loves to love
who loves to give and share whatever she has 'big or small'
who loves freedom
and knows now that she has it.

This woman,

My mother,

who has grown into a wonderful person through
time and experience, *no matter how hard.*

Has removed all the bad and come away
with only good stories to share.

Ever determined not to let the bad times surface
and consume her life, but to learn valuable
lessons from them

She is a go-getter
a teacher
an *ACT*er
a healer
a believer
a questioner
a forgiver
a lover
a dreamer
a motivator
an idealist
an enlightened soul.

SHE IS 'MY FUTURE.'

Dear Mum, you are the *giver of my life and* for the many lessons you have taught me
I am forever grateful. For the love you have injected in me, I am eternally fulfiled
and for the power you have instilled in me, I know I can conquer anything.

I will never deny you and am bound by fate to always love you!.

Marsha Moore (1997).

Through Dee's pain and anguish I reflected on the whole separation and realised that parents, whilst in their own pain, often don't recognise the pain they unconsciously inflict on their children, which stays with them for life. Parents may recover but the children go on suffering, simply because there is no substitute for parents love. Therefore, we must be mindful that we owe them a duty of care. Separation of any kind is a painful experience for all involved but:-

"I Thank God that the human-Spirit is strong and resilient. It bounces back, recovers and SURVIVES."

I'm proud of Marsha and Dee because they have matured stable, respectful, polite, confident, independent, happy, loving, caring, conscious, sometimes down right miserable and unbearable, because I have given them all of this and more. They will always be my greatest assets, best friends and proudest achievement; -

"Love - truly conquers all."

Additionally, making them aware of their spirituality, has instilled even greater strength and higher consciousness, that at times their faith in God and love for animals, astonishes and leaves me in awe. Many years later, I learnt that whilst we are in Spirit, we choose when we wish to return to earth and also choose the people whom we wish to become our parents. So, I'm truly glad that my children chose me, because their love and support has kept me strong.

❀ Divorce.

I couldn't wait to be unshackled. My solicitor advised that I could apply for a divorce once we had been separated for two years. My application was made exactly two years to the date and in 1989, I received the Decree Absolute. It felt great to be free and of course we celebrated in the usual manner. What my girls didn't realise was that I too was in pain, missed him terribly, felt desperately lonely and was going through hell, because

I also had the added pressures of trying to help them overcome their pains, deal with their adolescence and trying to survive on almost next to nothing. These were all new experiences for me and somehow I had to cope. It took me two years to come to terms with living alone; regained my confidence, self esteem and alas! I found myself.

❀ Living Alone.

I consciously chose to remain alone and celibate, until such time that I felt I'd overcome my husband and faced up to the problems I had caused in our marriage, before I could be ready to deal with a new relationship, without having to cast any blame or unconsciously take it out on him. I also felt that Marsha and Dee would need all of my time to heal and feel secure again.

I've always learnt from other people's experiences and had seen many of my friends take on new partners almost immediately after separation, primarily because of their need to feel wanted or desirable, which confused the emotions of desperation, loneliness, infatuation and true love. Too often their relationships ended and they moved on to another and so on. Their children's vulnerability was completely overlooked, no consideration was given to the emotional effects of being forced to accept one stranger after another as a father/mother figure. Sometimes they would come to like the new person, then the relationship ended, which messed them up. But their parents simply shrugged it off with an attitude of, *"they are young and will soon get over it."*

I knew that all three of us needed each other and a lot of healing time. It took 7 years for me to reach that moment of acceptance and stability; which may seem a long time but I gained additional strength from my ancestors, whom I had seen survive alone for many more years, whilst taking great care of their children. This was not being a sacrificial mother but simply putting my loved-ones first and meeting their needs. The period of healing also gave me time to mature, reflect on the type of person I needed and what I really wanted from a relationship. The seven years was worth the wait, because I found a committed mate, who loves and adores me and has since made my life blissfully happy.

❀ Unconditional Love.

Until I had my children, I didn't understand unconditional love, because I've only known abusive love, with the exception of my grandmother. Both my parents loved me but each wanted more from me. My father's vain pride, desperately needed one of his children to become a professional and as I was the only one who showed an inclination of being studious; he pushed me his way. My mother loved large houses but hated house work, as I loved to see everything sparkling clean and tidy; she pushed me her way. Then I ended up with a husband who was both intelligent and lazy and didn't want the responsibility of home, children or work; so he too pushed me his way. They all got what they wanted and I suffered to please them. Furthermore, 'colour discrimination' has always existed within the black race and those who have the courage to admit it, would agree that those with lighter skins are treated better than those with darker skins, even amongst families, loved-ones and friends. My husband frequently mentioned that he was luckier with lighter skinned women, even though his complexion was much darker than mine. My brother, sister and cousins, married English or Indian partners, so they had mixed race children who were favoured. This treatment was neither intentional or conscious but had grown out of habit... a throw back from the old slavery days, where white or light was looked upon as being superior or better, more beautiful, hence favoured. The same way blondes were favoured more than brunettes amongst white people. So it was not seen as discrimination or abuse, just a matter of fact.

In fact, the majority of African/Caribbean people tried hard to erase their African features, by preferring to mate only with lighter skinned men/women, who had straight hair and straight noses, so that their children could inherit these Western/Asian traits. They believed it would give them a better chance in life, as they would be more acceptable in the wider world. Although I was dark skinned, I never acquired this inferiority complex, because I've always been exceptionally proud of 'who and what I am;' plus with the guided knowledge that all of God's creations are beautiful, I was more than pleased with how HE'd created me. Unfortunately, many black people (men & women) suffered the consequences of this inter-racial discrimination, lowering their self esteem to the point of believing that they were ugly and destroyed their naturally beautiful dark features, by using chemical creams to try to lighten their skins. Unfortunately, this attitude amongst blacks still prevails throughout the world today. But fortunately, nature creates its own balance and 'black' has now become fashionable and the reverse is occurring within the white race, who in their desire to get as dark as possible, are destroying their skins by using skin darkening creams and also sun bathing to the point of getting skin cancers. 'Black' now represents beauty, sophistication and is so acceptable, that many white people are preferring to mate only with black people. So the saga goes on.

> ## *"Beauty is truly in the eyes of the Beholder."*

I was forty years old when my Mum told me, *"you are very photogenic, attractive and have beautiful features, especially your eyes."* This was the first time she had ever commented on my looks. Yet my light skinned sisters were always told how cute and beautiful they were. Here again, nature creates its own balance as *"beauty is only skin deep,"* both cuteness and surface appearance disappears with age but true beauty lies within, which is enhanced through maturity and is never destroyed.

Nevertheless, I was happy and loved them unconditionally and would forgive all their faults. Even though I became a stern disciplinarian, I'd always cover up my inner pain and tears and tried to avoid hurting their feelings. Nevertheless, my family relationship has remained in a perpetual state of unresolved feuding, which makes it extremely difficult to either be neutral or to ensure fairness. This experience has taught me that even amongst the ones you love, deep rooted bitterness is the most difficult to eradicate and which causes unnecessary anguish. Peacemakers generally end up in the firing line and can be slaughtered.

Falling In Love Again

I remained celibate for 7 years, taking care of my children, home and business; a complete workaholic. Then in July 1993, my mother who had been working with me for six years suddenly became ill. I'd never forget that terrible Saturday morning when Dad phoned to say, *"Mum is in hospital with severe stomach pains."* It turned out that she had advanced Ovarian cancer and passed away within 10 days. Mum and I had become very close over the years and I was not ready to lose her. She was only 68, strong, healthy and full of life. Her church had organised a two week holiday mission to Lourdes in France, which she was so looking forward to; that month was also Dad's birthday. Her passing was yet another painful passage in my life but one which reminded me that 'life' is both short and precious and should be lived to the full. She used to beg me to stop working so hard and to take a break. She would insist I should go on a long holiday, back home to Trinidad, as I'd not returned since leaving 30 years before. I was in a state of turmoil, my motivation, will to work and desire to succeed were all shattered. I felt lost, numb and confused and repeatedly asked God - WHY? Particularly, as part of my dream and determined drive, was to be able to give both my parents all they deserved and a grand lifestyle in their old age. However, for the family's sake, I had to be composed and stifled my grief. Being the only one with the ability to communicate on the other side (the Spirit world) brought both conflict and comfort. Nevertheless, Mum kept me busy and transmitted messages for a full 90 days after her death.

By November 1993, I was completely drained, exhausted and desperately needed to refill my energy. So Dad decided that we should return to Trinidad the following year to rest and recover.

Every year on the 31st December, I hold a private Thanksgiving Day to God, at home with Marsha and Dee. We would pray, give thanks and then ask for our 'wishes' for the new year. But, December 1993 felt different; for the first time since leaving my husband, I felt I was ready for a new relationship and as part of my New Year's wishes, I asked God to send me the right person. I've always believed that people don't need to go in search for a partner but if they'd first ask God to send him/her, then their true soul-mate would turn up at the most unexpected moment. Call it faith or just coincidence but it has always worked for me. I follow the philosophy, *"ask and you will receive."*

On 29th January '94, Dad and I finally left for Trinidad, the day after my 45th birthday. I'd dreamt of this moment for 30 years and could not believe that I was really back home. Feeling the hot tropical sun and cool breeze against my skin; I inhaled and exhaled deeply. Then Mum flashed across my mind. I imagined her joy as my feet touched the Caribbean soil, then the deep pain, grief, longing; missing her, all welled up inside me but this time my tears were soothingly healing and then, I smiled. It was terrific meeting and re-acquainting with all my family; retracing my sixteen year roots; our homes, schools, churches, etc.

The month of February is renowned for Trinidad's splendid carnival. I played mass for the first time and our band 'Mirage' by Wayne Berkeley won the first prize as band of the year. That was real fun, I was learning to let my hair down and having a ball. The week before carnival, we attended a crowded steel band competition called Panarama, when out of the blue in the midst of thousands of people, a gentleman named Rudolph Walker, the renowned Actor whom we both knew in England, turned up and greeted Dad. They were great friends to the point that he called Dad 'Pops' and Dad called him 'Son.' Rudolph and I had privately admired each other from a distance for many years but never got acquainted. We often met unexpectedly at special functions and the most we'd say was, *"Hello"* and *"Goodbye."* But on this occasion, something sparked and my heart skipped several beats. I tried hard to ignore my emotions but the next day I couldn't get him out of my mind and was acting like an excited school girl... grinning like a cheshire cat. Two weeks later, my cousin decided to organise a party and I telephoned to invite him. Whilst in conversation, his soothing, deep, velvety voice had me totally captivated... mesmerised; I simply melted. Getting ready for the party was something else, overwhelmed with excitement, it felt like ages but he arrived on time. After introducing him to everyone, we disappeared into the garden and spoke non-stop; covering every personal topic, only to be amazed with how much we actually had in common. We loved and believed in the same things; even down to what we were looking for or expected out of a relationship, careers or life. We both had two children and felt unappreciated by our previous partners. We connected 100% but cautiously concealed our true feelings and waited until we returned to England to start the relationship; by which time we were both head over heels in love. Neither of us could believe our joy or luck and continued to talk and talk, pouring our hearts out, releasing our inner most feelings without any fears, inhibitions or insecurities. In a very short time we became best friends and confidants. One evening he sat me on his lap and told me to close my eyes. When I opened them, he was holding a beautiful engagement ring and simply said, *"I'm totally committed to you, I've never been in love before but now I know I am."* Within six months we were living together. I never thought that love the second time around could be much deeper, stronger, better and more fulfiling than the first.

We were so compatible and spiritually connected that we frequently telepathise; in a manner of thinking the same things at the same time; or whilst in conversation, we'd find ourselves ending each other's sentences; or when he said something; I'd say, *"I knew you were going to say that."* At first, he was puzzled and couldn't understand how I knew what he was thinking before he said it and I couldn't explain how or why! I just knew that he was going to say precisely what he'd said. But two situations occurred which made us aware of this telepathic interaction. On our first date in Trinidad, whilst walking, we were about to cross over to the other side of the road, being the gentleman he is, he took my hand to lead me across. The moment our hands touched, I felt like a spark of electricity had instantly shot through my body, which startled me but I didn't say anything to him. About two months later, we were reminiscing about our first date and he happened to mention that when he held my hand, he felt an electrical 'shock wave' run through his body. I looked at him in surprise, then said that I too had felt the same thing. The other occasion happened about a year later, when Rudolph had to return to Trinidad to look after his sick mother and we were separated for one month. I was missing him terribly and decided that on his return, I would suggest that we take a few short romantic trips to various European countries. On the day he returned to England, I met him at the airport and as we journeyed home, he said how much he'd missed me and that the thought came to him that we should go on a short romantic weekend in Europe. Again I looked at him in dismay and said that I had precisely the same thought.

We believed that we were purposely brought together because our ways, needs and desires are uncannily similar. We met '7' weeks after I'd asked God in my new year Thanksgiving to send me the right person. Our birthdays fall on the same day 28th but on different months, our first date was on the 28th. Since then we've celebrated the 28th day of each month as our special lucky day and pamper each other. Rudolph is really the man of my dreams; romantic, supportive, complimentary, caring, passionate, affectionate and unselfish. He goes out of his way to make me feel totally secured in his love.

It took me over two years to get used to the idea of a man doing house work, shopping and taking care of me! I've never experienced such intense love, praise or devotion and for once in my life, I'm receiving exactly what I'm giving ...*"it is liberating to love and be loved."* This new experience taught me that no one should be afraid of letting go or of finding true love again; its never too late. If it could happen to me, it could happen to anybody. But building a good relationship takes conscious effort, compromise and understanding on both sides, even if the relationship is 'heaven sent' one still has to work at it. I've learnt to live again; my life is in balance and enjoyable, with so much more to look forward to. It feels great dressing up not just for myself but to look good for someone who appreciates me. Four years later, we agreed to jump the broomstick. On 28th August 1998, our marriage was a very special, sacred and private affair, where our children were the witnesses and gave us away. Everyone was overjoyed. Marsha and Dee said, *"Mum I've never seen you more beautiful, yourself and Rudolph look really happy together."* Having our children's consent, involvement and blessings meant a great deal, as it created a new pact cementing our extended family. As we were both previously married and divorced, neither of us believed that marriage would make a difference and were equally surprised to realise that it did. We became even closer and truly bonded. When I think or speak about him, I physically radiate and glow all over, my energy level rises to an all time high. So at long last, I'm living life to the full, truly happy and enjoying every minute of it. I've finally found my best friend, spiritual partner, soul-mate and knight in shinning armour, who treats me like a pure diamond.

The following year, I organised a surprise to mark his 60th birthday. For seven months, I collaboration with Pearsons Television, his family and friends, secretly collating information on his background and achievements. On the day of his birthday, a bogus meeting was arranged at Lords Cricket Stadium, with his celebrity cricket team (the Bunburys). Television presenter Michael Aspel and the camera crew hid in the background, whilst secretly filming his every move. A few minutes later, Michael Aspel appeared behind Rudolph and said those immortal words, *"Rudolph Walker, This is Your Life!"* No words could describe his shocked expression. Rudolph was then whisked off to BBC Television Studios, to begin filming the 30 minute live show; including live interviews of friends in Trinidad. The evening came to a close with a fantastic all night party. This was another glorious/unforgettable moment in our lives.

═ My Natural Heritage and Role Models ═

This might sound predictably corny but I always look to God first whenever I'm in need, in despair or looking for inspiration and guidance. Believing in HIM gives me greater faith in myself. However, for physical role models, I look first within my own family, for lessons on the art of survival.

I come from a family with a long history as Christians, Spiritualists and Natural Herbalists, not due to fashion or scientific changes but because it was the normal way of life, which goes back centuries. It was also my good fortune to be born during this wonderful period of existence, well before Western civilisation introduced their many pollutants; which has since poisoned mind, body, Spirit and the environment.

Seven members of my family has made a lasting impression on my life to date.

1.   **My Great Grandmother** (my father's grandmother).

   Jane Elizabeth Adams - (called Mam-Bucaud):

   was one of six wives of a wealthy African family, who came to the Caribbean (Trinidad) not as slaves but as free people. She belonged to the Yoruba African nation - her husband (Joshua Alexander) belonged to the Housa African nation. They were practising Muslims and converted to Catholicism when they migrated to the Caribbean. She was the only Spiritual/Herbalist and nursing mid-wife in her village and was more highly respected than the village doctor; well known for her home made herbal remedies and effective treatments. I am told that when anyone became ill, if she arrived at the same time as the doctor; she would be chosen to treat them or if a doctor was unsure of what to do, they would call for her help. They had complete trust and faith in her ability. She also kept all of her African traditions alive, which kept her family well rooted. I remember attending many feasts called 'The Nation Dance' held at her large home; where all our relatives from around the island would gather to pray, eat, drink, dance and sing to the vibrant rhythms of the African drums. Mam-Bucaud dressed in traditional clothes and jewellery, would take centre stage and out dance everyone from sunset to sunrise. She'd call on our ancestors; she spoke in tongues; gave spiritual messages, received medicinal instructions; blessed and healed her family. This was how most of our relatives kept in touch with each other. It was a time of tremendous preparation, merriment, reminiscence, story telling and also for new members of our clan (i.e babies) to be introduced to everyone. I remember once, when my Dad was introducing us (his children) to various family members saying; *"this is Uncle so and so?" - who is the son of so and so?* your 5th cousin; which went on to aunts, more uncles, nephews, nieces and cousins galore... 1st, 2nd - 11th, etc. As I grew older, I realised the significance of knowing *"who you are - who you belong too and where you come from... i.e. family, identity and strength."*

Mam-Bucaud was the family matriarch and historian, who by memory could recite her entire family tree. Every baby would be presented to her. She'd take a good long look at its features, take off its clothes to check for hereditary features and also signs of physical defects, illnesses and reflexes; then she'd bless it. She died at the grand old age of 112, retaining her mental faculties and without a sign of feebleness. She had lived purely the 'natural way'. I was only five years old when she died but remember vividly this young looking, tall, slim, stately, proud, alert and strong woman, with an encyclopedic mental capacity surpassed by no one I have yet come across.

She is also one of my Spirit-Guides. During the 1980's, African hair braiding became fashionable in the West, which also provided me with a regular part-time income, working from home. Mam-Bucaud often worked through me and I was able to recreate authentic African tribal hair styles, which enhanced their beauty. My clients who were unaware, would remark that they could hardly feel my hands working in their hair and also felt light headed, refreshed and soothed at the end of it. The styles were so neatly designed that strangers would run up to them in the street and ask, *"who did your hair, its beautiful, would she do mine?"* which gave me a regular flow of customers. In 1993 my youngest sister gave birth to her first baby and Mam-Bucaud gave me written instructions on how to bless and offer the baby to God in the ancient African tradition. This was the first time since her death 45 years ago, that this tradition was performed in our family and my father confirmed its authenticity.

These traditions have long been lost in our family, erased through the passage of time and the adoption of foreign habits. Many who dispersed overseas; lost touch with each other and their roots. I'm told that I have strong Fulani features which comes from my father's mother's side of the family.

2. **My Grandfather** (my father's father and one of Mam-Bucaud's sons).

<u>Andrew Joseph Bartholemew - Alexander</u>:

was a prominent member of the community and Head Master in Trinidad, who owned a private school. He was determined to rid the black race from their slavish dependent mentality, lack of leadership and effort, induced by their European slave masters. He wanted to re-educate them to achieve and become self reliant, by instilling a strong sense of pride and ambition. He was a hard task master and stern disciplinarian. Again, an extremely proud, powerfully built gentleman with a great sense of presence, deep voice, charisma, intellect and dressed exquisitely. He earned the M.B.E... (member of the British Empire) medal in 1953 for his personal contribution and service, in the fields of Education, Social Services, Federation of Agriculture, Fishing and various other Co-operatives. When he died it was recorded that 'Mr Alexander was a tower of strength and both the society and community has suffered a great loss.' A minute silence was held as a mark of respect. He too is one of my Spirit-Guides.

3.   **My father.**

<u>James Christopher - Alexander:</u>

was the first black man to establish a major Housing Association 'Trinity Housing' in Britain in 1969. His intention was to house all races, the only criteria being poverty, under privileged, in poor housing conditions or homeless. In those days, Housing Associations were the true philanthropists, fighting the Government to meet the needs of the poor, by providing decent housing with basic amenities and to destroy Rackmanism. This was when I learnt of the true plight of the poor working classes in England. Having lived in the upper/middle class area of Essex and in our own private home, I could not believe that there were British people (mostly Irish) living in absolute squalor and poverty. Seeing for the first time, a family of six, living in one small mice and roach infested room, riddled with damp. This one room was used as their living, dining, kitchen and bedroom. An equally squalid bathroom was shared with several of other families, who also occupied the same building and there was no hot water supply. This scene brought me to tears and has left a haunting memory. However, I was soon to realise that this was not an isolated case but merely one of hundreds in London, which also seriously affected black people. My father being a Christian family man, decided that every human being was entitled to live in privacy, with dignity and respect. This was how and why Trinity Housing Association was born. The word 'Trinity' represented the three protective mountains which surrounds our Caribbean Island Trinidad, called La Trinity, the Three Sisters or the Holy Trinity. My father established over 500 beautiful flats and houses and was able to help hundreds of people, before it was amalgamated with two other associations and renamed East London Housing Association. He then became one of the driving forces behind the plight of elderly blacks in Britain and in 1988 was personally invited and attended the Queen's Royal Garden Party with Mum proudly by his side. Dad has always had a competitive Spirit, renowned in his youth as a great athletic sprinter, ballroom dancer, charmer and classy dresser.

4. My Mother.

Beryl May-Rita, (Dallaway) - Alexander:

born and bred in Trinidad from a poor country background. Mum was exceptionally beautiful, a real classy lady who dressed magnificently. She was multi-talented; as a beauty therapist, hairdresser, fashion designer/seamstress and an excellent cook, which meant she knew how to take care of herself and others. She made all of our clothes including Christening, Communion, Confirmation and Wedding dresses, which also extended to other family members and friends.

Mum suffered a great deal during pregnancy, often putting her life at risk. I was one who caused her untold complications. As the story goes, she was seven months pregnant when she heard about the criminal trial of a child rapist. Mum became so distraught that she immediately went into spasms, lost consciousness; her jaws locked thereby destroying all of her back teeth... upper and lower, before going into labour. After my birth (weighing under four pounds), she needed months of convalescence, hence my grandmother's initial care. Mum used to say, *"you were like a little rat but you gave me hell to come into this world."*

She was also an Organic Gardener and Caribbean Food Consultant, who remembered most of the natural remedies learnt from her mother and stuck to the tradition. Wherever we lived, she'd cultivate a magnificent garden... a job she simply loved, which gave her enormous pleasure and was her best form of relaxation. Mum preferred gardening, cooking and sewing to housework, all of which kept those gifted hands extremely busy.

In making Britain our second home, her garden was filled with both Caribbean and European herbs (thyme, chives, sage, aloe-vera, vervain, basil, tarragon, oregano, mint, shallots, celery, rosemary, bay leaf, wonder-of-the-world, shaddon beni, West Indian hot peppers, sweet peppers and parsley, also vegetables and fruits such as spinach, carrots, tomatoes, cucumber, sweet corn, runner beans and potatoes; apples, plums, pears and cherries). We only felt home sick for family and friends but never for the food. She could cook every type of cuisine from Caribbean, English, French, Italian, Spanish, Chinese, Indian to herbal remedies; plus made superb cakes with exquisite hand made icing decorations.

As a strong, committed Christian and Spiritualist, she was forever praying and her shoulders were always available for everyone to cry on; giving endless support, advice, comfort and encouragement. I admired my parents' courage for leaving the Caribbean, where they had a comfortable lifestyle and ventured into a new unknown country (Britain) with their young children and worked hard to rebuild an equally respectful, comfortable lifestyle for us all. This took great determination, courage and faith. Mum worked in my business from 1987 to 1993, when she died and continues to help me in Spirit.

5. **My Aunt.**

Doris (Dallaway) - Alverez:

born and bred in Trinidad, my mother's only sister. Although only educated to elementary standard, Aunt Doris had a natural talent for property development and management. She married young, had five children and wanted to acquire a house for each of them before she died. She never did a day's work in her life but saved a little each day from her house keeping money and was able to buy her first property, which she helped repair, decorate and then rented it out. Putting aside more from the house keeping together with the new rent money, she was able to buy a second property and so on, until accomplishing her dream of five houses, including some land. She died in July 1988 aged 73, after undergoing heart surgery in England. Just before she died, she said to me, *"What I have done without education, could you imagine where I would have reached if I was educated?"*

6.   **My Great - Grand Mother** (my mother's grandmother).

Ma Winnie Loman:

I never knew Ma Loman but my mother told me this romantic story about her and my great-grandfather, which I admired for her love, courage and humanity.

My great-grandfather came from a family of African slaves, who got their name Dallaway from their slave-master. They lived in Portugal (Madeira) and were slaves to a rich white family called The Loman's. My great-grandfather used to drive the Loman's family buggy, to take them to church, shopping, outings etc. In those days, the black slaves were not allowed to get close to the whites. However, one of their daughters (Winnie) secretly fell in love with my great-grandfather and seduced him. She was a trained mid-wife but slaves were not allowed to have a mid-wife and delivered their babies alone. One night, she sneaked out to deliver a slave's baby. It was then she realised that there was no difference between black or white labour pains or child birth and that blacks were as human as whites and should not be treated like animals. Her love for my great-grandfather grew so strong that she was prepared to give up the family wealth, luxury and high society life for him. She hatched a plan for them to elope; had special papers made up for him, as if he was her personal slave and bought two boat tickets to the Caribbean. The next day she told her parents that she was going shopping and of course my great-grandfather had to drive her to town. They secretly boarded the ship; got married on board and came off at the first port which was on the Island of St. Vincent. Apparently she did not like the people there, so they sailed to Trinidad where they settled and had many children; one being my grandfather 'Johnny Dallaway' (my mother's father). Hence my mother was light skinned. Ma Loman never saw her family again.

7. **My Grandmother** *(my mother's mother).*

    <u>Wilhelmina Dallaway</u> (GRAMMA'S):

    made an indelible mark on my early life. Her encyclopedic knowledge of the properties and usage of herbs and plants; her love of God and unshakeable belief in the sanctity of nature's delicate balance, gave me an abiding respect for the old ways of 'bush medicines.' It was to be an inspiration for me, as a working mother in the heart of London, I began to look back to my roots for the blue-print for a less stressful and healthier lifestyle for myself, husband and children. I became immersed in the fast living high tech culture of the 70's, where the pill and prescription were the answer to all ailments. But, when it came to caring for my daughters health, I knew that Gramma's philosophy was not only natural but the best.

This is one of Ma's wise teachings on how to live; -

"As God is truth and love - always live your life truthfully and with love; share with love; give with a willing and happy heart; live life to the full and learn from it. Respect yourself, elders and all that is around you."

It was in her loving memory, that I named my business and products GRAMMA'S, in the hope that it would help to keep my feet firmly on the ground and remind me to remain a true child of God. I'm also told that I owe my life to her; being born severely premature, in those days such babies rarely survived and even though the doctors gave up on me, she never did. Apparently, she made a little pillow as I was too small to handle and placed it in a Bassinet basket which became my cot, nurser and carrier. With tender loving care, she massaged, breast fed and treated me with ancient herbal remedies. Therefore, I've survived as a direct result of folklore remedies, wisdom and love. In growing up, she took me under her wings and passed on much of her knowledge. She once said, *"what I'm teaching you now, you'd use in your later years and would then look back and laugh!"* These words were long forgotten and it was not until I started my business in 1987 and began re-educating people about the beneficial values of natural foods, herbal remedies and God, did I recall and realise what she meant all those year ago and then, 'I laughed.' Ma remained by my side, even after her death in July 1962, when she became my main family 'Spirit-Guide and Protector,' proving that 'through love, we connect to the Spirit world, because **love** never dies.'

In remembrance, I celebrate her birthday every year on 1st October, with a bunch of flowers and a lighted candle.

❀ Old Wives' Tales.

On reflection, the world has come full circle, because many of our ancestors' wisdom which was callously dismissed as 'old wives tales' by the Western-world, are now being acknowledged, accepted and adopted.

I remember Ma telling me; -

"When you decide to have children, if you want your child to be good natured and intelligent, then during pregnancy you must try to be good natured, calm, read intelligent books, relax, gently rub your belly and speak to your baby because it can hear, communicate with you and enjoys being comforted. If you want to know your child's true nature and personality, then observe your own mood changes. If you find that you are bad tempered or violent, then try your best to control yourself, as this would make it easier to control the baby after it's born. Once born, when ever your child is very sick or in any kind of trouble, you must band your belly tight, because you would feel your child's pain in the root area of

its birth (i.e. belly).   This banding protects you against serious illness (mental and physical) caused through stress and worry.   A mother endures many years of suffering as her children grows from baby to infant, adolescent to adult and onto death.   A mother's pains and tears for her children always attacks or hits her stomach; yet the pain for a lover comes from her heart.   She would automatically reach for her stomach when her child is in pain.   So the banding provides support and acts like a brace to absorb some of the shock-waves, whilst helping to strengthen her womb and nerves.   This is the major difference between a mother and a father, whose role is to give her added support and strength to help her bear the pain.   This does not mean that he does not suffer but he feels hurt rather than birth pains.   He is the one who generally keeps a strong head when there is chaos and brings balance and stability to the household.   But when there is no man to provide this balancing force, then the mother has to bear all the pain alone.   In this case, she should band both her 'belly' and 'head' for protection against the blows.   A very tight and firm full bodied girdle can be used as a belly-band."

Such simple wisdom, which all proved true in later years when I had my own children, I've felt every agonising pain they have suffered to-date. But it was not until I wrote this passage, did I realise that I forgot to band my belly (a direct result of modern western-culture) which could also be the cause for so many nervous breakdowns and stomach disorders.

I'm so proud to continue in my Grandmother's uneducated, uncomplicated, simple footsteps and also in my ancestors strength, tolerance, courage, determination and loving care. It will remain with me forever in my strive for excellence through God.

This is my personal philosophy, developed from the relationship with my ancestors and other Spirit-Guides;-

❀ A Sense of Purpose.

I believe that no matter how life turns out for us as individuals, whether:

high or low,

King or Queen,

beggar or thief,

President/Prime Minister or MP,

Magistrate or criminal,

homosexual/heterosexual or hermaphrodite,

mother or father,

able or disabled,

black/white or mixed,

democrat/nationalist/ communist,

famous or infamous,

working/middle or upper class,

aristocrat or vagrant,

artist or painter decorator,

singer or song writer,

sinner/atheist or priest,

first or third world,

loser or winner,

vegetarian or omnivore,

civilised or uncivilised,

child or adult,

fat or thin,

educated or illiterate,

sober/alcoholic or drug addict,

orthodox or unorthodox,

feminist/sexist/chauvinist/racist

we are all human beings, equally susceptible to all of life's ups and downs, including sickness, health and death but more importantly, we are all part of God's unique and wonderful creation. HE is the **respecter, non abuser** and **lover** of all and does not differentiate or equate in our comings and goings. In other words, we are all given life in the same way (birth) and leave HIS earth in the same way (death); **conceived**; bringing nothing and **die**; taking nothing. So if by good fortune or hard work, we are able to amass wealth for ourselves or even if we don't succeed: if we collectively try to 'serve a good purpose' by servicing and respecting humanity, maybe then, this world could be a better place for all to reside... i.e. humans, animals and plants.

"God & Food is Love & Life, so

LIVE and LET LIVE*"*

Andrew Joseph Bartholemew - Alexander;
my grandfather

Doris (Dallaway) - Alverez;
my auntie

Beryl May-Rita (Dallaway) - Alexander;
my mother

James Christopher - Alexander;
my father

● **1971:**
my wedding dress made by mum.

● mum working on wedding cakes.

90.

● Rudolph and I on our wedding day: 28 August 1998.

● with daughters,
Marsha and Dee.

Family photo: Darius, Sheona,
Rudolph, me, Dee and Marsha

● **1999:**
Rudolph's surprise birthday party
televised on **'This is your Life.'**

● After a tremendous evening with family
and friends, Rudolph accepts the 'This is
Your Life' red book from Michael Aspel.

CHAPTER II.

The Birth of my Business.

"In life, there are No Limitations,
With Faith, all things are Possible.

You hold the key to Success and therefore -

Possess the Power
to Determine & Create
your own Destiny."

The Birth of My Business

After that final dinner with my ex-husband in July 1986, I took a week off work to relax, contemplate and plan my future. Deep down inside I'd always wanted to do more with my life. I believed, I had something to offer, something to give or something important to share with others. But as my life had first been controlled by my parents, then later by my husband, whom I tried to please by doing whatever they demanded, desired or expected. Now at the age of 38, I realised that I'd lived trying to please everyone except myself. I'd never been 'free,' never lived alone. Although I still had my children, for once I felt 'free' because they depended on me but were not a burden. 'Free' to make my own choices. 'Free' to make my own decisions and 'free' to either make a mess or success of it. I decided that this was my life and I was going to make the most of it and live it my way. Not only mentally, spiritually, emotionally and physically 'free;' but I'd also acquired renewed self esteem, motivation, direction and was more focused than I'd ever been in my entire life.

I sat down for weeks and took a long hard look at my future and considered my options. I could either continue in a mundane safe 9 to 5 job, with its guaranteed monthly pay package or go back into a more professional career with all the hassles this entailed. However, the economic climate was in the process of change and long term job security was becoming increasingly fragile and insecure. I then looked at the lucrative prospects of setting up my own business. This idea excited me the most because it meant having to develop my own creative skills and to prove whether or not I really had what it took to make it. The more I thought about it, the more excited I became. Although I lacked confidence and experience, I was not afraid. For some unknown reason my vision and strategy was crystal clear, I knew what I had to do but I didn't know how I was going to find the ways or means of achieving my dreams. I was overwhelmed, bursting with joy and happiness. At last! I was 'free' and in control of my own destiny.

Once I'd calmed down and was sure of the full picture, I explained the detailed plans to Marsha and Dee. My intention was to make a mark on the World Food Market by recreating and manufacturing my grandmother's herbal foods and re-educate the British nation using her divine philosophy. They were instantly supportive and in total agreement, as they'd never doubted my ability. Marsha, being a Vegetarian, felt that it was about time vegetarian food got a bit of zing, zest and flavour. They also felt that the world would be a better place if exposed to my grandmother's philosophies. Therefore, naming the business was the easiest part; GRAMMA'S in her loving memory, to whom I owed my life and who also taught me about the importance of 'God & Food' and their connection with LIFE; -

1. 'Natural food' was originally created to both 'feed & heal' and is our best known medicine.

2. 'God is love,' so when cooking you must cook with love.

3. 'The simple Laws-of-Life and Nature through God.' This principle requires absolute faith in God as the Universal Creator and the understanding that life and healing originate from HIM. Therefore, when planting, growing, harvesting, preparing, cooking or manufacturing any food or medicine, the preparer must first pray to God for HIS blessings and healing, in the conscious knowledge that they are responsible for nourishing lives and improving health. Therefore, my business had to operate on these divine principles. Furthermore, my grandmother believed in the three gifts of life, FAITH, HOPE and CHARITY, which also had to be incorporated into the business.

I proudly told Marsha and Dee that I planned to get my products into Harrods. As far as I was concerned, they were the best and therefore belonged only in the best stores. In my naivety, I thought it would take ten years to get them on these prestigious shelves and I would have been more than satisfied if they were in Harrods for only one day. My plans grew even more ambitious, with great intentions of revolutionising black foods in Britain. Although I had no previous commercial skills or experience, nor any idea of what I was really getting myself into; yet somehow I instinctively knew that the marketing of black foods needed radical change. My strategy for the change would start by first educating people on the true beneficial values of our foods, which in turn would create a new awareness, gain their interest and acceptance. I felt inspired to challenge tradition and the status quo and envisaged great difficulty and opposition from the British Authorities. However, I believed that with God's blessings, if I was successful, it would not only benefit us but also the entire British nation and eventually the world.

I explained to the girls that it might take ten years to break the mould, during which there might be many times I'd lose heart and want to give up. But it was then that I'd need their strongest support to raise my spirits and their encouragement to go on regardless of the outcome. Marsha and Dee's response stunned me; *"Mum, you have been there for us all our lives, now it's our turn to be there for you. If we starve, we'll starve together and if we were to succeed, then we'll rise and celebrate together."* I'd always believed that when building anything you must have a firm foundation. My girls and my home were my foundation and with such solid support, I began to rebuild our future. This was before Dee's rebellion but even throughout her rebellious stages, she remained supportive and kept her promise.

The next day, I invited my parents over and told them about my plans. I can still see the look of pure pride on their faces. We prayed and gave thanks, so now I was ready to get started.

I set about the difficult task of learning business and how to actually begin the process of achieving this incredible dream. My research started with reading up all the literature on Food Laws, Regulations, Legislation, Labelling, Registration, the do's and don'ts in the Food Industry, whilst testing and perfecting my Gramma's Herbal Pepper Sauces, which was going to be my first product range. Then I had the products tested by the Food Science Laboratory and passed for human consumption; my kitchen examined by the Public Health Inspector and passed for Hygiene

& Safety Standards and finally obtained the necessary Public Liability Insurance cover. With these certificates, I could officially start to produce, market and sell my products. At this point, the real hard work began. I searched all over Britain to find suitable bottles, then designed the logo, labels and packaging; wrote the promotional literature and leaflets, label information, calculated the retail and wholesale prices and finally completed the full Business Plan. This was during the period of the Government's Enterprise boom, where faced with growing unemployment, both the Government and national Banks were enticing poor people to start up their own businesses as a way of securing their long-term future, with promises of all sorts of support, training, advice and funding. It was called 'The Spirit of Free Enterprise' created by the then Prime Minister, Margaret Thatcher and the birth of 'women-in-business.' They made it sound so easy but I was in for the biggest shock of my life.

After 27 years living in Britain, I came face to face with the so called 'True Brits' (the British Authorities) whose faces looked the same but whose attitudes differed from the 'Real Brits' I'd lived, worked and grown up with.

For the first time in my life - I came face to face with the destructive forces of racism, prejudice, sexism, classicism, superiority, jealousy, bureaucratic arrogance and ignorance.

For the first time in my life - I was confronting a strange bunch of people who seemed blind and deaf to my presence, ability or potential.

No matter how much I accomplished, their negative stereotyping kept me invisible. They were unable to comprehend a black, single parent, working class woman with ambition, vision, articulation and ability.

With hindsight and reflecting on my relationship with ordinary British people, the British media and British stores, I've come to realise that the negative propaganda, stereotypical images, racism and suppression, were created and cleverly perpetuated by the British Authorities... i.e. 'the powers that be.'

Therefore, I hope the following pages will encourage everyone, especially women and black people to;-

- Stop feeling sorry for themselves.

- Never give up, no matter how impossible it may seem.

- Realise that no one owes them anything in life but they owe it to themselves to be positive and know that it is up to them if they wish to improve their lives, they must work hard and fight to achieve their goals.

- To have faith, take direct responsibility and control their own lives.

"Dreams can come true - but only if you want them to."

Business Story.

SUCCESS or FAILURE is in the mind of the beholder.

Success and Failure is the result of hard work but the greatest adventure.

Nothing ventured, nothing gained.

Failure is an attempt to **succeed.**

Success is therefore the reverse of **failure.**

So, one never fails but always learns.

So, be proud of your **successes** and **failures.**

Since you'd have never learnt, unless you had tried.

My Dreams, Achievements & Nightmares

By December 1986, my products were beautifully packaged and ready for marketing. I registered the business under the name of Gramma's Ltd with Company House and prepared to meet my first Bank Manager. At the time I was still working full-time, where my then boss and most of the staff loved my Herbal Pepper Sauces. My boss had absolute confidence that it would be a best seller, so much so, that he wanted to become my business partner but I was afraid of his shrewdness. His firm dealt with one of the national Banks and all staff salaries were paid directly into their personal accounts held in the same Bank. So naturally, I approached the Bank for a start-up Loan of £3,000. I forwarded the Business Plan prior to the meeting. On the day of the meeting, when I arrived, I could see from the Bank Manager's expression, that he was surprised that I was black. During our conversation, he asked: *"which professional company did you use to prepare your business plan? I've never had such a thorough document, placed before him."* I replied, *"I prepared it."* He looked at me in disbelief and then said that since I had no collateral, he could not lend me the £3,000. This was my first heartbreaking disappointment. I remember walking back to work feeling that my world was falling apart. I'd built up so much hope and didn't leave any room for disappointment. The tears just streamed down my face.

When I arrived back into the office, I went straight into the toilet and refreshed myself. As I walked in, my boss immediately noticed the sadness on my face and called me into his office to find out how it went. I told him. He picked up the phone, called the Bank Manager, gave him a few well chosen words and on the spot guaranteed the loan, which went straight into my account the same day. He then took me to a lovely country pub for a celebratory drink, gave his blessings; drove me all the way home and told me to take the rest of the week off. His name is Sheraton Copland-Mander, a tough businessman with an infectious laugh but one of the most genuine, loving persons I've ever had the pleasure to work for. He really believed in me and was confident that I'd succeed.

So now, there I was in my little flat with my perfectly packaged Herbal Pepper Sauces (in four ranges MILD, HOT, EXTRA-HOT & SUPER HOT), proudly inscribed with the Vegetarian Society's approval logo 'V' and my £3,000. Then I thought, *"how will I get these into the shops and tell the world it's fascinating folklore history!"* I hated selling or cold calling (i.e. turning up at shops and trying to convince owners to buy). I'd never sold anything in my life, not even a pin, so how was I going to sell these sauces. Never one to be defeated, night and day I racked my brains thinking of a variety of ways. Then I thought, *"why wait ten years to approach Harrods, the worst they can say is NO!"* One of my grandmother's many sayings flashed through my mind, *"Don't put off for tomorrow what you can do today."* So by February 1987, off they went by post to Harrods and Fortnum & Mason, accompanied with an introductory letter.

I also read lots of magazines and newspapers and noticed that they always had interesting real life stories. The idea then struck me, *"if only I could get one of these nationals to write a feature about my sauces, then thousands of people would learn about them and buy them."* I telephoned one of the popular magazines and asked to speak to the editor. I explained that I was a newcomer in business and didn't know what the hell I was doing but had these fantastic products with the most exciting healing history; which I'd like to tell the world about and would she be interested in writing about it in her magazine? She was taken aback with such an honest, fresh approach and was very helpful and informative on how I should go about obtaining features. She advised me to send in a press-release. I replied, *"what is that?"* She laughed and explained; *"write your story on no more than two foolscap sheets and send it in."*

It took two weeks to write what I would call a good story. Back in Trinidad, my grandparents and the other older relatives were great story-tellers. In those days, there was no television and cinema was a once a year treat, so the older people kept us children amused with fables we called 'nancy stories,' acting out the parts themselves. I remember many nights going to bed terrified, after hearing a horror ghost story. They were brilliant. Seeing the same type of story on the big screen, was not as frightening as when it was left to the imagination. So, I used their imaginative story telling skills in the writing of my press-releases. Nevertheless, I wasn't confident with my english writing ability. So I gave the press-release to my brother-in-law, who was fluent and asked if he'd re-write it in proper English, which he happily obliged. Upon producing his version, I didn't like it... something was missing. It was perfectly worded but had no life, no soul, no feeling. So I promptly tore it up and sent mine with all the spelling errors intact. I remember using the word 'gold' instead of 'goal' when explaining my ambition and achieving my goal.

Anyway, I then thought, *"why just send it to one magazine, when there were so many others!"* With what little money I had left over each week, I bought every magazine and newspaper available, photocopied the press-release and mailed it out, accompanied with a jar of my Super-Hot pepper sauce to excite their taste buds and gain their interest. Within two weeks, I received a telephone call from the Observer Newspaper journalist Sue Arnold, who invited me to tea at a fabulous store called The General Trading Company, Sloane Square, in the heart of London's West End. I was excited; I didn't know what to wear, what to say or what to do. It was my first interview and it went great. She loved the story, because as she said, *"it was written from the heart."*

In March 1987, I had my first national newspaper feature in the Sunday issue, boldly printed on half of the back page. This was the start of a multitude of features to come. The very next morning, I received a telephone call from Mr Peter Whenham, the buyer of Fortnum & Mason who said that he had just read the feature and wanted to place an order. I asked, *"what do you like about my products,"* he replied, *"they are made with love."* I was stunned because there it was, my grandmother's spiritual influence, confirming her presence in my life. I immediately went and prayed, giving thanks to both God and Ma for making all this possible.

Straight afterwards, I telephoned the buyer of Harrods, to ask if he had seen the feature and confirmed that Fortnum & Mason had placed an order. He replied that he was very interested in the products but had not yet tested them and that I should call him the following Wednesday at 11am. I did and got the same response. He made me call him every Wednesday for three months, before finally confirming a meeting. I was elated, excited and horrified all at the same time, realising that this could be my moment of glory; again I thought, *"what do I do, what do I say, I've never negotiated or done a presentation in my life."* I couldn't sleep or eat, my nerves were rattled. But on the morning of the interview, I awoke calm and collected, had a bath, prayed and off I went. All the way on the train, I kept repeating the special prayer I say when I'm afraid which gives me strength; *"Lord, there is no one on this earth greater than YOU, therefore, there is no one I should fear."*

On arriving at Harrods, I took a deep breath and went straight to the Food Hall, from where I was later taken to the buying warehouse. It felt like hours. At long last, I was introduced to the buyer, Mr Stuart Gates, who proceeded with the interview. I cannot recall the questions he asked or my replies, because I was so nervous and praying so hard. In my mind, I kept saying over and over, *"Lord, please let him take my products."* After about a half hour gruelling interview, Mr Gates said, *"I'd like to order 50 cases of each."* I was praying so hard, I didn't catch what he had said and was about to automatically respond, as if it were yet another question. As I opened my mouth, I caught on and shouted, *"What did you say!"* He laughed and repeated it. I cannot describe my inner excitement, yet I remained outwardly calm. He then explained that the top people in Harrods were given samples to test and report back. Everyone reported that mine were the finest pepper sauces they had ever tasted. He asked, *"who designed and packaged the products so professionally?"* I proudly replied, *"my girls and I."* He was impressed. After which, we relaxed and discussed delivery arrangements etc.

Dazed with excitement, I returned to the Food Hall to look for something to buy for Marsha and Dee as a celebratory gift. I could only afford two small chocolate rabbits but I felt like a millionaire, as this was the first time I'd ever shopped in Harrods. I followed this practice, every time a store placed their first order; I'd buy a small gift for the girls in appreciation for their work, encouragement and support. On my return home, I'd also buy a take away meal and a cheap bottle of wine and we'd celebrate our success.

On the first week in July 1987, my products took pride of place on Harrods shelves. At the same time, the Guardian national newspaper was writing a half page feature. I called the journalist, told him that Harrods had placed an order and he included it in the article.

On the Friday morning when the paper was due to come out, I was late for work and decided to buy one and read it during my lunch break. As I sat down to start work, the phone rang and one of my colleagues answered it. She said, *"Dounne it's Thames Television News for you."* I laughed and replied, *"Stop messing about, its one of my daughters isn't it."* She passed the phone over and the voice said, *"This is Thames Television, we've just read the feature in today's Guardian and we'd like to film you at home, making your sauces, next week Wednesday for the news."* I was instantly petrified. I don't even like being photographed, much less being filmed. However, I realised that this was an opportunity not to be missed and said, *"yes."* I decided to worry about my fears later. Within half an hour the phone rang again, this time it was 'BBC News,' who said the same thing. In my naivety, I told them that Thames News were also going to film. BBC said they wanted an exclusive and if Thames were going to film, then they wouldn't. To which I responded, *"but I need both of you; I'm new to business and am not used to playing games."* To my surprise they agreed to film. So here again, honesty paid off.

Both television companies contacted Mr Gates of Harrods, who agreed for them to also film in Harrods. The next morning Mr Gates phoned me, stating that he needed to increase the order, as well as, learn more about the products. He was as excited as I was, because it was also going to be his first television appearance. Within an hour he phoned again but this time, he wanted me to come down to Harrods and choose my own shelf space. I was shocked, not only did I get my products on the shelf for more than one day; I could now also choose their shelf position and place... *"what a privilege and honour!"* Mr Gates was phoning me three or four times a day with questions. I went down to Harrods and met him in the Food Hall. He picked out the best top shelf and then said he'd remove all the products from either side of mine and replace them with Harrods own branded products, for better visual effect on TV, so viewers would know they were definitely in HARRODS! Mr Gates added excitement made me even more excited.

The next few days were extremely busy. In between phone calls, making more products; planning how to prepare for a television interview; thinking about what to say in one minute; what to wear; how to style my hair and make up; training Marsha and Dee on what parts they should play and how to do them; arranging my production routine in the kitchen for filming etc. I prayed non-stop because I was untrained in these matters and desperately needed guidance, help and strength. Once again those restless, sleepless nights and fears were becoming a regular routine. After many changes, I managed to write down precisely what I wanted to say in one minute... about me, the business, my grandmother, the products and their healing benefits. I rehearsed these words until I knew them by heart. Mum and Dad came down to help with the packaging and what ever else they could do. The atmosphere in my small flat was electric, everyone buzzing with eager anticipation, each face glowing with pride and joy. From time to time, we'd suddenly look at each other and just burst out laughing. We were ecstatic. We had never experienced such jubilation. My dream was coming true.

The day before the TV interview, we all got down, scrubbed and polished the flat... especially the kitchen from top to bottom. By midnight it was ready, with all the instruments, equipment and utensils in their right places. We also ensured that our outfits were ready. In the morning I awoke at 5am, had a bath, prayed; double-checked everything, rehearsed my lines several times and then woke up the girls. I was extremely calm. Mum and Dad arrived around 9am. Thames News film crew was due to arrive at 12 noon and BBC crew at 1pm. They were both on time. Every now and again, I'd get this incredible surge of intense fear, then the girls and my parents would hug and reassure me that it would be alright *"you can do it."* They were all praying for me. Again I hung onto my words for strength, *"Lord, there is no one on the earth greater than YOU, therefore, there is no one I should fear."* The set was ready, the cinema lights turned on and filming began. The Presenter took his cue, then turned to me and we went through the planned routine without a hitch. By 3 o'clock all was done and they left, each with their individual goodie bag of GRAMMA'S herbal pepper sauce!

My neighbours were very curious, seeing the television vans and people milling in and out of my flat. As I went back into the flat and sat down with my family, for a moment there was absolute silence, a strange stillness and peace filtered in the room. So we prayed, gave thanks to God, our Guides and then praised each other. *"We did great."* We then put everything back in place, ate, drank, celebrated and got the video ready to watch it all unfold that evening. It was going to be shown on both channels that same evening; 'Thames News' at 6 o'clock and 'BBC News Room South East' at 6.30pm.

It was great, they gave about 5 minutes; both stations trying to outdo the other, which worked in our favour, because it was one of the most inspiring and beautiful stories ever told about a poor, black, ambitious woman. The filming in Harrods was brilliant, which ended with the TV Presenter back in the studio, sitting at the News Desk with a jar in his hand... close up on to the TV screen. He then tasted it directly from the jar. The expression on his face when the heat unleashed its power, was a sight to be remembered; creating the perfect impact and a powerful ending.

Our elation increased the following morning when the phone rang about 11am. It was Mr Gates of Harrods. His words were, *"Do you want the good news or the bad news first."* My knees buckled with the thought, *"Oh God what could be wrong!"* I then said, *"The bad news."* He replied, *"I hope you have lots of products ready and can get them down here immediately; because the good news is - we have sold out."*

Apparently, people who had seen the TV show, were queuing outside the store before opening time at 10am, all demanding 'Gramma's.' An hour later, Fortnum & Mason called, they too had sold out and needed more. After which the people themselves started phoning with messages of congratulations but complained that Harrods and Fortnum's had both sold out. They desperately wanted to try the products and begged me to supply them direct.

As I had no transport, I called Dad to deliver the products and Mum also came over to help me make more sauces. Fortunately, the girls had taken the day off school. This was my Dad's proudest moment, because he wanted to personally deliver my products to Harrods. From then onwards, all hell broke loose in the flat; I needed more hot peppers, ingredients and bottles. My small pot could only produce 300 jars at a time, plus it took 48 hours to cook; 2 days to bottle and package by hand. So Mum bought me a larger pot. Every morning myself, Mum and Dad, went off to the wholesale market at 3am to choose, sample and buy fresh peppers; return home, prepared them and started the production; whilst Marsha and Dee kept busy labelling, boxing, folding leaflets. All this time, I was still working full-time. However, I realised I could no longer cope; so I called my boss; explained the situation and resigned. He was not happy to lose me but was overjoyed with my success and gave me his blessings. The massive sales went on for a month before orders started to slacken off. We were giddy from exhaustion and glad for the break. I thought that this was the 'rags to riches' stories I'd always read about but this time it was happening to me. I envisaged the beautiful lifestyle I was going to give my girls and my parents.

By the way, Mr Gates was instantly promoted up the Management ladder for doing a great PR job for Harrods. However, to my disappointment after 3 months, the orders began decreasing until the money was only sufficient to replace stocks and just enough to keep us... rent, food, bills. Fortunately, none of us cared about being paid a salary; we were only concerned about keeping things going. By the end of the fifth month, the sales were insufficient to live on, so at the age of 39 and after being in full-time employment for 21 years, for the first time in my life, I ended

up having to apply for State Benefit (Family Credit). I didn't mind because I believed it was only going to be short-term. However, still full of enthusiasm and ambition, I didn't realise that this was the start of a ten year nightmare.

> *"The roads into the real business world are not always paved with gold, for many they are paved with solid concrete, inlaid with sharp broken glass and surrounded by steel fencing"*

Although the State Benefit System has many pitfalls, it also has a few advantages; it paid my rent and gave just enough to feed us. To me this was most important, because at least, it kept a roof over our heads and food in our bellies... i.e. we could SURVIVE.

However, the nightmare and lessons was about to unfold.

LESSON NO. 1:

Being on State Benefit, I was advised by the Authorities that if I worked more than 24 hours a week (this includes the hours spent on business planning), I would lose my benefit. Furthermore, as I was living in a Council flat, it was also illegal to run a business from Council property and if found doing so, we could be evicted. This meant that I was forced to keep my business activities to the minimum. Therefore I decided to develop a 'plan of action' and the best 'survival strategy,' which would not get me into trouble whilst developing the business. By then, I was now well-known to the Council, so I went straight to the top 'the Director of Housing' and explained my predicament, detailing what had happened to the business; my dreams; inexperience, that the sales were only sufficient to replace stocks and declaring that I was not running a business but conducting 'market research' for future development. I promised that once the potential was proven, with guaranteed sales, I'd officially start the business and find proper business premises. He admired my ambition and drive but was also proud that I was one of his tenants. With that, I was allowed to carry on my work in peace, keeping to the minimum sales/market research plan. But my peace was short lived.

In the meantime, the tenants living in my block of flats, who had seen the television feature and newspaper articles, started showing signs of jealousy. I was the only black tenant. I remember one day, a tenant stopped me outside and said, *"When you become a millionaire, don't forget me,"* I immediately sensed her jealousy and told Marsh and Dee, *"our problems now begin"* and I was right. Most of the tenants secretly got together and formed an action group, to prevent me from succeeding. They wrote letters of complaint to the Council's Housing Department, stating that the smells from my sauces was getting into their flats and the machinery kept them awake at night. They insisted on remaining anonymous. The Council informed me of the complaints and stated that if I was causing a nuisance, then I must stop production. I immediately wrote to all the tenants, explaining that it would have been more neighbourly, if they had brought their complaints to my attention first and together we could resolve the situation amicably. I then invited the Public Health Inspector, the Housing Officer and all the tenants, to watch my production and listen to the machines, to prove that they were lying and that there might be other reasons for their complaints. On the appointed day, none of the tenants turned up, bearing in mind that they were all pensioners and at home. The Public Health Inspector and Housing Officer were satisfied that they had no grounds for complaint, especially as my production was too small and the machines were literally silent in operation. In fact, I was only producing once a month, which took no more than one hour of machinery use; the rest of the time was spent cooking and stirring. Unaware of the results and conclusion of the visit, the tenants continued to make the weekly trek to the Housing Department and complained every week for two years but the Council simply ignored them.

Throughout this period, we'd see them congregating and planning in the passage way or in the street. When we passed, they'd make indirect rude comments but made sure we heard. One evening, as Marsha was returning home from taking Zara (her dog) for a walk, I heard loud shouting outside my flat but when I heard Marsha's voice; I dashed out and saw Marsha confronting three tenants with Zara barking viciously at them. Marsha said, *"you touch my dog and I swear ****."* One of the tenants; a big man in his early 50's said to his wife, *"Call the police, she has threatened us, this is all they are good for,"* (meaning black people). I told Marsha to calm down and come inside. I'd never seen my daughter so angry. She replied, *"look Mum, you can remain passive and quiet. You know I've always respected old people but these people don't deserve my respect. No one threatens Zara and gets away with it. So please go back inside because the language I'm about to use, I don't want to say in front of you; its about time these people knew who they are messing with."* She was shaking. I went back inside and listened at the door. Well she was right, what swear words she didn't use, she invented and left them in no doubt, *"Don't mess with me or my family anymore, otherwise you'll have to deal with me!"*

After a few hours when she'd calmed down, I asked what had happened. She explained, that as usual they were talking about us, which of course put her back up but she ignored them. Then the man said, *"We should call the RSPCA to take Zara away on the grounds of cruelty."* Everyone knew Marsha's extreme love for Zara. I realised that because they had failed to stop the business, their next plan was to antagonise or force us to move out. Being aware of their past complaints, we were walking on egg-shells, trying our very best to avoid making any noise. So I sat the girls down, gave them a long talk and allowed them to express their anger. I explained the importance of not letting these people get to us or win, no matter what they did. Instead, we should utilise our karate training and practice to release all our pent up frustrations.

For months, we worked out intensely together both at home and in the club. It was great, we were battling and winning. The neighbours knew that we did karate, because we use to leave home in our karate outfits, plus hung them on the outside clothes line to dry. Hence, no one would challenge us physically, not even their young relatives who visited them regularly. One night on returning home from training, a notice was pinned to our front door stating *'RSPCA.'* The following week, there was an animal programme on television about rare cats with unusual tiger-like facial markings. To our surprise, one of our two half-bred Siamese cats (Banjo) had the exact same markings, colouring and looked identical as the ones shown. Now, Banjo was extremely placid and would go to anyone. Two days after the show he disappeared and was never seen again. Banjo was also Marsha's, the other cat (Zazu) was Dee's. We searched everywhere for him; put photos in every shop window; went around asking people if they'd seen him etc. We were convinced that our neighbours had taken him to spite us. Marsha and the other two animals sat by the front door all night for a week, waiting for him to come home. I had to give both girls another long talk, to enable them to come to terms with the fact that they may never see him again.

Banjo and Zazu were twins, they rarely left each others' side; Banjo was white and Zazu was black but Zazu was the aggressive one who always protected Banjo. For weeks Zazu wondered around the flat and in the gardens crying, pinning and searching for his brother. Zara on the other hand was Banjo's best mate; they used to groom each other and play for hours, whilst Zazu watched jealously, waiting to attack Zara at the slightest opportunity and then dart off and hide. Zara too was inconsolable. For weeks our home felt like a morgue. Then finally, I told the girls that we should stop saying Banjo's name in the presence of Zara or Zazu because it was prolonging their pain. It took almost a year for the animals to settle down but something strange started happening to Zazu. He began to act just like Banjo. He'd sit for long hours on top of the television and stayed in the house, where as before he mainly roamed outside, plus himself and Zara became best mates like Banjo. I told Marsha and Dee that I believed Banjo was dead and that he was communicating with both Zara and Zazu, hence Zazu's change in personality.

About six months later, Marsha was alone in her room quietly drawing. Suddenly, Banjo appeared, he jumped from the floor quickly onto her drawing board. Watching in amazement as he brushed his body against hers and darted playfully onto the bed, then disappeared. This was significant for Marsha, because it was exactly what both Banjo and Zazu did as kittens. After this incredible encounter, she came out of her room looking a little bemused and told me, *"Mum, I've just seen Banjo."* This experience finally made her accept that he was dead.

About a year later, Marsha became ill and was lying on the settee in the living room. She felt his fur brush against her arm. This time she just said, *"Banjo you've come to visit me again."* When she looked down, he was sitting beside the settee in all his glory, gazing up at her face. Marsha closed her eyes and fell back into a deep peaceful sleep. Another time, she was woken in the early hours of the morning because Zazu who generally slept on her bed, was playfully darting around. When she looked in the darkness, she could see the silhouette of two cats. She smiled and said, *"hello Banjo."* They continued playing and she went back to sleep. Neither myself or Dee has ever seen him. His visits brought tremendous comfort, as well as, confirmed that he was safe and still with us.

Eventually our neighbours gave up, the main instigators sold their flat and moved out, whilst the others tried to befriend us again. The experience left us cautious, so we continued to keep to ourselves.

In the middle of these trials and tribulations, I was slowly but surely making headway in the business. By the end of 1987, my products were not only in Harrods and Fortnum & Masons but I'd also negotiated them onto the shelves of other major Department and Fine Food stores such as... Army & Navy, Rackhams, Dingles, Kendale-Milne, Howells, Harvey Nichols, Bentalls, Neils Yard, Partridges. However, orders were still too small and the sales insufficient to keep us but I was absolutely confident of its potential. I then approached the Health Food stores and the major Supermarkets, who showed definite interest. But the Supermarkets confirmed that it was paramount to acquire business premises, as they would not place orders from a flat. So the prospects for expansion looked good. Therefore, the next course of action would be to raise the finance to rent and equip a small factory, in order to supply the Supermarkets.

LESSON NO. 2:

To gain the initial interest of the various stores, it was necessary to send an introductory letter with product samples; followed up with telephone calls and eventually an interview would be arranged at their Head Office... all of which incurred cost. For instance; the Head Office of Tesco supermarket was in Hertfordshire and the return train fare cost £15.00; Asda supermarket in Leeds - travel cost £49.00 and so on. However, my weekly State Benefit totalled £67.00, from which to live on, pay bills and feed us. Having no other income, I had to use my benefit to pay for the travel expenses. Therefore, after deducting the £49.00 to get to Asda, I only had £18.00 left to feed us that week. I was not allowed to reclaim any travelling or other unavoidable out of pocket expenses. These interviews were essential but did not guarantee the products acceptance in the Supermarkets; it's all speculation. Thank God my parents were always at hand to help.

So, it was back to the drawing board; I revised my business plan and approached my Bank for £50,000 start-up Capital. Everyone in London and the South East region of England, had by then, either seen the original two television features or read an article about me, including almost every Bank Manager. My Manager was most impressed with my achievements, proven ability and fast development. However, I was due for my next big disappointment.

LESSON NO. 3:

As I was no longer in full-time employment and living on State Benefit, plus had no collateral, security or savings; my Bank Manager said that although my business showed tremendous promise and great potential, because of the above factors, he could not lend me any money. I then approached every British Bank in the area and was confronted with the same rejections. They all used Head Office procedure as a convenient scape goat. None had the single-mindedness or vision to use their initiative.

Fortunately, by 1988 I received £15,000 settlement from the marital home, which enabled me to pay off my debts... i.e. furniture hire purchase, loan on Marsha's operation and the balance on the initial £3,000 business loan. The remainder went towards buying essential equipment for the business. I continued updating my press releases and issued stories to the media. Every month, I'd received calls from various journalists wanting to cover a new angle. The features mainly focused on my health re-education and awareness campaign on the true hot peppers and the benefits of my Herbal Pepper Sauces but it also covered issues surrounding small businesses, the difficulties experienced by women and blacks, parenting, divorce, women returnees, employment, etc.

LESSON NO. 4:

A female American journalist who worked for a British Television Company befriended me and did a splendid article in one of the national magazines.

We became very good friends (or so I thought). I was in the process of writing a book about hot peppers and she offered her journalistic expertise to help me compile and publish it. We conversed for an entire year and visited each others' homes. I began to trust her and divulged some of my most carefully guarded trade secrets. One day, I received a telephone call from Norman Parkinson (the world famous Royal Family and Celebrity photographer) who was then on location in America. It turned out that he had read the magazine article, which stated my products were in Fortnum & Mason. He had just got his famous sausages into Fortnum's and wanted to discuss a joint promotion deal. He was returning to Britain within the month and would call me to arrange a meeting. I was stunned.

As promised he called back, we had a lengthy chat and arranged to meet at his favourite dinning spot, Joe's Cafe in London. My friend wanted to come along, so I invited her and her Literary Agent. We arrived promptly at 8pm and was directed to his table. Norman Parkinson was by then an elderly gentleman, tall, handsome, casual, with a boyish mischievous personality. He greeted us warmly. We spoke at length. It turned out that he and his wife had been living in the Caribbean 'Tobago' for over 20 years, where he was not known as the famous society photographer but as the sausage man. In Tobago he could escape the trappings of society/celebrity life and be himself. I in turn, had lived in England for over 20 years; I knew more of what was happening in England and he knew more of what was happening in the Caribbean. So right there we had found a connection, which was going to be the source for our joint promotion... the English/Caribbean and the Caribbean/English. However, he was also mourning the loss of his wife a month earlier, plus his beautiful house in Tobago containing his fine art treasures and famous photos had been burnt to the ground. Whilst we spoke, he mischievously built a peculiar toothpick catapult and was flicking toothpicks at the guests on the other tables. This was when I spotted the boyish, mischief glint in his eyes and facial expression. He enjoyed it, because the guests couldn't detect where these toothpicks were coming from. Later, we moved over to the bar for drinks and my friend and her agent tried desperately to get acquainted but Mr Parkinson was not interested in them. Finally our meeting and discussions ended around 10pm and we went our separate ways. I was mesmerised. There he was, extremely wealthy and famous, yet down to earth, easy to talk to and very casual. My friend was babbling, *"I can't believe it, we met him in the flesh, he was sitting next to me!"* Two days later, after calming down, I suggested we ask Mr Parkinson if he'd be the photographer for my book. She was even more elated and felt that as we had clicked, he'd possibly do it, which would give the book prestige and guaranteed sales. However, realising the book's new potential, herself and the agent decided to try and steal it from me and make it their own publication. Behind my back they pestered Mr Parkinson's office trying to get an appointment, using the dinner introduction as their way in. Eventually, he suspected their scheme and refused to see them. He then alerted me, by sending a copy of the introduction of her proposed book, with other information she'd sent him. Our relationship came to an abrupt end, warning her that I'd sue if she ever published a book on peppers using my material. Unfortunately, the promotion venture with Mr Parkinson also did not materialise as his photographic work escalated.

Meanwhile, I was still trying to develop the business, doing numerous media interviews; raising my children; learning all the vital rudiments of business management; lecturing and searching for finance via Banks or Investment Companies. I came across a Government Funding Scheme called 'The Government Loan Guarantee Scheme' which was established for people in my situation but none of the Banks had either suggested or offered it. It provided finance of up to £100,000 for start-up businesses with recognised growth potential, where the Government guaranteed 75% of the Bank's security. Whilst researching the scheme, I was invited by the Greater London Enterprise Board, to lecture to a group of Bank Managers and Training Agencies about the difficulties faced in setting up a business and to offer solutions which could make life easier for entrepreneurs... particularly those who were poor. After detailing my achievements and horrendous experiences in trying to obtain Bank loans,

I went on to talk about the scheme. Then I asked each of the Bank Managers, whether or not they had heard of this scheme... some did, some didn't. I asked if any of their Banks operated the scheme. They all replied 'NO!' I then gave an embarrassing educational lesson, describing the scheme in detail ending with, *"This scheme is specifically designed to support poor people and is only available via your Banks. Please tell me how as Bank Managers, none of you have put yourselves out to learn about it. I'm not a Government employee, I'm an ordinary person but because I'm forced to scramble through your Enterprise Farce, to find the mirage you've promised us, I've had to find information to help myself and learn fast. From now on I intend to spread the word about this scheme and publicly embarrass every Bank that does not operate it."* They were all extremely apologetic and promised to put it into operation. I then reported the scandal to the press and the national newspapers had a field day. I began the campaign trail to expose the Enterprise farce and hypocrisy. It took me two years knocking on every bank's door, to finally find a Bank Manager willing to help me.

LESSON NO. 5:

By 1989, I eventually met the first and only Bank Manager who looked at my business plans purely on business grounds and potential, and not directly at me, my gender, race or class. He was the only Manager prepared to initiate the Government Loan Guarantee Scheme and so I was able to obtain financial assistance up to the full £100,000 secured under the scheme. This may sound great and at the time it was truly a victory but I was to realise later, that such borrowing was also the cause for the failure of many small businesses.

This new Manager was terrific and made me comfortable to confide in him. Before giving me the loan he told me straight; *"No British Bank would lend you money or support your business, because of who and what you are. Lets face it, you are black, a woman, a single-parent, on State Benefit and living in Council accommodation. Do you really think you'd ever be taken seriously? No! because you are in the highest risk category. Do you know what happens to Managers when we make financial mistakes, that cause the banks to loose money? We are demoted. No Manager would risk their career for anyone in your position, not even if you were white. But I have been following your achievements in the media over the years and after reading your business plan, I admire your determination and have decided to help you, because you would be good for my career. We can both help each other. If I lend you the money, I want you to promote my branch in your media features."*

I could not believe my ears. At long last! - here was a man who was sufficiently secure in himself, to speak the truth without fear of reprisals. God had finally led me to a friendly Bank Manager. He even went so far as saying, *"At the end of the day, if you succeed I'll get promoted but if you fail, then we are both out of a job."*

He was exceptionally friendly, understanding and supportive. Everything was conducted with his prior approval and consent, along with monthly progress reports. He was so confident of the business potential and my ability to make it a success, that he gave me his personal reassurance that the Bank would back me all the way to the top! He allowed me 18 months to try and get the business off the ground, knowing that the full loan would be quickly consumed mainly on the factory setting up cost, equipment, overhead charges and bank interest repayments. He informed me that the Bank had its own in-house Venture Capital division, who lent vast sums for a small Equity Stake (25% shares) in a Company and placed a member on the board to help run and oversee the business. He re-assured me that when the money ran out, he'd recommend the business for £250,000 Venture Capital Loan, which would repay the initial £100,000 loan; leaving me with a further £150,000 development funds. They had various repayment structures and easy terms, to help maximize business growth. Additionally, he also recommended and arranged for the hire purchase of the factory equipment through a finance company, whom he said they used regularly. I was to learn a year later, that it was actually one of the Bank's sister companies.

I was in seventh heaven, all my financial worries were over, (or so I thought). So now, I had to start the hunt for suitable factory premises. Because of the Government's aggressive advertising campaign, everybody who was anybody was setting up businesses, so small premises were difficult to find. Landlords were having a field day and gazumping was the norm. Every property I went for, someone got in before me or bribed the landlord and got it anyway 'gazumped.' Not one to give up, I approached my local Authority for advice on any properties they had available for letting. They sent me a huge list of addresses which was out of date. After weeks of searching, I finally came across a beautiful brand new factory which had been empty for three years. I learned that the Council had built this property, spending nearly a million pounds for an established business, who became bankrupt after its completion and had gone into hiding. Thus leaving the Council with a financial embarrassment. Therefore, I asked the Council if I could become the tenant, under a special rental arrangement... i.e. rent free for the first year, which would give me the time to get the business up and running, then to start paying rent from the second year. After a lengthy 'cat and mouse' game, the Council invited me to a specially arranged meeting. To cut a long story short, they really didn't want me to have the building and instead of being honest, they elected the only black senior executive present at the six man meeting to tell me that, *"no one is entitled to anything but everyone was legible to apply. If you intend to set-up your business out of Government charity, then don't bother. If you cannot pay the stated rent (£16,000 per year) from day one, you cannot have the property."* Then they offered me one of the poorest, filthiest sites in the area. I refused gracefully and went to Essex, where I'd previously gone to school and also grew up. Within a month, I found a perfectly sized property (1200 sq. ft.), negotiated through my Solicitor and moved in.

Having no time to waste, I commenced the arduous task of learning new production techniques, to cope with the proposed larger volumes, fitted out the factory unit with larger manufacturing equipment, shelving, other accessories and dealing with the real world of business. My brother-in-law, Robert and his cousin Colin, helped to put things in place. I'd grown accustomed to working seven days a week with only four hours sleep; but kept looking forward to the coming of that better day.

I immediately started following up the various supermarket leads; to commence proper negotiations, knowing that it could take in excess of one or two years, before new products are accepted and placed on their shelves. I only had eighteen months in which to do it and prove myself. Fortunately, they were all still interested and everything was going according to plan.

I came up with the great idea of having a grand factory opening in January 1990 and invite Lenny Henry (the famous British comedian) to launch it, along with the national media. I had previously met Lenny's wife, Dawn French the year before, when she'd asked me to take part in her first television cookery programme called 'Scoff.' She took me aside and gave some sound, valuable advice but also suggested that if I needed any help, to just ask. She was true to her word, because when I asked, Lenny came and did not charge me a penny.

I organised delivery of fresh Caribbean fruits and vegetables and my family... Mum, nephew Darren and eldest sister Pamela, prepared the most magnificent array of Caribbean dishes. Many like Soursop Punch, neither Lenny or the British journalists had ever tasted before. They all wanted to know when I'd be introducing these delicious foods into Britain. For me, the occasion was just to say a huge 'THANK YOU!' to everyone who had supported me; to share the joy of my new factory and to celebrate my success to-date, because they'd all played an enormous part in getting me to this point.

LESSON No. 6:

The Bank Manager and I were getting on great. He was thrilled to be involved with and also see a true success story unfolding before his eyes. Unfortunately, within six months my security, dreams and confidence were completely shattered, when he became seriously ill and went on sick leave. The Senior Manager who replaced him had a completely different attitude towards me and my business. He overturned all the arrangements and agreements of the Manager, which to my disadvantage were verbal, so I couldn't prove them. This Manager could not comprehend 'a black/British mainstream business,' nor did he understand supermarket negotiations or the food industry. By this time, the £100,000 loan was already spent and I was then told to seek external Venture Capital. His actual words were, *"find a friend who could lend you £250,000."* So completely inexperienced and naive, without any advice or support from the Banks' Business Advisory Service;-

"I was suddenly thrown to the lions and forced into a jungle of ruthless confidence tricksters, gold diggers, opportunists, unscrupulous manipulators and power hungry MAN EATERS."

This of course halted the business progress. The new Manager insisted that I strengthen my Management Team but didn't advise on how or why. I was confused, at a loss and did not know where to begin or turn. My staff consisted of myself, Mum, brother-in-law and daughters (part-time). I couldn't afford to pay them, much less bringing in so called 'professionals' who would certainly never work for free. I was advised to approach a well known Government funded organisation, who specialised in arranging Venture Capital for small businesses. During the initial two stage interview, I was confronted with open insider dealing and exploitation. Their consultants were creaming off businesses with good growth potential for their private business friends. I was given three options;-

1. (£50,000) Capital could be quickly arranged 'under the table' within a matter of days via their private business contacts, in exchange for a majority share holding (51% min). I must be prepared to lose complete control but to the outside world the business would still appear to be mine, as I'd continue to front it.

2. As an attractive single woman, I could easily find a sugar daddy, in

which case he was available. The meeting then transformed into his love for the Caribbean, cricket, rum, food and his many influential friends. He skillfully tried to convince me that this was how many big city business women survived. A month later, this fact was confirmed in a national women's magazine article, who reported the scandal on how many British business women were forced to use their bodies to finance their business.

3. Alternatively, I could go through the organisation's normal procedure, which could take up to six months without any guarantee and by which time I'd lose the business, as it required immediate funding. His actual words were, *"it's better to have 1% of something than 100% of nothing."* But when he phoned my home the following morning at 5 am to confirm that he had lined up a buyer. I told him precisely where to go. I was furious and hurt but when I thought of my daughters who also wanted to run their own businesses; I cried. I felt it was disgraceful that in a country which was then ruled and governed by two women who were both mothers (i.e. the Queen and the Prime Minister, Margaret Thatcher) that British Venture Capital meant prostitution for women trapped in poverty. The man had the nerve to phone me again two months later, stating he had just returned from holiday in the South of France at a nudist camp and how great I'd have looked beside him. I told him that if he called again, I'd expose him to the press. Needless to say, that did the trick. After this I was afraid to deal with any other Government Agencies, as they were all fronted by men. So to avoid similar situations, as well as, accepting my inexperience, naivety and vulnerability, I decided to employ the services of various professional private consultants; -

a. **Sales Agent**, to progress with the sales and supermarket negotiations, which I had already initiated with Tesco and Sainsbury.

b   **Financial Consultants**, to advise and raise the Investment Capital needed to finance the business.

This I believed would then free me to deal with the business management, administration, production, distribution and promotions. Unfortunately it didn't, because although claiming to have vast experience, both consultants turned out to be useless opportunists and tricksters, who attempted to use me to improve their credibility and with the hope of making a lot of money. One in particular was a born again Christian who really had me fooled. However, this also meant still having to continue handling all aspects of the business... including dealing with a now very difficult Bank Manager. Fortunately, past experience had taught me not to let go of the reins too early or leave anyone in complete charge or in control. Therefore, I kept an eye on their performance, which added to the stress and responsibility but luckily also opened my eyes to discrepancies and inadequacies soon enough to avoid disaster.

By April 1990, I'd secured test markets with Tesco and Sainsbury but had no finance to produce the products. I requested a small overdraft facility from the Bank Manager, who in turn advised that he would consider it on the production of a supermarket order. I phoned the Tesco buyer, explained my predicament and he immediately agreed to forward a 'letter of intention;' which arrived the following morning. I was back in the Manager's office but he refused to accept it as official proof. I turned to my parents and borrowed the money, which enabled me to produce the initial stocks. The Manager was aware that if at any time I was unable to meet the supply, I would run the risk of being de-listed by the supermarket and this would definitely ruin the business. However, he demanded more revised business plans which created even more stress but I managed to meet his request on every occasion.

Eventually, I received the official written Tesco order for over 9,000 jars to supply 25 stores. To my surprise, the Bank Manager rejected this stating, *"It's only a first order; it doesn't guarantee a second one."* The following week upon receipt of a second order, the Manager's response was still the same, *"it's only a second order and doesn't guarantee a third one."* The next week, not only did Tesco make a third order but also increased its store listing from 25 to 150 stores; in addition, Sainsbury supermarket placed its first order. Excitedly I thought, *"he cannot possibly refuse this time, because these orders prove that the products are selling over and above the envisaged projections and have also past the test marketing."* Anxiously I phoned and arranged a meeting for that week. On the day, I arrived with high expectations but to my horror when I showed him both orders, he was outraged and finally blurted out;-

1. *"You should have stayed small and remained in your kitchen."*

2. *"You are trying to get too big too soon."*

3. *"What's so special about your sauces anyway? After all, it's only a jar of pickle. Once eaten and thrown into the bin, it's as good as yesterday's newspaper."*

4. *"Take your product to a large British food manufacturer like Crosse & Blackwell and pay them to produce it for you."*

5. *"Employ YTS Trainees (i.e. unemployed youngsters) and work 24 hours manually to cut the cost."*

6. And finally, that he had no intention of financing the business beyond the Government Loan Guarantee Scheme. At which point he promptly froze the business account and told me to seek immediate legal advice on insolvency; and threatened that the Bank might demand full immediate repayment of the loan.

I questioned;-

- *"Why had they lent me so much money to set up my business, only to try and ruin me nine months later?"*

- *"How could I possibly negotiate contract packing (which I knew nothing about) at such a late stage? How would I protect my recipe? Furthermore, this would mean losing the supermarket orders as it would take months to finalise such negotiations?"*

- *"How could he expect me to be trading at a profit so soon after moving out of my flat, where I was producing only 250/500 jars monthly?"*

- *"Did he really understand or appreciate the problems of getting a new product established on the mainstream market?"*

- *"Did he realise that Supermarkets generally limit small businesses to only 1 to 10 stores and that I was exceptionally lucky to be granted 150 stores; this in itself said a lot about my products and their expected sales?"*

- *"What was the point of it all, especially as I needed to keep my recipe a secret and intended to be the first black person to commercialise our Herbal Heritage?"*

He smiled and said that I had **no choice, if I had no finance or facilities** and repeated the insolvency threat.

Again, I hadn't prepared myself for such a blow and could feel my head pulsating. I remembered walking out of his office but can't recall how I got home. I felt numbed, shocked, dazed. I didn't know whether to cry, scream, shout or curse. So I simply took a week off to gather my nerves, strengthen my thoughts, because I realised that I'd have to fight back.

I made an official complaint to the Bank's Chairman, requesting an immediate investigation, which was passed onto the Regional Head Office. They visited the factory and conducted a two hour interview. This was the first and last time anyone from the Bank ever visited my factory. Realising that this was a potentially damaging case and that I was no ordinary black person but an articulate woman; the entire Bank pulled rank and protected their Manager. The investigation became a farce and the Regional Head Office simply continued the merry-go-round. To show that they were co-operating, they agreed to submit my business for Venture Capital consideration via the Bank on the following grounds that;-

1. I revised my Business Plan (yet again).

2. Strengthen my management team but still not explaining how or why! (This actually meant seeking out more consultants).

3. That I also request the DTI (Department of Trade and Industry) to carry out their 'Manufacturing Initiative' and to include their report. The DTI generally took 2/3 months to conduct and complete such reports; costing £1,150, which I couldn't afford and the Bank subsequently refused to fund after the report was completed.

However, they rejected my application for Venture Capital Funding on the grounds that my projections were **unrealistic** and **over ambitious.** In other words, it was a deliberate merry-go-round, they had no intention of backing me, as it would have meant undermining their Manager. They simply wanted to show on paper that they'd consented to my request. The truth was, they were afraid of my media contacts and support, so in the event of possible exposure, they could twist the whole story around.

I then wrote to the Banking Ombudsman, the Confederation of British Industry (C.B.I.), Department of Employment, Department of Trade and Industry, Ethnic Minority Business Initiative Team, Prince Charles, my local Member of Parliament and the new Prime Minister (John Major) but none could help and most didn't respond. The Banking Ombudsman confirmed that he had no power to investigate complaints between small businesses and their Banks; he was only empowered to investigate 'private customer' complaints. So having reached a complete dead end, I finally wrote 'The Black Cinderella' document exposing my story and the plight of British Small Businesses trapped in poverty. It was sent to the Queen, every member of Parliament, the Press and those listed above. No one, except for a powerful Government political Institution responded.

Within a week, I received a telephone call from one of the top officials in the Institute, who said that he had been given a private copy of my Black Cinderella document by one of the Government Cabinet Ministers, who wanted them to act on it. I thought, *"at last, I'd found someone who had the power to make the Government listen and change the system."* Within the month, a private meeting was arranged. It turned out, that for years they had been waiting for a proven test case in which to encourage serious policy changes. To my surprise, I was to learn that the Cabinet Minister believed that I must have had someone from inside the Cabinet office, feeding me with Government information, because my apparent grasp of how the System operated was beyond that of an ordinary person, much less a black woman. Apparently, certain things mentioned in my document had only been discussed at Cabinet level. I was stunned but not all together surprised because although I had written it alone, the only advisers were my Spirit-Guides. I was also told that my document had created the biggest stir in the House of Parliament; all the MP's, especially the Government was afraid of its contents; if revealed to the public or the media. The two main topics of conversation which dominated the 'House' that month was the Falklands war and my document.

For months we collaborated. The plan was, they would use my document, combined with their statistics and Government information via the Cabinet Office; to compile a complete dossier in my name entitled 'The Black Cinderella.' They'd organise a Press Conference in the House of Commons, where I'd take centre stage and be permitted to question the Prime Minister on the issues.

A week before the press conference was due, I'd not yet seen their completed document, only parts of it. Three days before the set date, I received by courier, a document for me to sign; giving them the copyright and permission to proceed as agreed. I felt uncomfortable, so I telephoned their office and requested to have the completed document sent for proof reading and approval. When they started offering me various explanations as to why they could not send it, I became suspicious and refused to sign. They tried other ways to persuade me to sign but these simply heightened my suspicions.   Knowing that they could not proceed without my consent, I held out. The following day it was sent by courier. I patiently read through every page. The more I read, the more angry I became. My story was completely distorted to the point where I had difficulty relating to it. I phoned and questioned their reasons for changing it. They responded stating; 'it was necessary as they were dealing with intellectuals, therefore, it had to be presented intellectually.' After about 15 minutes of unsuccessful persuasion, I stated that my document was purposely written so that anyone from 5 to 95, academics to the uneducated, could understand it with ease. They tried in vain to convince me otherwise. I then realised that the whole exercise was not intended to create the changes desperately needed to help poor entrepreneurs but to gain political credibility for their Institution, as well as, to publicly embarrass the Government. However, my purpose was not to destroy or embarrass the Government in any way but to make all the political parties aware of the seriousness of our plight and to initiate policy changes which would improve our chances of survival. So I decided not to sign or participate. They were extremely angry that I prevented them from having their moment of glory. Although I was politically naive, I quickly realised the nasty back stabbing games played in the House of Common(er)s, even within their own ranks and I wanted no part of it.

In the meantime, my Bank decided to increase the pressure; I then found myself trapped and unable to change Banks due to a debenture agreement on my loan. I made several applications but no other Bank would touch a young business that didn't have the necessary **track record, had no assets, no security and with large debts... i.e. my Bank loan.** The all important Business Plan or long-term potential became invalidated, plus the deepening recession meant a scarcity of Private Investment Funds on the open market. To make matters worse, the Bank's debenture also meant that although my account was frozen and I had no facilities, every payment received had to be paid into the account, as it was legally binding by the original contract. Therefore, I could only deposit money into the account but could not withdraw from it to cover any expenses, not even for raw materials to manufacture or supply the products. Having nothing to live on, I was again forced to apply for Family Credit (State Benefit). My parents continued to feed us, so that I could keep going. I was still determined not to give up. Somehow, some way, I was going to achieve my dream.

By January 1991, sales through Tesco supermarket boomed with over 12,000 jars due to a BBC Good Food Magazine article and I was fast running out of stocks. I had confirmed written orders and invoices worth over £17,000 and requested a £1,000 overdraft facility for the purchase of raw materials. Tesco had ordered for three consecutive months and Safeway agreed to commence stocking by April 1991 into 200-300 stores, plus other supermarkets had confirmed their interest. The Bank Manager still refused my request. My then consultant (a Jewish gentleman) had his first confrontation with the bank.

The next page shows his angry letter dated 24th January 1991, expressing his emotion.

Consultants letter to my Bank Manager

24th January 1991.

Re: GRAMMA'S LTD.

I am writing to express my extreme annoyance at the discourteous treatment I received recently by you and your assistants.

I telephoned your office on three occasions and asked to speak to you as a matter of urgency regarding the above company. Each time I was told either by your secretary or your assistant that you were too busy to talk to me. On the first occasion your secretary said you would ring me back, which did not happen. The other two times I explained to your assistant the reason for my call and both times he said he would speak to you and one or other of you would telephone me. When I remonstrated with him for not returning my calls even though he knew the urgency of the matter, I was told the reason is that there was nothing the bank could do to help. I said that even if that was the case, common decency dictates that he should at least inform me of the fact rather than me having to call again. He said he could not comment.

I find your attitude and that of your assistant totally personally offensive and churlish to the extreme. I have been in practice for over thirty two years and have been Chairman of a Public Company, so I feel I can talk with some experience of dealing with bank managers and their staff and I have never been treated in such a discourteous manner.

Incidentally the decision not to increase the overdraft facility by £1,000 when you have been informed that the Company has a firm order from Tesco for over £17,000 baffles me completely. As I said to your assistant, apart from badly damaging a customer, I cannot see that it is in the interests of the bank itself, as surely if by taking that attitude you were to force the company out of business the bank would also lose money. I shall be obliged if you will please explain how this makes any sense.

Yours sincerely,

Again, I had to make another formal complaint to the Banks' Chairman, who advised the Regional Head Office to re-open the account and the overdraft facility was extended from £1,000 to £10,000. This enabled me to pay off essential trade creditors, in order to purchase the necessary raw materials to produce more stock. However, once the Tesco money was paid in, the account was promptly re-frozen and I was back to square one. They then called in Price Waterhouse (world famous accountants) to conduct an independent investigation on the business. During the investigation, Price Waterhouse representative advised me, that although the business had no assets or security, its products were established in two major supermarkets, therefore it had potential and in such cases, the Banks' were investing up to £500,000 into other British businesses. Therefore, I should revise my Business Plan again and re-submit it directly to the Bank's Venture Capital Branch. I acted promptly but it was rejected within 24 hours. When I requested a copy of Price Waterhouse's report; the Bank replied that it was a private independent investigation, called and paid for by the Bank and was therefore a private matter between the Bank and Price Waterhouse. I never saw the report.

So, for 15 months the Bank played a painful waiting game, knowing that without funds or facilities the business would naturally die. **The recession and not the bank would take the blame.** They suggested voluntary liquidation on several occasions, to which I rejected out of loyalty and responsibility to my supportive creditors. They were also hoping that one of these creditors would eventually force the inevitable liquidation and as none did, they finally used their own, (the sister-company who had the Hire Purchase agreement on the factory equipment) to commence wind-up and personal bankruptcy proceedings, which in turn forced me into voluntary liquidation. This was the only way to be released from the Government Loan Guarantee Scheme and a vindictive Bank. Furthermore, I soon realised that the only people who profit from business liquidations are accountants, solicitors and liquidators; they must all be paid in full before any creditors. I had to find over £4,000 to cover their costs even though I was broke. The company was officially dissolved in August 1991.

This experience left me totally drained, not just financially but also mentally and physically but even then, I still had no intention of giving up. In order to let off some of the the steam and vent my feelings, I sat and quietly penned this letter to the Prime Minister and sent copies to all of those in charge of the Establishment.

Copies to: opposition Leaders and the Treasury Minister.

Attn: Mr. John Major (Prime Minister)
10 Downing Street
London W.1.

16th August 1991

Dear Mr Major

RE: The Plight of the Poor.

I know that you are an exceptionally busy person with limited reading time, so my apologies for the enclosed extra wad of paper. However, it is essential you are made aware of the issues therein, as I do intend to make them public knowledge.

Lone Battle. I've battled long and hard to try and gain independence but face continuous brick walls not from the British people, media or stores but only from the Authorities. It is impossible to break centuries of fixed attitudes and indoctrination, so I am therefore, again requesting your direct intervention. You are part of the Establishment responsible for creating the 'laws' which control us and therefore better equipped to explain WHY? or help to remove some of these solid bricks.

The merry-go-round has got me completely dazed, for with every step forward I'm returned to the start of the maze. This is not just a black issue, as poor whites are also affected. I'm not a political animal, my life is based on the simple principles of TRUTH; just or unjust, right or wrong, good or bad.

I know that my business has the right ingredients to bring about effective, positive, conscious change, if looked at purely on 'Business Grounds' and not on race, gender or class, which had been trivialized for too long. When will the hypocrisy stop?

'Building a Better Future.'

My comments are in support of 'ordinary people living on Low Incomes and State Benefits' who would like to start up their own businesses as a way of securing their future. It is not another complaint about the current recession or banks insensitivity or pleading for sympathy or begging for charitable handouts.

It's about the reality of the tremendous business potential which exists in Britain but which has remained unexplored due to the lack of insight by successive Governments and their customary encouragement of keeping the unemployed and poor, trapped within the State Support structure. Furthermore, the so called Government Enterprise Initiatives have provided a false sense of security, thereby creating a 'Binding Contract for Failure' rather than Success! Unfortunately, those who have failed are left totally Soul-Destroyed, believing that they are failures instead of realising that it was the System which had failed them. There are many people who are, or will end up on Income Support/Family Credit or other State Benefits for years or even worse for a lifetime. Many are ambitious and have both the capacity and ability of becoming self-employed, if given adequate financial assistance and positive support.

It's a known fact that it takes at least 3-5 years to get a business off the ground. Even if the business only employs 1 or 2 people, it still means that it has generated employment and has taken 1 or 2 people out of the 'State dependency trap' and has also reduced the financial burden on the State.

It's another well known fact that the longer a person remains out of work, he or she gradually loses self-confidence and eventually becomes institutionalised, in the same way as long term mental patients and prisoners. Hence, State Support becomes their excuse for not wanting to find work and is turned into State

Dependence which;

1. DESTROYS: - personal drive, ambition, creativity, incentive, dignity, pride and responsibility.

2. INSTILLS: laziness, retardation and dependence.

3. INCREASES: boredom which in turn creates crime.

Coupled with the ever increasing cuts in education standards and poor discipline, it leaves little wonder what type of future generation is being created or why 'crime' is on the increase and 'respect' is on the decrease. Whereas when people are encouraged to help themselves, then personal **motivation, energy** and **enthusiasm** is revived and these are the main ingredients for 'success.'

My own story provides the evidence to back up these facts. During the initial four years, I employed myself and my eldest daughter (full time) my youngest daughter, mother, father, brother-in-law and cousin (part time). None of us received a wage. I am now looking to have a full time staff of five. My home-made food products are available in the top four department stores, supermarket chains (nationwide) and also in Ireland. So, at long last I should become self-financing, precisely five years from inception. However, without the hindrance of my previous bank, I might have done it all within three years.

With hindsight, I now realise that many (if not most) small businesses fail, because of the unrealistic time scales and inadequate financial assistance forced upon them, as well as, lack of positive support and understanding from the Government and Banking Institutions. People on low incomes, without collateral or personal savings, face special difficulties which have never before been properly explained and are therefore misunderstood. They should be set aside as a **'special case'** requiring special assistance. They are already living on the breadline and honestly cannot afford to pay any of the additional expenses, unavoidably incurred when starting up a business.

For instance: Over the five year period, my family and I had collectively invested £170,000 into the business (i.e. funds my parents injected and non-payment of wages).

The Bank loan of £100,000 guaranteed under the Government scheme, went towards the setting up expenditure incurred during the initial two year period 1989/91 when I acquired the factory, bearing in mind that for 15 out of the 24 months, I operated without any banking facilities.

Bank Interest & Charges	£34,000
Equipment & Fittings	£28,000
Factory Acquisition	
Overheads & Stocks	£162,000
Total Expenditure	**£224,000**

This is the realistic expenditure incurred by many new (Manufacturing) businesses in the two/three years from setting up. It should also be taken into consideration that I had previously conducted a thorough two years market research.

I was in receipt of £50.50 weekly Family Credit to support myself, two daughters, plus to pay 20% Council Tax, 20% rent, food, clothing, bills and travel expenses. In order to negotiate a sales deal, I had to visit the supermarket's Head Office at least twice, which is generally outside of London, i.e. Leeds, Bristol or Nottingham but this does not guarantee an order. It costs between £25-£39 return rail fares which comes out of my Family Credit and is not reclaimable. The introduction of the Government's new Council Tax on homes posed an additional problem both for myself and my eldest daughter... who is over 18 years. She too, having seen the possible long term benefits, decided to forfeit her wages and work with me full time to help build up the family business. She was honest and refused to claim any State Benefits. However, when she received her Council Tax bill for £449.00, she explained her financial position and requested exemption as a special case. All her pleas were ignored and she was eventually taken to court in July 1991 for non-payment. The Local Authority then explained that as she was working over the 24 hours weekly limit, she wasn't entitled to any benefits but could get assistance to pay her Council Tax if she stopped work. At the same time, since she was an adult, she must also contribute towards the rent payment of our flat, which in turn penalised me. My housing benefit was reduced by £13 weekly to cover her contribution. My daughter was forced to stop work to claim State Benefits in order to pay for the 'States' bill. So, on one hand, the Government is publicly claiming that they are doing all in their power to reduce unemployment, whilst on the other hand, Government employees are creating unemployment and encouraging dishonesty. It would cost the taxpayers £1620 per year to keep her at home, instead of the simple exemption of £449.00.

The Government is also injecting billions of taxpayers money in a desperate effort to regenerate employment, which is neither creating long term employment; career development; incentive or ambition. This is only the tip of the iceberg.

The **working classes; women** and **blacks** also face the additional unnecessary burden of bureaucratic arrogance, ignorance, discrimination, prejudice, racism, sexism, classicism, superiority, jealousy, greed and vindictive intimidation. All unfortunate elements which still exist but are impossible to erase, because they wear a 'cloak of invisibility.' It takes years of weighing up the evidence before it can be identified or recognised, yet almost impossible to prove in any Court-of-Law, so it is extremely difficult to beat the System. It is so extensive that one has to fight against becoming negative and paranoid. These elements are counter-productive and pose the greatest hindrance to progress and frustrates you into giving up. In my case I have spent 85% of my valuable working time breaking down these invisible barriers in order to progress.

The Government has introduced equal opportunities; unfair dismissal and racial awareness programmes in an attempt to control the problem. In my opinion there are no normal preventative solutions, as these are personal mental attitudes, indoctrinated from youth and reinforced by education. A problem can only be resolved by going to the root cause and not by masking over it.

The Government seriously needs to revive its entire Employment and Enterprise strategies and provide adequate financial assistance to those willing to help themselves out of the poverty trap. It makes sound common sense and in the long term is far more cost effective.

Furthermore, each small business created also supports the survival of many others... small, medium and large. The exact opposite occurs with business failures as the current recession is proving.

"Britain's economic and financial stability lies firmly in the hands of British small businesses, as recorded in the Government report in June 1980 by Rt Hon. Sir Harold Wilson, on the financing of small firms (command No. 7503) which emphasised that small firms generate more employment than big firms. Statistics show 86% of all businesses employ between 0 - 5 people, 96% employ less than 20 people, 0.05% employ more than 200 people. From 1985 - 87 small businesses created 1 million jobs, large firms created 20.000."

I look forward to your reply.

Dounne Alexander.

By September 1991, the business potential and future prospects was gaining momentum. My products were now into 150 Tesco, 200 Safeway's, 70 Asda's and 1 Sainsbury's supermarket, plus I was ready to launch into Ireland and had additional interest from the Health Food markets. My Solicitor advised, that a new company (Gramma's U.K. Ltd) could be legally formed in order to rescue and retain the business. This was done with my eldest daughter (Marsha) in charge. She had worked side by side with me; had sacrificed; suffered and endured every agony. We thought we had survived the worst but to our astonishment, we had more to come.

The Bank's (sister) Finance Company, decided to proceed with the personal bankruptcy case against myself and my brother-in-law. We had personally guaranteed the factory equipment and they were claiming payment for the full amount outstanding, £11,660. We tried desperately to renegotiate. As we had no money of our own, my brother-in-law, daughter and myself, offered our redundancy payment entitlement under the Employment Protection Act 1978, which we were told could amount to approximately £8,000 and to pay the remaining £3,600 over the next 12 months. The company rejected this offer just one day before the court hearing and insisted the equipment be removed immediately out of the factory and put into auction for re-sale, in which event they'd only recover scrap value. I explained that since we needed the equipment and as most were extremely heavy, incurring costly electrical installations; our new company was prepared to make an offer but that we'd still personally pay off the balance outstanding. They also rejected this. They insisted on the removal but said the new company was free to bid at the auction sale. Their negative, callous and irresponsible attitude confirmed our suspicions, that both the Bank and its sister company had conspired all along, not only to try and totally destroy my business but also to personally ruin me.

At the court hearing, I presented our case. The solicitor acting on behalf of the Finance Company, was surprised about the un-reasonableness of her clients. She turned out to be exceptionally supportive and requested a three month adjournment in which ten weeks were allowed for reconsideration. '*This experience proved to me that even in the midst of hell, there are still some fair-minded people.*'

I personally negotiated with the Solicitors and at the new Court hearing, the Finance Company accepted all of my original terms; requested legal fees of £750 and withdrew the Personal Bankruptcy Order. Therefore, if my terms were accepted in the first place, we need not have gone to Court or had to pay an additional £750, plus the extreme stress caused during the entire period.

With great determination and purpose in March 1992, I went ahead and self-published my book 'The Black Cinderella.' The following month, a General Election was held and the same Government was re-elected. I suspect to this day, that I was conveniently black-listed. I also received an anonymous telephone call from an employee of the Bank who said, *"you may be interested to know that the Manager has unexpectedly been given early retirement and has left."* Seven months later, the drastic failure rate of small businesses and the insensitive treatment they received from their Banks became national headline news.

It's a fact that Banks are known to lack business insight and vision but this experience made me realise that in the case of WOMEN, they become very short sighted and for BLACK PEOPLE, they become totally blind. Banks do hold the **controlling power**;- **FINANCE.**

Catalogue of Other Obstacles Encountered

❀ Appealing for my Livelihood.

In the midst of all these traumas, there were many other obstacles to overcome; like in the legal case with Marsha and the Local Authority. After the Authority had penalised her for non-payment of Council-Tax, they also disqualified my Benefit, therefore, I had virtually nothing to live on. I had to undergo a six month tribunal appeal to obtain Family Credit (State Benefit) and a nine month repossession Court Order Appeal to prevent the Authority from evicting me and my daughters from our flat, as I was unable to pay the rent. The Council was also insensitive and showed no sympathy or interest for my situation. My only income was £12.85 weekly (Child Benefit) and the weekly rent was £31.00. I conducted both appeals and won. The judge even awarded me £100 court costs!

❀ Trademark Registration.

This occurred just as I acquired the factory in 1989. I received notice from the Patent Office that my Trademark application to register the name 'GRAMMA'S,' made two years earlier conflicted with Campbells Granny Soup. My Solicitor advised me that legally I had no choice and must cease trading immediately and change my product name, as I was not in a financial position to fight an international company like Campbells. I had already spent a great deal of money on product packaging; labels, boxes, brochures and leaflets, plus the vast amount of national publicity on the business. I knew that if I changed the name, the public would not recognise the products and it would also be impossible to recapture the same level of publicity in order to make them aware of the new situation. So again I was at my wits end, with no one to turn to for proper legal advice. However, past experience had taught me that not all Solicitors were the same; some specialised in specific areas of the law. So I wondered if there were any who specialised in 'Trademark/Patent Law.' As luck or guidance would have it, my search led to a Patent

Attorney, who after going through my case simply asked, *"have you seen Campbells Granny Soup on sale in the supermarkets or elsewhere in England."* I replied *"no."* Then he said, *"I'd like you to go home and phone all the stores and ask them if they sell Campbells Granny Soup, then bring me your findings."* It turned out that Campbells Granny Soup was sold only in Scotland. The Attorney said, *"you can stop worrying now, we've found a loop-hole."* He wrote a short letter to Campbells, advising them that if they didn't agree to my registration, he'd apply to have them de-registered throughout the United Kingdom. Campbells instantly consented and GRAMMA'S trademark was officially registered. The Attorney's fees came to £500, plus I had to stop trading for three months until it was finalised. I've kept the Patent Attorney ever since and he has proved to be a valuable asset to the business.

❀ Stolen Recipe .

In 1991 an English woman who ran a respectable Health Food Shop in Wales, cleverly befriended me and I foolishly sent her a sample of one of my new product lines of Herbal Seasonings. She had it analysed, reproduced and sold it under her own label. She even went to the extent of using my information and had a major feature in one of the popular Health Food Trade Magazine. The product is excellent for dieters, candida sufferers and people with delicate or weak digestion. But as the old saying goes, *"cheaters never prosper,"* since then I've extend\range to four Herbal Seasonings.

❀ Medical License Department (1987).

This in fact was my first nightmare. After overcoming the awesome excitement of getting my products into Harrods, Fortnum & Mason and all the other Department stores, I received a horrifying letter from the Medical License Department, whom I had not heard of before. Apparently, they saw and heard the television features and read the many newspaper and magazine articles; where I'd spoken about the healing properties of the true hot peppers. Therefore, they acquired a jar of my sauce to investigate if I'd made any medical claims on my products. It so happened, that I had an information leaflet, detailing these historically known facts attached to each jar. It was all part of my Health awareness and re-education programme. So rather than explain the law on medical claims, their letter demanded that I immediately withdrew all my products off the shelves; threatening court action and heavy fine... £5,000. Therefore, I immediately telephoned their office to speak to the person who wrote the letter. A well spoken, elderly English gentleman answered. I asked him what was the reason for such a heavy handed letter; the claims on my leaflets had been substantiated for centuries and were used in private medicine. I politely explained my business, products and campaign. He became angry and said that *"to make any such claims on a food product is illegal; you need to apply for a Medical License through us; and I can tell now that you won't stand a chance in hell of obtaining one from us, withdraw your products immediately or I'll take you to court,"* I was shocked by his rude discourteous outburst but calmly explained the stores in which my products were in; the great pains it took to get them there and the difficulty I'd have; first to remove them and next to get them back in. The most likely outcome was that the stores might not take them back. He replied that he was fully aware of where my products were placed and insisted that they must be removed **NOW!** Then slammed the phone down on me. I detected from the angry tone in his voice that this had more to do with who I was and the prestigious stores my products were in, rather than the medical claims or food laws. I telephoned back and requested the name of the head-of-department; immediately sent him a written complaint, detailing the conversation with his staff; quoting his words; included the official proof of the claims and demanded a meeting. He telephoned on receiving my letter, was very apologetic and agreed to arrange a meeting with himself and the gentleman concerned, to discuss the law and figure out what assistance they could provide in supporting my campaign.

When I arrived at the meeting, instead of two people, I was confronted with a full boardroom of Government officials and medical experts (8 middle-aged to retiring gentlemen) all sitting around a huge oval table and I was directed to sit at the head of the table. They were extremely polite and hospitable towards me. Externally, I was calm and collected but internally I was shaking in my boots. In my mind I thought, *"what the hell is this?"*

The meeting started with the head of department explaining the reason why he had invited the various officials. They individually introduced themselves giving their respective professional titles. He then gave detailed explanations of the laws governing foods and medicines. It was then I learned that only medical products could legally make medical claims and these required a medical license; which was also very expensive. Therefore, by law it was illegal for any food product to make such claims. In response, I argued, *"but your medical products are synthetic (man-made) drugs; which suppresses rather than treat the symptoms; whereas natural foods are God-made and their historical factual benefits has been known since the beginning of time. Don't oranges contain vitamin C and minerals and good for preventing the common cold? Don't pulses contain protein, good for digestion etc. Don't the Hot Pepper contain capsaicin, good for hypothermia, breathing problems (like Asthma & cold), poor blood circulation, the heart etc. In fact, don't all Natural Foods & Herbs contain all the natural chemicals, nutrients, vitamins, minerals etc. which are essential for life and have sustained all our lives from the creation of the world. Haven't your man-made medicines destroyed and damaged both health and life? and lots, lots more?"*

They were shocked by my knowledge, as well as embarrassed, because they had to answer *"YES"* to all of my questions. They weren't prepared for such a barrage of factual information from an un-educated black woman. 'Never judge a book by its cover.'

What they didn't know, was that for the 13 years I'd worked for my father's Housing Association, I was not only the Housing Manager responsible for over 1000 tenants but also the driving-force, lobbying Government officials to change the law and provide decent housing for the poor working classes. I represented and handled all litigations in court on behalf of the Association and its tenants; prepared the Legal documents; liaised with solicitors and barristers and that I'd never lost a case... having dealt with over 100 cases in my time.

For two hours we argued, I put my case and won. Eventually they decided that I should re-write my leaflet, inserting a 'disclaimer' with these words;-

"This leaflet is to be read as a guideline on the medicinal evidence and reports on Hot-Peppers and not to be taken as a recommended Medical or curative claim for any of the ailments referred to."

Then I was allowed to list all the facts, as well as, put my name to it. So at the end of the leaflet I wrote:-

Written by Dounne Alexander.
'Creator of the famous Gramma's Concentrated Herbal Pepper Sauces.'

The whole purpose of the meeting, was for them to persuade me to disassociate my products with any of the medical claims I was making. But it resulted in not having to remove my products from the shelves and the revised approved leaflet, gave me more scope and still linked the claims to me, my business and my products.

❀ **Consultants.**

I'd tried using many consultants to advise and help sort out my Bank and financial problems. They had all personally approached me, after reading or seeing the many publicity features on the business; whose external prospects appeared to be great, so they wanted in. Naively and gullibly, I thought they wanted to help me, not realising that they were trying to help themselves. Fortunately, none were paid in the end, mainly because I had no money but also payment was based on results, which were NIL. However, one in particular came along with a friend and successfully manipulated their way into my business. They both sounded very credible, being a top Marketing Manager for one of the multi-national oil companies and the other a top Accountant for an International Bank. I thought, *"well! these men must satisfy my Bank's criteria of an improved Management Team."* After a couple of meetings with the Bank, they too realised that it would take 'super natural powers' to change the Bank's attitude. Therefore, they went away to devise a counter plan. After three months of working closely together, I became suspicious and felt that they were leading me down a dangerous fraudulent path. The week before finalising their deal, I had a dream where one of my Spirit-Guides told me to call off the deal. For the first time in my life, I could say that I came face-to-face with the Devil himself. The main-man was transformed from the perfect gentleman into a vicious rouge and in his great anger, exposed that his plan was a deliberate set-up to take over the business. It was then I learnt first hand, that he was not only power hungry but also dangerously manipulative. I felt devastated because I took them in as friends, divulged a great deal of secret information and had really pinned my hopes on them and they deceived me. I'd also wasted nearly two years trying to satisfy the Bank's demand to strengthen my Management Team, all to no avail. I was so deeply hurt that it made me feel weak and it was at this point that I felt I had no other alternative but to succumb to the Voluntary Liquidation in August 1991. What hurt me even more was that they were both black men. The following year one of them boastfully divulged the details of his plan to a business colleague, unaware that this person was a very good friend of mine. The full extent of his plan was even more horrifying, as I could have innocently gone to jail, leaving him in full charge and in control of my business under a new name. He also told my friend that I was lucky to get away because he intended to make a killing... i.e. make a lot of money. This experience taught me, *"the arms of flesh may fail you - you dare not trust your own."*

❀ More Bogus Financial Consultants.

However, a few years later (1995), I fell in the same trap of believing that qualifications or an important name made a person special. This time, through a very good and respected friend, I was introduced to what appeared to be a well connected, high powered financial consulting company. Headed by a middle aged, aristocratic English gentleman and a few other titled gentlemen (two were 'Sirs' and one a 'Lord') who had a seat in the House of Lords. At the first meeting I was duly impressed. The Chairman convinced me that they had direct and personal relationships with the Chairman of every British National Bank; the top Foreign Banks; various members of Royal families in the U.K. and overseas, as well as, many influential friends in Parliament and elsewhere. I was personally introduced to 'the Lord' who was one of the Directors of the Company and a member of one of Ireland's most famous family businesses. I was so impressed that I happily parted with the £2,000 initial fee requested in order to raise £500,000 Investment Capital. Two years later, they turned out to be fraudsters; they themselves had more financial problems than I and also proved to have poor business management skills. They promptly closed down the company and re-opened another 'Financial Services Agency' to con more people. Needless to say, on this occasion I lost my money.

❀ More Sugar Daddies.

On two separate occasions, I was befriended by two Jewish gentleman, both in the jewellery business. They had read about my achievements, sympathised with what I'd endured and offered to invest in the business. Again, I thought, *"This is great! at last I've found someone who understands business, it's difficulties and who is willing to really help me."*

However, it turned out that both were really after helping themselves to me. One merely desired a black woman to excite his ego. Unknown to me, the other had really fallen in love but was too shy to reveal his feelings until I'd met Rudolph and told him that I'd found the man of my dreams. In a state of shock, he told me how he felt and begged that if I left Rudolph he would leave his wife, children and religion. He offered to take me on a world cruise in the hope that I'd learn to love him. He also offered to invest £100,000 immediately into the business and promised I'd never want for anything again. I was broke but too much in love with Rudolph to give him up for anything or anyone. My love was not for sale or investment. Needless to say, neither of the two invested in the business.

● Working from my kitchen in 1987.

● My products in Fortnum & Masons

● First delivery to Harrods in 1987.

● On the first week 800 products were sold in Harrods.

Factory Launch 1990

GRAMMA'S HEALTH R... ...AUCES

- pictured here with my celebrity guest Lenny Henry, who opened my factory.

- pictured here with the late Bernie Grant - MP.

- invited guests enjoy the Caribbean style spread prepared by mum and the family.

● above: with mum and dad.

● below: my family; also my daughters Dee and Marsha.

● Uncle Gus singing his rendition of 'Bless this House.'

● **1990:** First factory unit in Hainault, Essex.

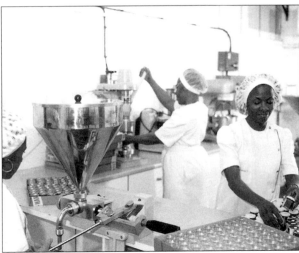

● right:
Mum, Marsha and I making the pepper
sauces for delivery to department stores
and supermarkets.

The Good and the Funny Times.

The Good and the Funny Times

In between the bad times there were lots of good times, which boosted our motivation. For instance:- in 1989, I received a call from a television researcher who said, *"I'm researching for a new Channel 4 Food Programme called SCOFF, which will be presented by Dawn French. I'm interviewing about 500 people to select for the show but Miss French insists that there is no need to interview you, she wants you on her show. She's a great fan of your products and said that I must get you, so please say you'll come."*

My mouth dropped open and I said, *"WHAT? Dawn French loves my products and wants me! But she's a real celebrity and I'm a huge fan of hers."* Well! on the day, they sent a car to collect and take me to the filming site. As Dawn French was in my opinion, the best female comedian in Britain, I expected to spend the day in fits of laughter. But privately she was serious, professional, warm and friendly. She then played the best trick on me. She got me to relax and drop my business PR presence. Then we did several takes, when at times I'd say things like *"oh shit"* and laughed out aloud. She kept saying, *"don't worry about that; it will be edited out, just be yourself."* Well the outcome was, she used the out-takes instead, which turned out to be the most memorable feature of the whole programme. The people loved it because they saw the real me and not the business woman. I'll always be eternally grateful to Dawn and the entire British Media for providing me with such super positive and all inspiring coverage.

That show led to another call, this time from the BBC for a business programme called 'Women Mean Business,' presented by Glenda Jackson. I said, *"you mean THE GLENDA JACKSON, the greatest female actress that has ever lived, is going to come to my little flat!"* My mouth fell open once more and said, *"oh God, who's next!"* On that fateful day, the camera crew arrived early, then there was a knock at the door. I was nervous and anxious. I peeped through the spy hole, only to see Glenda Jackson standing there. I opened the door, she was dressed plainly, with no make up. I thought, *"Glenda Jackson is really standing in front of my door looking at me. Pinch me, am I dreaming?"* She too was delightful and made me relax. After we'd gone over the filming sequence she said, *"I need a cigarette, do you mind if I go outside and have a smoke."* I said *"no but you can have it in here!"* However, she also wanted some fresh air. So we both went outside and sat on the back step. Well, my neighbours mouths fell open even wider than mine. During the filming, we had a real dinner scene and I thought, *"Glenda Jackson, in my flat, at my dinner table, eating food I've cooked with my own hands and saying it was delicious! I must be dreaming."* That was how the entire day felt. She was so nice, so down to earth, sincere and real, with no super star ego.

As the old saying goes, 'luck comes in threes!' The following year, I received the third call from the BBC. Another business programme called 'Move Over Darling,' presented by Pamela Stephenson. This time filming took place in my new factory.

Then came the icing on the cake, when I received a letter from Options Magazine to say I'd been nominated for their national 'Women Mean Business - best newcomer Award.' However, this involved a real competition and I had to undergo two gruelling one hour interviews by a panel of first class judges... The Director of Finance for TSB Bank, Editor of Options Magazine and a Corporate Business Executive. Each nominee had to demonstrate her knowledge, overall awareness and understanding of business based on; general acumen, management, finance, leadership, national and global markets, business potential, product uniqueness and dynamic entrepreneurial personality. It was terrifying because no one was informed about the questions they'd be asked. I arrived and was ushered into the interview room, sat before these judges, who just fired question after question, each requiring spontaneous responses, so you really had to know your stuff. To my surprise and delight, I won the regional heat **unanimously** representing London and the South East Region of England and went onto win the national heat **unanimously**. Now this meant a lot to me personally, because all the nominees were white and excellent.

On the day of the final national heat, we were all invited to stay over night at the extremely posh Hyde Park Hotel... marble bathroom and all the trimmings. I took Marsha with me and we had a ball being pampered. In the morning, Marsha styled me to perfection... i.e. my hair, make up etc. I told her, *"don't worry, I know I won't win, so lets just have a good time and enjoy the day."* She answered, *"why not, you are as good as the others."* I replied, *"yes I know that but I'm the only black woman. There's no way I could win. If I'm lucky, maybe third runner up."*

The national press, plus some 100 guests were invited to the posh luncheon ceremony with Piloma Piccaso to present the Awards, which comprised of two categories 'Best Newcomer' and 'Corporate Business.' After the end of the various speeches, the Magazine Editor started to announce the Best Newcomer Award, (my section). She started with the third runner-up and whilst stating the name, I started to get up feeling certain that it would be me but someone else's name was called. Then she announced the second runner-up and again called another name. I looked at Marsha and said, *"Oh well that was expected."* Then she announced the winner and called my name loud and clear but I didn't hear it. Then Marsha said, *"Mum its you,"* I replied, *"stop kidding - it can't be,"* I noticed everyone clapping and looking at me. I looked at the Editor and tapped my chest, mouthing *"me!"* She nodded back, *"yes you!"* I just burst into tears, I couldn't believe it and walked up to collect my award. Whilst walking back to my seat, I noticed most of the guests and the press also wiping tears from their eyes. It was a moment of glory to savour. Afterwards, a gentleman came up to me and said, *"you made grown men cry."* All the winners and runners up went into the hotel garden for the press photo shoot. Every national newspaper was there. The next day my photograph was in all of the main papers. When I looked at it, I couldn't believe my eyes, it was the best picture I had ever taken in my whole life. It showed me in my full glory; reflective, calm and happy. It holds a very special moment in time.

On reflection, another great but funny experience was my first supermarket interview with Tesco. Being naive, as well as not having attended such interviews before, my first thought in preparing for the presentation, was to take my products in a Tesco carrier bag. To me, this made perfect common sense, as the Tesco Buyer would believe that I was a regular Tesco customer. However, on arrival at Tesco Head Office and posh reception room, I found that not only was I the 'only woman,' but I also observed that each of the ten impeccably dressed male sales representatives in their pin-stripped suits, also had neatly stacked at their feet 'identical black leather product cases.' These reminded me of tomb stones. I then thought, *"WHOOPS! This is what I'm supposed to have and not a carrier bag."* Trying desperately hard not to look stupid or conspicuous, I confidently walked right through; sat in the middle of them; placed my carrier bag down on the centre table, which was laden with all the national newspapers;- picked up the Times (to look intelligent), and sat up straight pretending to read.

However, I was to learn later, that at these interviews, if you received fifteen minutes of the buyers time, you were extremely lucky. Well, my interview lasted two hours. The Buyer was wonderful. I've always believed in being myself and not to emulate others. I'm also proud of who and what I am, and not ashamed or afraid to ask for advice, help or to admit that I'm inexperienced. The buyer gave me all the advice I needed to deal with other supermarkets. I think he was completely surprised at being confronted by someone who was outside the usual text book training. The result was that the buyer agreed to stock my products. On leaving the building, when passing the remaining salesmen with their identical cases, I wondered just how many of them would have been as successful as I was that day. I realised then that I was unique and had a unique approach. So I kept my original approach and it worked everytime. By the way, I think *"businessmen would look both stupid and unprofessional with a carrier bag, which looks perfectly normal and natural on a woman. After all, aren't we expected to be the house-keepers and shoppers?"*

Later on, I also learnt that the big food companies paid the supermarkets huge sums of money (six figures) and also brought the buyers expensive gifts or took them to lavish dinners, in order to get their products onto these shelves. I'd never paid or bought anything, mainly because I'd always revealed the fact that I was poor and had no money but I was also unaware of these private dealings and even if I was, I'd be too scared of making such offers in case they backfired. So my products had to sell for themselves and compete with others; their uniqueness, superior quality and superb packaging, won every time.

Furthermore, I also learnt that it could take two years or more, to get a new product into any one of the supermarkets, because shelf space is extremely scarce and in great demand. I got my products into all the 7 major supermarkets in under two years. A feat never achieved before single handedly by an individual and definitely not by a black person. Additionally, a small business with new products would only be allowed space in 10 to 20 stores; black products were limited to 1 to 5 stores and only in areas which had a large black population and were placed on ethnic shelves. At each interview I told the buyer, *"although I'm black, my products are for everyone. Therefore I'd like them placed everywhere and shelved amongst the European Cooking Aids."* They were all extremely generous and placed them into stores nationwide from Scotland to Wales:- Tesco (150 stores), Safeways (200 stores), Waitrose (70 stores), Asda (70 stores), Co-Op Leo's (50 stores), WM.Low (50 stores) and J.Sainsbury only (1 store), plus Northern Ireland.

However, there was a down side to supplying supermarkets; unless you had millions of pounds at your disposal to provide continuous advertising (on television, newspapers, magazines, radio, billboard posters, exhibitions and in-store promotions) in which to create constant consumer awareness, it's difficult to compete or maintain the sales requirements. Multi-national companies spend in the region of £5 - £30 million on promotions every year... *"that's a whole heap of pepper sauces."* Furthermore, my products were also in the 'speciality' category, which required specific marketing. My only source of promotion was via free features from the national media, who were exceptionally accommodating but *"how often could they be expected to repeat the same story."* *"Where there's a will, there's a way."* They were willing and I found many ways of keeping in the front-line. Within 7 years I'd become the highest profiled small business in Britain, grossing over 76 Television features, over 250 Magazine and Newspaper features, over 60 Radio shows, as well as, featured in 16 mainstream books. I wrote every press release, made every phone call to become my own PR machine. This was yet another area where I was untrained but realised that writing from one's heart and with passion, was not only very effective but also touched the hearts of others.

❀ Driving.

One of my greatest achievements was learning to drive, because I had an extreme phobia... I was petrified of driving. I made every excuse under the sun to get out of it. I was quite contented to travel everywhere by public transport. However, circumstance and necessity dictated. My factory was in an area called Hainault, situated in a rural industrial estate. The journey from my home took two hours by public transport, whereas by car it was only twenty minutes. I often needed to get into the factory in the early hours of the morning (5 or 6am) and left late at night (up to 11pm); but during these hours the area was dark and desolate.

My parents and daughters nagged me to despair, until I plucked up the courage to start taking driving lessons. *"Confronting one's fears is no easy deal."* I could only afford one lesson a week and decided, *"no matter how long it takes, I'm going to pass."* Three failures and one year later, I finally passed.

My brother got me an old Toyota car for £600. Although I had passed my test and knew how to drive, I was still terrified to drive on my own. The car was permanently parked outside my flat; I'd pass it straight and still took public transport, even down to carrying my heavy shopping home. My daughters thought it ridiculous and it was! but I was scared to get into the car. They hatched a plan and decided that every evening after school, they'd accompany me until I gained my confidence. The first time we did it; my hands were shaking whilst trying to open the door. When I sat in the driver's seat, my heart was beating so hard, I could see its vibration against my clothes and my legs turned to jelly. The girls said, *"come on Mum, you can do it."* After several false starts, we were finally off. They would look all around to ensure that the road was clear and instruct me, *"go now Mum"* and off I went. This went on for a month and gradually they took me further and further, until I was able to drive confidently on my own. Within two months I was whizzing to and from work; shopping, here, there and everywhere. But to this day, I still don't like to drive and continue to escape when ever I get the chance.

The Black Cinderella.

Extracts from my first book 'The Black Cinderella,'self-published in 1992, after my business was forced into liquidation.

Specifically written to expose the plight of the poor entrepreneur and the British Enterprise farce.

Copies of the book were sent to;-

(the Queen, Prince Charles, The Prime Minister, Opposition Leaders; every member of Parliament, the Department of Trade and Industry, the Confederation of British Industry, the Chairman of the four main national Banks, the Banking Ombudsman, the Home Office, the Ethnic Minority Business Development Team and the National Media).

"Through her struggle for **truth** she encountered **light;**

through the light she found **knowledge;** through knowledge

she understands truth; - *the key to her* ***freedom***"

Marsha Moore.

THE UNFAIR SYSTEM

"I'm consciously aware of the 'Powers that Be' and know that these revelations may risk the destruction of my business but risk taking is a peculiar instinct of true Pioneering Innovators and is often a necessary sacrifice to cause and create effective -

POSITIVE CHANGE!*"*

The Plight of the Poor

- Working Classes
- Women (in particular single parents)
- Blacks (and other minority groups)

In the past, many feeble attempts have been made by Governments to try to create **social and economical changes** to improve our situation and position in life. All these policies were written by intellectuals and academics who have never experienced such a lifestyle and from using second hand information. Policy after policy lacked sensitivity and basic understanding, therefore each have mainly been ineffective, leaving the poor to become poorer.

This unique little book is a first time, first hand, non academic but hard hitting and factual account, gained from my own personal experiences as a black, working class, single-parent attempting to establish a high quality British mainstream business and the difficulties encountered from the British Authorities... i.e. Banks, Financial Institutions, Government Ministers and other bodies, responsible for enticing ordinary people into setting up small businesses. It exposes years of authorised Government Enterprise hype! I passionately believe in the enhancement of racial harmony, equal opportunities, individual development and have used my business at every opportunity to prove these points. I would equally fight to expose any hint of injustice or lack of fair-play which hinders personal growth.

This book may be offensive to many people, especially those at the top but shock treatment is necessary to revive a conscious awakening in order to prevent further suffering. Additionally, the book creates awareness and reveals many serious questions on morals, human rights, equal opportunities, equal access, fair play, status and ethics. It provides the reader with independent food for thought.

History Repeating Itself

'The injustices of the ruling minorities.'

Blame should not be levelled against everyone. It is said that
"There is good and bad in ALL races" The majority of ordinary
citizens of every nation are fair-minded people.

The EVIL, CORRUPTION, RACISM, PREJUDICE and INJUSTICE
stem from the **ruling minorities** and their wise counterparts (the planners
and controllers) responsible for the clever brain-washing, re-education
and indoctrination of us ordinary citizens, yet, they are equally
responsible for making, controlling and enforcing the laws with which to
punish us for the very same deeds. However, even among the ruling
minorities some fair-minded people can still be found.

Since the beginning of time, women have been;-

Undermined

Abused

Controlled

Exploited

Taken for Granted and

Under valued.

We have experienced prejudice from inside and outside of the home.
When we try to gain independence we are branded;-

Feminists

Radicals and

Over ambitious.

Civil rights, human rights, equal rights or **equal opportunities** have
not freed us from centuries of brainwashing, conditioned up-bringing and

reinforced education. Even when we've proven our ability beyond a doubt and gained public recognition and acceptance, the authorities still refuse to take us seriously. Single parents in particular, are still seen as unstable and looked down on;-

- For centuries, black achievements, talents, innovations, initiatives, knowledge and potential have been wilfully, deliberately and purposely undermined or hidden in order to keep us down. The Western World has profited enormously by capitalising on us.

- The disabled and homosexuals have always been treated as social outcasts and still cannot gain full recognition, acceptance or access.

We are all equally entrapped and enslaved by bureaucratic arrogance and ignorance; people who believe that they have a God-given right to dominate.

History has repeated itself for far to long and it's about time the **tears, exploitation** and **hypocrisy stop!**

The Entrepreneur and Business

The reality is:-

It's extremely difficult for anyone regardless of race or gender to set-up, run, maintain and sustain a business. However, the level of difficulties encountered depends on four major factors;-

1. Gender
2. Race
3. Social Class
4. Economic Status.

For instance;-

(a). **An upper-class married woman** (of any race) would have financial security in the form of personal savings, property, collateral and social influence. She would experience little or no difficulty in obtaining development finance, plus the control of her business and destiny is more or less in her own hands. However, she would still experience some traditional negative female prejudices!

(b). **A middle-class married woman** would have less financial security... i.e. Personal Savings, collateral and influence. She would experience more difficulty in obtaining development finance; the control of her business and destiny is half and half. She will also experience a bit more traditional negative female prejudices.

(c). **A working-class married woman** would have little financial security... i.e. Personal Savings or collateral but no influence. She would experience greater difficulty in obtaining development finance; greater scrutiny, would have less control of her business and her destiny would be in the hands of the bank and or investors. She would experience a lot more traditional negative female prejudices.

(d). **A working-class, single parent or black woman** would have No financial security whatsoever... i.e. no Personal Savings, no collateral and definitely no influence. She experiences the greatest difficulties of all. If exceptionally lucky, limited development finance is dependent solely on a sympathetic bank or private investor, no matter how great her potential or proven ability. Her business and destiny is at the mercy and control of the bank. She also experiences the full force of traditional negative female prejudices, stereotyping and is never taken seriously. She undergoes perpetual scrutiny, simply because she's at the lowest level of the social ladder and has no back up support.

However, if she's fortunate enough to survive the exhaustive obstacle course and merry-go-round, she emerges as the better and stronger business-woman, possessing all the vital survival techniques! i.e. natural business instincts.

British Enterprise Initiatives
(A poor investment)

'Success is the **Prize,** not the **Price.**'

For once the issue is not just one of
RACISM or **PREJUDICE** but also
Bureaucratic **ARROGANCE**
and **IGNORANCE.**

It's REAL LIFE!
In its TRUE PERSPECTIVE.

- Achieving against the odds.

- The truth behind the success.

- The tears behind the smiles.

- How and why the System is failing us.

- Will women ever be taken seriously.

- The destructive forces of discrimination and jealousy.

- The plight of the poor working classes, women and blacks.

- The untapped potential of women living on Low Incomes.

- Building a better future.

A lone voice crying in the wilderness and pleading support for British Small Businesses. As usual, everyone's talking but no positive action is being taken to -

CHANGE THE SYSTEM.

Achieving Against the Odds;-

She is;- A Woman

Black

Over 40

Single parent (with 2 daughters)

Working class

Living in a council flat

On income support

Had no money or collateral

A TRUE SUCCESS STORY which should have a happy ending 'from rages to riches' but under the Government Enterprise Scheme, it ended 'from rags to ragged.' In my case, success only means accomplishing all I had set out to achieve and that's more valuable than money. I have also learnt that 'one creates one's own luck and opportunities.' Through this, I can now continue to excel un-hindered to fulfil and hopefully realise my true potential.

"Success is the Prize not the Price."

I've spent four years trying to break down the negative stereotype barriers which were blocking my progress but bureaucratic arrogance, ignorance, prejudice, racism and jealousy from the British Authorities were and still are the most difficult and stubborn barriers to remove. These negative attitudes are not only counter-productive but also destructive and whilst they exist, will continue to pose the greatest hindrance to the success and progress of the poor working classes, women... especially single parents and blacks. Additionally, blacks are classified as ETHNICS. This new negative stereotype further undermines and devalues us and our businesses. It's quite clear that the British Authorities place strong emphasis on the classification BRITISH, therefore full access and facilities are only made available to **British Businesses.** Hence the importance for blacks to fight for official recognition of **Black British Status** and call for the abolishment of the negative **Ethnic** label. Blacks have been in Britain since Roman times, long before the fashionable slave trade of the 1500's. Our fathers and forefathers belonged to the British Empire. They have also fought and died in many wars, from the Roman conquests to the two world wars, to protect and safeguard Britain's Independence and Sovereignty. **We have paid our dues, contributed, served this country well and therefore we belong.** This sense of belonging is also extremely important for the protection of our British born black and mixed race children, in order to instill pride and make them feel an integral part of the society. For too long our inherited rights have been denied. For too long we have remained complacent and have allowed the British Authorities to trample and keep us down.

1992 (the European Common Market) is now upon us, if we cannot get into the mainstream or obtain recognition in Britain, how can we expect European recognition?

How are we to market our businesses in Europe or Worldwide? What do we call our Businesses, 'Ethnics?' I truly fear for the many racial European uprisings and wonder if this is yet a further extension of the divisional process. Who is really behind it? A United Europe where British Blacks are denied entry, access, status, recognition and acceptance, even in the European country where they were born? Isn't this their birthright? Are they trying to resurrect another Super-Race or to guarantee that the term European only means WHITE? Years of traditional brainwashing have left Britain and Germany fearful and unable to trust each other. The principles and application of the 'divide and rule' strategy is violence in its worst form. There are so many deceitful human mind-traps, that blacks must also avoid falling into the 'special needs' trap, as this would mean we need special treatment or charitable handouts, which in turn would keep us dependent on State Support and in perpetual deprivation. We should demand fair and equal treatment; equal rights, equal opportunities, equal access, positive support, recognition, acceptance and official Black-British status.

"Justice must be seen to be done and not appear to be done."

Britain needs to get its House in Order.

It's about time Britain showed equal pride in its black community, by effectively embracing us as an important integral combination and accept the inevitable, that Britain is a multi-racial society which can survive in harmony. As in the 1991 Tokyo World Games, the 4 x 400 British Relay team consisted of three British blacks and one British white, whose surname coincidentally was Black. Their magnificent Gold winning performance saved Britain from ultimate disgrace and world embarrassment. On the rostrum, they all sang the British National Anthem with true pride and joy; the world saw:-

British Pride

British Spirit

British Power

British Ability

British Unity

British Harmony, Joy, Jubilation and Equality.

British-Black Athletes have repeatedly brought world pride, respect and recognition for Britain. It's disgraceful that only on these occasions blacks are proudly called British, not even Black-British, just BRITISH. The word Black or Ethnic is totally omitted. Only then is Britain referred to as our home. This is our only true moment of glorious acceptance. Why can't such harmony, acceptance, respect, recognition and equality, be demonstrated to all of us on a daily basis? The games showed that whether Britain is to be called the United Kingdom or Great Britain, collectively we can all make it more 'united' and even 'greater'. Equal opportunities or a classless society will never become a reality, because there will always be the haves and have nots, discrimination and racism.

These negative elements are too deeply rooted in tradition. Furthermore, fair-play is not a game accustomed by the men in control of our lives, they have created, as well as, perfected the strategy of 'divide and rule.'

The Authorities must be made to realise that Britain is losing a great deal of raw talent and tremendous potential by denying the poor working classes entry, access, recognition, respect and adequate support. In our hands, lies the creative and competitive future of the British economy.

"Small business are of key importance to the economy as a whole. They are a source of new ideas, new products and new jobs."

Rt. Hon. Michael Howard Q.C. M.P.
Secretary of State for Employment

Attn: Gillian Shephard
Minister of State Treasury
TREASURY CHAMBERS
Parliament Square
London SW1P 2AG

27th June 1991

Dear Mrs Shephard

An Enterprising Proposition

With reference to your working breakfast invitation on 2nd July 1991 to business women.

As mentioned, my present focus is solely concentrated on the development of my business. In view of the Government's desperate effort to regenerate employment by injecting more capital into training, which is not creating long-term employment, career development, incentive or ambition. I'd therefore like to appeal directly to you, to use your Ministerial influence to encourage the Government to initiate a **Winter Warming Campaign**, by supplying one jar of my Herbal Pepper Sauce to the elderly, as an additional warm-hearted Christmas bonus.

N.B. There are some 10 million pensioners in Britain, out of which over 50% are living in poverty, unable to feed or keep themselves warm. The Government could show a gesture of goodwill, concern and genuine care by initially setting up a regional survey say in London, Devon and Scotland on 500,000 pensioners via Doctors or pensioner groups such as Age Concern or Help the Aged. If proven satisfactory, then to make it a permanent annual gift nationwide. I've spoken to hundreds of pensioners over the years and all have asked me to keep pressing the Government to take up the campaign.

Setting aside the important health benefits, the economical results are equally beneficial;-

1. Government orders 500,000 jars, £1.30 each. = £650,000.

    This order would immediately create stability; jobs and job security, whilst we continue to improve sales on the open market, thereby reducing unemployment and the overall long term cost to the State. Staff will be paid the appropriate rates for the job.

2. The establishment of a unique British Industry. The first Traditional Health Food Manufacturer, which in time could develop other plants in depressed areas. Hence more job creation.

3. Create many responsible career jobs. The company controls all its affairs internally... i.e. product design, promotions, marketing, quality control, sales, distribution, packaging / warehousing, manufacture and administration, which could expand into separate departments.

4. The company also supports other British businesses. Increased orders mean more raw materials like; bottles, boxes, printing, herbs and spices, machinery, machine maintenance, pallets, transport carriers, all of which are supplied by British companies.

5. The Government's direct support could enhance racial harmony and revive HOPE!

In my opinion, this is a far more cost effective, economically viable and sound, 'Healthy Enterprise Investment,' whilst still encouraging free enterprise.

I look forward to our meeting on the 2nd to discuss this challenging proposition.

British Enterprise Initiatives

'A Poor Investment?'

As usual, everyone is talking about the failure of British small businesses but no positive action is being taken to change the System. Therefore, I've decided to reveal my five years business and personal experiences encountered as a test case, in order to expose the injustices within the System and also prove that the nineteen years of Government Small Business Initiatives have always been a farce. Since 1973, successive Governments have introduced various Initiatives to encourage ordinary people to set-up and run their own businesses (in particular the so called Ethnic Minority Initiatives) but with each passing year, more and more small businesses fail, leaving many enthusiastic individuals shattered, believing that they were failures. Little did they realise that it was the System that failed them. Even worse, those who became bankrupt were left with a lifetime of shame and disgrace, also enforced by the System.

The **Small Business Initiatives** have always been ineffective and inadequately financed, purposely and deliberately designed to ensure **FAILURE**.

1. **Billions of Pounds** of tax-payers money are allocated but none or very little of it reaches those to whom it was intended and who need it the most. Instead, it is totally controlled and recycled within the System. Maybe this is the Government's 'real' Environmental Policy - RECYCLED WASTE. Their Initiatives have created only one big business and that is a huge Government Service Industry (Lip Service) and long term job security for millions of well paid Civil Servants, who are prohibited from exposing any found injustices as this would jeopardise their jobs. The money is spent on their own staff training, wages, office administration, rent, machinery and equipment, stationery, staff expenses and the mountains of printed Government Literature etc, etc. In 1991 alone, £250 million was spent on supporting so called Enterprise Initiatives.

2. **Business Advice and Training** are provided by staff who have had no practical experience but who are advising equally inexperienced people on how to set up and run a business. The training deals with basic business administration, which does not relate to real business problems. Therefore, the intended business person only receives free inadequate advice and training, tons of free leaflets giving information on where additional help and aid can be sought and are finally left in a maze of confusion of **where** to find more help and **how** to apply!

Professor Ellis Cashmore is one of Britain's leading authorities on race relations. He is also a researcher at Aston Business School in Birmingham and Professor of Sociology at the University of Tampa, Florida. In 1990 he spent six months interviewing successful black entrepreneurs and found that although many black women had used retraining programmes, the most successful were those who had rejected training and grants offered by race relation groups, seeing them as irrelevant and possibly dangerous, because of the role they played in encouraging a dependence on organisations.

Professor Robin Ward of Nottingham Business School supports much of Professor Cashmore's study and also found that an average of a third of the black and Asian people setting up companies were women, which is roughly the equivalent of the figure for whites.

3. **The DTI Initiatives** is another Government Department which spends £18 million a year on advertising. There are about six individual initiatives each costing between £2,000 - £6,000 for 5 to 15 days Professional Advice with 50% paid by the Government. Therefore, it could cost the Small Business in the region of £6,000 to £18,000 for Professional Advice.

4. **Finance.** The only financial provision is 'The Government Small Firms Loan Guarantee Scheme;' up to a maximum of £100,000 obtainable from Banks, who do not support it and which is therefore not on offer, unless the intended Business Person is fully aware of its

existence and insists upon it. The scheme has a seven year repayment term, where only interest is paid for the first two years. However, seven years is far too short a period for a new business starting from scratch and with no other source of capital.

- Its a well known fact, that recent High Interest Rates (16%) were a major contributor to the bankruptcy of many larger established businesses... who generally get rescued by other large companies or Banks. Yet under the 'Government Small Firms Loan Scheme,' the small business has to pay an additional 2% above normal Bank Interest Rates (no matter how high or low) throughout the repayment term. There is no rescue plan available.

- It's another well known fact, that it's unwise to set-up and run a business on bank loans, yet the Government Loan Scheme is precisely that, a bank loan. The dangers are not advised to the inexperienced business person, who only learns from hindsight, to their detriment.

- The third well known fact, is that it takes at least 3-5 years to develop a new business but the Government and Banks expect this to occur within the first year.

Therefore the Government's Enterprise Initiative operates with;-

Limited finance

Limited advice

Limited training

Limited back-up

Limited support

Limited time

No wonder they get limited Business success. "

5. **Sugar Daddies** are on offer to attractive single women and single parents as a financial alternative. It is absolutely disgraceful when

self-financing or Venture Capital means prostitution. Catch 22 or Trap 22. Is this how we acquired the phrases:-

"Lie back and think of England"

or *"Britain is the old man of Europe"* and

"BRITAIN is used to playing second fiddle."

6. **Personal Commitment** to a Bank Manager means only one thing 'Your personal financial security' (cash or collateral) or how much money you are investing into your business... i.e. putting into their bank. This is supposed to prove how committed you are to your business, not withstanding that you may have;-

(a). spent all your life savings on the business;

(b). have worked seven days a week;

(c). had no wages or holidays in years,

(d). endless sleepless nights;

(e). have to find continuous effort and self motivation;

(f). limited time to spend with your family;

(g). your relevant business experience and expertise;

(h). your business viability or commercial potential.

At the end of the day, when you approach the Bank for finance to set up your business, you will find that these factors have -

NO BEARING ON YOUR PERSONAL COMMITMENT!

Therefore people on Income Support (or any other State-Benefit) could never set up a business of their own, as the Government's qualifying criteria are that;-

(a). One must be out of work and have no money to take care of themselves or their family.

(b). Your entitlement ceases, if at any time you work for more than 24 hours a week... paid or unpaid. So even hours spent on planning out your business are taken as unpaid work.

(c). Most people on Income Support are living in Council accommodation. It's illegal to run a business from Council private accommodation. If a nuisance is caused, you are forced to stop, or could be evicted. So the most you can achieve is a limited market research exercise, which means you lose even more money than you gain.

(d). The majority of people on Income Support are single parents, most of whom are **women.**

So where would someone in this position find the **Bank's personal commitment**... *finance?*

Furthermore, little does the inexperienced business person realise that Bank Managers also have no real practical business experience and that their only training is in Banking administration. They are procedure followers, insecure and afraid of taking risks because their careers or promotions are at stake and they can quickly be demoted if financial errors are made. They are not businessmen, promoters or accountants and cannot understand the basic difference between the practical realities and the theory of running a business. Communication can become limited or one sided, generally in their favour because they know they hold the controlling power... **Finance.** One is left feeling vulnerable, with no choice but to listen and obey or be destroyed.

This has been precisely my situation for the past five years. Fortunately, I've succeeded without having to yield to temptation but also without any;-

Support

Assistance

Back-up

Encouragement

Advice or

Recognition -

from Authorities, who appeared to do everything in their power to silence me or destroy my business.

- Even though I had personally negotiated and obtained orders from Harrods, Fortnum & Mason, Tesco, Sainsbury, Safeway, Asda and Ireland.

Even though my business;-

- would create a unique and exclusive industry for Britain;
- could create hundreds of jobs;
- has colossal worldwide potential;
- could increase Britain's exports;
- could improve the nation's health;
- supports many other British businesses, the third world and the environment;
- brought national recognition to British black foods;
- could enhance racial harmony and;
- offers real inspiration to others.

The Authorities remained adamantly non-supportive and I was left trapped within the Government Small Firms Loan Guarantee Scheme. Although the Government spends billions of pounds on their so called 'NEW Enterprise Initiatives,' they refused to release me from this noose. In addition, the Government rejected my offer to initiate a

Winter Warming Campaign for the elderly, claiming they don't get involved in commercial enterprise as its unethical. If this is the truth, why then encourage New Enterprise or Initiatives? Doesn't the Government pay subsidies and provide other financial aid to keep British industries alive? For example: British farmers; (milk, meat, butter, vegetables, fruit), The National Health Service (Drugs Companies), British Aerospace, Rolls Royce and many others. Also is the Government really consciously concerned about the nation's health?

✿ Redress.

Small business-owners who are unhappy with the treatment they are receiving from their Bank Managers have only one recourse and that is to ask the Bank's regional or head office to investigate their situation, with a view to overriding the Bank Manager's decisions. If this fails, there is nothing else they can do. Unlike the private customer, a small business owner has 'no right of appeal' to the Banking Ombudsman. It is a right they should have if small businesses under severe financial pressure are not to feel that they are being unfairly treated.

✿ The Risk Factor.

It's another known fact that not everyone has the capacity or ability to succeed. Setting up a business is a big gamble, one is taking a huge risk. For most, it's the biggest gamble of their lives as they could end up losing everything.

"The Government Initiatives were introduced to try and minimise these risks but instead have maximised them, hence the real reasons many small businesses have been and are still failing."

Change must start from the top, *"you can't teach an old dog new tricks;"* old men are slow and lethargic, set in their ways and behind the times. Britain needs new blood, young energetic, enthusiastic and adventurous people; *"one cannot be progressive, creative, innovative or competitive, if one is backward."*

Britain has lost all its sense of adventure. How can we compete after 1992 with a forward thinking and progressive Europe in which small businesses are actively encouraged and supported by their Governments?

The successful running of a business depends on the ability, knowledge and financial resources to manage it well. The same goes for the successful running of a country. The current crisis state (recession) of the British Economy and the extensive reports of bank's mismanagement are adequate proof of bad management. The Government has the best economic and management brains in the country and all the financial resources (our money) at their disposal and have still failed, yet are too arrogant to admit it. They relentlessly continue to complicate the issues in order to deceive and confuse us. Surprisingly, we are left with the guilt of explaining why our businesses are failing.

The simple truth is -

"We have not failed - **they have failed us."**

> *They have set the rules,*
>
> *the regulations,*
>
> *the guidelines and*
>
> *the training programmes for us to follow,'*

In other words;-

"A binding contract for failure."

The billions of pounds incurred on the Government's 'Poll Tax Initiative' and the continued expenditure required to try to sort out this administrative mess, could have probably saved thousands of viable businesses and secured millions of jobs. The Government has made this country **Bankrupt.**

I am personally grateful for every disappointment and rejection, because each has taught me many valuable lessons. I now enjoy making my own mistakes and learning from them. I've single-handedly fought my own battles and found the solutions to my problems. Unfortunately, each step forward has meant ten steps backward battling with the Authorities; then recuperating and regaining the strength in order to progress again.

The setbacks have cost me dearly but time is a great healer and I've become;-

> stronger
>
> more consciously aware
>
> more sensitive
>
> more committed
>
> more feminine and
>
> a more confident and capable human being.

A natural business person acts from 'intuition'... i.e. inner feelings or gut reactions which is called initiative. No amount of book training alone can make anyone a dynamic business person or entrepreneur.

"The uniqueness comes from within, hence the importance of encouraging individualism."

My most valuable lesson learnt is: do not ever trust, believe or depend on Banks or Governments, as they are the greatest hinderers of progress and will hamper your success. But, if you are fortunate enough to find a good Bank Manager, treat him/her like a precious gem.

> **"I was exceptionally lucky to have survived."**

I sincerely hope that these revelations will identify the root causes, awaken people to the reality and remove the double standards, injustices, hypocrisy and false sense of security. I hope it will encourage the Authorities to review their current Enterprise Policy and offer real hope, real incentive, adequate financial provisions and bring about serious change in attitudes in relations towards women, black people and small businesses alike.

The Solution

SELF-HELP Employment Incorporating Government Investments.

*''There is a solution to every problem,
but WHAT is that problem?''*

Enterprise needs MONEY

In business, one needs to *speculate in order to accumulate,*
but **speculation requires money.**

Enterprise means business expenditure, which means spending money before you make a profit. This is why small businesses fail... they do not have the finance to set-up and run, in order to make more money.

Even your ideas cost money. If you are an enterprising person or entrepreneur, it costs you to think enterprisingly.

For instance;-

You've got a brilliant **idea** which you believe could be a money spinner. To prove its **potential,** you must first conduct a **market research**. *"This costs money."*

Once proven, you must **market** it (or sell it). *"This costs even more money."* Once you've obtained the market place, you must **promote** it, in order to keep up the sales and create more demand. To **commercialise** a product *"costs the greatest amount of money."*

To start a business successfully, **first** you must have the money.

"It's the chicken and egg situation."

The Government is playing the part of the chicken and the small business is expected to lay the *'golden egg,'* but due to such poor, ill prepared nesting, once laid, the eggs have no chance of survival. To make matters worse, the poor working-classes do not belong to the 'old boys network' which only opens 'financial doors' to the elite.

I'd like to offer the following solutions to help the poor entrepreneur:-

1. The Government should allow 3-5 years time scale for any business to get off the ground.

2. Remove the 24 hours working limit for people on State Benefit trying to set up a business.

3. 3-5 years Child Care Grant for those with young children.

4. 3-5 years Business Grant (£5,000 to £50,000) for market research and setting up expenses.

5. Machinery and Equipment Grant (50% minimum).

6. 3-5 years Council Tax exemption on private dwelling and business premises.

7. 3-5 years Housing Benefit allowance on private dwelling... owned or rented.

8. 2-3 years Business Premises Rent Grant.

9. Business Premises Repair Grant (50% minimum on privately rented commercial properties and 100% on Council owned properties).

10. 2-3 years Exhibition Grant for small manufacturers (50% minimum).

11. D.T.I. Initiative - 100% Grant for all of their Enterprise Initiatives- (design, marketing, business planning, quality control and manufacturing).

12. Loan facilities. The Government Loan Guarantee Scheme should be increased (maximum £250,000); 3 years capital and interest holiday, plus an extended repayment term of up to 25 years.

13. Action should be taken to encourage Venture Capital Investment in

equity holdings, to reduce the current dependency of many small businesses on bank lending.

14. Small business should have the right to have complaints investigated by the Banking Ombudsman.

15. Free business advice and training, as currently provided by Enterprise and Development Agencies or free professional business management courses provided by Colleges or Universities.

In order to monitor progress and prevent abuse of the suggestions made from 1-10, each business will need to apply annually for the continuation of their Grants/Benefits. This will also provide an indication of the cut-off point for Grant-Aid.

I believe that this package is not only realistic but also offers greater incentive for long-term success. Additionally, it allows for time to build up the all important 'track record' insisted upon by Banks and others.

Business should be a long-term investment and not the short-term interim measures currently being exercised.

The Government is bound to claim that they don't have the funds to finance small business. Drastic measures call for drastic action. In the final analysis, in order to stop fooling the nation, the Authorities will have to stop providing parasitic training, which ultimately means the abolishment of their entire Enterprise Initiatives and Business Training Programmes, replacing these with properly structured long-term professional Business and Management Training Courses provided by Colleges or Universities. The vast amount of money which would be saved, could then be re-invested in those who need it most, (i.e. small businesses), which should still leave a huge financial surplus. The removal of the obstructive bureaucratic red-tape, creates further natural savings caused from unblocking the System.

Finally, Britain has been set in its ways for far too long and needs to be reminded that opportunities missed can never be recaptured. If unemployment is going to continue to rise, then 'self-help employment incorporating Government Investment' could be the best viable alternative to put Britain and the British inhabitants back on their feet.

I didn't know that I had real business potential, so how many like me are there, OUT THERE?

By Dounne Alexander

© Copyright, 12th August 1991

"The power to dream and the ability to hang on to your dreams has been lost, due to a climate of continuous depression, unemployment and a sense of hopelessness - why bother!

Ordinary people and kids need impossible but realistic dreams in order to forge ambitions and drive. It takes an underdog to encourage, motivate and inspire others."

FOOD AND DRINK

Dounne Alexander-Moore's utter determination to put her grandmother's Caribbean recipes on the supermarket shelves is starting to pay off.

Carol Dix spoke to her

Woman with sauce

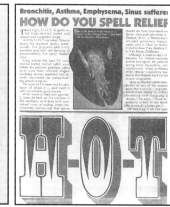

Bronchitis, Asthma, Emphysema, Sinus sufferer
HOW DO YOU SPELL RELIEF

H·O·T

CT: Supporting the community

'There is no glory without pain, hard work and sacrifice'

The taste of success

Caribbean sauce is a winner for businesswoman

by Geraint Smith

WEEKEND

FOOD & DRINK 39

THE INDEPENDENT Saturday 8 October 1988

The fruits of getting in a pickle

Jeremy Round meets women who have found home-cooking means business

FOOD

EXPRESS

TELEVISION
4-PAGE ESSENTIAL VIEWING GUIDE

Risky business

High fliers reveal the secrets of how they made it to the top

ENTERPRISE MONEY MAIL

Early success is rewarding

Small Business Diary

GUARDIAN FOOD AND DRINK

Friday July 17 1991

The spice of life

195.

Insight

The four high street banks are all blaming small business for their poor...

Why are the banks over providing for the debts of small businesses?

SUE ARNOLD

Some like it super hot

THIS is all a bit awkward. I was instructed this week to tell you about a magnificent new recruitment drive to get more women into Parliament where, of course, they should rightfully be, but I missed the introductory session last weekend. I was up in Scotland nosing malt whisky for the equally magnificent, though I suspect more uproarious, introductory celebrations thrown by the Grant family to commemorate the founding by their great grandfather William Grant of the famous Dufftown distillery 100 years ago. I'm sorry about this, and I swear neither wild horses nor Glenfiddich will keep me from attending the next meeting of Miss Aleksander's Grooming Academy For Young Ladies Who Want To Grow Up Like Edwina Curry.

Talking of curry, I had an intriguing letter on Tuesday from a Mrs Moore who said that for the last 15 years she has been producing hot pepper sauce in her East Ham kitchen and distributing it at the rate of 250 jars a week to friends and acquaintances. Mrs Moore believes passionately in the healing powers of hot peppers. According to the instructions that come with the stuff, they can alleviate 35 different conditions including fever, chills, gout and fatigue, as well as preventing blood clotting and expelling wind and poison. I believe it. For some time now I have been persevering with Dr Bach's well known homeopathic flower remedies and, like some ancient medieval alchemist, spend many an evening mixing the contents of the Good Doctor's 38 bottled substances to suit my personal requirements. I've tried most of them in various unlikely combinations, *but* neither I nor my loved ones have noticed any discernible improvement in my health or my temper.

Mustard for emergencies

I'm clearly too far gone for flowers, but hot peppers—that sounds more likely. We're a family of spice lovers. My mother takes Tabasco in lieu of cough mixture, and my ex-mother-in-law carries a tube of Colman's mustard in

HOW SCHOOL DUNCES MADE IT TO THE TOP

Who needs O-level, we've got GO-levels

A woman's place is in the world of big business

PROFILE

22 WEDNESDAY, JULY 3, 1991

BUSINESS NEWS

Treasury Minister Gillian Shepard yesterday hosted the first of a series of White... women to hear what lies behind their success—and to discuss their economic problem... Moore (left), of Grannms Catering, and Pat Marsh, managing director of A...

WEDNESDAY, SEPTEMBER 19, 1990 ★ 5   DAILY SALE 876,824 (avg)   25p (Republic of Ireland)

Today

FOR A BRIGHTER TOMORROW

We're dishing up success on a plate

issue No: 379 January 23 1990

THE VOICE

Britain's Best Black Newspaper!

40p weekly

L'S MAGIC

WNK radio

103·3

'LONDON'S FIRST BLACK RA...

VS IS BAC...

Get your free... next week in No 1 Voi...

The Weekly GLEANER

THE TOP CARIBBEAN NEWSPAPER

2434   WEDNESDAY, OCTOBER 14 1998   PRICE...

INTERVIEW   INTERVIEW   ENTERTAINMENT

Mission in progress

Successful businesswoman Downie Alexander who founded Gramma's Herbal Pepper Sauces in the '80s tells Colette Hibbert why she is pushing to get a herbal drink she has developed officially recognised

● NEWSPAPERS AND MAGAZINES FEATURES: 1987 - 1999. *(cont....)*

197.

198.

199.

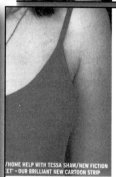

Labour's election manifesto

April 1992

It's time
to get Britain
working again

Your
land,
my
land

Time for a change

**Made in
Britain**

- **1992** General Election.in support of the Labour Party.

above right:
Neil Kinnock (Leader of the Labour Party).

- **Tony Blair MP**
Secretary of State for
Employment.

- **John Prescott MP**
Secretary of State for
Transport.

- **Gordon Brown MP**
Secretary of State for Trade
and Industry.

- **Robin Cook MP**
Secretary of State for
Community Care and Health.

- **Jack Straw MP**
Secretary of State for
Education.

- **Margaret Beckett MP**
Secretary to the Treasury.

- **Bryan Gould MP**
Secretary of State for
Environment.

- **Jo Richardson**
Minister for Women.

● **1993:**

Preserving a family tradition, mum, myself, Marsha and cousin Yasmin.

Resurrection After Liquidation.

BUSINESS UPDATE.

- *The following nine years from 1991 to 2000.*

Pressure

The entire first five years in business contained so many major obstacles and problems, that it makes me weary just thinking about it. I simply can't believe what I was put through. I keep asking myself WHY and refuse to put it all down to racism because the human experience is far more complex than just one simple issue.

However, this was just a taste of things to come, in the following five years I received the full treatment. In order to retain a sense of balance, sanity and to keep grounded, I continued to lecture regularly around the country, sharing my experiences and exposing the System. It was the only way of fighting back, by making others aware. At all times, I kept my composure intact and was never nasty, rude or arrogant to those in Authority, not even when they tried to annoy, hurt or ruin me. I remained respectful in their presence, primarily because it is my nature but mainly because I don't have an ego problem. On reflection, all the consultants I'd employed were men, who had only experienced a couple of difficult confrontations with the Authorities, yet they immediately lost their cool and got angry. They didn't last long because they couldn't handle the pressure and always questioned me, *"how can you take so much? How do you withstand it? WHY don't you give up?"*

However, the more I understood the System, the more frustrated I became. *"How is it that I and everyone else could see the potential of my business but the Establishment remained blind?"* Knowing that I was not the only one hurting, made it worse. This pain has a ricochet effect and I was concerned about my health and the general welfare of my daughters. Still I had to remain positive to keep them from becoming negative... the fight had to go on.

Publicity was an essential tool, not only to keep the business in the news but also for maintaining sales. I was fighting for survival in more ways than one; chasing sales to meet my monthly factory rent of £1,000, plus other overhead costs. At the same time, I was desperately trying to get into more Supermarkets, which took months of negotiations;- dealing with the day-to-day administration, manufacturing, bottling and packaging products; in order to keep up with the current orders (up to 5,000 jars); lecturing, handling the Solicitors, Accountants, Creditors, Liquidator, etc. I had to cope with everything on my own, as there was no one available with the experience or expertise to advise me. The only helpers was still my Mum and daughters, who worked happily without pay and never once complained but continuously nagged me to rest. They could see the frantic pace I was going at but I couldn't. It was all new experiences for me and I knew that somehow I had to handle it. During the night, instead of sleeping, I'd read over legal documents and also dealt with the daily administration, letters etc. Thank God, I was used to working seven days a week with 3-4 hours sleep. Prioritising and time management was essential but difficult, when there were insufficient hours in the day to do everything.

Once the liquidation had ended, there was still no time to rest and still no money. I now had a 'newly' reformed business with the same factory, expensive overheads, the lot and I had to immediately plan the re-building process. This simply meant even more work and still only one person and one brain to do it. I felt like I was in the middle of a battle field, with both the allies and enemies firing every weapon full blast at me. Somehow I had to find a way out to survive. I worked myself to exhaustion.

But fortunately, the good times and a little luck always overshadowed the bad times. My father, cousin (Noelena), a dear family friend, the late Mrs Shuffler, a white customer, Ms Nora Wingate and my close friend, Gillian Bush all personally lent me the money to restart the business. Many of my customers called regularly to keep my spirits up but on the day I received the call from Nora she simply said, *"if you need any help, just ask."* A few months later, I desperately needed £10,000 and thought, *"I dare not ask for so much!"* It was on a Friday morning, she called just at the moment when I was feeling very low. She said, *"how much do you need?"* I said £10,000. She replied, *"it's in the post."* The next morning there it was, a £10,000 cheque with a post card. I was dumb struck.

As I sat alone in the factory, looking at the cheque in disbelief; I cried, gave thanks to God in prayer, then called Nora to thank her. She said, *"Don't thank me, Thank God."* I was able to meet my commitments. To this day, I have not been able to repay them but I know that one day I will fulfil this promise.

To restart the business I also needed to find a new Bank. By this time, they were all aware of me because of the publicity and were most eager to get my business, until I revealed that the business was liquidated and I had no money. Their attitude swiftly changed to my 'personal security' and as I had none, I was back to square one;-

i.e. **NO money - NO security** = **NO LOANS.**

Realising that none of the Banks were any better than the other, I decided to open an account with one and then try to rebuild a good working relationship. I really believed that in time, if I proved my ability, I'd gain their confidence and in turn regain my credibility. So I prepared myself to re-start from scratch.

The new Bank had a business section with a Business Manager in charge, to whom I immediately got acquainted. One day, I decided to test the level of his expertise by asking, what advice he could give me on negotiating with the large Supermarkets or Department stores; How could I find and negotiate Venture Capital; How to organise my day to day administration and production? After beating around the bush and fumbling for a half hour, he finally admitted that he hadn't a clue; but he could give me all the advice I needed on Business Banking matters and produced his Bank's ready-made 'Business Pack' complete with ready-made cash-flow forecast. I simply asked him, *"how could you ever help me, when you don't even understand what I'm dealing with?"* I smiled and left, visualising the difficulties ahead.

Before the year was out, I'd notched up an incredible amount of publicity and accolades, listed below:-

- Invited to a private luncheon in Pall Mall, hosted by The University of the West Indies, whose Patron is Princess Anne. I obtained permission to have my pepper sauces on the tables to accompany the meal. It was there for the first time Princess Anne tasted and loved it. In her speech she acknowledged me as an outstanding British/Caribbean woman of achievement. Through the Chairperson she requested for me to send her a private supply of my sauces.

- I obtained official recognition for my business to be identified as a 'British Speciality Food Producer' rather than the general 'ethnic label' used for all black and other minority businesses.

- Nominated for my second award 'The British Food Processing Awards;' but this time I was the second runner up. The winner was the Chairman of the British Food & Drink Federation and the second runner up was the Chairman of the British Meat & Livestock Commission. At this presentation held in a posh London Hotel, myself and Marsha were the only black people invited, everyone else were middle/upper class white people. We both felt extremely proud.

- I became a Vice President for 'London Youth Clubs' whose Patron is the Queen's Mother, whom I also met that year at St. James's Palace.

- Won the 'Black Achievement Award' from the Business Federation.

- Invited to launch Parkside Health Authority's conference '*Look After Your Heart Charter and Food Guidelines*' with Sir William Doughty and I gave the key-note speech.

- I obtained lots more television, newspapers, magazines, radio coverage plus my photo was on the front cover of two mainstream British books 'Women Mean Business' which accompanied a BBC television series presented by Glenda Jackson. The book cover picture was also made into large posters and displayed in all 'Job Centres' nationwide; I was also on the front cover of 'Enterprising Women' by Carol Dix.

At the beginning of 1992, the country was ablaze with election fever. The main battle was between the Conservative and Labour Parties, both fighting for the female vote. By now I had become a high profiled black female, plus they were all aware of the contents of my book, which I'd planned to publish around election time. Therefore, they wanted me on their side. I was a complete political ignoramus but my father was a Conservative and my mother a (die-hard/card-carrying) Labour supporter. So, now I didn't only have the two political parties on my back but my parents also fighting for which one I should support. Needless to say 'Mum won!' Therefore, it wasn't my choice, it was hers and Dad respected my decision.

I must say, I thoroughly enjoyed learning about politics. The Labour Party wanted me to support them at the highest level. I was suddenly mixing with Cabinet Ministers (i.e. the late John Smith, Neil Kinnock, Majorie Mowlam, Margaret Becket, Gordon Brown, John Prescott and others) and was personally invited to take the front stage, side by side at press conferences and television interviews; manifestos were being couriered to me in advance of being announced to the press; my advice on business and women's issues were sought and recommended for policy change and was also allowed to answer press questions. I remember replying to a question on the issue of the cost of living, *"you can fool some of the people all the time but you can never fool a housewife."* I wrote an article for their magazine 'Your Land - My Land.' I was privileged to be present at private consultations with the Cabinet Ministers. It was there I saw the real Neil Kinnock (sincere, open and passionate). He was driven not by selfish ambition like most politicians but I saw the deep, strong love for his party, country and people; with the poor holding a special pocket close to his heart. I also saw the devastating pain experienced when they lost that election, which surprisingly lessened my own pains and struggles. It was consoling to realise that one had to be even stronger to withstand public humiliation and defeat. They too were all fighting for their livelihood, political ambition and personal pride. It exposed me to what it meant to be committed to a cause; fighting for what you believe in and fighting to win. I will always admire Neil for opening me up to the heart of a true politician. To my dismay, it was later rumoured that Neil did not win because Britain would not accept a Welshman as its Prime Minister. However, within a couple of years the then elected Prime Minister (Margaret Thatcher) was brutally back-stabbed by her own Conservative Cabinet Ministers and thrown out of office. Although, I was not a fan of hers, I respected her as a woman and for the strength she displayed. She worked hard for her party and country and this was how her dedication and loyalty was repaid. This too decreased my pain because it made me come to terms with the fact that discrimination, prejudice and injustice was not only exclusively a 'black-thing.' Nor has it changed my mind that politics is a dirty game and that discrimination exists even within their own ranks.

In between all of these happenings, I'd also completed my book, **The Black Cinderella** and it was ready for publication but no British publisher would touch it. I thought, *"could it be that bad?"* So I sent a copy to Ken Follett (Britain's renowned best selling international author) for his opinion. He loved it so much that he attached his personal endorsement and told me, *"you are a writer,"* then advised on how to publish it myself, which I did within two months; establishing my own publishing company called Unity Books.

Ken Follett's endorsement;-

> ***"This book is like Dounne herself; inspiring, controversial, shrewd, likeable and quite, quite unique."***

The book created the desired impact; political recognition and policy changes, which were recorded in both the Labour and Conservative Party manifestos. However, the Conservative Party won the election for the third consecutive time and therefore continued with their policy of keeping down the poor.

The book effectively caused the following changes;-

1.   It exposed 20 years of Government Enterprise hype, corruption and conspiracy; revealed the truth behind small business failures; under capitalisation; sub-standard training and why the recession became a convenient scape-goat to cover up gross mis-management, insensitivity and the exploitation of the vulnerable poor, who were being mis-treated, trapped and left unprotected, with no form of legal redress.

2.   It exposed the Banks' insensitivity to Small Businesses, especially towards women and black people.

3.   Created a new position for a Banking Ombudsman to investigate Small Business complaints. However, I later learnt that the offices and salary of the Ombudsman are paid for by all the National Banks, hence impartiality remains questionable.

4.   Increased the Government Loan Guarantee Scheme from £100,000 to £250,000 and extended the repayment terms from 7 to 10 years. However, whereas all small businesses were previously entitled to apply, the Government cleverly curtailed the entire scheme limiting it only to manufacturing businesses who had been trading for two years. This directly affected all Retail Traders and new 'start-up' businesses. Hence, although more money was injected into the scheme, those who needed it most (i.e. the poor) were no longer entitled.

5.   Improved business training by setting up the Training & Enterprise Councils.

6.   The Business Initiatives carried out by The Department of Trade and Industry (DTI) was abolished.

7.   It also brought an abrupt end to the Government and Banks (hyped-up) small business advertising campaigns.

8.   The Ethnic Minority Business Development Team which operated from the Home Office was disbanded.

Not surprisingly, I received no credit for exposing or bringing about these changes. However, the changes made were still grossly inadequate to meet the training and financial needs of the poor entrepreneur. The Government also cleverly restructured the same advertising funds into establishing more guango organisations to fleece the poor. For instance, the new Training and Enterprise Council (TEC) provides a two day 'free' Consultancy Service, after which the small business has to pay £50.00 per day for any additional advice required. Small businesses were still drowning in a sea of paper-work on 'how to access information,' but in their search on how to 'access finance,' they still reached a dead end, because **finance was never available.** Poor entrepreneurs should always keep in mind, that this country was built on deceit, an art which they have carved, crafted and perfected.

(Achievements continued);-

- By the end of 1992 my products were in other supermarkets... Asda, Co-Op Leo's, WM Low and Waitrose.

- I received the 'European Women of Achievement Award.'

- Won an 'Honourary Award' for the most outstanding Black/British Business Woman from the Black Women's Promotion and Research Project.

- Invited by the Conservative Cabinet Office to register for public appointment.

- Suffered my first major health scare, suspected Breast Cancer.

- Invited to all the prestigious events and functions; such as the 'Women of the Year' luncheon, held at the Savoy Hotel.

- Became a member of the following organisations:-

    UK Federation of Business and Professional Women

    British Association of Women Entrepreneurs.

    Parents at Work.

    Federation of Small Businesses.

    Black Women's Promotion and Research Project.

    Women of the Year Association.

    Network 2000.

    The International Institute for African Research.

    Tastes of Anglia; subsidiary of the national 'Food from Britain group.'

    Footprints.

Yet still, my credibility was questioned. I still could not obtain financial help from my Bank or anywhere else. However, in that very same year, it was reported on BBC Television that the British Banks had re-financed the Mirror Newspaper Group, to the tune of £250 million to secure it from bankruptcy and took the majority shares after a major 'staff pension' fraud was committed by its owner; who was an international figure and multimillionaire. Another report exposed that the Government had subsidised the jailed American Entrepreneur to the tune of £800,000 towards the cost of producing Deloren cars. This man was later caught selling cocaine to further finance his business. Yet I couldn't raise £50,000 to run an honest business. These reports also exposed that the Banks' recession losses were caused by their friendly alliances with big businesses and not from the pittance they'd spend on small businesses;

the likes of Olympia & York (a Canadian company) who also went bankrupt, leaving the Banks with billions in debts and having never occupied their enormous brand new building (in London's Docklands) which became a Government embarrassment. The Euro Tunnel is another fitting example, with over £9 billion in debt, which may never be repaid and with a strong possibility of bankruptcy. Nevertheless, my expertise was good enough to advise Government Cabinet Ministers, Bank Managers, Universities and Enterprise Training Agencies but inadequate for British Banks or Financial Institutions, **WHY?**

My new Bank proved to be no better than the old one. They were just as negative, blinkered and non-supportive in every way. In the end I had to resort to foul play, literally forcing them to lend some money. I eventually used blackmail or was it 'black female' to twist their arm. No matter what I did, they would not budge to help me. They knew that I was under extreme pressure and it appeared as if they were gloating, waiting to see how long it would take for me to give up and close down. But I battled on. Although the supermarket sales were going quite well, I had continuous cash-flow problems, caused by their late payment of invoices... up to three months. By December 1992, I had been with the Bank for one year and over £70,000 had passed through the Bank, plus I'd submitted quarterly progress reports. I desperately needed an annual overdraft facility of £10,000 to tide us over. I invited the Manager to visit the factory for inspection and to see the operation in progress. We sat in my office and I explained how the cash-flow problem materialised. For example, the supermarkets would place an order this week, for delivery of the products within seven days; therefore, the raw materials had to be bought, then the products made, bottled and packaged in advance. Hence, it was imperative to keep a certain amount of prepared stock always available. On the other hand, I didn't receive payment from the Supermarkets for between 30-90 days. Furthermore, I had other supermarkets interested in taking the products but would find it extremely difficult to supply them without an overdraft to meet the cost of supplies. I showed him the weekly invoiced orders, which were more than adequate to cover the overdraft. The Manager still turned me down, because I still had no personal security. The invoices of seven Supermarkets, with regular weekly orders for over six months was still not good enough to secure finance. So I was forced to remain at a stand still, unable to develop or grow beyond where I'd reached.

By 1993, the business showed all the signs that it was on the verge of a boom. I was certain that this was going to be my year. Then in July, my mother suddenly became ill and died shortly after. My whole world turned upside down. I was totally devastated, which naturally affected the business and my ability to perform with the same enthusiasm. For once success had no meaning. This shock, coupled with the additional stress, began to take toll on my own health, which I with-held from my family. By 1994, my doctor diagnosed lower spinal damage which was causing extreme sciatic pains in my legs and I also had repetitive strain in both hands. I was in constant pain but loosing Mum was the greatest pain of all. Then my doctor warned that if I didn't stop working, I could damage myself beyond repair. Although I was frightened, I still kept going. These injuries were caused by the heavy manual work required to manufacture the products. Having to make, fill and label up to 5,000 jars a week (by hand), plus lifting heavy boxes and stacking pallets. My poor lifting skills made matters worse. Hence, both my business and I was now in a crisis and slowly grinding to a halt. However, after returning from my first Caribbean holiday, (where I'd fallen in love) I felt well rested and re-motivated but the financial crisis still loomed.

By October 1994, I was invited to be the key speaker at a high powered finance seminar, where to my surprise, my Bank's Regional Manager was also a speaker. After my speech, an American delegate asked, *"has any of the British Banks recognised your charisma and PR potential? Have they ever approached you to promote their Bank?"* When I replied *"no,"* she could not believe their short sightedness.

During the speech, I detailed my achievements, as well as, the treatment I'd received from my Bank but I never revealed the name of the Bank. The entire delegation of 300 white financial consultants were appaled and frequently gasped in dismay. After the seminar ended, the Regional

Bank Manager asked me (in private), to tell him the name of the Bank who had been so insensitive and difficult. I replied, *"yours."* He thanked me for not embarrassing him and insisted I call him if I had any more problems with my Manager and gave me his business card.

By January 1995, sales were falling, the local Authority was now pressing me for rate arrears due on the factory and threatening to issue a Bailiffs warrant to seize my equipment, if payment was not made within seven days; plus my Landlord's £3,000 quarterly rent was also due. To my good fortune that month, Marsha's dog (Zara) who was diagnosed with terminal cancer six weeks earlier; given not long to live and no medical treatment because the Vet believed that nothing could save her. However, through spiritual intervention I developed a special Herbal Drink; treated her with it and she made a full and complete recovery. This unexpected recovery gave us all (including the business) a new lease of life. I desperately needed £15,000 loan to clear my debts or be forced to close down and also to set-up research on this seemingly miraculous drink. So armed with the Vet's report in hand, I arranged a meeting to see the Bank Manager. By now, I was so used to refusals; I expected it. But then I thought, *"any fool with the slightest amount of imagination would see the potential of this drink and would want to be involved."* But this time when he said "**NO**," I returned home and decided that it was time to turn the tables and give the Manager a dose of his own medicine. *"How would he feel, if his career was put on the line?"*

I telephoned the Regional Manager, explained the situation and threatened that if something was not done immediately, I was going to expose their Bank to the national press. He telephoned my Manager and within hours a meeting was arranged with the Local Area Manager and my Bank Manager. The Area Manager went out of his way to impress me about his seniority and to show that I was being taken very seriously. He explained, *"I'm the Senior Manager who oversees all the local branches in the East London area, therefore, I'm senior to the Business Manager (i.e. my Manager) as well as, senior to the actual General Branch Manager, which means that whatever I say GOES. Above me there is only the Regional Manager, who you complained to and after him is the top man himself; the Chairman of the Bank."* I was duly impressed because they were at least now prepared to listen. My Manager looking extremely nervous and uncomfortable, sat in silence throughout the meeting, whilst I put my case, detailing the number of times short-term loans were rejected, producing back up letters etc. He said that my internal file was the largest of all their business clients. I was able to clearly articulate that the Bank has never given me *'fair treatment* or a *fair hearing'* and questioned **WHY** were they so deliberately negative and destructive? I closed my statement saying, *"over the years, I've never revealed the names of any of the Banks who had mistreated me but this time I intended to expose your Bank, if this money is not approved today, because I've now had enough."*

They were cornered and couldn't give a convincing reason as to **WHY,** because there was none. Realising that they were in danger, they had to bow to my demands and my Manager experienced 'first hand' what it felt like to have the rug pulled from under his feet... his career and livelihood was in jeopardy. The £15,000 was sanctioned immediately as an unsecured long-term overdraft and was placed into my account that same day. I dictated my own terms which they agreed to. This money allowed me to pay my debts and set-up the research on the drink.

However, I knew I needed more money and continued to search everywhere to raise venture capital. Each one praised my business plan, product quality and future potential but the liquidation and lack of security remained the big question mark against my credibility. I continued to be taken for a long ride and at face value. I was told by a well known Investment Institution who finances British companies, that my business plan, product quality and personal achievements were incredible but they could not invest because of my lack of management qualifications and experience; but, if I had worked within one of the big British Corporations, it would have given them more confidence in my ability, plus the liquidation proved that I couldn't make the business profitable. He advised me to amalgamate with a large food company, who had the necessary management expertise, experience and finance in hand. In other words, sell to a British company.

Unfortunately, by the following year, sales continued to decrease, because I had no money for advertising or promotions and my health had gone down hill. I was in extreme pain; almost losing the use of my right hand and could not stand up for no more than two minutes. My doctor compelled me to rest. But my landlord was now on my back and becoming quite aggressive. One morning, I arrived only to find the locks on the factory door had been changed. This was his way of demanding payment, by seizing the factory and my possessions. Therefore, I was forced to vacate the factory and cease trading.

So finally, by 1995 I had gone full circle and was back working from home and living on State Benefit. I focused on re-establishing the business as a 'mail order' operation and continued with the medical research on the drink. The rest gave me the opportunity to review and redirect the business. *"Yes!"* I still had no intention of giving up. This was just one of those timely minor set-backs that make you reflect and re-focus. Although I had no regrets, one of my many mistakes was not concentrating on or developing the mail order alongside the retail trade. I believed that the supermarkets would have created and provided sufficient sales to keep us forever. This was a fallacy but I thank God for the experience. No amount of book education or training would have given me such great knowledge and expertise.

Throughout the years, people from all over the country and overseas would telephone or write, asking if I would supply them direct as there were no local stores where they could buy my products. On checking our mailing list, we had accumulated over 1000 customers and within the following two years, this grew to nearly 2,000. Furthermore, as my products were still exceptionally unique; plus their superior quality and superb packaging placed them perfectly into the mail order quality market, which opened me up to a wider vision. It's potential was now much greater than that of the supermarkets, **the world was now my Oyster, within which I could visualise my PEARL.** So with my Spirit-Guides by my side, I prepared myself for a new but much greater adventure.

> ## 'In my darkest hours, the Lord always gives me a LIGHT.'

This special light came in 1996, in the form of a direct/divine mission and the realisation that there was a purpose for all my sufferings, my humility and my gifts. So armed with this great knowledge and awareness, I thought that my misery had finally come to an end but again I was wrong. There was still more disappointments to come but this time I was so filled with joy, that I felt no pain or anger, because I knew that this too was for a reason.

For the two years up to 1997, after not obtaining any medical support, I decided to set up an independent research on the Herbal Drink, using my own customers and their pets and kept the Bank fully informed. Zara herself provided the best testimony of all because she had survived the cancer without drug medication or any other medical treatment and continued to maintain good health. My customers stood by me with support, encouragement and prayers. By mid 1997, I received spiritual confirmation that the drink was an effective **blood cleanser and preventative**; safe and should be made available for worldwide distribution; (the full story is detailed in the next chapter 'For the love of Zara').

I was now ready to start all over again but this time round, I had the experience and confidence that my future was secure, and that *'I would survive!'*

Fortunately, I still had most of my factory equipment stored in a small warehouse. So I got down to the nitty-gritty, worked out the minimum amount of money required to set it up and resume production (£50,000) and revised the Business Plan. I then arranged yet another meeting with my Bank Manager, to present the full proposal to him, except for the Spiritual messages. This time, although I knew that he'd refuse my request, I still had to hear it for myself. I knew he would never forget or forgive what I did to him two years earlier. No amount of potential could ever overcome 'willful spite.' Bearing in mind, he had received regular (written) quarterly progress reports, coupled with quarterly meetings, plus I'd kept up the monthly interest payments on the overdraft. So he was fully informed and updated.

On the day of the meeting, I gave the presentation of my life because I felt confident that either way I was going to fulfil my purpose. I detailed the strategy and potential, including the proposed publication of this book for worldwide distribution and had already secured interest from the major national book store (W.H Smiths) anticipated good media support, plus I was to be presented with a special 'American achievement award' that month.

Anticipating an instant refusal, I concluded my presentation by asking if he was aware of the Government's new Enterprise Initiative called 'Race For Opportunity,' which involved the participation of several major corporate companies, who had agreed to support minority businesses to access the mainstream markets and that his Bank was one of the companies involved. He replied, *"no"* and asked me to explain how it worked, to which I gladly obliged;- *"as your Bank is involved, you are supposed to sit down with me and go through my business strategy plan in detail; review its long-term potential (say over 5 years). If agreed, then consider and support the necessary finance and work along with me to develop it. The £50,000 I'm seeking, is to repay your £15,000 overdraft; set up the factory, purchase a sachet filling and herb blending machine; publish the book, re-package the products and cover overheads. I'll continue to work for no wage until the business was in a financial position to pay me."* He then said that he'd investigate with Head Office and come back to me with a decision, reminding me in the process that the Bank had already given support in the past and it was extremely unlikely that they'd lend beyond the £15,000. I'd heard this reply so many times before that I was mimicking his every word in my mind. He could never tell me **NO** to my face, it was always the Head Office decision, not his.

Bang on time, he called two days later and as expected, the answer was 'NO.' Once again, lack of personal security being the same nonsensical reason. I couldn't resist testing him one more time. So I said, *"OK, how about financing it under the Government Loan Guarantee Scheme to cover the security obstacle."* That threw him, he wasn't expecting a counter. After fumbling he said, *"but you'd have to prepare a lengthy Business Plan, it could take months to process as this system is now very complicated and there is no guarantee that it would be approved."* I then reminded him that it was really a Bank loan and if he as the Manager had faith in my business and recommended it; the loan would be approved. Now being cornered he replied, that *"the Bank won't give a loan to repay a debt (i.e. their overdraft)."* My response was, *"you won't give me a loan regardless. Never mind, I'll find a way."*

His final statement was, *"you have an excellent product which has enormous potential; why don't you sell the recipe to an international company to raise the capital you need for the business."*

Unfortunately, the previous Regional Manager who had supported me two years earlier had been transferred to a new position and it would have been pointless complaining to his replacement, as he'd more than likely back up the Manager.

So I was back on the trail of trying to find a Bank who would be willing to support my business.

Seeking a Fair Hearing

In 1990, I came across this true story about a black American doctor (E. Bates) in the 1950's, which I keep as a reminder that fifty years on and society has not really changed.

Dr. Earnest Bates was typical of many blacks in the 1950's. He worked hard in school and in the army to become a Nuero-Surgeon. He developed a successful practice in California earning $500,000 a year by the 1970's but he knew that many hospitals couldn't afford to purchase expensive diagnostic technologies like CAT-SCAN Machinery, so he invested in a business to lease mobile diagnostics to hospitals.

Like many start-up companies his firm ran into difficulty but Dr. Bates says that one of the greatest difficulties he had was getting 'a fair hearing' when he went to the Small Business Administration, to Venture Capitalists and to Investment Banks on Wall Street. Once they saw he was black, interest in his business plan simply evaporated, until he met Michael Milken, (a Jewish man) who provided the capital he needed to expand. It's now one of the most successful medical leasing services in America.

"If a successful Black Neuro-Surgeon can't get a fair hearing when he looks for support for a business proposition at this point in 20th Century America, then where is an under-educated twenty year old black male supposed to turn? So don't be fooled by the theory that; anyone with a good business plan, with viable commercial potential and good entrepreneurial Spirit is able to find capital."

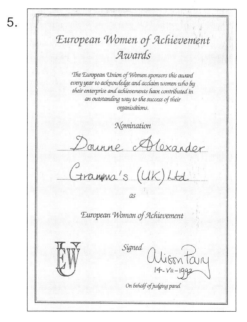

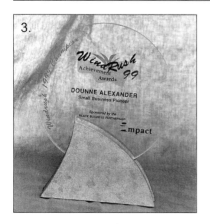

1. Voice Community Award; 1999

2. Black Womens Promotions Award; 1993

3. Windrush Award; 1999

4. Black Achievement Award; 1990

5. European Women of Achievement Award; 1992

and Federation of Black Women Business Owners; 1997, *(picture not included)*

The Black Cinderella

BLACK LONDONERS 1880-1990

NELSON BUSINESS ENGLISH

BUSINESS CLASS

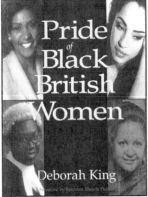

Pride of Black British Women

Deborah King

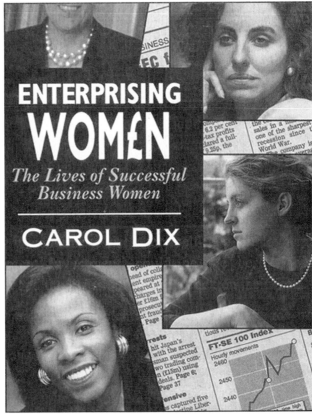

ENTERPRISING WOMEN

The Lives of Successful Business Women

CAROL DIX

ROOTS OF THE FUTURE

ETHNIC DIVERSITY IN THE MAKING OF BRITAIN

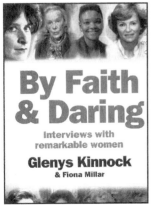

By Faith & Daring

interviews with remarkable women

Glenys Kinnock & Fiona Millar

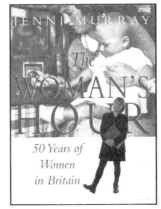

JENNI MURRAY

The WOMAN'S HOUR

50 Years of Women in Britain

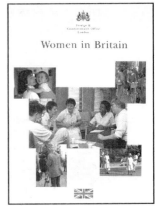

Women in Britain

Peppers

AMAL NAJ

A STORY OF HOT PURSUITS

THE PERFECT PICKLE BOOK

DAVID MABEY AND DAVID COLLINSON

THE BOOK OF THE BBC tv SERIES

TIGER LILY

FLAVOURS OF THE ORIENT

Henrietta Green's

Food Lovers guide to Britain

The finest producers and the best shops in England, Scotland and Wales

FOREWORD BY DEREK COOPER

The Authentic Food Finder

a new guide

to finding and buying traditional, organic and fine foods direct from the maker and grower

FOOD BY POST

The Best of British Food Delivered to Your Door

edited by Bernice Hurst

EXPRESS DELIVERY

WOMEN MEAN BUSINESS

BLACK WOMEN TAKING CHARGE

Profiles of Black Women Entrepreneurs

Emete Wanogho

Foreword by Chrystal Rose

THE UNEMPLOYABLES

CHRIS LEWIS

Alan Sugar
Mirman · Si
Harvey-Jon
Ashcroft · E
Marco-Pierr
Lennox Lew
Conran · W
Tony Gordo
Gabriel · Bo
David Sulliv
Chorlton · L
Grace Igwe
Stockford ·
Alexander-M
Andrew Wi
Brown · Ke
Fiona Price
Fiennes · M
Colin Jacks
Pinter · Ton
Marc Weink
Bader · Bri
Howard Hodgson · John
Harrison · Linda Beard ·
Peter Parfitt · David
Northrop · Bob Payton ·
Tim Wilkinson

THE ENGLIS SAINT BERNA CLUB

Millennium Yearbook

❀ **More Obstacles Encountered.**

Up until 1993, I was repeatedly called upon by the Establishment to support and represent British Small Businesses and womens issues, plus Government Ministers frequently talked about racial harmony and support. So I decided to put them to the test. I wrote to both the House of Commons and House of Lords to introduce my products for their dining room tables, as well as, for use in their kitchens. The gentleman in charge on receiving my letter, immediately telephoned the factory. Fortunately, we were not in, so he left an angry racist message on my answerphone. His voice sounded like a middle aged aristocrat, so I knew he was well schooled and in a position of authority, which goes to show that racism can make even the well bred forget their status. I called a journalist friend who worked for a well known national newspaper and sent her a copy of the taped message, she was horrified. I asked her to arrange to meet with him and demand a face to face apology, otherwise the message would be publicised. The meeting was arranged, he was extremely apologetic and bent over backwards to accommodate my request. He went so far as to take me on a tour of the 'House,' showed off its lavish kitchen and even introduced me to the head chef. In the end, I didn't bother to pursue it because I was sufficiently satisfied seeing the fear on his face and hearing his apology. Anyway, I'd have found it difficult to work with hypocrites, who grinned with their teeth incapable of projecting a genuine smile.

❀ **Local Authority**:- *(Hardship Relief).*

In Britain, all businesses whether small or large are charged an annual tax rate by the Local Authority, for the property they occupy within the district area. This rate is called the Uniform Business Rate and amounts to quite a large sum of money. My bill for 1993 was £2,500.

However, in that year, my arrears had accumulated to £3,700 which I couldn't pay. I called The Federation of Small Businesses to find out if there was any hidden assistance I could apply for. I learnt that there was an allowance called 'Hardship Relief' which the Local Authority could grant to any business who was in genuine financial difficulty. The Authority could cancel the full debt and then reclaim a refund from Central Government. However, because of the Government's Poll Tax scandal the previous year, when they tried to change the national rating system on private dwellings, which showed that poorer districts were being charged far more than the wealthy ones, thus causing many protests and eventually led to violent riots. This new system had cost the Government £21 billion which they were forced to quickly abolish and also had to refund £2 billion back to the general public. Therefore, in order to avoid further payments, the Government advised the Local Authorities not to make small businesses aware of the 'Hardship Relief Scheme.' Furthermore, as an incentive for the Authorities co-operation, the Government agreed to refund 100% of any unpaid rates, if a business became bankrupt or was closed down but only to refund 75% - if the Authority granted the business 'Hardship Relief.' So to obtain the full 100% refund, Authorities were recklessly forcing small businesses to close down. This was the period when the recession was at its worst and the majority of businesses were in serious financial difficulty. Mine was just one of thousands in the same position. I then wrote to the Prime Minister, the Minister for Small Firms and my 'Local Member of Parliament' for help. This was their response;-

a. The Prime Minister.

I received a compliment slip acknowledging my letter.

b. Minister for Small Firms.

said that, *"No Minister has the power to intervene"* and advised me to complain to the Government Ombudsman, who in turn had no power to enforce his own decisions.

c. Local Member of Parliament.

replied, *"Time is running out, pay up now."* Then wished me all the best.

I pleaded every which way with my Local Authority but nothing worked. Within a few months I was taken to Court and told that if I did not pay the full amount in three months, the Local Authority would send their Bailiffs to remove my machinery, which would then be auctioned to recover their debts. I explained that this would force me out of business. They just said that it was my problem not theirs. All I had was my State Benefit of £65.00 a week, which I offered as a last resort but they refused it. The 'Federation of Small Businesses' also pleaded on my behalf and they too were ignored. In the end, they asked if I was prepared to use my business to highlight the problem on national television. I agreed and the full situation was exposed. The television presenter went into the Authority's building and confronted those in charge. In embarrassment they declined to comment. I still didn't receive any relief.

This was yet another scandal on Government's insensitivity and the hidden reasons for the failure of many Small Businesses. It leaves little to the imagination as to;-

- how many businesses really died because of the recession or were conveniently executed by the Government or Banks? (without any course of redress),

- how many were stolen via greedy and ruthless Venture Capitalists?

- how many mental breakdowns or suicidal casualties had occurred as a direct result of the tortuous pressures and stress?

There may be many cases entitled to compensation for the false sense of security, false hope and lack of, or misleading advice given to inexperienced poor entrepreneurs by Banks, Governments and so called Professional Advisors/Consultants.

The 1997 national business statistics report revealed that 50% of new businesses were still failing in their first year.

❀ **Bribery.**

Whilst having a heart-to-heart chat with a local chemist (an Asian gentleman), discussing the negative attitude of Bank Managers towards blacks and minority businesses, he suggested that I should offer the Bank Manager a bribe. I was shocked and said, *"I wouldn't know how too."* He then revealed that this was how many of them obtained money. Apparently, when he started his business he needed £20,000. He discussed his plans with his Bank Manager and told him openly, *"lend me £22,000, (£20,000 for me and £2,000 for you)."* He said, British Bank Managers would give you anything, if there's something in it for them. *"This way we all survive, you have to know how to play THE GAME."*

❀ Drugs and money laundering.

Like the Deloren car entrepreneur, many businesses become involved with drugs or launders drugs money to finance their enterprise. From my experience, I can appreciate how easy it is to become corrupt in order to maintain a business.

❀ Further Achievements.

(Between 1993 to 1997, I'd notched up a few more records);-

- Negotiated my products into North Ireland.

- My factory and products were approved by a Jewish Rabbi as Kosher Parve. The first black food to obtain Jewish kosher approval.

- In an independent national survey, my products were voted 'NO.1' and 'The Hottest Pepper Sauces' on the British market.

- Became Patron of the 'Black Women's Promotions and Research Project.'

- On the 75th Anniversary of 'Women's Right to Vote.' I was invited to chair the 300 Group - City Conference on 'Women into Decision Making,' as well as, the key note speaker for the University of North London - International Conference on 'Access into Europe.'

- Featured in 18 mainstream books below;-

1988 **The Perfect Pickle:** (BBC television series and book).

1991 **Women Mean Business:** (BBC television series and book, photographed on front cover).

1991 **Enterprising Women:** (Bantam Books) - photographed on front cover).

1991 **Food Lovers London:** (Macmillan) - top quality British foods.

1991 **Food by Post:** (Longdunn Press) - top quality British foods.

1992 **Peppers**: (USA International Book) - the history of peppers.

1993 **By Faith & Daring:** (Virago Books) - Britain's most courageous women.

1993 **Black Women for Beginners:** (USA) - prominent black women in history.

1993 **The Food Lovers Guide to Britain:** (BBC) - top quality British foods.

1993 **Business Class:** (Nelson Business English).

This book was significant for me because it is educational (with accompanying radio cassette tapes). It is a skills based university course for business professionals and students at upper-intermediate to advanced levels of English, to develop their oral and written communication skills, while at the same time broadening their knowledge of the business world. I occupy the entire chapter on 'The Entrepreneur' and am invited every year to lecture at the University of Westminster. Other companies included are Grand Metropolitan, Marks & Spencer, Levi Straus,

Rowntree Mackintosh, Glaxo, Nike, Euro Disney and The Body Shop. It is sold to universities throughout Europe.

1994   **The Unemployables:** (Britains most extraordinary people).

1994   **Woman In Britain:** (the British Foreign Office) promotional book for international reference.

1995   **Pride of Black British Women:** (successful black women in Britain).

1996   **BBC Woman's Hour:** (to celebrate BBC Radio 4) - 50th anniversary and the history of British women since 1945. I'm in the chapter 'Women Who Led The Way.'

1996   **Roots of the Future:** (Commission for Racial Equality) - launched by Prince Charles at St. James's Palace.

1996   **Flavours of the Orient:** (the two authors claim that I was their inspiration).

1997   **Black Women Taking Charge:** (an inspiration to Black British Women).

1998   **Black Londoners 1880-1990:** (history of black people in London).

- Met six members of the Royal family. The Queen Mother, Prince Charles, Princess Anne, Princess Margaret, The Duchess of York and the Duchess of Kent.

- Became a member of the American Chilli Institute and my name is recorded in its Hall of Fame.

- Introduced my products on QVC (Europe's first television home shopping station).

- The National Asthma Society launched Britain's first

'Low Allergen House' officiated by the Duchess of Gloucester. I was asked to prepare a healthy Caribbean lunch for 150 special guests and the press. But I went one further to include live steel-band music (by Ebony) and a fresh Caribbean floral display by (Jessie Hunnigan, a bouquet was presented to the Duchess).

- Invited to judge, present and speak at the 1994 Prince's Trust Enterprise Awards, where I met Prince Charles.

- Received a 'Special Achievement Award' from the National Federation of Black Women Business Owners in America, Washington D.C.

By July 1997, I celebrated my 10th anniversary in business and remained on the shelves of Harrods and Fortnum & Mason. I also launched my divine mission, 'The Celebration of Life' and from then onwards kept a low profile, focusing on my missionary work and the development of the business with a new Bank. But this time I concealed my passed history, achievements, experiences and potential. Within a year, my new Bank Manager began to gain confidence and to my surprise authorised an unsecured loan. Since then, he has increased my lending facility four times. This goes to prove that if my previous Bank really wanted to assist, it could have done the same. This also goes for all of the four British Banking Institutions, as they follow the same facility criteria. Hence I reiterate, that *"its not the Bank but the Bank Managers who discriminate."* This experience reminded me to, *"never give up or lose hope."*

The Labour Party won the general election that year and restored the 'Government Loan Guarantee Scheme' for all new start-up businesses.

In 1998, I received a surprise invitation from the Governor of the Bank of England, Mr Eddie George, to a private dinner at the Bank, to discuss the problems black businesses still faced with British Banks; how to unblock these obstacles; how to re-educate Bank Managers and the ways forward to improve relations, cultural understanding and financial access. Mr George was promising a better millennium for minority businesses. Also invited were Managers from each of the 4 National Banks and 14 minority business owners - 11 Asian/Indian - 2 African/Caribbean, I made up the third.

At the end of the meeting, I left feeling disheartened because after fighting for 11 years, I realised that 'POSITIVE CHANGE,' if it were to ever materialise, would still take a very long time, simply because those at the very top of the Establishment, cannot accept or comprehend that in the main, they are racist and also discriminate against women.

Here is an extract from my letter to Mr George after the dinner.

20th July 1998

Attn: Mr Eddie George (Governor)

Bank of England

London EC2R 8AH

Dear Mr George

RE:- URGENT INTERVENTION

Black/British Business

I refer to your dinner invitation and our meeting on 17th June 1998, along with 14 other Black Businesses, to discuss the particular problems we face with the British Banking Institutions.

BACKGROUND.

You may recall I mentioned that my past 10 years experiences were exceptionally difficult, even though I'd achieved tremendous success and had sought recourse from the highest level within the Establishment; none was forthcoming or supportive, which led to the total suffocation of my business.

Moreover, due to Political naivety, I was called upon by Mr Neil Kinnock to publicly support the Labour Party during the 1992 General Election, to which I happily obliged. During the same period, I'd also published my first book 'The Black Cinderella;' which gave a first-hand insight into the real difficulties of blacks, women and poor-working-class entrepreneurs and how the 'System' was failing us. My recommendations for improving the facilities for small businesses were taken up and recorded in both the Conservative and Labour Party election manifestos but I still received no support or credit. However, once the Conservative Party had won the election, I realised the dangers of so called 'Democracy and Freedom of Speech,' especially if you are black and in business. I've been refused any form of development/investment finance by every British Bank on one ground only - NO COLLATERAL for SECURITY, even though I was supplying prestigious department stores such as Harrods, Fortnum & Mason, Selfridges, Harvey Nichols, Army & Navy, Rackhams, Dingles, Bentalls, Howells, Kendale-Milne and the top 7 supermarkets; Tesco, Safeway, Asda, Waitrose, Co-op, WM. Low, Sainsbury), was officially recognised as a British Speciality Food Producer;' won national business awards; proved my natural PR talent with an unprecedented portfolio of over 75 television features, 300 national magazine and newspaper features, 60 radio shows and included in 16 mainstream books and was called upon as a key note speaker and advisor from the Government at Ministerial level to Government Business Agencies, Womens Groups, Universities, Schools and other British Organisations. My track record, proven ability, experiences, achievements, business potential and support of the System count for naught where finance is concerned, no one is prepared to help me. Hence, my only satisfaction is that I've achieved beyond my wildest dreams and am therefore successful but have been hampered from the rewards of obtaining financial success.

Considering my personal background as a single parent, on State Benefit and living in a Council flat, without any business experience or training and personally accomplishing all of the above within my first five years in business. I believe that I am ample testament of the opportunities which exist, even within a negative society and what is achievable if one is determined. I often wonder, what more am I expected to do to gain credibility. Although I'm a direct casualty of Mrs Thatcher's 'Spirit of Free Enterprise' hype and still carry some of the scars, I refuse to become a victim; heartened by the reality that hundreds of thousands of other businesses have been conveniently destroyed but at least I'm still ALIVE!

Furthermore, I'm not seeking sympathy, curry favour or handouts; just 'a fair hearing and equal treatment.'

The fact remains, that unlike Asian businesses, blacks and working-class whites do not have a network of rich families and community financial support and are forced to depend solely on their Banks. Although the System itself is not racist, unfortunately the people who run it are, hence we are doubly disadvantaged.

I've lost all confidence in the 'System' and it would take a miracle to restore my faith, although I take your word that you are serious about re-educating British Bank Managers, removing any racist barriers and providing better financial support for black businesses. However, I must confess that I've been hearing these very same promises for the past eleven years and to date nothing has changed. In fact, it has become worse with even more quango organisations fleecing the poor and inexperienced, whilst maintaining the pretence, under the umbrella of 'Opportunity 2000' and 'Race for Opportunity.' *"Actions speaks louder than words"*, therefore, I welcome your new initiative and can't wait to see the results.

The details in my first book covered just the tip of the iceberg but my new book will tell the full horrendous nightmare, which I hope will provide a glowing insight to encourage real change.

My business still has tremendous global potential and I remain totally committed to achieving my dream. It's a fight I'll never give up, as well as, to see the abolition of the negative word 'ETHNIC,' to ensure that my black/British (born) children's birth-rights are not only respected but also officially recognised as BRITISH - with equal status, equal access, equal opportunities and on 'a level playing-field.' There comes a time when hypocrisy must stop and I do hope our entry into the new millennium will be that turning-point for Britain to *accept,* appre*ciate and value* it's multi-cultural inheritance.

It was both a privilege and pleasure meeting you.

Yours sincerely
Dounne Alexander

The Last Hurdle

By year 2000, I was guided to start preparing the business for the commercial market, publish the book and establish the mission for the year 2001... the 21st century. So I got down to updating my business plan (revealing all) in readiness to test the Banks' millennium financial promise. The business had by then evolved into a three-fold operation... commercial, spiritual and charitable.

By August, I sent the plan to my Bank. The Manager praised it and was most impressed with my achievements but finance was rejected because *"the proposal does not make an attractive lending proposition to the Bank."* But when challenged to clarify, it turned out that he had no faith in my ability to achieve the projected sales. Knowing that I had no money, he said that he'd only consider funding if I had some of my own money to invest, or if I could find other investors. Although I had £25,000 worth of machinery, this was not considered as collateral. He was not prepared to submit the plan for Government approval.

The next step was to approach a new Government organisation called The National Endowment for Science, Technology and the Arts (NESTA). They were set up in 1998 and given £200 million of National Lottery money, specifically to bridge the funding gap and invest in talented individuals, small businesses (with under 5 employees) and the disadvantaged... targeting minorities. According to their mission statement;-

- To help exceptional individuals, so they can pursue their ideas and fulfil their potential.

- To help people develop ideas that can be exploited for commercial and social benefits.

- To help communicate the importance of creativity in our lives.

I had to submit a brief description of my business aims, objectives and potential. Their response was... *"Our assessors commented in particular that you are over ambitious. In practice, it could be extremely difficult for you to manage and coordinate all three projects."*

Bear in mind, that this organisation is supposed to provide professional advice, mentor-guidance and back-up support in excess of 5 years, aimed at guaranteeing success.

After three months of time-wasted negotiations, I eventually persuaded the Bank Manager that I had found a publishing company to publish my book and a marketing company to manage the mission. I then halved the costing to £50,000 to meet my minimum requirements. This amount barely covered the cost for renting a small processing unit, renovations, additional machinery, utility installations, product ingredients, packaging materials, wages and other overhead expenses. Surprisingly, this necessitated two more lengthy meetings in an effort to reduce the cost even further. He finally decided that the maximum he was prepared to lend was £30,000, deducting wages, marketing and promotions, trade mark registration. This in effect meant that we'd have to continue working without pay until the business could afford to meet these expenses from its sales, plus some of my products would not be protected and to develop the business without a marketing budget. I also had an outstanding 'business loan' of £6000 with the Bank and suggested increasing the amount to £36,000 to repay this debt, in order to reduce my overall monthly repayments. My request was refused on the grounds that the Government scheme did not allow for the repayment of existing loans. However, to help businesses get off the ground, the scheme provides an affordable repayment term in two stages;-

(1). The repayment of 'Interest only' during the first 2 years.

(2). then 'Capital & Interest' repayment over the following 8 years.

Hence, improving the business chances of success, by reducing its overall expenditure and allowing a 2 year period to develop and grow.

My Bank Manager refused to sanction the full term, allowing 'Interest only' for one year, followed by 7 years full repayment. Therefore my actual monthly repayments combined with the outstanding £6000 loan are as follows;-

YEAR 1 - Interest only:

 £30,000 repayment = £90 per month
 £6000   repayment = £145 per month
 Total monthly repayments = **£235.**

Whereas, on £36,000 the 'Interest only' would just be £91 per month.

YEAR 2 - Capital & Interest:

 £30,000 repayment = £482 per month
 £6000 repayment   = £145 per month
 Total monthly repayment = **£627.**

Whereas, if the second year 'Interest only' was allowed, I'd be repaying £91 monthly.

Furthermore, 'Interest only' on the full loan initially requested (£50,000) would be just £150 monthly for 2 years and approximately £600 for the remaining 8 years. In any form of business language, this does not make sense and the conclusion is blatantly obvious. The 'Government Loan Guarantee Scheme' provides a maximum of £100,000 for new start-up businesses and £250,000 for businesses in operation for over 2 years. Bear in mind that in 1992, I was the one responsible for raising the scheme's limit to £250,000 and increasing its repayment term.

Therefore, I reiterate that at the end of the day, **finance** is available but almost impossible to obtain. I believe this final hurdle was to prove beyond a doubt that when it comes to raising 'serious money' to establish a 'serious business' we are still not taken 'seriously.' However, I'm still not defeated because I know where I'm going and will reach my destination. I will not allow other peoples' limited imagination to limit my dreams, aspirations, expectations or purpose.

I hope these revelations will not only provide concrete evidence to the British Establishment that they 'seriously' need a change of attitude but also to anyone who has a dream, to endure the difficulties and pursue it regardless. By breaking down the barriers for yourself, you will also be helping others now or in the future. There is always another stone waiting to be turned.

You too can make a DIFFERENCE

(BIG or SMALL).

I believe this is the first detailed account of how the Government and Banks are supporting small businesses and what it really means to be black, female and ambitious in today's 'NEW BRITAIN.'

The Final Lesson

Finally, although its been 14 exceptionally difficult years, at the end of the day I've accomplished over and above my original dream and exceeded far beyond my own expectations. I've also come to realise that one has to take direct responsibility for one's own choices and actions. So although the Authorities and others gave me a hard time, I must accept that it was my choice to go into business in the first place and as such, I must accept the consequences, (good, bad or indifferent), as well as, to recognise and value the tremendous lessons learnt from the experience and the positive end results. Hence, instead of doing harm, it gave me greater wisdom for the future. Furthermore, it's comforting to also realise that the majority of great innovators, inventors, entrepreneurs and the like, experienced untold difficulties before realising their dreams. They succeeded because they never gave up and nor would I.

My future looks brighter than ever. I've always been ten years ahead of my time and had visualised 'global home shopping' years before this has now become a reality for the 21st century. So the world has now caught up. I'm therefore looking forward to the challenges ahead because I'm certain that - **I will survive.**

❀ **Business Collaboration.**

It is my intention to collaborate with other gifted individuals and help develop their unique products via my business, which I hope will eventually lead to the establishment of their own independent businesses. To show by example that it is possible to combine commercialism with conscience. I truly believe that the purpose of our God-given gifts are to share and support others in their quest to 'survive.'

I wrote the following passage whilst 'in the spirit';-

"I'm now personally happier and mentally stronger than I've ever been in my entire life, because I know and understand that

my God-given talents are only just beginning to blossom. I still have a long way to go before reaching full bloom and to scatter the knowledge and experiences gained for the benefit of those who need it. I know that I must try to keep myself true to the purposes for which I was sent to TEACH."

❈ The Millennium Dome.

I could not end this business section without adding my comments about the Government's show piece 'the Millennium Dome.'

Despite the fact that the majority in Britain voted against this idea, the Government in its infinite wisdom, still went ahead and invested millions of tax payers money to erect this monstrosity to celebrate the year 2000... built to last only one year. The Dome was the Government's way of showing off to the entire world. They alone believed it would become a major tourist attraction and that millions would flock in their droves to visit and experience what it had to offer. The Government spent a whole year playing silly games with the media and public. However, the game back-fired and it soon became an embarrassment... but this still did not deter them.

Within the first month of opening in January 2000, its management called for more funds (£60 million) and sacked the Chairman. By May, they called for a further (£38 million) to rescue it from bankruptcy and sacked the second Chairman. The total cost reached £758 million.

It was reported that the Dome was a 'complete failure' and financial disaster. Yet some of Britain's finest business minds were involved in its planning. The 20 million visitors (weekly) initially envisaged, showed that it did not have the capacity to hold this amount of people. By May 2000, after failing to make their estimation, the weekly average was reduced to 7 million. A further television poll showed that 80% of the nation voted to have it scrapped. Once again proving the Government's lack of business acumen, insight, foresight and was out of touch with the nation. These are the same people running the country, legislating business policies and advising entrepreneurs.

The Dome is a true symbol of VANITY. Why? because vanity only sees itself, considers itself and is oblivious to everything and everyone. In other words 'vanity considers no one but itself.' They never listened or intended to listen to what the people of Britain wanted or had to say. If they did, they would have heard voices from all over asking for money to be put towards: better health care, more hospitals beds; education; the elderly, to which the Government only saw fit to increase their pension by 75 pence a week; war veterans who are struggling to make ends meet; poverty, combating homelessness etc. When the public questions why the Government are not putting money into these issues, their answer is always, WE DO NOT HAVE THE BUDGET! yet they somehow found £758 million to salute the new millennium and glorify themselves.

To our humane and caring leaders,

I SALUTE YOU.

- My products highlighted on 'GMTV' with presenter Lorrainne Kelly and celebrity guest chef.

- below: presenter of 'This Morning', Richard Madeley assists in making my hot toddy drink whilst Judy samples a glass approvingly.

Both presenters Richard and Judy taking advice from Dr Chris Steel on the subject of cold remedies and how to combat Britain's annual flu epidemic.

SYBIL RUSCOE

- 'Good Morning' breakfast show.

- First spate of television coverage was London Plus, and Thames News; which helped propel the business into the media spotlight also prompting sales in Harrods to soar (my hands could not produce fast enough).

Needless to say the reactions from both the press and public was astounding. The most memorable being, when both reporters decided to try the pepper sauce neat 'LIVE' on tv.

● 'Scoff;' presented by
Dawn French

● 'Coffee Break':

Presenter David Hamilton,
sampling a variety of dishes
I prepared using my Herbal
Pepper Sauces.

● BBC Food & Drink's presenter
adding my Hot pepper sauce
to his recipe.

● 'Granada Live':

Marsha and Zara on the their debut television appearance; sharing Zara's incredible cancer recovery story and sampling Zara's Herbal Tea.

● Special guest:

On Gloria Hunniford show (left), and 'Kilroy' (below).

248.

● Dilly Down Town.

● BBC - 'The Perfect Pickle.'

● Cooking on 'Nite Bites.'

● 'QVC,' Home Shopping Channel.

● BBC1's Women Mean Business, presented by actress Glenda Jackson (pictured above).

● Showing Glenda the preparation process for making the herbal pepper sauce.

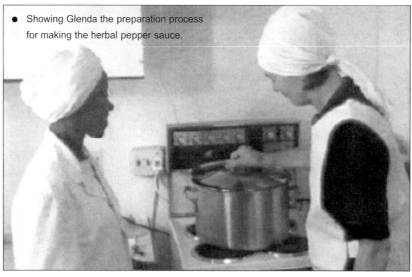

● Dining in my living room.

250.

BBC EDUCATION

WOMEN MEAN BUSINESS

Meet these women in *Women Mean Business*, 6 programmes looking at some of the issues facing women returning to paid employment. BBC1 Sundays 10.45-11.10pm. Starting 22 April 1990.

MOVE OVER darling

Women in the Nineties

THE JOHN BULL BUSINESS

A 5-part series for BBC2 about the culture of British Business

Episode 1 - SELF-MADE Tuesday 18* August 9.45pm

Episode 2 - FEAR & GREED Tuesday 25* August 9.30pm

Episode 3 - THE BIG GAME Tuesday 1* September 9.30pm

Episode 4 - THICKER THAN WATER Tuesday 8* September 9.30pm

Episode 5 - WELCOME CHANGE Tuesday 15* September 9.30pm

PANOPTIC PRODUCTIONS

Television features profiling my business; The John Bull Business (on Britains top entrepreneurs); Women Mean Business (presented by Glenda Jackson); Move over Darling (presented by Pamela Stephenson).

Motivational Speeches & Lectures.

"It is good to know your history or past,
not to be drowned by it,
but to learn from it, in order to achieve greater
things and progress forward"

Motivational Speeches & Lectures

The speeches and lectures included in this section makes me sound a bit feminist, anti-male, anti-establishment or even nationalist, none of which I am. I am simply an **ACT**IVIST.

I write purely from spiritual or intuitive inspiration, in an effort to make people consciously aware of themselves, their surroundings, the problems they would face in business, to empower them to take action and free themselves.

In other words, to get people to ACT for themselves by showing them that, I always ACT on my own behalf, as well as, fight my own battles, whilst knowing that my *actions* may help or benefit others in some way.

At the time of writing, I didn't realise that I was being specifically directed. With hindsight, I was invited to speak to people from all walks of life; the working-class to the upper-class, children to adults, as well as, females and males of all nationalities. At no time did any of the meetings consist of just one race. If it was a predominantly white group, there was always one or two other races present and vice versa; or a good cross section. I lectured every month up to 1995. My speeches are written in an unorthodox manner.

● 1994, with Prince Charles at Lancaster House

Personal Lessons Learned

This is the list of my own personal lessons which I generally pass on at every lecture.

1.   Be a good listener.

2.   If you want to be 'taken seriously,' you must 'first take yourself seriously.'

3.   Be Assertive but not Aggressive.

4.   Take no one for granted.

5.   Never become too relaxed; always be Alert and Aware of what is going on around you and in your business.

6.   Never believe that you know it all, because this leads to complacency.

7.   Always be competitive and try to keep up with the times, because every decade brings a new generation with new attitudes and you have to be able to bridge the generation-gap, in order to stay in business.

There is an old saying *"The world doesn't change but people do."*

8.   Be ambitious - THINK BIG.

9.   Set your own High Standards.

10.   Think and ACT Positively.

11.   Be Self Motivated and Self Confident.

12. Take responsibility for your own actions.

13. Set the Right Examples for others to follow.

14. Above all else, just be yourself and try to make the most of your new found talents and abilities. Remember our ancestors motto of life - FAITH, HOPE & CHARITY. Have FAITH in God, in Yourself and in your Dreams. Never lose HOPE; as Jesse Jackson puts it **'KEEP HOPE ALIVE.'** Always give in order to receive. Along the way, help a brother or sister up the ladder of success.

15. Understand that there is nothing you cannot do, if you put your mind to it and your energy into it.

16. Whatever you can visualise - you can create.

17. Only you can change the course or direction of your life.

18. Be passionate, stay focussed, committed and love what you do.

19. WIN or LOSE, Succeed or Fail, it is all down to you.

THE CHOICE IS YOURS

"So be your own best role model, rise above yourself and take control of your destiny."

I was invited to give the key note speech at this top London Hospital. This was my first major speech in the presence of British dignitaries and I was the only black person in attendance.

LOOK AFTER YOUR HEART WORK PLACE CHARTER

INCORPORATING FOOD GUIDELINES

SIGNING AND OFFICIAL LAUNCH PROGRAMME

Location	-	St. Mary's Hospital McRae Function Room Queen Elizabeth, the Queen Mother's Wing South Wharf Road, London W2
Time	-	12.40 - 2pm
Date	-	Monday 15th April 1991
12.40pm	-	Introduction Dr Leila Less of, Director of Public Health
12.50pm	-	Food for Health Dounne Alexander Proprietor of Gramma's Pepper Sauce
1.00pm	-	Signing of Charter and Food Guidelines Sir William Doughty, (Chairman of the Regional Health Authority), Michael Hatfield, (Chairman of Parkside Health Authority)
1.20pm	-	Photocall Introduced by Gordon Hemsley (Director of Human Resources)
1.30pm	-	Lunch & Displays

Speech by Dounne Alexander
Parkside Health Authority.

15th April 1991

FOOD FOR HEALTH

It's not just a question about what we eat but many other questions about food, society, changing attitudes, lifestyle and education.

WHY we eat; To live, to satisfy hunger, to sustain prolonged healthy lives.

WHAT we eat; Correct combination and do we eat quickly or slowly? Do we chew thoroughly, eat in between meals; relaxed or rushing around. How often do we eat.

WHEN we eat; Time of day or night.

WHERE we eat; At home, the work place, schools, colleges, day nurseries, restaurants, fast food chains and take - aways, cafes, snack bars or hospitals.

All these are relevant for good health.

I always speak about my Grandmother because she has taught me so many valuable lessons; which I've lived by, brought up my children by but which also prove that; *"some things don't or can't be changed"* - i.e. **TRUTH.**

She also liked quoting parables or wise passages, therefore I'd like to start with the old English sayings;-

"Have Breakfast like a King,
Lunch like a Prince and
Dine like a Pauper"

"A little of everything does you good,
All things in moderation"

All very wise words.

- I watch with great interest the increasing confusion our NEW FOUND, FAST WORLD is creating.

- What a price we are paying for a World of Convenience and Plenty,

- Life is now valued more in terms of Quantity rather than Quality,

- This world has existed safely for millions of years, yet in less than 150 years of MAN MADE;

Synthetics
Chemicals
Experiments and
Interference

We now live in fear of total destruction.

Financial gain (money and greed) has always been man's motivation. As my Grandmother used to say;-

"Money is the root of all evil."

We must therefore look at the **root causes**, in order to find the true solutions.

"For every action there is an EQUAL and OPPOSITE REACTION."

Hence, our wonderful disposable world of plenty, has not only changed our lifestyles but also our attitudes. We are now exceptionally;--

Absent minded

Complacent

Careless

Reckless

Thoughtless

Destructive

Aggressive

Disrespectful

Wasteful

Greedy

Abusive

Excessive

In other words

A World of Self Destruction.
Here today, gone tomorrow.
Longevity is now out.

Fashion too, plays a great part in changing attitudes and lifestyles. The young, adolescent and inexperienced, have always been the exploited victims of fashion. In my youth it was the Twiggy look-alike, I was alright being a natural twig but my two elder sisters in whose youth it was the Jane Mansfield, Marilyn Monroe and Diana Doors look alikes, their lives became a living hell and still are.

STOP THE WORLD, I WANT TO GET OFF!

Other root causes are;-

ECONOMICAL CHANGES

More working Mums, no time to teach or feed the kids properly,-

Talking is out,

Watching TV is in.

I'm not against working Mums as I'm one but I do believe in shared responsibility and I know that quick, easy, simple, convenient, economical and healthy meals are still possible to prepare everyday for all the family. I've done it myself and neither myself or my daughters now 22 and 17 have ever needed to diet or fall prey to any of the fashionable exercise or diet crazes. We simply eat properly every day, which has become routine or habitual.

Health Education in schools including healthy school meals. These are almost non-existent due to continuous Government cut-backs. Children are now left to their own devices.

Have you ever known an untrained child to eat or do the right thing?

They also need to be educated at the school dinner table, given and shown the right things to eat and not left to the mercy of fast de-vitaminised foods. We all know that the forming of a strong healthy body starts from the mothers womb (the root), then from childhood and throughout life. These children are our future generations; What or how would they teach their children? We can see the degeneration occurring now! In my day, it was a proper sit down hot meal at lunchtime (meat and two veg, deserts with plenty of fresh water) but nowadays children are more:-

STREETWISE THAN HEALTHWISE!

Commercial foods and medicines also play their part;-

1. **Fresh fruit and vegetables.**
Grown using synthetic chemical pesticides and fertilisers, added chemical sprays for long term storage, irradiation -

'further de-vitaminisation.'

2. **Meats.**
Animals reared for fast growth, chemical hormone treatments to increase or reduce fat and speed up growth. Artificial feeding, antibiotics, no form of exercise.

3. **Fish and Sea-Foods.**
Surviving in a totally polluted environment, chemical and nuclear waste, untreated sewage, all manner of poisons dumped into the seas and rivers for disposal but yet this is their feeding ground and habitat.

4. **Food Manufacturers.**
More de-vitaminisation. Fad foods plus even more chemical additives, colouring, flavourings, preservatives used only to assimilate taste, colour, flavour and to extend shelf life. Many foods and drinks made up of completely artificial ingredients are **cheap,** therefore highly consumed especially by kids who get an acquired taste, habit forming etc.

5. **Environmental Pollution.**
Air and water pollution, acid rain, global warming etc, caused by even more chemical discharge from industries and motor vehicles into our environment.

6. **Synthetic Drug Medicines.**
General medication made from strong 'synthetic drugs' which suppress illness rather then treat or heal the condition; many having dangerous side-effects that could result in causing more harm than good (i.e drug addiction, disability, death, food allergies, eating and behavioural disorders, suicidal depression etc).

All these are approved by Governments for our convenience!

We are what we eat.

Now do you still wonder why food scares, aggression, allergies, eating disorders, food obsessions, perpetual dieting and mental problems are starting at a younger age and are on the increase? **Our bodies have become living chemical factories, addictive food junkies, showing all the symptoms and signs of drug addicts.**

I'd now like to quote the Bible.

JOB CHAPTER 12;12

> **"With the ancient is WISDOM and in**
> **length of days UNDERSTANDING."**

I believe that the gentler philosophies,

> Sense of purpose
> Responsibility and
> Balance

of our ancient ancestors need to be re-introduced. Their simple uncomplicated *'laws of life and nature through God'* can bring back a little sanity and by **combining the best of the OLD with the best of the NEW, we can create the best of Both Worlds-**

> still progressive
> still convenient
> but
> More consciously aware, caring and harmonious.

There is nothing NEW under the Sun. All the things we make and eat now, were made and eaten then; meats, vegetables, soft drinks, alcohol, water, sweets, cakes, pickles, jams etc. But the difference came from the roots! The raw materials, feeding and cooking processes were all pure and natural.

•

Food has its own 'life force' essential fuel and energy which is our 'life source,' hence there was also NO need for artificial vitamin or mineral supplements.

Equally important was regular:-

Exercise (preferably Yoga), walking and swimming

Massage
Relaxation
Meditation and
Faith.

To enhance discipline, self control, respect and love. Good, sound, old fashioned grass roots - common sense.

These are the principle concepts, primary aims and objectives of my business GRAMMA'S, named in loving memory of my Caribbean Spiritual/Herbalist grandmother. To re-introduce concentrated natural, pure foods just like Gramma used to make and to re-educate the nation.

The Recipe for Good Health & Harmony is

'EDUCATION.'

SCHOOLS

In 1994, I was invited to talk to a class of teenage girls, mainly because they were extremely disruptive, aggressive, low self-esteem and lacked ambition. The headmistress repeatedly warned me not to be surprised if they did not pay attention, were rude or non co-operative. She and the other teachers were very nervous about one girl who was particularly bad and appeared to be the ring-leader.

The school was situated in London within a beautiful old Victorian building, with pleasantly landscaped surroundings, more like a grand stately home. The children were predominantly black. The headmistress chose the assembly hall to hold the talk and set out the chairs exactly like a classroom; with my chair presiding at the head of the class.

When I entered the room, it felt cold, impersonal and formal. I asked if I could rearrange the setting; removed all the chairs and asked the girls to sit in a close circle around me on the floor. Once we were all comfortable, I started to talk to them as a friend, about my school days; what I didn't like; having to work so hard all the time; parental pressures and expectations; about my daughters and how I taught them to be independent, responsible, about loving themselves; recognising the subjects they loved most and why they should work hardest at these; the importance of school in preparing them to enter the wider-world with confidence.

Every now and then the Headmistress or a teacher would peer into the room, with shocked looks on their faces, because not only were every child totally focused, they showed absolute manners, discipline and courtesy, when they wanted to ask a question.

The talk was supposed to last one hour but it lasted 3 hours and continued in their class room for the rest of the day. I arrived at 10am and left at 4pm. The children opened up; spoke about deep problems they were having at home; adults not understanding them, hence their 'don't care' aggressive attitude. But more importantly, the one who was supposed to be the most disruptive, was the one who asked the most questions. She would not leave my side all day; begged me to stay longer; could she carry my bag, hold my hand, have my autograph; and at the end she gave me a big hug, kiss and said, *"when I grow up, I'd like to be like you."*

I left feeling satisfied, because I'd left them filled with a sense of self worth, ambition and personal responsibility. The Headmistress and teachers could not believe the turn around and asked; *"what did you do."* I replied, *"I gave them the love, attention, respect and understanding they needed. You have to learn how to communicate at their level and to know when a child is screaming out - HELP ME!"*

Another memorable school lecture was at an all white school in March 1992. Yet another beautiful school in a posh conservative area. On this occasion, it was the celebration of International Women's Day and I was being honoured for my motivational work and business achievements. I first had to lecture to the entire school in the assembly hall, then moved on to speak privately to a group of fifth formers (older teenagers) in their last year of school; again to lift up their spirits and prepare them for life after school (i.e. work).

This time the class room was used, so they sat on their chairs and I sat on the teachers desk, mingling with them whilst speaking. I recreated the same atmosphere of one to one openness and again ended up spending the entire day. To break the ice, I generally say the things I tell my own daughters and it works every time. My favourite opening statement to teenagers about ambition is, *"I tell my daughters, I don't care what you want to be, just be good at it. So if you choose to become a prostitute, just be a good one."* At first, the teachers are shocked and horrified but the children roll up in laughter. Then I get down to the serious stuff but in a relaxed jovial manner; allowing them to interrupt and ask questions at any point of the talk; thereby turning it into a two way friendly conversation, where we all learn from each other.

However, there was one very timid girl, who wouldn't leave my side and within an hour she too was asking questions. After lunch, the school had arranged a photo call with a local newspaper. When they were asked to position themselves around me, she dashed to my side and put her arms around me. At the end of the day whilst in private conversation with the headmistress and teachers, I learnt that this girl had lost her entire family (father, mother, sister and brother) in a car accident about two years earlier and went into herself, didn't speak or participate in class. In other words, *"she was there but not there."* Consumed with grief, not even counselling helped. This was the first time she came out and was back to her old self again. I was so overwhelmed that it was difficult to hold back the tears, because I could feel her depth of pain; all she needed was a mother's comfort, love and a good hug. Herself and a few others had ambitions of becoming writers, plus the class had started its own little business, making badges.

I was about to launch my first book the next month. So I asked them to make me a few badges using the business logo and invited the 'would be writers' to the launch. I also invited Britain's most famous international author, Ken Follett and introduced them to him. Well!, no words could write their excitement or expressions. Ken spoke with them privately for over an hour. Coincidentally, I'd also invited a young black journalist who had just graduated and got her first job with a newspaper. When she saw Ken, she said, *"This is the man I had hoped to meet one day and personally thank; because of him I'm now a journalist."* She then explained that in the last year of study, her student grant abruptly stopped, which meant she couldn't complete the course. She wrote to Ken pleading for assistance and promised to repay him once qualified and working. Within the week a cheque covering the full course fees came through her letter box. So anxiously, she introduced herself; thanked him for his kindness and offered to repay. He gracefully refused her offer saying, *"It is payment enough to know that you've qualified and can start your career as a writer; just be a good one."*

BLACK BUSINESS IN BIRMINGHAM (3B's)

(3rd October 1991 -mixed audience)

I was invited to be the key-speaker, together with a Government Minister, to launch this new Government Black Enterprise Agency, in the presence of a mixed audience of 500 people.

LAUNCH SPEECH

I'd like to speak about the 'real issues' facing Black/British businesses TODAY, YESTERDAY & TOMORROW, which can only be changed by the Black community themselves.

There is a solution to every problem.

But **NO Problem** could be solved

or **NO Battle** could be WON

without first understanding and re-assessing the full situation, then devising the strategies to ensure and secure long-term success.

One of our main problems is that we have become mental slaves, afraid of our own shadows and have also remained complacent far too long, preferring others to fight our battles. We complain a lot but then sit back and don't act. Britain's long standing strategy of 'divide & rule' is still effectively in force within our race. No Battle can be won without solidarity and total unity;-

Unity brings **Strength**

Strength brings **Force**

Force brings **Power.**

So in order for Black-Britons to win their new battle for business success, we need to **unite**, not only in word but also in **deed**;-

"Actions speak louder than words"

Black People talk more than they ever Support.

So in order to COMPETE,

GAIN RECOGNITION

and or

ACCEPTANCE.

We need to build up our own 'Economic Power Base,' or financial resources, which in turn means *'actually putting our hands into our own pockets'* to raise the funds necessary to finance the development and expansion of Black British Businesses.

This is how other races have succeeded, by supporting their own and this is what we have continuously failed to do for ourselves, hence we have remained stagnant whilst others progress.

We must therefore re-learn;-

PARTICIPATION, CO-OPERATION, SUPPORT

&

TRUST.

Recent statistics have shown that;-

97%	of	Chinese buy from Chinese businesses.
92%	of	Jewish buy from Jewish businesses.
84%	of	British buy from British businesses
82%	of	Asians buy from Asian businesses and only
19%	of	Blacks buy from Black businesses...

Even my own family don't buy my Pepper Sauces, unless I give it to them free. They'd go out of their way and buy others. This is the general attitude of our people.

This is FALSE Economy.

You are *starving-out* your own!

In order to become a noticeable force, our businesses must get into the mainstream of Britain and Europe. Why stop there! Worldwide too.

But I also believe that we must learn to creep before we can walk. So let's first creep through Britain and conquer this market nationwide; then we'll be able to walk through the rest of Europe; run through America and sprint throughout the world, just like our powerful world champion athletes. In order to do so, we must also be recognised, which means becoming more visible. We cannot afford to continue to remain in the background, visual image is important. It's about time our businesses were advertised on national television and bill board posters; not just as MASCOTS for others but as role-models for ourselves.

We invented Carnival to mimic and laugh at our slave-masters. Now the laugh has back-fired on us. We have become ONE BIG JOKE. We'll never be taken seriously, unless we take ourselves seriously. Therefore, we not only need to re-evaluate ourselves but to VALUE ourselves.

- We are the only race who have FAITH in everyone else, except in ourselves.

- The only race who TRUSTS everyone else and not ourselves.

- The only race who RESPECTS everyone else and not ourselves.

- The only race who is LOYAL to everyone else and not ourselves.

- The only race who VALUES everyone else and Under Values ourselves.

- The only race who BUYS everyone else's Goods and Services and not our own.

- The only race who allows others to Capitalise on everything we possess (our Lands, our Religion, our Knowledge, our Talents, our Inventions and our Initiatives) and have even failed to Capitalise on ourselves.

- The only race who BLAMES everyone else for our Mistakes and never blame ourselves.

- The only race who has allowed others to steal or destroy our great culture to become a divided, scattered and alienated groups or 'A LOST RACE' - who was once called the 'Fathers of Civilisation,' now we are called uncivilised.

- We are the only race who continuously CRY FREEDOM and keep ourselves in Mental Slavery.

The Biggest Joke of all is that none of the other races either Value, Trust, Respect or have any Faith in us.

NO wonder we are SEEN and TAKEN as FOOLS. We have proven it.

We have become the only Re-cycled Race.

A USEABLE COMMODITY, TO BE USED & RE-USED

DISPOSABLE

DISTRIBUTABLE

NON Essential

NON Vital

NON Important.

We even fall into the category of OTHERS in the national statistics; and are **classified** as ETHNICS; meaning 'none status citizens' who do not belong.

We have become the led instead of the LEADERS. Even though black people have been in Britain since Roman times and Queen Victoria's Great Great Grandmother was a black woman - *Queen Charlotte Sophia.*

Our Pharaohs of Yester Year

are now the COWARDS of Today

What a disgraceful LEGACY for our future GENERATIONS.

As Martin Luther-King once said **"How Long!"**

When will we 'wake up!' and realise that -

Our Future

Our Faith

&

Our Destiny

Lie within our OWN HANDS.

and if we don't take a strong hold, we'll continue to fail, or like me, be thrown to the lions and forced into a Jungle of ruthless tricksters, gold diggers, opportunists, unscrupulous manipulators and power hungry man-eater.

The business world is full of corruption and immoral practices.

There is tremendous business potential and talent amongst blacks in Britain but these have remained unexplored due to a lack of insight by ourselves and successive Governments in their customary encouragement of keeping the unemployed and poor trapped within a State support structure, creating a false sense of security.

The most valuable lesson I've learnt is that *"If you wish to succeed in business, do not trust, believe or depend on Banks or Governments as they are the greatest hinderers of progress and will hamper your success."*

I was exceptionally lucky to have survived.

Therefore, I'd personally like to endorse any Initiative of 3B's which will;-

CREATE

PROMOTE

ENCOURAGE

ENHANCE

DEVELOP

or

ADVANCE

Our Independence in this Country.

We have already made significant contributions to the world but most of our inventions were credited to others, who also received all the wealth. If the wealth was fairly distributed from inception, we would not now be begging for SURVIVAL.

The 'Traffic Lights' are the best shinning example of our brilliance. So let it be a constant reminder that we've been taken for a 'long long ride.'

We can stand proud and equal to any race.

Finally, remember that historically the colour **black** meant

POWER - BEAUTY - MYSTERY & LUCK

It was a black man, who helped Christ carry his cross, proving our naturally soft, sympathetic and supportive nature. Now its time to TAKE UP YOUR OWN CROSS, because the bleeding and tears must stop!

BIRMINGHAM'S WOMEN
ENTERPRISE DEVELOPMENT - AGENCY-25/09/1991

(a mixed audience; filmed by BBC Television)

'In Celebration of Women.'

THIS IS BUSINESS

Women are NATURAL MANAGERS.

We have been fully trained, schooled and prepared for Business from birth. The moment a girl child is born, everyone automatically accepts and expects that when she grows up her natural place in life is:-

1.   To get married

2.   Look after her husband

3.   Run the home and

4.   Have children.

Therefore, from day-one the automatic 'natural training' for her future role begins. Not only by Mum and Dad but by everyone else who knows that she is **female**. So with regular day-to-day training and good practice she learns:-

1.   How to manage and run a home (i.e. dolly house games).

2.   How to take care of and consider others.

4.   How to take and accept responsibilities.

5.   How to make ends meet... budget.

6,.   How to be organised and well co-ordinated.

7.   How to reprimand and discipline.

8.   How to be forever in demand (children, husband, family and friends).

In other words, HOW TO COPE and *'girls haven't we coped well!'* We can 'think and do' ten things all at the same time without falling apart.

So in their traditional efforts to turn us into the Perfect Wives, Mothers and Housekeepers, they have accidentally created the 'Perfect Managers and Bosses' without them or us realising it.   We are the true Civil Servants and Silent Partners.

Therefore, all the organisational, administrative and managerial skills needed for business, can be found in good old fashioned house work.

THIS IS BUSINESS

Over the years I've watched my mother cope with the;-

STRESSES

STRAINS and the

PRESSURES.

of raising six children, (I could call my father the seventh) plus deal with all the other daily problems of;-

MARRIAGE

HOUSE WORK

FAMILY and

FRIENDS.

and at a moments notice, be transformed into the;-

PERFECT HOSTESS

ENTERTAINER

CHEF

MASCOT and

SKIVVY.

for my father's business colleagues and clients or for our birthday parties and weddings. There was no situation she couldn't cope with; forever in demand; the first to be called on; the least to be noticed and the last to be considered.

She gave us her all and sacrificed herself for our happiness.

THIS IS BUSINESS

So you see girls, we have always been in business; self sufficient and independent. But watch out, men are wising up. They are now trying to create the 'new 90's man,' i.e. the man who shares the household duties; responsibilities and can take care of himself but don't worry because we are still light years ahead! However, do not get too comfortable, relaxed or complacent.

Business is also instinctive; since most of us have not been subjected to acquiring 'high academic qualifications', we have been able to develop our natural instincts and intuition, hence making us natural survivors.

THIS IS BUSINESS

So what else do we need, in order to complete our refined, qualified business skills;-

1.   Confidence

2.   Book Administration

3.   How to handle big money (in business terms, cash-flow).

The 'confidence' comes with time and also when you come to terms with yourself and realise that;-

a.   You are unique and creative.

b.   An individual in your own right.

c.   You have value and worth.

d.   This is your life and you can make your own choices.

e.   It's up to you to take full control and responsible charge of yourself.

Anything else, you can always learn from any good Business Training course or book. So be proud of your **woman-hood** and superior skills which have taken you a life time to master. Practice makes perfect and we are well practiced. Men have good reason to be very worried about the future world of business women!

They know that they are losing their grip and power-base and are frightened of the repercussions or reprisals. For the first time in history, they feel insecure! The laws of Karma, *"do unto others, as you would have them do unto you."* For centuries this world has been run mainly by men and what a mess they have made of it. Maybe if given a fair chance, we could put it right and as the nurturers, nourishers and managers of life, we may value it more and be less destructive.

Men must be made to realise that without women, they would not have come into this world. We have laboured, suffered tremendous pain and even died to give them free entry and easy access to life. Why then must our lives and paths to access into their business world be met with abortive blockages.

It is recorded in the Bible that the Virgin Mary conceived and gave birth without a man. We possess the most powerful weapons in the world **'our bodies.'** It's the only vessel or medium in which the Human embryo can develop and grow, yet we have never once held the 'world to ransom.' What would men have done if they possessed such a precious weapon?

Yes, we have immeasurable value and worth.

The greatest asset of all time.

We possess the controlling power of the world.

Without us it could never be Multiplied.

THIS IS BUSINESS

We are coming to the turn of the century, a new decade; the year 2000 may be our turn to rise and show our true potential.

THE BIRTH OF A BUSINESS

Finally I'd like to end with another touch of womanly wisdom. It is said that when you go into business it becomes your BABY. Being an experienced mother, I can testify to these facts. With hindsight this is my analogy of the birth of a business, to which all mothers would be able to relate; (those of you who are not, just use your imagination);-

It's frightening at first

It's continuous anticipation

It's perpetual guessing and hoping

It's constant anxiety

It's exciting

It's depressing and stressful

It's restless, sleepless nights

It's handwork and tremendous energy

it's panicking

It's pressure

It's taking a high risk

It's expensive

It's agonisingly painful

It's PUSH, PUSH, PUSH all the way

But once delivered, it could either be

total devastation - caused by death or serious illness but if healthy and strong,

it's RELIEF, JOY and GLORIOUS HAPPINESS, because it stands a good chance of survival. This feeling of elation is only short lived, because before long, you find that it has taken over your life and these emotions start all over again and continue throughout its growing years.

These I call *'the growing pains.'*

But you also soon find that you are left *'holding the baby'*

This I call *'taking care of business.'*

It's a big responsibility but in time you grow in self-confidence and learn how to juggle several tasks and include them into your daily routine. Organisation and timing become second nature, then normality is restored.

This may sound awful but ask any number of mothers, if they'd go through it a second time around and the majority would say YES!

now **'that's serious business'** and **'that's life!'**

'A WOMAN'S WORK IS NEVER DONE.'

LADIES FORUM CONFERENCE

(14th October 1994 - all white audience)

Last May the Daily Express newspaper carried a major feature headed;-

"Positive moves for the Hard-working Woman"

It reviewed research on the results of our 20 year battle for equal rights and commented that after 20 years fighting for equality, the rate of success has been limited and that women's lives have not improved by much.

SURPRISE! SURPRISE!

Furthermore, the predictions for the year 2000 are even gloomier as career divisions widen.

For example:-

1.   **Women without children;** will reach further up the organisation ladder.

2.   **Single Parents and Older women returnees;** will not find it easy to build a career.

3.   **Women will still have worse jobs than men;** in terms of pay, prospects and security and men will still continue to hold most of the top jobs.

An American survey also concluded that;-

4.   **The women who make it to the top;** are more likely to be living alone, childless and still earning less than their male colleagues.

WELL Ladies - What's NEW!

Life hasn't changed much for us and if we want to get CHANGE; then we've got to CHANGE;-

> If we want EQUALITY
>
> If we want a CAREER
>
> If we want a FAMILY
>
> If we want WHATEVER.

We know that sacrifices must be made.

We have been fighting for centuries to find our true place or position in society and to regain our identity. Therefore, we must realise that if we want to succeed at anything; we have to fight for ourselves -

> Be prepared to take RISKS
>
> Make the necessary SACRIFICES
>
> and create our own OPPORTUNITIES.

But we must also realise that to succeed takes tremendous hard work and having achieved it; the end result is generally an anti-climax. Success is never what you really expect it to be.

However, **ambition** is self fulfiling, self motivating, self challenging and self propelling, which sets you on a roller-coaster-ride or never ending journey and pushes you beyond your natural limits. Hence, you never achieve your ultimate goal, for with each new goal set; once achieved; you set another. Therefore, it also takes great imagination, determination, commitment, patience, courage and staying power to succeed.

Nowadays, with the grave unemployment situation and lack of long term job security, self employment or running your own business is a good option for future independence.

NATIONAL FEDERATION OF BLACK WOMEN BUSINESS OWNERS (NFBWBO)

(13 October 1996 - black audience)

FINANCING YOUR DREAM

THE REALITY:

As an Entrepreneur with nine years experience, I've now come to terms with the fact that **finance** whether it be for paying the bills, wages, buying a British Rail travelcard, food or for business development; is a perpetual nightmare which no business person can ever dream of escaping.

This realisation goes for all businesses regardless of size, race or gender.

You see! The moment you think business you are thinking 'money,' but generally in that initial thought process, your mind-set is reversed, because you are only thinking about how much money you are going to make; which is a great motivator to get you geared-up and start dreaming. Once you begin to realise that you are truly on to a good thing, you can get carried away and then start formulating strategic plans, in which to turn this wonderful mirage into a reality.

Then suddenly with a bang! Reality hits home.

> *"In order to make money,*
>
> *you first have to find the money*
>
> *to make it."*

and although your imagination can continue to run wild; you soon realise that it too, has to be curtailed and controlled in accordance with what

finance you have available and only then, you begin to think within your budgetary limitations.

In other words; you are in the classic chicken and egg situation.

Your focus is then reversed from the initial amount of money you planned to make;- to how to find the money to get started and eventually **raising finance** for whatever purpose, becomes the focus of your dreams. Hence, progress throughout, is limited to the amount of money or finance available to activate your vision.

Whatever you want to do, even the smallest step getting from A to B requires financing.

Before long, you soon also realise that to turn this grand dream into a real business would take great imaginative, creative, intuitive and persuasive skills. You begin to **eat, sleep** and **drink** your **dream** which then starts to consume your whole life.

At the end of the day, the business becomes YOU because;-

> YOU have to nurture its personality
>
> YOU have to deliver its potential
>
> and
>
> YOU have to cultivate its Life.

After all, it is your dream and therefore, requires your energy.

However, if we were to realise that every entrepreneur's journey starts precisely at this stage (A DREAM) invariably going through the same fearful emotions, before eventual **success** is attained years later, then this would give us the motivation to hang in and not give up.

Unfortunately, most success stories generally focus from the point of victory, without detailing the many disappointments, obstacles, failures, disillusions and mistakes, before reaching or attaining gold.

SUCCESS takes tremendous hard work, discipline, commitment, risk, determination, patience, failure, sacrifice and is never easily achieved .

FINANCING YOUR DREAM

Therefore, initially you should look to **finance** your dream via;-

1.   your own personal savings or

2.   Private loans from family and friends, which do not tie you down to a specific repayment period. Of course! donations should always be welcomed.

3.   There are various Grants available via for example:-

      (a).   **The Prince's Youth Business Trust** (£1,500), if you are under 24.

      (b).   **EEC Grants for Women and Minorities** (up to £5,000).

These could take in excess of six months to obtain, if you are lucky.

4.   Furthermore, there is Institutional Finance via bank loans /overdrafts, which is not advisable until you are sure that you have a viable proposition, say one to two years down the line.

    LOW INTEREST LOANS; (up to £5000) via -

    (a)   The Prince's Youth Business Trust.

    (b)   The Greater London Enterprise Board - up to £10,000.

5.   **The Government Small Firms Loan Guarantee Scheme:-** up to £250,000 for established businesses. But be careful, because this is a bank loan, where the Government provides the all important security always requested by the Banks - up to 70-85% guaranteed Security;- you have to find the remaining 15-30%.

Many businesses like retailers do not qualify and you must have been in business for 2 years, hence the majority of you wouldn't qualify.

6. **Investment Capital**: via wealthy private individuals, Business Angels, or large Corporations. Once your business is up and running and has good long-term potential with a healthy balance sheet, i.e. profits, you can raise substantial finance for expansion to the tune of millions in return for an equity stake or share of the business. That's if, you use a white person to front your business.

7. Ladies, there is also the more seedy route of the sugar daddy. Yes! This too is available to attractive women and I don't need to explain the 'criteria - laid down!' Although I know that we are sitting on a GOLD-MINE, our treasures should lay within our businesses, personal pride, self respect, dignity and integrity. This I most certainly don't recommend. And Yes! I've had many persuasive offers in the past, so I know they exist.

I'd like to elaborate a little more on 'Institutional Finance.'

"Is it available to everyone? Yes and No."

Gender and race are still very much a hindrance to equal access in Britain, primarily because of old fashioned, outdated dogmas and stereotyping, which are perpetuated from the very top... i.e. the Establishment or 'the powers that be,' those in direct control of our lives.

No matter how polite or nice we'd like to be, the truth is; 'Britain is a racist society.' If it wasn't, there would be no need for any Equal Opportunity programmes, as we'd be seen, respected and treated equal to our British white counterparts.

In my own personal experience, I've never had any form of discrimination from;-

1. The British Department stores or mainstream Supermarkets and easily got my products into exclusively white areas.

2. **Nor** from the ordinary British people, in fact 95% of my customers are white and we have an exceptionally good relationship.

3. **Nor** from the British National Media, who have featured hundreds of positive, pro-active, inspirational and informative stories about me and my business. In fact, far better than our own Black Press has done to-date, with a few exceptions like Candace Magazine, Black Beauty & Hair, the Gleaner and Success! Hence, the white community is more aware of my achievements and struggles than the black community.

For example;-

This week I received an advance copy of a new BBC Book called 'Woman's Hour,' celebrating the 50th anniversary of the BBC Radio 4 programme, featuring positive women in Britain since 1945. I'm included in the chapter 'Women Who Led The Way.'

This is only one of the 15 British mainstream books featuring me. This month I'm also on the front cover of a British international business magazine called 'Business Opportunity World.'

PUBLICITY is another essential ingredient for financing your vision, because in any business, you'll need to create continuous consumer awareness, which leads to increased sales, hence more money. In my nine years, I've attracted over 400 national media features on television, magazines, newspapers, radios and books, which have carried my message and business nationally and world-wide. Hence, 'communication' is also another vital key to your success... your ability to communicate or get your message across.

ACCESSING OURSELVES

In terms of any form of access; whether it be finance, new markets or publicity;-

You have to create your own opportunities.

Take the initiative and utilise it to your advantage.

So be very careful, when allowing others to formulate your **identity** or create access opportunities on your behalf; because they'll surely continue to place limitations on your potential.

'You have to try and stay in control of your DESTINY.'

For example; on the point of **Identity & Limitations.**

Last year a London University was funded to devise an Ethnic Minority Enterprise Training Resource Manual (a huge book) and I was invited to be on the executive committee. At the first and only meeting I attended, I questioned, "*why yet another Ethnic Minority Enterprise Training programme was necessary?*" because I was concerned about:-

- the continuous Government Investment programmes devised to perpetuate the Ethnic Minority Business stereotype... i.e. the Business under-classes.

- The many consultants and organisations earning a healthy living from these programmes.

- I was sure that the provision of so called Ethnic Minority Enterprise Training was sub-standard and inferior to that of British 'white' Enterprise Training Programmes; plus access to all facilities was severely curtailed or not available to us.

- From an outsiders view point it would appear that we have access to business training. But no one questions the **quality** of that training. The same goes for **finance** but no one questions the **levels of finance** provided and the extreme difficulties encountered in obtaining it.

I finally questioned - "*why do we need separate training? - when business acumen or entrepreneurialism is **natural** and derived from* *personal intuition, which has no race, gender or class."* Hence, the huge amounts of Government investment funding, would be better spent on developing a National Business Training Programme incorporating all entrepreneurs and the surplus funds, should then be given as grant-aid to small businesses who desperately need it to get started.

Needless to say, I refused to participate. However, a year later when the manual was completed, I was asked to launch it and further told that my name was essential to give it credibility.

This was my response at the launch; pertaining to;-

IDENTITY & LIMITATIONS.

"Firstly, in your programme, you've described me as 'an effective case study of an Ethnic Minority Enterprise.'

Before I start, I believe that it is important for all individuals or businesses to get their description correct, because you must have a clear identity of **who or what you are and what you are all about,** in order to have a sense of pride in yourself and in your career. This pride is further strengthened by the feeling that you belong, involved and are an integral /essential part of the community and country. It also helps to strengthen you for the battles ahead.

The word ETHNIC MINORITY is the Government's chosen description for all of us and one which I do not relate to, as I truly believe its the starting point of demarcation or barrier, in which to fence us into a convenient group. I'm not pompous but this is one term that I do have strong views on. The correct, official and recognised description of my business is a *'British Speciality Food Producer.'*

Joe-Casely Hayford and Bruce Oldfield are recognised as British Designers. Naomi Campbell as a British Supermodel and not as ETHNIC MINORITIES.

Therefore, those of you who are in or planning to go into business, must first in your own minds, decide what is your true identity and not be labelled as something else.

For instance;-

On my business letterhead, if I were to put 'GRAMMA'S - ETHNIC MINORITY ENTERPRISE,' this would immediately undermine my business and limit its potential.

However, having 'GRAMMA'S - *British Speciality Food Producer,*' immediately improves both its status and the potential becomes unlimited.

Therefore, you must recognise Double Standards. If you want to be taken seriously; you must first take yourself seriously. In business, you are in the 'people industry,' catering for everyone, therefore, **race** should not matter. An Indian/Chinese/Italian/French or British Restaurant is a correct description, plus they cater for all races and genders. My younger daughter (born in Britain) has just started her own Fashion Design business and would also be identified as ETHNIC, because she is black. Fortunately she's aware of her true identity and will refuse to be pigeon-holed.

Therefore, I believe that the entire business community should first be fully integrated, as we are all part of the economical strength of Britain. The only segregation should be in size... start-ups, small, medium and large businesses.

I hope that this has provided food for thought, as well as, broadened your vision on the importance and implications of IDENTITY, which would prevent you from obtaining 'equal access' to all business facilities.

> I'd like the University to know that I'm not offended by their description, because I do understand the Establishment's focus.

Another example on how ACCESS is limited to Black Businesses.

I've been privileged to attend many Black Business Seminars where Bank Managers and Government Ministers were invited as guest speakers to show, how much they really want to assist us and what efforts they were making on our behalf.

I've heard Bank Managers patronizingly say, *"if you came to us with an invoice from Harrods or Tesco, we'll happily give you a loan."* Of course the reason being, is that they were speaking to an all black audience and want our business but in their minds they don't see us as real businesses capable of ever getting into the top British mainstream market. We are expected to be only one-man operations, markets stall owners or small shop keepers, never corporate, national or international businesses. In other words, if we achieve the impossible they would finance us.

But to their surprise, seated in the audience at one of these seminars was a small black woman, who not only had an invoice from Harrods but also from Fortnum & Mason, Army & Navy, Tesco, Safeways, Sainsburys, Waitrose, WM.Low, Co-op, Asda, Selfridges, Harvey Nichols, and they still refused me a £500 bridging loan. The small loan I eventually obtained two years ago, was only given after I went over my Branch Manager's head and formally complained to the Regional Manager, called for a face-to-face meeting and threatened to expose the Bank via the media. The loan was agreed immediately.

Many black businesses have had to resort to using 'white people' to front their businesses in order to obtain 'institutional finance.'

As our brother Malcolm X said, *"by any means necessary."*

Therefore, financing your dreams would continue to take much longer than most, unless we adopt the strategies developed by other disadvantaged groups such as the Indians, Jews and Chinese, who have demonstrated perfectly, the results of having independent financial resources with which to fund, develop or rescue their own businesses.

However, before we can achieve this, black people have to first develop trust and respect toward each other; join forces instead of having hundreds of small splinter groups, each with limited memberships, limited resources and all struggling to survive.

Our people also need to change their shopping habits, exercise their spending power. This has been talked about for years, yet I still see no improvement. We appear to be the most complacent race on this planet and unless we take the bull by the horns and stop blaming others or the past, we'll never move forward.

> *"We owe an individual responsibility to ourselves and a collective responsibility to our race."*

> We have to devise our own financial strategies, whilst taking advantage of any external resources available. We should welcome and embrace all new initiatives... like Race for Opportunity who's mandate is to change the status quo but also get involved in these decision making processes to ensure that *'Full and Equal Access'* at every level becomes accessible. The majority, if not all of these initiatives, have been cleverly devised to create credibility for individuals or organisations and at the end of the day, this does not help us.

Therefore, our vision has to be unselfish, going beyond ourselves and extend globally.

If we want our lives to change we cannot expect others to change it for us, we have to take the lead ourselves.

> *"We must learn to 'Spread the Word*
>
> *give committed SUPPORT*
>
> *and SHARE the knowledge and WEALTH."*

EXPOSING THE SYSTEM TO FREE OTHERS.

I've been asked by many black business men;-

"Why do you persistently expose the System?"

"Why don't you wait until you've made it, then talk?"

"I can't wait that *L-O-N-G!*"

I can't sit back and see hypocrisy and exploitation continuing to destroy our people, leaving us to believe that we are failures, instead of realising that it's the System which is failing us. I also know that the System would listen, if we have the courage to speak out rather than compromise.

'WOMEN INTO DECISION MAKING'

(In celebration of the 75th Anniversary of Women's Right-to-Vote).

(all white audience).

In 1993, I was invited to chair this major conference held in the city of London and organised by the most powerful women's organisation called the 300 Group.

<u>SPEECH</u>

"Good Morning ladies and welcome to our aptly titled conference;-

'WOMEN INTO DECISION MAKING'

Perfectly timed and falling on the week of the 75th Anniversary (6th Feb.) when women were given the right to vote.

75 YEARS ON:
and that RIGHT many of us take for granted and some of us don't even use.

75 YEARS ON:
and although we are now over half of the population, we are still grossly under represented in all the Houses-of-Representation... The House of Commons, the House of Lords, '*well that name speaks for itself, doesn't it*' and the European Parliament. Even in the financial institutions, the heads of all the National Banks have always been chaired by men.

In our own conference lists of speakers, those who are on

Corporate-Boards are referred to as Chairmen and not Chairwomen. Now this is a directive that needs to change.

75 YEARS ON:
and women can now be ordained in the Church of England. What moral dilemmas that has brought?

75 YEARS ON: and we have had -

HUMAN RIGHTS

CIVIL RIGHTS

EQUAL OPPORTUNITIES

and even OPPORTUNITY 2000.

all this has still not **FREED** us from centuries of MALE DOMINATION and we are still fighting for;-

RECOGNISED INTEGRATION

JUSTICE

FAIR PLAY and a

FAIR HEARING.

Women are still UNDERMINED

still taken for GRANTED

still not taken SERIOUSLY

still conveniently kept in our PLACES.

To make matters worse, many women who are in positions of power, also consciously undermine other women and keep them down.

As a Black/British Business Woman, I've had first hand experience of this many times, which I've found insulting, abusive and irresponsible.

Furthermore, **75 years on** and some of the description have changed, with new words brought in such as:-

SEXUAL HARASSMENT

SEX DISCRIMINATION

SEXISM

RACISM.

and even ETHNIC MINORITIES, a word which infuriates me, because I know that in the Caribbean (where I was born), I was brought up more British than the average British child... even by name! I also know that my father, his father and his fathers before him, gallantly fought and died in many wars including all the World Wars, to protect Britain's sovereignty and independence, which confirms that we've paid our dues and that they have given us an INHERITED RIGHT to be HERE! **I Value their lives** and **I also value their inheritance,** just as much as I value the suffragettes inheritance giving me the 'RIGHT-TO-VOTE.' Therefore, I deny the classification ETHNIC, as it is negative, insulting and disrespectful.

- I am Black/British.

- My children who were born here are **British**.

- and my Business which is based here is also British and I'm proud of it.

Cohesiveness or integration will only be established, when we are accepted as what we were indoctrinated to believe. Now there is a decision to be made.

Nevertheless, FEMALE DISCRIMINATION and PREJUDICE are still rampant in 1993 and ladies a great deal of committed work awaits, in order to turn these decisions in our favour.

Finally, I hope many more women will take direct responsibility for their own livelihood, by playing an active part and getting involved in the decision making processes which have so far:-

Kept us under Control

Suppressed our Talents

Stifled our Ambitions

Suffocated our Dreams

and also kept us continuously Dependent and Deprived.

I believe that our destiny is in our own hands; singularly and collectively. We must also recognise our tremendous value and worth. We create a wonderful stabilising force and balance.

So without any further ado, we have some dynamic guest speakers as well as, workshop speakers. They are not women into decision making, they are the decision makers. I'd like to introduce you to our first key speaker, BARONESS JEAN DENTON of Wakefield - The Under-Secretary of State at the Department of Trade & Industry.

1.   **Baroness Denton's** list of career experiences is exhausting but I'll try to give a brief summary of a lifetime of hard work.

2.   **Stephanie Monk;** (of the Granada Group).

Closing statement;-

To date, women MP's have done us proud and have conducted both their public and private lives in an exemplary manner. Never do we hear of any sex or corruption scandals involving them. The male MP's would do well to follow their example.

To echo Baroness Denton's speech;-

"We all have the freedom to choose and the RIGHT to make our own

decisions. These rights should always be respected."

As Stephanie Monk inspirationally confirmed in her speech;-

"We also have 'unique, valuable and precious' skills which we need to recognise and boldly use to our own advantage"

But, you also need to re-evaluate yourself and assess your time well. What ever you choose to do. I wish you every success.

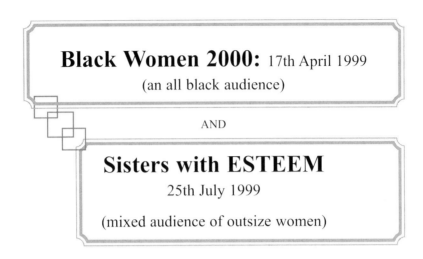

Black Women 2000: 17th April 1999

(an all black audience)

AND

Sisters with ESTEEM

25th July 1999

(mixed audience of outsize women)

Good evening friends,

Many thanks for inviting me to share some of the positive lessons that have helped me to survive and succeed and to also elaborate on this important theme - **ESTEEM.**

Esteem relates to **self,** which goes beyond size and points directly at the perception you have of yourself, which extends to every part of your life; your relationships (family, friends, colleagues), your career, your dreams and your expectations.

So you see, **self esteem** is a vital part of your life process which cannot be developed unless you are prepared to grow. In fact, it's larger than life itself and without it you hinder and stunt your own growth. In other words you hold yourself back.

Everyone regardless of size, needs **self esteem** and here girls! - I'm speaking from personal experience.

I had my first 'wake-up call' in 1986, when my eldest daughter (then only 15) said;-

> *"Mum! when I grow up, I'd never let anyone treat me as if I have*
>
> ***NO VALUE or WORTH."***

The painful truth but made even more painful, because she was speaking about her Dad, whom she also loved dearly.

You see! I thought abuse was only a physical thing. I didn't realise it could also be mental. At the time, I was thirty eight years old and a puny seven stone weakling with a great deal of pride, extremely ambitious but I also had low self-esteem because I was in an abusive relationship, where I allowed my then husband to control my life and although on the outside I appeared strong, holding down a high-powered professional job but on the inside I was weak, because I loved him too much and was afraid of losing him.

My daughter's words made me realise that I had to take back control but in this process my husband became violently aggressive in his effort to try and keep control. Realising that I'd have to protect myself and my children, I decided to take up martial arts and for six months, trained extremely hard to ensure that I could defend me and mine. When he found out that I was practising karate, his aggression immediately stopped because no macho man would run the risk of his wife beating him. Like my Grandmother use to say, *"You have to fight fire, with fire."*

However, although I did not change physically but my confidence had grown so much that I became stronger in every way.

I looked strong

walked strong

talked strong

yet still remained gentle and feminine.

So with this new found confidence, I picked up my two daughters, our dog and two cats, walked out of my home (unopposed and unchallenged) and have never looked back or allowed anyone else to ever abuse me or steal my power again. I then took full charge, complete control and personal responsibility for my own life and turned what was then a frightened, shy, nervous wreck, into the strong, confident, positive and successful woman I am today.

So, **self esteem** also relates to **courage** because it takes tremendous courage to consciously face yourself, look boldly into your own eyes and admit that you don't like what you see and then have the **will power** to do something positive about it and turn your life around.

The reality is, no one else can do this for you but YOU.

This experience made me realise that **fear** is our greatest obstacle and that many of us need to be kicked up the behind, to allow us to **let go** and **move on** in order to achieve our full potential and or fulfil our purpose.

That was the beginning of my new life and from then onwards, I have grown from strength to strength. As an unknown single-parent, living in a small Council Flat in London and on Government Welfare, I've become one of the most respected, inspirational and influential women in Britain today. All because I decided to take control of my life and make the most of it. More importantly-

> *"I've achieved all this without having any form of*
>
> *business training, advice, experience or qualifications."*

Therefore, **self esteem** is one of the most vital building blocks of life. It needs to be nurtured in order to help us to develop and grow. This nurturing starts with **SELF**;- **self-love**, **self-appreciation**, **self-respect**, **self-confidence**, **self-value** and **self-awareness** to bring us to the realisation of our true **self-worth**. **Self esteem** enables us to achieve our deepest desires and soar to unlimited heights. Without it we would remain weak, unfulfilled, fearful and unhappy.

Now I'd like to say a little bit about **success** and share the survival lessons which keep me motivated and well grounded.

The above tells its own story and shows that **success** in anything you choose to do takes dedicated hard work, discipline, determination, pain, sacrifice and love.

I didn't realise I could make a difference to myself, my children or others and have since helped and encourage everyone to rise above their own expectations, because people need support to help them make it.

1. If you wish to succeed, it is up to you to set your own agenda and standards.

2. You must make a conscious CHOICE, then ACT on it, in other words

"POSITIVE THOUGHTS & ACTIONS achieve RESULTS."

Remember, the one who fails, is the one who gives up.

3. Not every disappointment you encounter is because you are black or fat or female, instead, it is often a necessary lesson you need to learn, in order to grow.

4. TRUST your natural instincts and follow your own mind. Remember, whatsoever your mind can conceive - you can achieve.

5. Keep an **open mind,** don't be afraid to make mistakes but learn from them, because these are your best lessons.

6. Don't blame someone else or make excuses for where you have reached in your life but take the responsibility, come to terms with, realise, acknowledge and accept that it is all your fault because you have continued to live in some form of fear. So always point your finger at yourself.

7. You will also find that success is an anti-climax and does not always mean making money. As long as you've achieved your dreams - you have succeeded.

8. Along the way, try and help another brother or sister (of any race or creed) up the ladder. Always keep in mind and follow the ancient principles of our ancestors; *"the more you give wholeheartedly and unselfishly, the more you will receive."*

9. Take the initiative, create your own opportunities and utilise them to your best advantage.

10. Try and keep both feet firmly on the ground and your life in perspective. With all that I have achieved, my children and my new husband (Rudolph Walker) come first because a business or career can fail but once you've become a parent - *"you are a mother or father for life."* So don't lose or forget yourself, whilst in pursuit of your goals.

    We generally only see the glory of success and not the many difficult years leading up to this final GOAL;- the struggles, doubts, disappointments, failures, obstacles, dedication, sacrifices, painful tears. Furthermore, the extreme stress can also lead to nervous breakdowns, marriage breakdowns, loss of your home, bankruptcy and even suicide. So be careful, keep balanced and protect yourself 'spiritually, mentally and physically,' because **success** is not all glitz and glamour as is often portrayed.

11. **Success, Fame or Fortune** means nothing without good health, happiness and love in your life. So learn to value yourself, those around you and all that you have.

12. **LIFE is precious, fragile and short**; So Live it, Enjoy it, Cherish it, Make the most of it, Take good care of it, Treasure it and know that YOU deserve the BEST.

13. Never be ashamed of WHO or WHAT you are, because this gives you a history on which to build. In other words:- a story... YOUR STORY.

"Every success starts with a good story."

Just as I'm telling my story to build your **esteem,** so should you! By telling your story, you too can make a difference to yourself and others.

Every stage in your LIFE should be;-

"Saluted, honoured, acknowledged, claimed, respected, appreciated, loved and celebrated, because it's a declaration which affirms that **YOU EXIST."**

14. Size, colour, gender or creed mean nothing when you DIE but what you leave behind does. So leave something worthwhile.

15. Remember, watch your step, tread carefully and present yourself admirably, because where ever you walk, you are reflecting the shadows of your nation. So set a good example and open a space for the next one who follows you.

I'd now like to end on a business note.

The most vital and essential element in any business is **the product**. Equally important is the 'quality' of that product. It is pointless having a quality product without it being beautifully packaged. Therefore, a product's quality is valued according to what is inside and outside.

Now I'd like you all to visualise yourself as

a Product of the highest *and* finest Quality

INSIDE *and* OUTSIDE is superbly packaged.

You look so good that everyone wants you.

But realise that unless 'you love *and* value' yourself FIRST.

No one else, would either - know, understand, appreciate
or see YOUR TRUE WORTH

Believe me this is serious business girls, so know that

you are PRICELESS.

Thank you, God's blessings and success, in all YOU choose to DO

for YOURSELF.

THE LAUNCH OF BBC TELEVISION'S
DIVERSITY DATA-BASE (1st October 1998).

(audience:- BBC Television Head of Programme Makers and Producers).

GOOD EVENING: - ladies and gentlemen.

I was delighted to get involved when first approached about this new **Diversity Data-Base**.

But, I must confess that I was also somewhat surprised, because in ignorance, I believed that this was already established, considering that we've had over 20 years of equal opportunities and race relations legislation.

But then I also realised just how much I'd taken for granted and how fortunate I have been, having had over 400 national media coverage in my 11 years in business, including 80 television features, covering not only business but the full gamut of women and family issues, politics, health, food, education, self employment and the like, attune to the entire country and not marginalised or pigeon-holed as a minority. The BBC in particular, was most supportive.

To mention a few;-

1. I was called several times to review the national newspapers for **BBC Breakfast News.**

2. Included in many major documentaries and series, like the **John Bull Business**, featuring such notables as Richard Branson, Anita Roddick, Allan Sugar, Sir John Harvey Jones, Freddie Laker and of course, ME!

3. **Women Mean Business** presented by Glenda Jackson, well before she became a Politician. It accompanied an educational book and motivational poster which were on sale in all major book shops, as

well as, displayed in every Job Centre nationwide. The book cover and posters featured all the participants, with my photo taking central position, surrounded by the others, who were all white.

4. Another BBC series and book was **The Perfect Pickle** and so many others, even including **Kilroy**, not as a member of the audience to make up numbers but as a special guest speaker.

I've never been portrayed as a BLACK-TOKEN but as a successful business woman and an inspiration to everyone. It just so happened that I'm 'BLACK.'

However, unlike most people, I know how to put myself about. *Don't get me wrong, I'm not that sort of a girl!* I mean, as an entrepreneur, I realised that television provided the most valuable platform for my business, on a national level and was partly instrumental for its success and continues to be so.

I control my own P.R, write and mail out the Press Releases, then politely pester or should I say, nag them to death. After all, its expected, I'm a WOMAN and a black one at that and if you really want to know about nagging, then speak to a black mother.

But seriously, from humble beginnings, as a single-parent with two gorgeous daughters, living in a small council flat in East London and on Income Support, you turned me into a positive house hold name. Now, we all know what **bad press** can do. It could have been the exact opposite picture and portrayal. So I'm grateful, not only for your support but also for your HONESTY.

• **Therefore, as a Business Woman, Professional and British Speciality Food Producer:**

I can confirm that effective programming is not only useful, but an essential tool for our trade and also a valuable life line.

• **As a British Citizen, Mother and Minority:**

I can also confirm that its vital for embracing all of Britain's communities; essential for putting across positive images and paramount for creating national awareness, which would go a long way to defuse bias and improve harmony.

- **Now here's some food for thought:**

  We are now approaching a new millennium and are still being referred to as **ethnic minorities**. This may be acceptable to the likes of those who have dual-nationalities but what about our British born children who knows no other culture and in the case of those with Caribbean backgrounds like my children, whose surnames are more British than native Britons. How would you differentiate them on your Database? Bear in mind that they will not be as passive as their parents, after all they are British - born and bred.

As our Prime Minister, Tony Blair said this week - **ONE NATION**

The BBC should consider taking the lead, by developing programmes, which **unashamedly** and I repeat **UN-ASHAMEDLY** embraces the whole British Nation, without exception or hidden agendas;- ensuring equal access and a level playing-field, on which we could all

PLAY THE SAME GAMES.

You hold **the eyes of the Nation**

but in future, we will now have to keep **a watchful eye on YOU.**

I therefore, whole-heartedly support your **Diversity Data-Base.**

Readers Letters.

- **ON MY FIRST BOOK -** *'The Black Cinderella.'*

B. Ferguson,
Northampton.

15th February 1993

Dear Dounne

I have recently read the most interesting article of your personal experiences in running a small business and thought I must write to congratulate you on your sheer determination to succeed at all costs. This must give heart to others who are struggling hard to survive in the present economic climate.

The reason I am writing is to inform you of my own predicament. Recently my husband and I had to place our own Logistics Company (Warehousing & Distribution) into voluntary liquidation based on recommendations from our Accountant and the Bank. The shock and trauma of actually going through the process of winding down the company as well as coping with personal financial problems was horrendous and has left us both feeling physically drained and mentally exhausted.

To my horror we found that there is a lack of professional advice and assistance to give guidelines and possible counselling to those who really need help. Another shock was that we had to pay a very substantial fee up front to the Insolvency Practice before any work was carried out, whether this was because there were very little assets available to the Creditors or this is just standard practice. Although the company was a Limited Company we still dread the knock on the door or what the morning post will bring!

The purpose of this letter is to ask you how you personally coped with liquidating your company before starting afresh, did you have any professional assistance for guidance? I am still finding it hard to come to terms with what has happened and constantly feeling guilty about letting myself and the Creditors down. I would like to join some sort of support group or start my own group because there must be a lot of people out there who just don't know where to turn to for advice.

I have enrolled with the London Writing School and would like to research into writing a book later, on the difficulties of starting up a business and above all the personal trauma of Company Insolvency, together with all its unforeseen problems. Perhaps I can interview you at a later date!

I am sure your business will continue to be a success and if you could find time to reply to my letter it would be most appreciated.

Kind regards

M. Farmer
Norfolk

8 February 1993

Dear Ms Alexander

I have just finished reading the Maureen Cleave article in the Telegraph Magazine about you and felt compelled to write.

I have recently started a small business of my own and am up against many of the same problems you mention in the article. However, your story has been a source of inspiration as well as advice.

I am a fully qualified architect and in 1990, I was involved in a car accident. The injuries sustained left me unable to work for two years, consequently I lost my job and then my house. Once recovered, I was unable to get any sort of job because I had been off work for so long and because of the economic climate.

Then one day I saw a programme on the TV about SUCCESS in which you were featured and I decided there and then that I would follow your example. I now run a small business designing fanciful and luxurious homes for animals. Like you, I first went to Harrods who now hold a portfolio of my designs in the Pet department so that they can offer 'the complete architectural service for animals.' With the Harrods name behind me, I have found that people take me more seriously now and the interest generated has amazed me, I have been in the local paper;- The Lady, Period Living, Dogs Monthly, Dogs Today and Architectural Design Magazines. I have been on local radio and have been asked to go on Anglia TV. I will also be in the Telegraph on Saturday 13th or 20th February (in Celia Haddon's Pets column).

Before I saw you on television I would never have thought this possible- However, I have not yet made a profit and was beginning to get downhearted when I saw your article in the Telegraph. Yet again you have encouraged and inspired me.

I would therefore, like to thank you most sincerely for the inspiration that you have provided and I wish you all the very best success in the future, when perhaps we may some day meet.

Could you tell me where I can buy GRAMMA'S in Norfolk?

With many thanks and best wishes.

Yours sincerely

1996

Dear Ms Alexander

I have just started a degree in integrated engineering at Manchester University.

I have just read the article on you and your 'Hot Pepper Sauces' and I have to be honest, I was so moved I just had to put pen to paper. My heart moved and I almost broke down in tears. I am so happy for you, right now I feel as though I'm glowing.

I didn't actually buy the October copy of 'Business Opportunity World,' I just saw your smiling face on the cover at one of my friends houses.

I am so proud to be black and you have just given me one more reason.

I think I'll use you as an inspiration, I hope you don't mind.

I think you are brilliant and I hope Gramma's keeps going for a very, very, very, very long time.

My class is 70 strong, there are 5 blacks in this class.

This is a good representation of the whole university.

Testimonies.

Buckinghamshire.

7 February 1993

Dear Ms Alexander

I have just read the article about your business and was so struck by your experiences and comments regarding banks etc. that I felt I had to write to say how pleased I was that you had not given up.

I started a small business in 1984 and I encountered exactly the same types of attitudes. I also was very naive and assumed that orders equated to success and expected support from our bank to finance our growth. This actually was the case until about the middle of 1990, when attitudes seem to change. Unlike you, I gave up the struggle at the end of 1991 and have now a job which at least pays me a regular sum, without me worrying whether or not the bank will authorise it!

I would be very pleased to help you out in any way I can (also for nothing, of course!). I have at least seven years experience in trying to run a small business against all odds and now work for the *Inland Revenue (!)*, so there is probably something I can do.

By the way, I'm white and male and they forced my company under due to a lack of even a modicum of vision or common sense. To be honest, I don't think the average modern banker has the imagination to differentiate between black, white, male or female.

Keep at it.

Best regards,

J. R. Sharp

M. Reece,

Essex.

Dear Ms Alexander

How wonderful to see the face of a black woman on the front cover of a predominantly white magazine. All too often we are led to believe that the black race are underachievers. It is with great pride that I wish you every success in your endeavours. With your continued determination and motivation I hope all of your dreams will come true.

Having embarked on a home-based business only recently. I now feel a renewed impetus to keep on going regardless of the setback.

Thank you for your inspiration and I look forward to seeing your face prominently displayed on other magazines.

Very best wishes to you.

CHAPTER III.

For the Love of Zara.

A heart wrenching story which shows the miracles of faith, hope and love and how a herbal remedy combined with a healthy Vegan/Vegetarian diet can save the lives of animals, humans and the environment. Through Zara's suffering comes an amazing - **Gift of Life.**

● picture taken April 1995 – Zara aged 10 years.

For the Love of Zara

On top of so many other problems, within 14 months of my mother's death, Zara was struck down with mammary cancer which was terminal. I remembered Marsha phoning me at the factory saying: *"Mum, Zara is dying, she has got cancer."* I instantly responded with, *"that is not funny, don't mess about."* Tearfully she said; *"I am not joking Mum, I have just returned from the Vet, who has examined her and said, she hasn't got long to live. Oh Mum, why me? why my Zara?"* Marsha was serious, so I told her to drop everything and come straight to the factory. I knew she would be terrified and would need my support.

She arrived around 4pm, extremely distraught and collapsed on the floor. I was not sure of what to do or say, as no words could possibly bring any comfort. She was in shock and somehow I needed to soften the blow. So I picked her up, sat her down and said, *"talk to me, just talk, say what ever is going around in your head."*

"Mum, I have tried to be good, I have never hurt anyone. You know that Zara is the one special thing I have always wanted. Why is God punishing me? We have only just lost Nan, I can't handle another death. Why me, why me? Mum I can't take it."

I held her tight and allowed her to pour her heart out. She cried herself to exhaustion. In a brief moment of calm, I tried to explain that she was not being punished but somehow she would have to come to terms and deal with it. She then pleaded, *"Mum please help me, you have got to do something, make anything that might help her."* I said, *"I don't know what to do but lets pray and ask my Guides."* I also called on my mother to help strengthen Marsha. They all spoke to her and within three hours, she was able to laugh a bit and was much less tense. Then I took her home.

That night in prayer I spoke to God; *"Father, I am afraid for my child. You know how much she loves Zara. I have taught her to love You above all else. I have taught her to always look to You for help. I have taught her that You are the only true miracle worker. Father, I fear that if Zara dies, Marsha and possibly Dee too, would turn away from You forever. Marsha has already suffered a great deal with her deformity. She has suffered losing her grandmother. She really cannot handle this pain. You know she is extremely strong willed but this would break her Spirit. Father, please, please, please, show her that You are real and not a figment of her imagination. Grant her a miracle and save Zara's life. She is young and needs proof that You really exist. Father, have mercy on Zara for Marsha's sake."*

I fell asleep still praying and was then instructed on what to do. The next morning, one of my customers phoned and told me about a product which was reported good for cancer but it only contained four of the fourteen herbs I was given through Spirit. Instead of re-writing the whole story, I have copied below, the original leaflet written by Marsha two months after Zara's recovery, as it details the depth of our emotions at the time.

(Written by Marsha).

All I ever wished for as a child was to have my own dog, therefore when my mother finally felt that I was old and responsible enough to have one, I was overcome with joy. To my complete surprise on Christmas day 1984, I was given a beautiful Pedigree Labrador-Retriever pup, whom I named ZARA... I was then fifteen years old. From that day on Zara became my soul-mate; the love we both shared was both unconditional and exceptional in every way.

ZARA has always been in excellent health, however, in June 1994, I noticed her gums were irritating her. By September a small growth had developed in her mouth which I assumed was an abscess, so I took her to the Vet to have it examined. The Vet confirmed that it was not an abscess but a growth and decided that it was best to remove it. The growth was successfully removed but the Vet did not send it away for testing because she said it did not look like anything unusual. Apparently this type of growth usually occurred in Boxer dogs and not Labradors. However, she further said that it may re-occur, in which case she would continue to remove it and that this was quite normal.

At the end of October 1994, a week before Guy Fawkes night, I decided to get some tranquillisers for Zara, as the fire-works usually made her very nervous. My regular Vet was then on holiday, so she was examined by a new Vet. To my horror, after examining Zara, the Vet told me that she had mammary cancer and showed me the cancerous growths all over her chest, breasts, stomach and groin... with a particularly large/ prominent one on her top left breast. My heart sank, I couldn't believe it because at home my sister and I always checked her body for anything unusual but we didn't notice or feel any lumps. I asked the Vet if the growth in her mouth could have been cancerous and if by cutting it out could have caused the cancers rapid spread. The Vet denied that this was possible and stated that it was just an unfortunate coincidence, most likely due to the fact that Zara was not sterilised and getting older. However, she was reluctant to tell me how far gone the cancer was, so I had to wait another week for my regular Vet to return from holiday. Zara was then re-examined and it was finally confirmed that the cancer spread was too far gone for an operation to be considered. The best we could do was to make her as comfortable as possible and to relieve any pain and discomfort as her condition worsened... but it was inevitable that she was going to die.

The news devastated my whole family but my own feelings and fears cannot be put into words. I grieved constantly, everywhere I went (at home, on the bus, walking in the street), I was inconsolable. But my mother and sister were there for me all the time, trying to keep my spirits up. Mum would tell me to remain *"positive, faithful and to pray; to never lose hope, right up until the very end but also not to lose sight of reality."* So with this advice my main aim was to make the most of the valuable and precious little moments we had left together. I gave up my job to devote every minute to her. All we could do was pray, meditate and give her spiritual healing in the hope of a miracle. Since Zara had nothing to lose, I asked Mum to make something which would help her. Instead of re-assuring me, Mum reinforced the inevitable, mainly because only a year earlier, we had all watched helplessly as her own mother died within 10 days of ovarian cancer.

Mum then prayed and meditated for spiritual guidance on the correct herbs and on how to prepare them. It took a week to get all the herbs and a further three days for her to complete the brew. In the meantime, Zara's health was rapidly deteriorating, the cancer growths were both much larger and spreading fast. She became incontinent, dehydrated, her stomach swelled up and was extremely hot, her breathing became erratic and her chest would cave in as she desperately fought for air. By now, we had received Zara's blood test results which confirmed that her kidneys, liver and lungs were also deteriorating, her blood was abnormal and her heart was getting very weak. The Vet stated that these were the usual symptoms for advanced cancer and if the pain became too unbearable, I'd have to make the decision to put her out of her misery and have her put down.

The stress of the nightly fireworks leading up to Guy Fawkes night made her worse. She became so weak that she couldn't walk; collapsing every time she tried. I was worried about giving her the tranquillisers, so I called the Vet to seek advice; who confirmed my worst fears and told me not to give them to her, as it would most definitely be fatal in her weakened state.

The 4th and 5th November '94 was my worst experience. Fireworks were going off every minute, Zara was so petrified that she suddenly started going into fits; became doubly incontinent and could hardly breathe. I thought she was going to have a heart attack and wouldn't survive the night but thank God she did. I stayed awake with her night and day up to the 9th November, trying to comfort her whilst she tried desperately to sleep, her stomach was burning up and she was panting constantly. Her whole body looked like it was giving up on her. Her breathing was shallow and short and as her chest caved in, it sounded like it was slowly filing up with fluid. Laying with Zara in my arms, I watched every breath she took. I felt so helpless, all I could do was cry and pray that she'd make it through another night. On three occasions Zara stopped breathing. I watched... holding my breath in total denial. I cradled Zara in my arms; rocking and rubbing her gently; trying to fight back the tears. I called to God, asking Him not to take her away from me, not like this;- I stared hard at her chest for signs of movement; I kept on watching until she'd catch her breath and began to breathe erratically again. Then on the 10th November, Mum finally finished brewing the herbal drink and gave her a cup full. Mum then instructed that;-

1. Zara must only be given this drink in place of water or any other drink.

2. Every morning on an empty stomach, the drink must be given (NEAT) one hour before breakfast and last thing at night, one hour after eating.

3. Add it to her drinking water but the water must first be filtered then boiled.

4. Changed her diet to plenty of vegetables, pulses and wholegrain

(cooked with a little Gramma Herbal Pepper Sauce and Herbal Seasoning), plus fresh fruits. **NO** meat or dairy products whatsoever.

5. Exercise her as much as possible, to keep her energy levels high. This she insisted was part of the vital healing process.

6. Draw a diagram of her body and pin-point every lump.

After taking the herbal drink for one day, her condition literally changed overnight and she slept like a baby. After the first week her eyes were bright, her breathing had improved, she showed no sign of pain, discomfort or nervousness, was on her feet and walking properly. The incontinence and dehydration stopped, her temperature was back to normal, stomach swelling stopped. Zara was looking alive again.

By the second week she looked fit, healthy, her breathing was almost back to normal; coat shiny, stomach size also reduced back to normal (shed all the excess weight and swelling), her energy level very high and she was bounding around the house like a puppy. I was able to take her for very long walks. However, because she still had the lumps, we were convinced that she wasn't going to make it to Christmas. So I decided to celebrate it early, put up the tree and all the decorations. Mum bought me a video camera to film her as a keep-sake remembrance.

By the third week (beginning of December 1994) whilst examining the growths, I felt that there was a distinctive reduction in their size, especially the very large prominent one on her chest; it had become softer and at least half the original size. My heart sank in disbelief. We all examined her and were equally stunned and excited.

By the fifth week, her condition continued to improve but now the large growth was down to a third (no longer prominent) and all but two of the many smaller growths appeared to have disappeared altogether. I phoned the Vet and explained her condition, she too was amazed by her remarkable and speedy recovery.

On the 3rd January 1995, Zara had a full examination including a blood test. The Vet confirmed that all the cancers had disappeared and only a very small pea-sized one remained. Her blood, kidneys, lungs and heart were all back to normal. Her severely defective liver was half way improved. The fur on her chest, stomach, groin and inside legs which had previously gone bald were completely re-grown, plus her entire coat was thick, shiny and in beautiful condition. The Vet wrote a full report and even featured the story on BBC Radio and newspapers. Zara's condition has gone from strength to strength, she has not had any form of side-effects and looks great. So now we wait to see whether or not the cancer will be completely cleared and for how long she'll continue to live. This has also given me the time to come to terms with the fact that one day she would leave me. Since she became ill, she has had no other medication therefore, I can only thank God for answering my prayers and my mother for producing a 'miracle,' giving me new hope, stronger faith and a Christmas present I never thought was humanly possible.

I personally believe this miraculous drink should be researched and quickly released to all those suffering from this deadly disease, as well as, for the healthy, so that they too could benefit from its wondrous properties.

- Imagine the implications of a safe drink which could possibly cure or prevent cancer or reduce tumours.

- A drink which could reduce the risk of getting cancer altogether.

- A drink which could do away with painful treatments and operations to surgically remove growths.

- A drink which could thoroughly clean the blood.

- A drink without side-effects or drugs.

- A drink which makes the sufferer feel good, revitalised and pain-free.

- A drink which could improve and maintain general well-being.

"The possibilities are endless."

My mother has decided to name the drink after Zara.

ZARA'S HERBAL DRINK

A fitting tribute to a beautiful and loving 'Spirit of God,' who has brought so much joy into my life and I sincerely hope that the result of her suffering and her drink will bring **new hope, improved health and joy to the world.**

Independent Research.

ZARA'S HERBAL DRINK.

- Zara's follow-up story after cancer recovery.

- Difficulties encountered with Medical Research.

- A Gift from God.

Independent Research

❀ The Follow Up.

With hindsight; Marsha and Dee left home in December 1993 and although they had only moved a five minute drive away from me, the area in which they lived was a relatively new site, developed during the 1980's 'Yuppie' property boom era. However, it was previously a waste refill dump site, which was never treated. By the late 1980's, residents were warned not to grow any food in their gardens, because tests had shown the earth contained high levels of dangerous toxic chemicals. Unfortunately, Zara loved eating dirt. The tap water in their house was also cloudy and tasted foul. Furthermore, a busy motorway ran close to their property, which was always jam-packed with traffic and exhaust fumes blew in their direction. I truly believe that these three elements were the main factors which caused Zara's cancer. She'd lived with me for nine years, ate a lot of dirt from my garden, yet got cancer within six months of moving and would have died within one year.

Anyway, after Zara's miraculous recovery in December 1994, not only did we have a new Zara but also a renewed Marsha. Her strength and faith grew stronger by the minute, she was so grateful to God and our Spirit-Guides, that nothing could describe her glow, she'd simply radiated with joy. For her birthday that year I asked, *"what would you like;"* to which she replied, *"Mum , I don't need anything else, I've been given the best gift I could ever want, I've got back my Zara. Every morning as soon as I open my eyes, she greets me with a huge smile and a big kiss and I thank God for each new day with her."*

By February 1995, I started the long search to find out how to get the drink medically tested and research it's full potential. To my surprise, Doctors were privately very open and admitted that cancer had reached epidemic levels in animals and humans. Statistics showed that 1 in 3 people, would die from some form of cancer. It was still a medical mystery and they had not yet found a cure or effective treatment.

Operations, drugs, chemotherapy or radiotherapy had not proved successful, as the cancer eventually returns. Furthermore, long term chemotherapy treatment damages the immune system, destroys blood cells and vital organs and gradually poisons the body, which in turn kills the patient. Therefore, they were keen to look at any safe alternative which could be beneficial. They believed that herbs were in many cases more effective and superior than drugs and that this drink could prove to be 'a vital key to better health care' in the future.

However, when it came to putting pen to paper and supporting the research of the drink, they all backed down. Professionally, they could not publicly get involved or support, even though it could benefit health and prevent suffering.

Instead they encouraged me to set up an **Independent Research Programme** and to ask the users to notify their Doctors/Vets and get them to participate by monitoring their progress. Again, I found Doctors were encouraging but still reluctant to endorse. I also learnt that medical trials were extremely expensive (in excess of £500,000), which I couldn't afford. Therefore, left with no alternative, I proceeded with the independent research amongst my own customers and the results proved to be clearly incredible and without any side-effects.

Having had first hand experience of the intense stress, pain and trauma associated with terminal illness, mixed with feelings of helpless, hopeless despair, as I watched my own mother die from Ovarian cancer, plus being personally diagnosed with suspected breast cancer. Their attitude angered me to such an extent that I started to delve into the reasons **why** Doctors were so fearful of speaking the truth; fearful of those in Authority and or of losing their jobs; thus causing an over protection of their profession, rather than protecting their patients. **Why** were Doctors so sceptical, stating that because the drink was effective on an animal, it didn't mean that it would be effective on humans as their systems were different. I questioned, **why** then were they spending billions annually testing all their drugs on animals first, before they were approved for human use? I was baffled by their double standards, moral and ethical principles.

I later learnt that it was not in the interest of Drug Companies to find a cure for any illness, as they'd lose billions from their continuous fund raising research campaigns and also from the sales of their drugs. Therefore, it would not be profitable to have a healthy nation. One Scientist told me that there is a known 'natural compound' in the laboratory which is believed to be a cancer cure but the Drug Companies would not research it because they would not make any money from anything which comes from a 'natural source.' I replied, *"so you mean, my mother could have been saved?"* He said, *"get real! the Drug Companies are running a money making business, they are not interested in saving lives."*

Being in the food industry, I was already aware of the callous disregard the industry has for its customers health... **putting profits before health and safety.**

I then reflected on Marsha's drastic personality change, weight gain and suicidal depression, after being prescribed steroids (without consultation), which also exposed her to possible breast cancer. I became even more angry because I could have lost a beautiful child through no fault of our own. As a mother, humanitarian and businesswoman, I paused and asked myself **WHY?** Where is all this leading too? What are they trying to create? What was going to be in-store for my grandchildren? I then reflected on God and my grandmother's practical but simple teachings; compared the 'quality of life' then to now and realised that tampering with nature leads to disaster.

Like myself, people nowadays have been indoctrinated to believe in 'the quick fix,' that doctors can 'cure' every illness, that 'quick, ready-made meals and fast foods' are the answers to all our health and cooking problems, whilst we search for a more relaxed, wealthier and sociable lifestyle.

In 1996, I returned to the Caribbean (Trinidad) where I met a Scientist, who informed me that the West (especially Germany) were conducting extensive research on ancient herbs and herbal remedies. He explained that Western Scientists were fully aware that their many years of chemical drug experiments had been a total failure and that 'the future key to health' now rests with ancient herbs and traditional remedies. I also met an incredibly healthy, alert and intelligent 95 year old lady called Ma Henry, who gave me her many secrets for longevity and cooking tips for good health. She reminded me very much of my Grandmother, who was always ready to teach me how to protect my health and to live life in 'God's ways, by putting Him first in everything I do.' She said that I was especially blessed to be in the *"natural food business because I'm charged with the responsibility of nourishing and healing others, plus it is necessary to protect the innocent and teach the truth to future generations."* We spoke at length about the modern food and drug industries. Her observations and knowledge was most enlightening and worthy of sharing.

Ma Henry said, *"food nowadays tastes bad because it no longer has the rich, full bodied flavour or natural nutrients as it used to in my younger days, before all these chemicals were developed and introduced. When we ate the natural foods in the old days, we used to get full up real quick and were totally satisfied for hours with only a small amount. We didn't need to be constantly eating snacks in-between or afterwards. But I notice that nowadays, people eat twice the amount or more to feel full and it doesn't seem to satisfy them for long because they are snacking all the time. They seem to be continuously hungry; this is not normal! and it's obvious that the chemicals they've put into the food have caused some kind of abnormal eating behaviour. Milk for instance, has completely lost its true taste, God only knows what they have done to it, so I do not drink it. If you were bought up on natural foods and then taste modern foods, you could actually taste the chemicals in them and its awful."*

Her eyes lit up as she reminisced about the sweet taste of the many fruits and vegetables back in those early days.

She continued;-

"Your modern Scientists have even invented artificial vitamin and

mineral supplements, these could never substitute or be better than the real thing which has nourished us since the beginning of time. I'm not at all surprised with the huge increase in sickness, crime, aggression, food allergies, eating disorders and behavioural problems. I blame it all on modern Scientists, they cannot be trusted. A Doctor's vocation should be to HEAL; sickness can be controlled with proper diet (natural foods), exercise and herbs."

To qualify this statement she explained that, for most of her working life she ran a boarding house for professional people (Doctors, Lawyers, Ministers, Judges etc) and had personally cooked for them. She claimed to have successfully healed many from serious sickness using her simple (old fashioned) herbal remedies, combined with the correct diet of natural foods and even Doctors would enquire of her methods when theirs failed. Ma Henry has survived four generations; with 10 children, 48 grandchildren, 74 great grand-children and 9 great, great grand children. She went on, *"I've lived long enough now to understand what was said in the Bible. In the end, the trees would refuse to yield its good fruits."* She use to believe this meant that the trees would stop bearing fruits but now she recognised its true meaning; *"that man would destroy the soil and drain it of all its nourishment, so the trees, plants etc, would no longer yield its full strength (ie. energy) for us or the animals to eat. God provided us with all the nourishment we needed and it was in the soil.* ***Poison the soil and you are killing yourself,*** *there is no getting away from this, it is evil. You can clearly see the difference in people's behaviour today. There is a distinctive change in the younger generation. They are prone to more disease, always sick, has low resistance, irritable, poor concentration, lack respect, violent and difficult to discipline. They act more like drug addicts. The Lord made our body like a car, every part needs each other to function properly. So you must maintain every part in good working order, to keep fit and healthy. Sickness can be controlled with proper diet, that means the natural foods that God has given us and not the poisonous ones that man is inventing for us;* ***Prevention is better than CURE."***

Her final advice was, *"look after your body and your body would take care of you; Put your life and trust in Jesus hands and God will bless you. The Lord said, Jesus will return again in the year 2000 to renew the world from all its confusion.. There will be pestilence, floods, fires, earthquakes, violence, (look at what's happening in America) today. The world has become a dangerous place. We are close to the year 2000."*

I continued to question Ma Henry about love and marriage. Her eyes twinkled, as she remembered her youthful courting days; life with her wonderful husband and gave me some very sound advice but this was her funniest one; *"if you notice that your man likes to look at the pretty ladies in the road! don't get angry, just gently take his hand and lead him straight into the nearest lamp post, he'd soon stop staring and look at where he's going in future."* At 95 she keeps abreast of world and domestic affairs, politics, sports etc. **She is simply an incredible lady with an encyclopedia of valuable memories, worthy of listening to, learning from and preserving**. She gave both myself and Rudolph her blessings. I truly treasured our moments together, as it reminded me of the sharing relationship of our ancestors. I often agonise over the tremendous amount of knowledge and cultural traditions we have lost, in return for so little gained, in the pursuit of Western vanity and greed.

Surprisingly, when I returned to England, one of my customers sent me a book called 'The Betrayal of Trust,' by Dr Vernon Coleman, who explains in depth, how the Drug Industry has had the entire world (including the animals) on a massive experiment without our knowledge or consent; why they've failed and that we'd be better off without the majority of prescribed drugs. My grandmother used to say, *"the Lord always sends proof when the truth is spoken."* This book confirmed my discussions with Ma Henry, as well as, provided concrete medical evidence. It's a real eye opener and if you want to learn the truth about what is really going on behind your back and wish to protect yourself and family, then I recommend that you buy and read it... details are given on the information listing at the back.

Shortly afterwards, whilst watching television (Sky Satellite);-

'The Book Programme' reviewed an American book called 'Spontaneous Healing' by Dr Andrew Weil (M.D.) who was being interviewed. Apparently, he is an orthodox doctor and also a botanist who believes in Spiritual healing; medicinal plants; positive attitudes and dietary changes as a process of 'self healing.' He explained, *"people should seek out others with similar illnesses and find out how or what healed their condition and follow the same route. Conventional drugs do not always work and alternative methods should be adopted by Doctors more often. Prevention is sometimes better than cure; the body can heal itself, all medicines should be integrated."*

Another satellite programme reported on an American doctor, Dr. Joseph Gold who was a former Nasa Scientist... discovered a virtually non-toxic drug 'hydrazine sulphate' (60mg) derived from 'rocket fuel' which was effective on his cancer patients. The recovery results were clearly incredible. It is not a cancer cure but a preventative. The drug was approved and is used in Russia and Europe. However, the American Food and Drugs Administration (FDA) refused to license or approve it, because it originated from a natural substance, in which case the Drug Companies would not benefit financially, (see back information page on where to obtain this drug in Britain).

These revelations propelled me into setting up the 'Independent Research' on Zara's Drink. I informed all my customers, explaining that it was only a trial and that I was not making any medical claims that it would cure cancer or any other illness but was researching the effects on as many people/animals as possible, to investigate or prove whether or not it was effective. I also advised that they were free to notify their Doctors or Vets and if possible get them to verify their condition and or any results. My customers as usual, responded positively and through them I was able to gather sufficient evidence proving that the drink was also effective on a huge range of other conditions affecting humans and animals. It is **not a cure for cancer but a preventative.** It reduced tumours and other growths and seems to keep it contained and under control. It was also effective on diabetes, incontinence, high blood pressure, breathing problems, congestion, like (flu, colds, asthma, hay fever, bronchitis, emphysema), food poisoning, tiredness, constipation, fluid retention, indigestion, sickness, inflammation and swelling, menopause, sleeplessness, septic wounds, irregular and painful periods, cuts, bruises, skin and kidney problems and some pain. It was particularly noticeable on animals, that it quickly cleared any skin irritation and infections, plus their fur regrew glossy, thick and completely reconditioned. They showed no sign of pain, discomfort or sickness; became more alert, confident and energised. Three dogs who were incontinent, stopped in just one week. **On the human side,** everyone noticed a major improvement in their energy levels; feelings of nausea quickly cleared; faded dark shadows around the eyes, cleaned the face and restored their complexion; also improved relaxation, alertness and general well being (see testimonies at end of the book).

However, Zara did have her ups and downs. **By May 1995** her general health continued to improve and the cancer effectively kept under control with the Herbal Drink. Then she had her first menstruation since contracting the cancer and suddenly all the original tumours reappeared on the same parts of her body but she showed no sign of physical illness or weakness. So off we went to the Vet for more tests. Her blood test results showed that it was even cleaner than before and the cancer tumours had remained inactive. The Vet simply told us to continue giving her the drink as she was absolutely fine and in good health.

❀ November 1995.

She had her second menstruation and we noticed the same inflammation of the tumours. It was then I concluded that it was Zara's own natural hormones during her menstruation cycle, which was causing the tumours to re-generate and inflame. The very same thing happens to women when we start menstruating; we become bloated and our mammary glands (i.e. breasts) swell up because of the hormone changes occurring in our bodies at that time. Since Zara was female and had mammary cancer, this was the most logical conclusion. From then onwards the tumours stayed but throughout she still showed no sign of ill health, pain or discomfort and remained healthy, energetic and happy. We celebrated her 11th birthday that month and enjoyed another very merry Christmas. Needless to say; we continued with our prayers, meditation and spiritual healing, *(just in case)* and also to keep the other side busy on her behalf. We remained hopeful and thankful to God, for HIS immense generosity and believed that Zara's life had been given a meaningful and useful purpose. Each new day was a blessing and a bonus.

❧ March 1996.

Zara suddenly started showing signs of becoming gravely ill again and naturally we feared the worst. We thought it was the development of secondary cancer. She started shaking and almost stopped eating. So, straight back to the Vet for more blood tests and x-rays. To our surprise, the x-ray showed up an extremely infectious swollen womb, which the Vet said had to be removed immediately, as it could burst within the same week and she'd die. The Vet was amazed with her general condition, fitness and health. Apparently, for the extent of the infection, she should have been looking far worse. He was even more amazed to find that when she was cut open, there were no signs of any internal *secondary cancers,* she was absolutely clear and the womb safely removed. The x-rays also showed that all her organs (lungs, liver, kidneys, heart) were strong and functioning perfectly. The cancer tumours still around her chest and stomach were away from her organs... well contained and under control. Zara walked out of the surgery hours after the operation, looking extremely happy and pleased with herself. She gave Marsha a big kiss, as if to say, *"thank you Mum."* On her return home, she dashed into the kitchen, lapped up a bowl of tomato soup and wanted more. She was back to normal. The next morning, we had to stop her from jumping up in fear of bursting the stitches. Within a week she was fully healed and recovered. Two weeks later, we noticed that the tumours were beginning to soften and shrink. So now with her womb removed, she'd no longer have menstrual periods to aggravate the cancer and we hoped that the tumours would completely disappear again. But more importantly, Zara was alive, healthy and fit.

❀ October '96.

The cancer tumours still continued to inflame periodically but by now the original largest tumour had become ulcerated, causing irritation which she continuously scratched and eventually cut it open. To avoid infection, the Vet suggested its removal and we agreed. However, when we returned to collect her, we were horrified to see the aftermath of the operation. The whole side of her body was opened and all the tumours removed, she looked like she'd been through a train wreck. The Vet had previously told Marsha, that removing all the tumours on the same side all at once was the best plan of action. We accepted his decision as he showed so much care and love towards Zara. But seeing how she looked, we then realised that it was far too traumatic. By now, Marsha's nursing skills were second to none. Again Zara healed rapidly but we noticed that she had become much weaker than normal. The Vet had diagnosed the on-set of arthritis in her spine and hind legs, which he said was a condition that affected Labradors when they began aging; apart from that she was fine.

❀ March '97.

Since her last operation, we held our breaths and kept a watchful eye to see if the cancer would spread but it didn't. None of the tumours which were removed, showed any signs of returning but the ones that were left on the other side of her body, continued to periodically inflame. Her arthritis had deteriorated rapidly and both her hind legs were becoming weak and painful. We felt that the three large tumours should be removed but did not want the Vet to open her up as he did before. Therefore, we went to seek his advice. He agreed with the individual removal of the tumours but advised that it could wait until they became irritable or made her uncomfortable. He was more concerned about the arthritis and prescribed some mild 'steroid based tablets,' to ease the discomfort and reduce the stiffness. Zara, not being used to taking drugs started to experience adverse effects within the first week. She became extremely ill and hot, (stomach and ears were very red); itching all over; bringing up her food and her legs got so weak that she could no longer walk. We immediately stopped giving her the tablets and were guided to treat her with a new product **(Gramma's Willow Drink)** plus warm baths, massages, spiritual healing and to include seaweed, fresh aloe vera gel and extra virgin olive oil in her diet. Within two days she began to improve, five days later, Zara was running up the stairs, although she still had a slight limp. Within one month Zara's improvement was astonishing and she looked great. That very same month, whilst watching television, a Scientist reported that he had found seaweed contained the highest levels of natural antibiotics and was looking at developing it into a new drug.

❀ 23rd May 1997.

An early morning television news programme reported, that a group of British Scientists had been researching the 'African Willow tree' for its effects on cancer. Their test on cancer patients had shown beyond a doubt that the 'willow' definitely destroys cancer cells; only small dosages were required and there were no side-effects. These Scientists were hailing their discovery as an amazing medical breakthrough for cancer treatment and that they were embarking on recreating it into a new synthetic cancer drug. *"When will these Scientists learn that the side-effects are caused from their man-made synthetic drugs and not from the natural plant? Why can't they invest their time, energy and money into growing more natural plants and provide people with the natural God-given remedies."* This may have been a new discovery for them but the 'Willow tree' is not new, it has been on earth since the creation and used successfully in traditional African herbal medicines for centuries. It is also one of the ingredients in Zara's Herbal Drink.

❀ Late 1997.

Zara's sight began to fade and again the Vet put it down to old age. The pupils of her eyes turned quite grey, she was definitely going blind. She'd bump into furniture and miss see her food bowl. This was a sure indication, as Zara was very greedy and could always find her food. Again, I was Guided to include lots of pumpkin in her diet, preferably the Caribbean or African variety which has a stronger orange colour than the European type. Within a month, her sight began to improve. Further, her diet of 'natural whole food' proved effective not only for improving and maintaining her health but also her weight. Although Zara was greedy and ate a lot, she remained very slim. The same goes for Marsha, Dee and myself.

❀ 1998.

Her sight continued to improve but the arthritis worsened. I was guided to give her regular swimming exercise to increase her mobility. The Guides explained that at her age, swimming was much better than walking, as it is detoxifying, rejuvenating, improves circulation, strengthens and tones the muscles, heart and respiration; it also reduces stiffness, stress and would help her body to heal itself. Unfortunately, dog swimming pools were rare, far away and expensive. The nearest one was a one and a half hour drive, way out in the countryside and impossible to reach without a car. However, we managed to get there once a week... during the summer months. The improvement in her mobility was quickly noticeable. We were forced to stop once the cold winter weather began.

❀ July 1998.

The Government published an official report on food poisoning, revealing that over 2 million people were poisoned each year. These figures were grossly under-estimated as many cases went unreported and claimed that many people died, particularly the very young and elderly. They were voicing serious fears, as the so-called 'super bugs' were now resistant to antibiotics and getting out of control, because they no longer had an effective treatment to remedy the situation. Having personally witnessed three complete recovery cases of chronic food poisoning, I immediately wrote to the British Medical Association, offering them the

Herbal Drink. As expected, they did not take up my offer.

Attn. Dr E.M. Armstrong (Secretary)
British Medical Association
BMA House
Tavistock House
London WC1H 9JP   27th July 1998

Dear Dr. Armstrong

Salmonella Super-Bug (Antibiotic Resistant)
(Deadly Food Poisoning Fears.)

I come to you, not as a medical person but as a missionary, concerned about the latest medical news report on the above life-threatening health scares and wish to bring to your attention a special 'Herbal Drink' which could be of benefit.

I've personally witnessed three cases of 'chronic food poisoning' (i.e. violent vomiting, diarrhoea, cold sweats and debility) swift and complete recovery in less than an hour, after drinking one cup of this Herbal Drink, made into a tea using just one tablespoon topped up with hot water. I'm willing to offer it 'FREE on TRIAL' to any hospital to test the effects against this 'super-bug' and any other food-poisoning strains.

In light of current medical fears that there is no medication available to treat this condition; plus it's resistance to antibiotics, coupled with recent medical calls to reduce the general over-use of antibiotics, then it is my belief that something is better than nothing. You or I have nothing to lose, however, the potential gains (if it worked, even on just half of the cases) are immeasurable in terms of 'future health protection' which does not damage or weaken the immune system but improves it. It could also safeguard the most vulnerable (i.e. the very young and the elderly) from the deadly effects of food poisoning, as well as, save billions of pounds on NHS expenditure.

By coincidence, I initiated a nation-wide 'Health Awareness Campaign' in June '98, in the hope of drawing medical attention of the many beneficial aspects of this drink. Enclosed is a copy of the Press Release entitled 'Can FOOD really HEAL?' It also includes some testimonies which were circulated to the national media. It's my greatest dream to have it medically researched, tested and approved as a 'safe, self-help remedy.' However, I'm opposed to turning it into a 'synthetic-drug.' It is my hope that this new confirmed health scare, could be the opportunity I've been long awaiting.

I know that it is difficult for the Medical Establishment to come to terms with 'natural herbal remedies' but I can assure you that my motives are sincere and my concern is genuine.

I look forward to hearing from you.

❀ October 1998.

'National Breast Cancer Awareness Month' was covered extensively in the media, featuring many cancer recovery stories, as well as, the tragedies and warning signs. A popular television programme featured several triumphant cases, all but one had orthodox treatment. The one exception explained that after surgery, the chemotherapy made her so sick that she felt she was going to die. She learnt about a natural herbal remedy in Brazil and decided to go over there for the treatment. She said it effectively cleaned her blood, controlled the cancer and made her feel great. The resident British Doctor on the show, arrogantly dismissed her claims, which she gallantly defended. She went on to say that it was unfortunate that this drink was not available in Britain to promote an alternative to chemotherapy.

❀ February 1999.

Zara's legs were becoming increasingly lame and I was guided to get a large water tank to use as an indoor swimming bath, so that she could swim every other day. However, Marsha and Dee needed to look for new accommodation, so the water-tank plan had to wait until they moved.

❀ April 1999.

This was a particularly stressful month for Marsha, who was also in the process of moving home. I believe that animals sense and absorb any tension or stress from their loved-ones. Zara, for this reason became equally stressed out. This in turn could have lead to her contracting a strong flu-virus the week before Marsha moved house, which knocked her health sideways. Flu knocks down the best of us and is seriously dangerous for the very young or elderly, many of whom die as a result, because they are not strong enough to fight off the disease. To make matters worse, the new house was cold and drafty. Zara's condition worsened and by the second week she'd almost stopped eating, began sleeping a lot and was loosing weight rapidly... in fact, she became a bag of bones. The Vet's examination showed that her blood and organs, with the exception of her liver were in good condition. Her liver for some unknown reason had deteriorated badly and he confirmed that she was on her way out and gave her an antibiotic injection. That week the weather was beautiful, so Marsha decided to sit with Zara outside in the garden to get some sun. Unfortunately, this action had the opposite effect and by the next day Zara slipped into a coma and was rushed to the emergency animal hospital. The diagnosis was grave and the Vet advised immediate euthanasia because he felt that her liver was beyond repair and even a drip would not prolong her life. There was also blood in her stool. He gave her no more than 2 to 4 days to live, then left the room to allows us to consider putting her down that day.

Once again Marsha had come to this cross road of decision but this time she knew that Zara was old and death was inevitable. Marsha stared that painful lost stare of helpless sinking agony. Holding Zara tightly in her arms she cried, *"God please don't let me have to do this, please don't let it be this way, I want Zara to die with me, I can't leave her here with strangers."*

Then she looked at me and said, *"Mum I can't do it, if she is going to die, I'm taking her home, I want her surrounded by those who love her."*

She called the Vet and asked if Zara was in any pain and if she was likely to be in any pain before she died. He said that she was completely comatose and would not be in any pain whatsoever. She'd simply sleep longer and longer and would eventually die in her sleep. So Marsha decided to take her home to die.

The hospital Vet then gave her 3 booster injections... an antibiotic, one to increase her temperature and an appetiser. He advised us to give her lots of liquids and try to get her eating. By the time we returned to the taxi, Zara started coming around. My Guides had previously instructed me to make her 'a pureed vegetable soup' containing garlic, ginger, onion, celery, tomatoes, carrots, pumpkin, potatoes, yellow lentils , seaweed, a little pepper sauce, vegetable stock, olive oil, cooked and liquidized, then mix in a little cod liver oil or flaxseed/linseed oil. To also make up a porridge of boiled oats, strained and add a little honey. The porridge would provide slow release carbohydrates for energy, which would help to build her up quickly and the soup with the warm herbs to help her circulation, appetite, stimulation to heal the cold and the lentils to provide easily digestible proteins for muscle strength, plus her Herbal Drink diluted with water. Having my own home-grown aloe-vera plant, I also made her a special fruit juice using the fresh aloe-vera gel, to stop any internal bleeding.

We nursed her around the clock, feeding her fluids using a 20ml syringe. The Vets warned that vomiting and constant sleeping indicated further deterioration of the liver. Within 24 hours she was awake, alert and did not vomit. She stayed awake for sometime, yawning, stretching and smiling again. Then my Guides advised me to make a spinach soup, include papaya, potato, celery, pumpkin with seasonings to stimulate her appetite and digestion. That morning my Guides informed me to produce these soups and porridge as high energy foods for sick, convalescent humans and animals. The following night, Zara was looking good and for the first time when tempted with ice cream, she opened her mouth to eat it. This was a sure sign that she was getting back to normal. By the forth day, Zara was snapping and trying to chew the syringe. By the forth week, we started her on the indoor swimming... half an hour for 2 - 3 times weekly. We also got her a magnetic collar for arthritic animals. By June, the Vet confirmed that Zara had improved tremendously and was doing well, even though she could no longer walk. By July, the regular swimming exercise was making a definite improvement on her health. She looked forward to it, especially as it meant a good rub-down massage to dry her off at the end. Although she was never constipated, the swimming motions would open up her bowels and she'd start going to toilet straight away. So we had to keep a watchful eye to quickly take her out to finish, then put her back in.

In next to no time, her front legs gained considerable strength and she'd paddle away for 15 minutes at a time. Her hind legs (which were lame), began to strengthen after four weeks. The more strength she gained, the brighter she became and we remained hopeful that she would walk again.

Zara was now a grand old lady of 14½ years, still looking elegant, youthful and dignified, when her time comes we will be happy to **let her go** into God's safe keeping and loving care, comforted by the assured knowledge that -

---

LIFE is ETERNAL

TRUE LOVE never dies but lives FOREVER

So we'd have her 'spiritual visits' to look forward to. In the meantime, we'd continue to monitor her progress and give her all the 'love' she deserves. But no matter how well one is prepared or ready, the moment of parting or separation will always be a difficult and painful experience, which only time and fun memories heal.

On reflection, Zara's happiness and beauty has always shone and attracted others. Ever since she was a puppy, when ever we took her out, people (i.e. children, men and women) would stop and say, *"she's so beautiful, can I please give her a hug"* and we'd allow them. They'd then make a big fuss of her with lots of hugs and kisses. So, Zara has been giving love and healing people from birth and this healing will continue after her eventual death with her very own special drink, as a lasting memorial to PURE LOVE.

❀ Conclusion.

Although Zara had her ups and downs but after taking the Herbal Drink, (from 1994) she maintained good health. Even though she had two major operations to remove some of the tumours and her womb, the cancer did not spread but remained contained and controlled. Additionally, over the years we noticed something significant. All the tumours gradually merged together to form 3 to 4 large clusters, which could have been easily removed by surgery and would not have re-grown. Zara also had no form of conventional treatment (like chemotherapy or radiotherapy) and we stuck rigidly to **a vegan diet** instructions. I wonder if this is one of the ways forward for cancer treatment. All in all, the best treatment to date was the natural foods and remedies with minimal use of conventional drugs. However, **wheat pasta** was the only food which seemed to aggravate and cause the tumours to swell considerably. They'd reduced almost immediately once she was taken off it. Furthermore, since her initial recovery, all other illnesses which followed were not cancer related. It's satisfying to know that Zara would eventually die from old age rather than cancer. At fifteen years old, she has survived the average stated age for Labradors which is twelve.

Although our story focussed mainly on cancer, the Herbal Drink is not exclusively for cancer but is a general 'preventative' for a wider range of conditions. Our independent research only touched a limited number of cases but it was a large enough indication to prove that it should be taken seriously. My Guides also stated that **liquid medicines** are far more effective and efficient than tablet medicines, because they are readily absorbed through the body's microscopic membranes, travel directly into the bloodstream, and are then easily transported to vital organs. Hence, the reason Zara's Herbal Drink should be taken first thing in the morning on an empty stomach. I believe that the only possible CURE is one's faith in God, as HE is the only true miracle worker and that part of the healing process incorporates; **a zest for life, positive attitude, correct diet, exercise, spiritual healing, prayers and love.** I really believe that one must want to live, in order to survive. At the end of the day, we must not fool ourselves into believing that we will live forever, as 'physical death' is inevitable and is a stage we must all confront when the time comes. Since God is the ultimate controller of *'life and death,'* then it stands to reason that we should always first look to HIM for the help and guidance to heal us.

❀ Lessons Learned.

This heart wrenching experience has given me a greater appreciation of life, as well as, a unique insight into cancer. The subsequent five years independent research has also provided additional insight into the suffering of animals and their subjection to chronic drug abuse.

Their lives are not valued, respected or taken seriously, hence euthanasia is legally and readily available, because they are expendable and easily replaced. However, in our case, Zara was not only our pet but also Marsha's baby and an integral part of our family. Therefore, the emotional and physical stress and trauma was deeply rooted as for any member of my human family. I realise that unless one has had personal experience fighting with cancer or any other terminal illness, then one cannot truly appreciate the depth of pain, fear, stress, HOPE or even the release when death occurs. When Zara became lame, my guides explained:-

"Once the brain is active, alert and conscious, then the animal or person is still ALIVE. People like the actor Christopher Reeve and many others who are totally paralysed, still have useful lives to serve or to be of service to others. In other words, their experience can bring about effective treatments and also give strength to others undergoing the same difficulty. Everyone, including animals have a useful purpose, so we should not be so hasty to destroy."

Having already faced medical scepticism, it would be interesting to hear the medical professions' response, when they learn of the spiritual aspects of these products. Would they also poo-poo God's words? - or come to the realisation that **even animals have Souls and Guardian Angels too**.

After more than five years of trying to obtain medical approval, I'm left feeling convinced that neither the Medical Establishment, Drug Companies or Government are honestly concerned about the nation's health. Therefore, I no longer care for their approval because I truly believe that the Herbal Tea will stand the test of time. So, I've chosen to place my trust in God's hands because I know that HE knows best.

A Gift from GOD

A few months after experiencing my first encounter with God in 1996, Marsha, Dee and myself were meditating together when God gave this message:

"Zara is being used to teach humans humility and respect, that through an animal comes our healing. Animals may be dumb but they are not stupid, they are highly intelligent creatures. Zara is also being used to show that HIS medicine is for all HIS creations (humans, animals, plants and the environment). Therefore, we should stop the abuse. At times she may appear to be suffering but she's not, because she's protected and being loved not only by us but also by those in the Spirit-world including her mother, Betsy."

> **"Zara's purpose is to bring healing to the world and to show us the Power Of Love."**

On 16th November 1996, God finally confirmed that;-

"the Herbal Drink is a universal food. It contains herbs from all over the world, to prove that no race, food or country, should ever claim that they are better than each other. It also shows that singularly, we are created with power and strength but when combined (or collectively) we become a much greater force; DYNAMITE. The Herbal Drink 'cleans the BLOOD-of-LIFE' and is essential for everyone in this time, to neutralise the toxic/poisonous effects of man-made environmental pollution and would restore 95% of all illnesses. It is vital for both the sick and healthy as a daily preventative."

❀ November 1999.

Television reports confirmed that cancer treatment in Britain was sub-standard, inadequate and below expectations, especially in Scotland, where 40% of machinery and equipment were outdated. There was a serious lack of Government investment, machinery, specialists and ancillary staff in every field to cope with the increasing demand. Therefore, people were dying because of the long waiting list this has created. The Government allocated £93 million to improve the facilities but the leading cancer specialists stated that it required ten times this amount.

✿ ON REFLECTION.

To this day, I receive calls/letters from new customers using the drink for different illnesses and I'm am still being amazed with the speed of recovery. It just seems to work on everything.

A Scientist once suggested that the results could be psychological but when I explained that this is not possible with animals, who showed even quicker improvements, he could not comment.

✿ Toxic Shock Syndrome.

When my Spirit-Guides first advised me about the drink, they also stated that it should be sprayed on sanitary tampons, to prevent 'toxic shock syndrome.' I hadn't heard of this condition before but within a few days it was reported on the television news that an American woman had almost died from wearing tampons. Apparently, a common bacteria grows rapidly because of the warmth inside the virgina during menstruation, producing a deadly toxin which is quickly absorbed into the blood stream. It then damages the immune system, weakens the entire body, causes fever, vomiting, headaches, muscle pains, diarrhoea, dizziness, hallucinations, hair loss, kidney failure, collapsed lungs and even cardiac arrest. It can all happen in a matter of days and if the patient survives, she may take months to recover.

✿ Vegan Diet :- *to reduce cancer risks.*

9th June 2000, a scientific research claimed that by cutting out meats and dairy foods can protect men against prostate cancer, because it reduced the levels of a body chemical called I.G.F - 1, which has been linked to the disease. A study of 696 British men found that vegans had I.G.F - 1 levels, 9% lower than meat-eaters and 7% lower than vegetarians. Prostate cancer is less common in people who consume little meat and dairy produce.

The Passing of an Angel.

The Passing of an Angel

❀ **September 1999.**

One day, out of the blue God said, *"There is going to be a miracle."* I was excited and hoped it meant that Zara would be up and about... walking again, as she was doing well and swimming quite strongly. A couple of weeks later, Marsha caught the flu and passed it onto Zara, who again went down hill rapidly. So we were back to the nursing vigil. By the end of September, she seemed to be on the mend but was still weak, so we planned to resume the swimming the following week.

On the morning of the 5th.October 1999, I was just about to wake, when 'in Spirit' I saw Zara walk through my front door. I followed her into the living room where she sat up proud and strong, looking at me with a big smile on her face. I said, *"so you've come to say goodbye?"* Looking at me once more, she smiled and then disappeared. Zara had been completely transformed and was a picture of perfect health. I began to pray, then immediately opened my eyes and continued praying.

That same day, Marsha had to attend a business meeting and pre-arranged with me to take care of Zara. When Marsha left, I sat quietly with Zara and spoke of her spiritual visitation that morning. I told her that I knew the time had come for her to return home to heaven; that her work here was complete; expressing what a great job she'd done; how she'd served her purpose well; how much she had taught us and what a beautiful gift-of-life she was leaving behind for the world's benefit. I started reminiscing about the wonderful times we all had together; how blessed and enriched we'd been by her existence; how much we all loved her; how difficult her leaving would be, especially for Marsha and that it would be easier if Marsha was with her at the end and she should try to visit Marsha regularly after her passing. I then told Zara that she was truly 'an angel, heaven-sent' and I was personally honoured, grateful, thankful to have known her and it was a pleasure looking after her.

I sat there talking and crying for hours but Zara simply listened, looking at me with peaceful contentment in her eyes. Zazu (our cat) spent the entire day snuggled up to her thick coat and was unusually quiet. The customary strange stillness filled the room. Marsha returned, all bubbling and happy but I refrained from telling her about Zara's visit or my thoughts.

The next day (6th October) was Zara's 15th birthday, so I spent the day with her whilst working on the book with Marsha. Around lunch time, I noticed there was a change in her breathing rhythm, (slightly laboured) but I still said nothing to Marsha, as I didn't want to alarm her. Again, Zazu spent the day quietly laying beside her. By the time I left that night, her breathing was still laboured but she looked fine. I returned home, said my prayers and asked God not to prolong her suffering; *"if she is dying, then please take her out quickly but let Marsha be present with her to the end."* I felt uneasy, so before going to bed, I phoned Marsha to check if Zara was alright and she was fine.

❀ ZARA'S LAST MOMENTS :- *(written by Marsha).*

Before I got Zara ready for bed, I tried to give her some food (from the bottle). She would only take a little down and kept turning her head to the side, so it would dribble out of her mouth. I laughed at her and said, *"no you don't matey"* and turned her face upwards, so that she would automatically to take it down. I tried again but she was having none of it, so I gave up, laughed at her cheekiness and then cleaned around her mouth. I then turned her body over and placed a warm towel under her face. Zara looked quite contented and fell asleep. This was after midnight.

Feeling hungry myself, I put some dinner to heat in the oven, then settled down in the living and whilst watching television I fell asleep. I suddenly woke up to see smoke in the air. Realising what had happened, I jumped up, took the food out of the oven and opened all the windows. The food was charred, burnt to a crisp. I'm not quite sure of the time but I believe it was around 2:30am.

Zara was up and my first thoughts were to get her and Zazu out of the smoky room; so I took them into my bedroom. I noticed Zara looked uncomfortable and was breathing deeply, so I picked her up and placed her on to my bed. I moved her head slightly to see if the way she was lying was restricting her breath but it made no difference. I then laid close to her, put my arms around her, staring into her eyes. After about what seemed like half an hour later, I noticed that her breathing had not changed. It only then dawned on me that something else was really wrong. The thought of her dying flashed past my mind but I couldn't actually believe it. I began to cry as I thought to myself, *"should I take her to the animal hospital?"* But this time I thought *"No,"* if this was indeed her time to go, then it would not be fair to drag it out any longer. I just looked into Zara's eyes and said, *"Zari, if its time for you to go, you must go, do not stay here any longer for me. You have done and suffered enough; I don't want you to stay a minute longer for me."* Zara was watching me as I spoke, her breathing getting more laboured but soft, not gasping for breath, her breathing pattern was slow and soft. I then phoned Mum and when she answered, I broke down and said, *"Mum, can you come over, I think Zara's going."* Mum replied, *"I know darling, I'll be right over."* I phoned Dee and I told her. Dee anxiously asked if it was the cold that was causing her to breathe deeply. I was confused as to whether it could be the cold or the inevitable. I knew in my heart that it couldn't be the cold as I had checked her nose for any blockages that evening... as always. Whilst speaking with Dee, Zara's breathing became worse. I called out, *"oh God,"* Dee asked me to keep the phone line open, so I put the phone on my pillow and kept on talking and stroking Zara, telling her that both Mum and Dee were on their way but if she had to go now and couldn't wait, then it was okay.

Mum arrived first, the time seemed to last forever...

When I arrived, Zara was lying on Marsha's bed, her breathing was shallow but looking peaceful and calm. Marsha was gently stroking her, whilst crying and speaking to Dee on the phone. She put the phone to Zara's ear and I heard Dee say, *"Zara, please wait for me, I'm coming, I love you."*

Zara's breathing was gradually getting deeper, yet she was not struggling and showed no sign of pain, discomfort or fear. I lit a candle and quietly prayed. In tears, I listened to Marsha painfully saying her goodbyes:- *"Zari, I never thought this moment would ever come but baby it's alright. I don't want you to suffer anymore. I don't want you to go but I must let you go. I'll be OK. I love you so much. Thanks for coming into my life. Thanks for teaching me so much. Thanks for choosing me to be your Mum. You are so beautiful. You have never been a burden. I love you. I love you."*

As her breathing deepened, Marsha cried out, *"Oh God, please take her now, don't make her suffer. Zari don't be afraid, it will be alright. You are going to be so happy. You'll be able to walk and run again. You'll meet all your family and friends. Zari, I hope you are happy with how I looked after you. If I did anything wrong, I'm sorry, please forgive me. You are all I've ever wanted. I'll never forget you. Oh Zari, my Zari, I love you, I love you, love you. Please come back and visit me."*

"Please hold on for Dee, she's on her way, she won't be long."

All the while, stroking, kissing and comforting her. Then she noticed that the arthritic stiffness in her front leg was gone and she could circle both legs with ease. Marsha said, *"look Zari, your arthritis is gone, you are being healed already - you are free, look for the bright light and follow it, God is waiting for you."* Then she called on my Mum, *"Nan, please come and help her, look after her for me."*

About this time Dee arrived and she too was crying, kissing, cuddling and comforting her, *"thanks for waiting for me, Zara I love you."* Dee placed her head on Zara's forehead for a while and communicated with her telepathically one last time. A little after she had finished, Zara's breathing then rapidly changed and became much shallower but throughout, she remained calm, peaceful and pain free. Zazu laid by her side all the while. Suddenly, Zara stretched out both front feet to Marsha and stared into her eyes. Marsha held her paws, then Zara's mouth dropped open and without struggling, took and gave out her last breath. She passed away with her eyes loving fixed on Marsha, her pupils were no longer a cloudy grey but bright and shinny. She looked completely at peace, dignified and majestic to the end. The time was 7.07am. We were all crying, cuddling and hugging Zara. Zazu ran out of the bedroom and hid under the chair in the living room. About 5 minutes after, Dee brought Zazu back into the bedroom and placed him on the bed, next to Zara. We watched in amazement as Zazu walked up close to Zara's face and placed his forehead against hers, staring deep into her opened eyes for a while, then laid right beside her and fell asleep.

In the silence, Marsha said she heard a dog bark outside. This was unusual, as no dogs lived on her street and it was the first she had ever heard a dog bark.

Marsha washed Zara clean for the last time and placed her on clean sheets. I blessed her and she laid peacefully on Marsha's bed for 5 hours. In the privacy of our own home, we were able to love and talk to her, before driving her to Wood Farm Crematorium... Marsha held her in her arms all the way.

The 'Chapel of Rest' in the farm was beautiful. Marsha gently laid Zara inside the coffin wrapped in her sheets. As soon as the Farm owner saw Zara she smiled, commenting on how peaceful she looked. Stroking Zara softly, Marsha fell to her knees, crying quietly repeating, *"oh Zari."* She didn't want to leave her alone in a strange place surrounded by strangers. It was the first time they would be separated and she knew that it was the last time they'd be together. I placed my hands on her shoulders and comforted her whilst trying to persuade her to leave. But she quietly asked to be left alone.

Before leaving, Marsha expressed to the Farm owner to treat Zara gently and with great respect when it was time for her to be cremated. Around that time, two dogs who had been previously playing outside in the grounds, came into the office with their owner. One of the dogs strolled over to Marsha and rubbed its head against her leg. She smiled, stroked it gently, before leaving for the long journey home.

Zara was to be cremated at 6pm that day.

On returning home that evening at precisely 7pm, the atmosphere changed and we all suddenly felt happy, started laughing and talking about her. Recognising her spiritual presence we celebrated her life.

The next day, we collected her ashes, which were also blessed. In true ancient fashion, we prayed for three days for her safe journey home. On Sunday 10th October, her ashes was scattered in the nearby river with a beautiful floral wreath, prepared by Marsha the night before. Marsha's wishes were granted, because Zara died peacefully in her arms, surrounded by loved-ones and not from the cancer but from old age.

I spent the first week with Marsha to help her through the grieving process. Trying to get her to open up and to talk it out but she refused. She had spent the last six months sleeping in an arm chair, watching Zara every night and did not realise how tired she was. She slept for the first time in her bed and just slept and slept for hours. The flat felt empty and lifeless. Zazu would not leave Marsha's side, constantly kissing and trying to comfort her. She had spent the last 15 years taking care of Zara. Her entire life was Zara, who was not just a friend or mutual companion but the greatest love of her life. Zara was her main topic of conversation. Whenever she felt down, Zara was always there to perk her up. Whenever she needed something to hold, she held onto Zara. If you ever wanted to find Marsha, you'd only have to look for Zara and vice versa, they were inseparable. However, the day she feared most for years had finally come and Zara was no longer there. Yet she consoled herself with the fact that Zara had survived 5 years, so much more than we'd ever expected and was thankful to God for that extended time and for taking her in the manner she had asked for; **in peace and pain free.**

For the first two weeks, none of us dreamt of Zara and wondered how long it was going to take before she communicated. On 22nd October, I arranged to collect some paper work from her in the morning after gym training. I arrived at 9am to find Marsha beaming with joy and asking, *"guess who visited me this morning?"* Not thinking about Zara, I answered, *"who?"* Well, Marsha almost could not contain herself with excitement, hopping around and laughing, whilst relaying this amazing encounter.

"My eyes have seen the truth, and it has filled my heart with the kind of happiness witnessed only from the very first day Zara entered into my life."

Marsha Moore.

• aged 10 years.

• zara, holiday-ing in Scotland aged 2 years.

• with brothers Zazu and Banjo.

Page 354: YOUNGER YEARS -
A selection of pictures of Zara from age 2 years and upwards.

Page 355: LIVING WITH CANCER -
Zara at various stages in her life ' living' with cancer.

Page 356: NIGHT BEFORE, MORNING AFTER, RECOVERY -
Pictured here the night before and after surgery to remove her womb. The whole procedure took alot out of her but in true 'Zari' style she came back fighting fit. Amazingly, 2 days after, she was bounding around the house.

Page 357: THE WONDER YEARS -
Zara on swimming sessions to improve her arthritic legs.

● 1998.

● 1995.

●1996.

● February 1996.

● cancer tumours.

355.

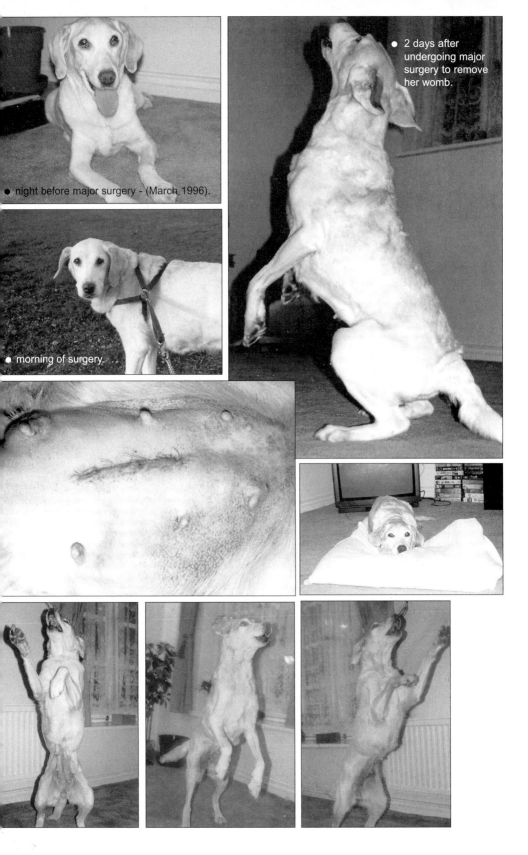

● night before major surgery - (March 1996).

● morning of surgery.

● 2 days after undergoing major surgery to remove her womb.

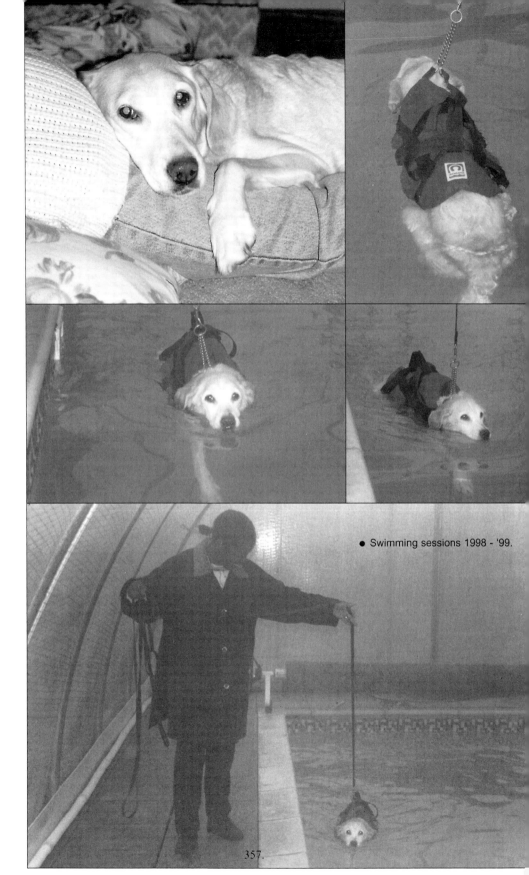

● Swimming sessions 1998 - '99.

357.

Marsha's Miracle

'21st October 1999.'

Written by Marsha).

Last night I was feeling quite defiant and despondent, didn't want to say my prayers, even though my Guides kept nagging me to say them. So I just said a quick prayer of protection before going to bed.

I woke up in the early hours of the morning, it was still dark in the room but as I opened my eyes, I could see Zara lying down with her head on her paws, sleeping... facing me. She was laying just beside my wardrobe which is opposite my bed. I thought in my head, *"Zara"* and instinctively went straight over to touch her... mainly to see if I was indeed dreaming or if she was a Spirit. To my surprise, I could feel her fur perfectly as I ran my hands through it. This woke Zara up and she immediately looked up at me and began jumping and spinning around. I couldn't believe it but I wasn't scared, it was then I knew that I was awake and this was not a dream. Zara led me to the living room jumping and walking at the same time. I don't know which of us was more excited. I could see everything around me, my television (which I'd left on that night), the table with Zara's picture and flowers on it, I could see my settee, her chair, even into the kitchen. I hugged and kissed Zara, saying aloud, *"I should call Mum"* but in my heart I thought I'd wait, just in case Zara left early. Then I had an even bigger surprise. As I sat down, Kenny (my Nan's dog who had passed away about 4 years ago), also appeared and sat beside me. I put my arms around him saying, *"Kenny,"* I just couldn't believe he had come. As I hugged him I could feel every bone in his body, I could see and feel his black fur, I could see his ears, everything. Then, I was stroking who I thought was Zazu but as I looked down, a white face looked up at me, it was Zazu's brother Banjo! I looked at Banjo in disbelief and just said *"Banj."* All their faces looked calm, happy and contented. Even though Zara was as elated as me, there was also a calmness in her excitement. Zazu at some point had gotten up and joined us but I did not see him physically come into the room, I just remember him being there.

I remembered thinking to myself that I should check the time to tell Mum, as she always told me *"when Spirits visit, they usually came at a certain time."* I remembered thinking this whilst standing up and looking towards my clock which is situated in a corner by my bookshelf and thinking, *"I'll check it later."*

Then I was asleep again. I don't remember going back to my bed.

The next thing I knew I woke again, the room was still dark; Zara was laying in the same place but this time, watching for me to wake up. I arose and we both returned to the living room.

I can't remember anything else after that...

Bits of what I did or said during the time Zara, Banjo and Kenny were around, I can't remember exactly everything but when I finally woke up in the light of the morning, Zazu was lying directly behind me with his paws outstretched on my back. I woke up and remembered what had happened. I gave Zazu a huge, kiss and said, *"good morning"* and a big *"thank you"* to Zara, especially for bringing Banjo and Kenny to see me.

Whilst saying my prayers, I broke down in tears but this time I truly had joy in my heart and not so much sadness. I know that I will always miss her but to see all of the things that I had wished and actually asked for, materialise right before my eyes, is a blessing greater than I'd ever imaged. The feeling is indescribable. I feel light, I feel relief, I feel Zara is okay and is happy. I feel that she is with me now; *"I have the confirmation, the proof, the evidence; in my soul I can truly say I have experienced true life eternal! No matter what people will say or think, in my heart, **I know the truth**. My eyes have seen the truth; and it has filled my heart with the kind of happiness witnessed only from the day Zara entered into my life."*

My house no longer feels so empty and I no longer feel so alone as I did before. I look forward to her and (the others) next visit and for the time when we can communicate together freely on this earth, until my time

come to join her in the next life.

This miracle happened 14 days after she had passed away.

Later that day, God suddenly revealed, *"there is the miracle I promised. Marsha has witnessed that the Spirit truly lives. From now on she knows, understands and believes that I AM ALIVE and active in hers, yours and any one else's life, who calls on ME. I never desert my children."*

❀ Further Visitations.

On the morning of the 11th November, I awoke and while preparing to get out of bed, I felt a strange force preventing me from moving. I could only open my eyes. I knew something spiritual was taking place, so I waited. I could feel that something quite heavy had come on the bed and could see the physical weight impression on the bed but when I opened my eyes I couldn't see anything. So I closed them again. Then I saw Zara's front paws placed into my hands and I said, *"Zara, you've come to see me?"* She then snuggled up, gave me a big kiss and I heard her say, *"Thank YOU."* As she was getting off the bed, I opened my eyes in the hope of seeing her but all I could see was her weight impressions as she moved off. The force was then lifted and I was able to get up.

(Written by Marsha).

The morning of the '7th' November 1999... exactly one month since Zara passed away.

I woke up to find, Zara lying on the bed, watching me. At first I thought it was a trick of the light but I looked again and realised it was indeed Zari. I rose up sharply, letting out a gasp at the same time and said her name. I turned to Dee, (who was also asleep in bed) and nudged her to wake up. That's all I remember, before falling fast asleep again.

I also remembered seeing everything in the room.

Later that morning, when we all woke up, I told Dee what had happened. She said that I'd frightened her and Zazu out of their skins. She described seeing me shoot up from my sleep and heard me moan, my eyes were closed (which really creeped her out) and that I was nudging her. She thought at the time that I was trying to tell her something.

This happened pretty early in the morning... before 5am.

Zara has since appeared to both Marsha and Dee on several occasions, even showing them how her Spirit moves in and out of Zazu to communicate with them on a daily basis. Since then they have noticed distinctive changes at times in Zazu's mannerism, which look suspiciously close to Zara's. I guess it is her way of showing them that she is ever present.

Although Marsha is still getting over Zara's passing, this experience lifted her Spirit to such an extent that she looks forward to the day when Zara would be able to visit her everyday, because she now knows that *"with faith, all things are possible,"*

It should be noted that Zara died on '7th' October precisely '7' minutes past '7' O'clock.

• ZARA MOORE •
6th October 1994 - 7th October 1999.

CHAPTER IV.

Health 2000.

• PRESERVING OUR ENVIRONMENT & HEALTH.

The Way We Were

'before man-made interference, exploitation and global commercialism.'

From 1995, immediately after Zara's cancer recovery, my Guides started to talk about environmental and health issues. They referred to the dangers of scientific experiments and the importance of preserving the environment in the natural state in which it was created and how essential this is for our health and general sustenance.

Mother Earth -

"The EARTH is our MOTHER; breathing, nurturing, nourishing and yielding her 'Full-Life-Force' (energy/strength) to feed us. Therefore we must love, cherish, respect and protect MOTHER EARTH, because she is the womb of the world."

Our ancestors were taught these values at an early age and grew up with the understanding that they owed their lives to God and the earth. Therefore, they appreciated this direct relationship and interdependence with everything which was purposely placed in the universe for our benefit, enjoyment, pleasure and life.

To correspond with these teachings, my Guides related this picture of God's original plan for HIS universe and the increasing dangers science is exposing us to.

❀ Paradise Re-Visited.

"God took many years planning and designing HIS best works (i.e. the creation of the world... paradise). HE carefully placed every natural plant (i.e. vegetables, fruits, herbs) containing all the essential nutritional and medicinal ingredients we (i.e. humans and animals), would need for our food and medicine to keep us in the best of health. HE then placed us in this wonderful, pure, natural, clean environment,

with clean air and clean water, to live in harmony; each depending on the other for LIFE. This is how HE hoped it would remain throughout eternity, because HE visualised a world of love, appreciation, care and mutual respect."

Hence, when we die (i.e. humans, animals and plants) we all return back into the earth to decay; releasing our natural nutrients to further enrichen the earth for use by future generations. Therefore, we all replenish the earth, to enable it to continuously yield its full riches to all life forms, forever (perfectly recyclable).

LIFE is essentially ENERGY,

therefore, we survive by transferring,

supplying and filling each other with ENERGY.

In my school days, I loved science lessons and remembered being taught how animals, humans and plants also supplied each other with the 'breath of life' (air), whilst at the same time keeping the environment balanced and pure.

(a) Plants need **rich soil** to grow strong and healthy, plus they breathe in 'carbon dioxide' and breathe out 'oxygen.'

(b). Humans and animals eat these **energy-rich plants** to also grow strong and healthy, breathing in their 'oxygen' and breathing out 'carbon dioxide,' which the plants in turn breath in. This cycle of air exchange forms a vital part of our life process.

(c). In time and after many years, our rich compact accumulation in the earth, eventually yields precious stones, gems, metals, gases, oils etc, for all our benefit.

In order to receive the **full life force** of food, we should wait until the earth has nurtured it long enough to release its full strength. In this way, we'd be eating full bodied nourishment (i.e. energy or all its essential vitamins, minerals & nutrients). Hence, we should only pick or reap food when its fully ripe and ready to eat.

In olden days, people were physically strong, fit, mentally alert and lived long healthy lives. Sickness was rare because their immune systems were strong and able to build-up resistance to fight off disease. They showed no sign of feebleness, had excellent eye sight and incredible memory. Like Ma Henry at 95 years old, who claimed she has never had a headache, backache, toothache or any kind of pain, all of her joints were in perfect working order with no swellings or stiffness. She demonstrated her agility by swiftly raising from her chair without using her hands for support, rolled her shoulders round, stretched her arms in the air, touched her toes and did some squats. My father's god-sister who was also in a her late nineties, lived alone and was fit enough to look after herself. She, like other elderly folks who lived by the ancient principles, had perfect teeth; each absolutely strong, white and clean; with no form of decay or plaque, yet she has never used toothpaste or a toothbrush throughout her life. They used a special plant which the old folks called 'that one.' In fact, it is Trinidad's national flower called 'the double Hibiscus,' which grew wild and abundant in every garden. They'd cut off a small stem, scrape off the surface skin and chew on the end until it frayed into a brush, which was used for brushing, then simply rinsed with clean water and that was it. From time to time they'd rub their teeth and gums with ashes (from burnt wood) and rinse with water or sometimes salt water. In fact, dentistry was a rare profession.

Both my Grandmother (73 years) and Great Grandmother (112 years) died with every perfect teeth in their mouths. I, myself never had a toothache or decay whilst living in the Caribbean but within one year of moving to Britain, I was in a dentist's chair and my teeth have deteriorated ever since. Thinking about it, animals in the wild never use a toothbrush or toothpaste or visit the dentist but check out their teeth! I'm not saying that dentistry isn't a necessary or worthy profession but we must look into the inventions of commercial products which may be purposely designed to cause deterioration in order to make money. In the old days healthy teeth were a sign of good health, but nowadays tooth decay is the norm, WHY? Furthermore, due to Western influence, this very special plant which was also used for fencing gardens, is being cut down, thrown away and replaced with modern concrete walls, plus the Caribbean people have taken to using only toothbrush and toothpaste, thereby creating a Dentistry boom! This is yet another example of false economy, Western reverse psychology and the so-called great advancement in scientific technology.

Furthermore, people did not need complicated science to tell them what the various foods contained, because they trusted God. As my Guides explained;- *"just follow God's simple rules in your daily diet and you can be sure you'll receive sufficient balanced nutrients. God filled the earth with a beautiful array of colours to fill us with joy, calm, peace, balance, happiness, pleasure and health. Therefore, when cooking, simply choose a variety of different colourful foods to make up a complete meal, surround it with plenty of greenery (i.e. fresh raw vegetables).*

The colours of the rainbow are a good indicator of HARMONY"

They went on to talk about drug medicines. *"If you continuously feed people on drugs, then they'd become dependent and will end up taking all forms of drugs, whether legal or illegal. It is a vicious circle. The 'Western-Powers' have cleverly placed the entire world on a mass drugs programme, similar to that of organised crime (i.e. create a demand; feed the habit and then maintain the 'users' supplies).*

In the old days, you simply had to boil and cook food thoroughly, in order to kill germs and bacteria but no amount of boiling or thorough cooking could destroy the deadly chemicals that are being used today. It is so sad that man has lost sight of God, for the sake of greed."

Can Food Really Heal?

'Let thy Food be thy Medicine and thy Medicine be thy Food.'

(Hippocrates, one of the ancient fathers of medicine).

The answer to this important question is a resolute YES! Food can heal, repair, restore, re-balance, condition, maintain, control and sustain our bodies in the best of health, from birth to death. All that is required is to have an awareness of the nutritional content of foods (i.e proteins, carbohydrates, fats, sugars, vitamins and minerals), plus how to prepare them correctly, when to eat them and which are more digestible.

❀ Life Stage Re-balancing.

Every stage in our lives calls for re-assessment, in order to keep control and to maintain a healthy balance. We need to re-balance our daily diet according to our age, our body's metabolic rate (i.e. digestion) and lifestyle (i.e. energetic or lethargic). Food provides us with essential fuel and energy which our bodies use to keep us going. Hence, **energy intake** (food) versus **energy output** (exercise) is the key to balanced health and weight control. For example- babies, active children, adults and athletes, require a diet high in proteins, carbohydrates, fats, vitamins and minerals, to cater for their rapid growth, excessive energy and fast digestion. They quickly burn up these energy rich foods, leaving little or no reserves in-store and also need to eat a lot more to maintain a reserve for their continuous high energy output. Whereas children, adults or the elderly who have a lazy, lethargic or sedentary lifestyle, require a diet low in sugars, fats and carbohydrates but high in proteins, vitamins and minerals. Sugars and fats need to be reduced considerably, in order to compensate for their inactivity or lack of exercise. Otherwise, these food reserves will simply be stored in the body. Hence, such people soon become overweight because they do not exercise sufficiently to burn up their fat and starch reserves, so the pounds pile up. Furthermore, as we grow older our body's metabolic rate and energy levels slow down gradually, therefore, it requires foods which are easily digestible and in much smaller portions.

In the main;-

1. PROTEINS -
   are for muscle and bone development and are found in pulses, all meats, tofu and dairy products.

2. CARBOHYDRATES (starchy foods) -
   are for energy; found in bread, rice, potatoes, pasta, cereals, corn, cakes, wholegrain, wholemeal, wheat, flour, ground provisions, (such as yam, dasheen, eddoes, sweet potato, green banana, casava, plantain etc). Undigested carbohydrates turn into sugar which is dangerous for diabetics, therefore, they should control the amount they eat.

3. SUGARS -
   are for energy; found in honey, fruits, raw cane sugar, certain vegetables (sugar beet) and the herb stevia.

4. FATS -
   are for lubrication; protects organs and cells; found in oils, butter, margarine, cream, milk, egg yolks, nuts, meats, cheese.

5. MINERALS & VITAMINS -
   are for dilution or flushing out the system and to make 1,2,3,4 above, more efficient and are found in water, fruits, vegetables and herbs. Water in particular helps to purify the body.

❀ Digestible and Indigestible Foods.

Most people eat meat primarily for protein, but the tough muscles in meat (particularly red meats) are extremely difficult for our delicate stomachs to break down and digest properly. In fact, most of the time, the meat remains undigested and eventually rots in the gut, which leads to fermentation, indigestion, constipation and other stomach problems and sometimes long-term illness. Whereas, pulses and vegetables contains a much higher quality protein than meat and are easily and thoroughly digested. Milk and other dairy products contain high levels of animals fats and proteins which are also indigestible and should be avoided. Humans are the only creatures in the universe who continue to drink milk after weaning. Animals who are much stronger and fitter than we are, **do not,** proving that this practice is absolutely unnecessary. Mother's milk is important for the babies of both animals and humans (i.e. their own children). Therefore, animals milk are unnecessary for humans, especially as we do not know how the animal was reared. Whether or not it was sick, infected or had a contagious disease (like cancer, BSE, flu, tuberculosis) or fed on drugs etc; all of which can be transmitted to us through the animals milk and meat. Whereas, vegetable milks such as soya or coconut contain a richer source of the same nutrients (including Calcium) and are more digestible. However, animal milk is excellent for external use, to cleanse, nourish and moisturise our skins.

❀ Chronic Illness.

In the case of chronic illness, it is advisable to stop eating dairy products and meats (including fish and chicken) and go on a vegetarian/vegan diet, until fully recovered, or alternatively remove meat/dairy products from your diet altogether.

❀ My Personal Experience.

Soon after turning 45, I began gaining weight primarily because of spinal damage and also hormonal changes due to menopause. I was forced to stop my daily jogging and aerobic exercises, opting for swimming, yoga and weights instead. My normal exercise routine was drastically curtailed and of course, falling in love did not help either. Therefore, I needed to re-balance my eating habits to compensate. I reduced fats, dairy products, meats, carbohydrates, sugars, snacks and alcohol and cut my meal portions by half. Instead of using my normal size plate, I changed to a small tea plate. I also increased my in-take of water, fresh fruits and vegetables. On reflection with my conversations with Ma Henry; she said that as we grow older, our bodies need the minimum amount of food to sustain it. Eggs in particular become increasingly difficult to digest and the elderly should avoid them.

Now that I've passed 50, I'm beginning to follow my Guides 'vegan diet' by cutting out all forms of meat (red, white or fish) and dairy products, using pulses instead. This way I've found to be far more balanced, healing and most effective for improving digestion, weight control and general well-being. However, I still love meat and dairy products, so I have these as a once a week treat. Additionally, when I'm being really good, I 'fast' for 12 hours, once a week drinking water only. I believe that just as we need to relax and rest our body from stress, we also need to give it a break from eating. I cannot emphasize more the importance of drinking plenty water (at least 1 litre, boiled then cooled), herbal teas and eating lots of raw foods (vegetables, sprouted seeds, nuts, seeds and fruits) daily, to improve our general health.

I try to avoid alcohol, coffee, fast foods, snacks and refined processed foods (such as white sugar, white flour etc) and use wholefoods (such as brown bread, brown sugar, honey, wholemeals, wholegrains) as these are wholesome, nourishing and more filling. Moreover, 'organic' foods and products are best. I also try to exercise at least 4 to 6 times a week and have become interested in crystal healing and magnetic therapy to help balance my energy levels.

NB: It is necessary to become aware of the 'nutritional value of food' and its importance in maintaining, sustaining and controlling our health throughout our many life stages. It's equally important to become aware of our bodies and its changing cycles. We are all unique individuals, with different body types, needing different things to keep balanced. At the end of the day, life is to be enjoyed. So enjoy not only your food but also your life and try to keep both REAL!

Natural Foods

'Our best medicine'

Here is a short list of just some of the nutrients found in natural foods.

VITAMINS/ MINERALS	Found in these FOODS	Essential for a Healthy Body
Vitamin A	Oily fish, dairy foods, Liver margarine, green vegetables, yellow fruit, (peppers, pumpkin and carrots).	for growth, eyes, bones and healthy skin, hair.
Vitamin D	Sun light, oily fish, butter, margarine, eggs.	teeth, bones and nervous system.
Vitamin B1	Yeast, wheat germ, meat, soya beans, whole grain foods, green vegetables.	growth, conversion of carbohydrates into energy, nervous system, muscles.
Vitamin B2	Yeast, wheat germ, meat, soya beans, eggs and green - vegetables	growth, skin, mouth, eyes.
Vitamin B6	Yeast, wheat germ, meat, fish, wholemeal products, milk, cabbage, nuts.	Essential for body's use of protein, healthy skin, nervous system and muscle.
Vitamin B12	Liver, meat, eggs, Sardines.	nervous system and skin, body's use of protein, growth.
Biotin ('B'Group)	Liver, kidney, vegetables, nuts, oats, whole-wheat.	skin, nervous system and muscles.
Folic Acid ('B' Group)	Green vegetables, yeast.	for all growth, healthy blood, reproduction.

Niacin	Fish, liver, meat, poultry, wholegrains, peanuts green vegetables.	growth, healthy skin, digestion of carbohydrates, nervous system.
Vitamin C	Citrus fruits, other fruits, raw vegetables.	healthy cells, blood vessels, gums and teeth.
Vitamin E	Vegetable oils, wheat germ, wholemeal bread, egg-yolks, green vegetables, nuts.	heart, muscles, testes, uterus, blood adrenal and pituitary - glands.
Calcium	Milk and other dairy foods, green vegetables, soya milk	strong bones, nails & teeth.
Iron	Egg yolks, nuts, molasses, beans, oatmeal, dried fruit.	Essential for life and for the production of haemoglobin in red blood corpuscles which carries oxygen to the tissues.
Potassium	Dried fruits, green leafy vegetables, sunflower seeds, bananas, potatoes, avocados.	Works with sodium to regulate the body's water balance and to maintain the heart's rhythm.
Sodium	Salt, shellfish, carrots, beets, artichokes.	for growth; works with potassium.
Zinc	Wheat germ, brewers yeast, pumpkin seeds, eggs, non-fat dairy milk, shell fish.	Takes part in the formation of insulin and the development and maintenance of the reproductive organs.
Magnesium	Figs, yellow corn, nuts, seeds, dark green vegetables.	Bones. It works with calcium to maintain muscle function and a healthy nervous system. Important for converting blood sugar into energy.

Manganese	Nuts, green leafy vegetables, peas, beets, egg yolks, whole grain cereals.	Bone structure, digestion. Important for reproduction and central nervous system function.
Selenium	Wheat germ, bran, onions, tomatoes, broccoli, tuna fish.	antioxidant
Copper	Dried beans and fruits, peas, whole grain, prunes, shrimps and seafood.	converts the body's iron into haemoglobin, builds bones and red blood cells.
Phosphorous	Fish, poultry, meat, whole grain, eggs, nuts, seeds.	Present in every cell in the body, bone & teeth, essential for Kidneys.
Protein	Meats, fish, seafood, milk, cheese, eggs, tofu, pulses, (lentils, soya beans, kidney beans, butter beans, chick peas, pinto beans etc).	bones, hair, nervous system, skin, growth and muscles.
Carbohydrates	Wholegrain, wheat, barley maize, rice, bread, oats, flour, oat meal, millet, potatoes, cereals.	for digestion, fibre, general health and energy.

Another valuable book detailing the importance of eating 'live (raw) foods' is **Living Food for Health** by Dr Gillian McKeith. I came across this book in July 2000, whilst in my local Health Store, when my Spirit-Guide pointed it out and instructed me to buy it. Upon reading page 6, Dr McKeith writes, *"I am on a divine mission to share this essential information with as many people as possible for the good of civilisation. I believe that the spiritual purpose of our lives is to 'share' not to just* *receive for one's self alone."* I instantly recognised our connection. I personally recommend it as another valuable 'gift of life' which shows that we can really heal ourselves.

Although no one can guarantee total prevention from sickness, but our chances of prolonged health will be greatly improved by **what we eat.**

Modern Foods

'Chemical Abuse.'

The 'modern foods' today have been totally altered from its natural God-made state and changed to become either completely artificial or scientifically engineered/modified and are therefore **void of all energy**. Furthermore, modern farmers also use highly toxic chemical pesticides, fertilisers, hermicides and insecticides, which are absorbed into the natural foods whilst they grow. Although we are told to clean fresh fruits and vegetables before eating, this only removes some of the surface chemicals but you cannot remove what has penetrated into the food itself. The majority of us don't even bother to wash fresh fruits because they look so clean and natural when purchased. From time to time the dangerous over use or abuse of these chemicals are reported on the news as 'health warnings.'

For instance; in the 1980's, apples sprayed with a chemical called 'ALA' were found to cause cancer. It was banned in America but continued to be used in Britain.

In March 1997, apples sprayed with a chemical insecticide was said to cause a similar condition as the 'Gulf War Syndrome' which attacks the nervous system... causing 'the shakes.'

Now, just think of all the other foods including vegetables, cereal, grain, meats etc, in fact, everything we eat is being treated with an overdose of chemicals and other artificial synthetic substances.

My Guides went into great depth about the state of food and medicines in the world today and the madness of scientific technology, under the guise of progress. What continues to amaze me, is that whenever they talk about an issue; shortly afterwards the information is confirmed by experts, which is brought to my attention in various ways... either television, newspapers, books or whilst in conversation with others. Moreover, only half truths are generally revealed to the public, whereas my Guides always give a full, detailed picture. Here are some of these facts on foods and chemical abuse, to prove that we are being systematically poisoned.

Nothing we are eating, not even raw vegetables is doing us any good, except if it is farmed 'organically.' You can easily overdose on multivitamin tablets. For example; it is dangerous to take excess vitamin A tablets, which are used to prevent aging, wrinkles and promote healthy skin. Too much can cause headaches, hair loss, bone and joint pain and liver damage, plus pregnant women increase the risk of birth defects. Yet, avocados and pumpkins contain an abundance of natural vitamin A, which can be eaten to your heart's content. So-called artificial high fibre supplements put into foods like cereals and bread, can increase bowel cancer. An excess of vitamin B6, can cause irreversible nerve damage. Zinc tablets are taken to improve sexual performance and the immune system but too much can shrink red blood cells and impair rather than boost immunity. Sardines contain a massive amount of natural vitamin B12. Food manufacturers also remove the natural vitamins, then replace these with synthetic ones. Fruit juices are dried for easy transportation and long storage, after which water and synthetic vitamins are added to turn it back into juice, then they boldly advertise on the packaging 'with added vitamin C,' etc. Additionally, they include an abundance of artificial additives, preservatives, flavour enhancers etc, simply to assimilate taste, colour, flavour and to extend shelf life. None of these are designed to improve our health. WHY?

❈ Abuse of Pesticides.

In August 1996, I met an English gentleman who was an ex- farmer. He explained that the Government lays down rules and guidelines, stating the amount of pesticides farmers should use per acre of land. In most cases, farmers were ignorant of the dangers and often doubled or trebled the approved limits. One of his colleagues could not even read or write, much less to work out complicated quantities per acreage. No Government official monitored the use or abuse of these pesticides. Therefore, he was not surprised when in 1995, the Government declared that the quantities found in carrots were 25% higher than their approved limits and advised the public to peel, top and tail the carrots. In fact, the entire carrot crop should have been destroyed, because they are root vegetables and therefore absorbed the full strength of the chemicals in the ground. He went on to say that the only people who regularly visited farmers, were the pesticides sales representatives, who were only too happy to encourage more use, as this increased their sales. The same thing occurs in the Food Manufacturing Industries; there are Government guidelines, but no proper monitoring procedures or follow up controls to guarantee public safety.

In November 2000, a horrific meat scandal was uncovered. It was reported that tonnes of condemned meat (chicken) destined for pet-foods was being cleaned up and re-sold for human consumption to supermarkets and butchers all over Britain. Apart from being rotten, the meat also contained cancerous ulcers, high levels of antibiotics as well as other drugs. It was reported that this find was just the tip of the iceberg and was known to have been going on for well over ten years. The report also highlighted the total lack of monitoring by the Government Health Inspectors within the food industry. Giving way to suspicions that this practice was still active all over the United Kingdom. The thing I found most disturbing about this report was the fact that although the Government accepted that rotten food was not acceptable for human consumption, they have legalised its use in pet foods. I wonder just how long our nation of animal lovers have been (unknowingly) poisoning their pets through their food? The truth could be more frightening than we realise.

Now let us take the BSE (Mad Cows Disease) crisis, known to the Government for some 20 years and deliberately kept secret from the public. However, once this scandal was exposed, everyone focused on the diseased meat sold to the public, but no one considered the transmission of the disease through the cows milk. In 1996, it was reported that BSE could be transmitted through the blood of the diseased cow to their unborn calves and could also therefore be transmitted via infected pregnant women to their babies. Yet there were no discussion on the 'milk' transmission issue, because the country would lose too much money and jobs. So again, making money becomes more important than safe-guarding our health. My Spirit-Guides have been warning me to stop drinking milk for the past three years, but didn't say why, so I continued drinking it because I love a cup of tea. After a while I realised that my body would swell up when I drank too much, the same thing happens when I eat Chinese food, caused by the artificial flavour enhancer 'monosodium glutamate,' therefore, I'm allergic to something in the milk. I now only use 'organic, rice or soya milk' and have reduced my consumption drastically.

I've also noticed that old people in Britain suffer from 'the shakes.' For years the British Government has given pensioners 'free Beef' taken from their huge stock-pile of old frozen meat; BSE attacks the nervous system and causes the 'shakes?'

On 16th July 2000, the Government reported that the high incidence of CJD deaths amongst young people, could have been caused from infected baby foods and school meals eaten 20 years ago. However, children used to be given half a pint of 'free' school milk daily, (also Government approved). CJD is the human form of BSE caught from cows and sheep. CJD and BSE can incubate in both animals and humans for over 20 years before being detected. Farmers would not notice an infection until it has spread to many of the animals. In fear of losing money, farmers may not report infections until it becomes an epidemic. Farmers and Vets also treat infections with antibiotics, steroids and other powerful drugs, which simply suppress the illness and does not cure it. Therefore, proving that BSE and hundreds of other contagious infections and diseases like (foot & mouth, swine fever etc.) have been incubating in animals for years and the effects of this transfer to humans is now showing itself on a massive scale. Hence, the nation has become chronically sick (eg. CJD, cancer, tuberculosis, arthritis, inflammation, influenza, etc). Antibiotics and steroids, have not only destroyed our immune system but also the animals. Therefore, disease is now rife and out of control.

- Whatever is **God-made is dissoluble.** Hence once it dies, it easily breaks down and is naturally recycled back into the soil for enrichment. Therefore, the earth readily consumes it, leaving no left over waste.

- Whatever is **Man-made is indissoluble.** Hence impossible to break down; cannot be naturally recycled, therefore, the entire world is now overloaded with junk waste. Like the mountains of plastic piling up everywhere, impossible to destroy and can only be recycled by remaking even more junk-waste.

Talking about the plastic issue, did you know that this wonderful, light weight, cheap and convenient product, used in almost every food packaging, contains 'artificial synthetic Oestrogen,' which is released into the food from these packaging and causes cancer cells in the body to multiply rapidly? It is also the cause for the reduction in male sperm (i.e. infertility and impotence); reduced the size of their genitals and caused deformities. It has turned male fish into females and boys into hermaphrodites?

"What a Catastrophe!"

Whereas soya beans and yam contain natural oestrogen which is good for us, especially women during the menopause, as it replaces this important hormone and avoids the use of HRT... yet another drug.

Now! think of the millions of other legal, artificial drugs on the market given to us daily by doctors or purchased over the counter in Chemists, Pharmacies and Supermarkets for every type of ache, pain, cough, cold, flu, to prevent pregnancy, stress, skin problems, stomach upset, allergies, depression; to name just a few of our everyday problems. When you consider that in Britain alone there are approximately 56 million people, of which over three-quarters of the population are taking some kind of artificial drug every day; (hence over 50 million tablets per day), now multiply this by one year, then by the past fifty years, only then you could begin to see the huge problem we all face. Once we understand that everything we **take in** (i.e. eat daily), we also **let out** as waste daily (i.e. excrement and urine) which all goes back into the soil and water supply and eventually returns to us to be consumed in whatsoever we eat or drink.

"Whatever you put into the earth, it will yield itself back to you."

There is no other place for waste to be disposed but in the ground or in the atmosphere and its all recycled back to us.

This is only the tip of the iceberg, because we have not considered the development and dumping of nuclear and industrial waste in rivers, seas or buried underground. This proves that the Scientists are fully aware that their man-made inventions are dangerous and insoluble because they attempt to conceal them in reinforced concrete or thick metal castings, then try to bury them as deep into the ground as they could go. However, **the earth eventually devours whatever is put into it.** So, no matter how long it may take, these deadly poisons will be released one day onto future generations.

In 1998, dolphins and other marine animals in the Mediterranean sea were found with large cancerous tumours. Never before in history have these animals ever had cancer and Scientists claim that they don't know the cause, but the reasons are obvious. Many conscious doctors openly admit that 'Science has unwittingly exposed us to, chronic drug abuse' with a lethal mixture of chemical cocktails and that these drugs have dangerous side-effects; many are placebos just to counteract side-effects; whilst most simply suppress the illness rather than treat the condition. Many people have lost faith in their doctors because in some cases, the drugs had resulted in disability, permanent health damage, addiction and even death. For instance, antibiotics were once hailed as the wonder drug of the century, but continuous over-use has weakened our bodies to such an extent that they've become virtually ineffective. Therefore, major diseases (like Tuberculosis) once believed to have been cured, are now back in full force. Even hospitals have become breeding grounds for un-treatable deadly bacteria. Scientists have now woken up to the fact that they have come full circle and are faced with the same deadly diseases which existed for centuries, but this time round their ferocity is much greater because our bodies have become dependent on drugs to do its work and they have also destroyed our immune system. Therefore, we no longer have the ability to build up resistance, in which to fight off disease, in order to repair/heal ourselves. Unbelievably, these same Scientists are desperately experimenting to invent even stronger drugs, in the hope of preventing a much bigger epidemic. God only knows what would be the results of these new powerful drugs. We are already hearing about mutations in frogs... born with three eyes and missing limbs. My Guides also commented on the new impotency drug 'Viagra.' There are many safe, herbal plants available for this condition. Viagra makes a nonsense of so called Government medical license, legislation or approval, as it by-passed all laws by creating an open black market through the internet. The huge increase in male impotency caused by the same scientific man-made inventions was a well known fact to the scientific world and therefore VIAGRA was a welcomed invention to stem man's fears of losing his manhood or masculinity; even though they know there would be possible dangerous side-effects. In the long-term, Viagra's powerful potency could lead to permanent impotency. Modern man prefers speedy results. *"The results of high speed leads to dead ends."*

❁ Genetically Modified Plants: - *(Dead Foods).*

Taking this impotency issue deeper. Did you know that the genetic Scientists have removed the reproductive genes (i.e. the sex organs), from the seeds, so that these plants would not be able to produce 'fertile seeds' for cultivation? Therefore, by removing the natural 'life force' in the genetically engineered plants, you will be eating **dead infertile foods.** The long term health implications are obvious. Again, this has been done solely to make more money for the genetic companies. Natural plants produce fertile seeds, which farmers use to cultivate new crops every season. So re-planting costs them nothing. The genetic companies have patented their dead seeds, so that farmers will be forced to buy these seeds every season, hence making food more expensive.

  ✿ **Legal Drug Addicts**:- (*Substance Abuse*).

Many over the counter drugs such as paracetamol, co-codamol, ibuprofen, aspirin, codeine based medicines, cold remedies and even cough sweets are highly addictive and are part of a hidden epidemic of substance abuse. It was reported, that by the end of the year 2000, the number of 'over the counter drug-addicts' will be on par with heroin addicts. People assume that these medicines are safe and harmless because they are available in shops. Eight high strength codeine tablets taken daily, produces the same amount of morphine as for a heroin addict. Continuous use of cold remedies can lead to permanent liver, pancreas and gall bladder damage or death. Six paracetamols taken daily for ten days can make you an addict. To relieve the pain in my spine, my doctor prescribed (high-strength) co-proxamol daily for the rest of my life, without informing me that this was highly addictive and could cause long-term internal damage. There are millions of people addicted to pain-killers and they don't know it. These drugs are called NSAIDs (non-steroidal anti-inflammatory drugs). The chances of sustaining a major gastro-intestinal complication from NSAID treatment starts almost immediately after swallowing the first pill. In the UK, this drug alone is killing 2000-4000 people and damaging countless others every year. The four biggest killers in US and UK hospitals are heart disease, cancer, lung disease and prescription drugs... 1,700,000 prescriptions are issued daily in the UK.

For decades, Third World countries have been secretly used as guinea pigs for the Western world, to test the results and side-effect of their drugs and vaccines. So when doctors claim that millions of tests have been conducted to prove the efficacy and safety, you should request; (a). the exact records; (b). in which countries; (c). on which race and (d). what treatment was given to those who had side-effects. It would provide interesting reading to learn how many people have suffered, in order to benefit Western countries scientific advancement.

On 4th November 1997, the British Medical Association openly admitted on television that doctors had been over prescribing antibiotics, which have seriously damaged our immune system and have become ineffective. Medical practitioners were advised to stop prescribing these for general use and encouraged people to return to natural remedies to overcome disease. This was a welcomed turn around for the future.

As my Guides explained;-

> *"Modern Scientists are not concerned with the long-term damaging effects; they simply want to prove that Science is essential for life, under the disguise that it is necessary to provide for a growing world population; pest control, improved health-care and cheap convenient foods. But the truth is, that it is all being done purely for the commercial gain (WEALTH) of the Producers and Providers. Hence, your health has never been taken into consideration in their money making evaluation or planned scheme of deception."*

It is fearful that in less than 100 years, since the introduction of these artificial ingredients, that the younger generation have been brainwashed into believing that these are **natural** and have become dependant on them. Therefore, in order to restore the balance, re-education based on the TRUTH is vital, especially in the light of increasing behavioural problems and social breakdown.

The Truth

'Reversing the process - consumer power.'

Unfortunately, man's greed for wealth, control and power has now taken precedence and is destroying God's beautifully balanced paradise. This imbalance is purposely designed to benefit a few through the sustained suffering of the majority. Their desire for wealth and power has also infiltrated the top power-stratas of society (i.e. Governments and other decision making Authorities), so that policies are made in their favour (i.e. legalised). Therefore, any effort to change these policies becomes extremely difficult, if not altogether impossible.

"Man-made MUST NEVER PREVAIL over God-MADE."

When 'Scientists and the Powers that be' attempt to play God with their re-inventions, one always find double standards, with no moral or ethical principles involved (i.e. reckless). However, we as consumers still collectively hold the most powerful fighting weapon... MONEY. Therefore, if you demand that they **respect your health** as much as they **respect your money** and refuse to buy anything which is artificially produced or tampered with, then you'd soon find that policies would quickly change in your favour, because these people only **respect their wealth.** So, you must reverse the process and affect what they value most, 'your money.'

❀ **PROFITS before HEALTH & SAFETY;-** *(Experiments).*

The food and drug industries are continuously conducting experiments which have no regards for consumer health. These Scientists are employed solely to create artificial substances, simply to suppress illness and or extend shelf life. On the other hand, the same amount of effort or finance is not being employed to conduct equally extensive medical research, to show the long-term results or possible dangerous side-effects. These Scientists are obsessed with preventing **decay** (or rotting).

Here again, this is not for the benefit of your health but for making more money, because if a product (fresh or processed) could last longer than its natural life span then:-

(a) the 'sell by date' would be extended.

(b) they would add some artificial vitamin supplements.

(c) tell you how good it is for your health and well being.

(d) reduce the price to entice you to buy. Hence a new increased Mass-Market of cheap 'fad-filled' foods is thus established.

"The end justified their means."

Initially, the experiments started with -

1. **'Synthetic drugs'** for medicine, then they moved onto -

2. **'Artificial ingredients'** for farming and food processing.

3. **'Irradiation'** for fresh fruits and vegetables.

4. and has now progressed onto **'Genetic engineering/ modification (GM)'** for all natural foods.

Not satisfied with just adding chemicals to natural-foods or creating substitutes, they now want to change the genetic structure of natural foods, so that it looks and tastes the same but **will last longer** than the real thing. Thereby taking their **decay obsession** a stage further. Their replications are so good, that you cannot differentiate the 'natural' from the 'un-natural.' These scientific experiments cost the industries billions every year, which in turn is included in the price you pay for their products. It would take many years for them to recover the cost, which goes to show how long they plan to keep you fooled. It also makes it easy to identify the culprits, because it is only the large wealthy industries, who would be able to afford such huge experimental costs.

The real danger is that **every natural food** on this planet, has already been 'genetically engineered/modified' and ready to be secretly placed on the shelves for you to buy UNAWARES.

PEOPLE BE WARNED!

"Modern Science has put the world on a mass-human experiment as Corporate Guinea-pigs.

- *You are on a scientific universal holocaust.*

- *Your health is being ransomed, hence your LIFE is at risk.*

- *Therefore, you can no longer afford to remain complacent or trust your Leaders. You must try and stop this abuse from going any further and prevent these dangerous irreversible processes."*

The following month, after receiving these explanations, an American Scientist involved in such experiments, visited Britain in July 1996 to lobby Parliament, in an effort to stop the sale of 'genetically modified foods,' because he feared that insufficient research had been conducted to ensure their safety or serious long-term implications. A month later, Government Scientists (the same ones who claimed that mad-cows disease (BSE) would not endanger humans) approved genetically modified 'soya beans' and 'tinned tomatoes' from America, stating that because they had not altered the natural shape or appearance of the food, there was no need to include the words, **GENETICALLY ENGINEERED /MODIFIED or ALTERED** on the product label. These products were then quietly placed on the supermarket shelves. This also said a lot about our so called 'consumer rights, protection and choice.'

Furthermore, America later threatened a world trade war, if Europe rejected their genetically modified 'maize,' as it involved billions of dollars in annual revenue (i.e. money). Therefore, if countries would be blackmailed or held to ransom in this way, then what would they be prepared to do next? For the sake of making money and in fear of creating a trade war, Europe would bow to America's (bullying) demands. Although European Scientists had voiced grave concerns about its long-term safety, British Scientists approved genetically modified 'maize' and its import from America commenced in November 1996. Supermarkets immediately printed free customer information leaflets, declaring its safety and why there was no need to record it on food labels.

It is important to note that 'maize' is an essential ingredient used in animal feed, breakfast cereals, margarine, snacks, baking and brewing products and many other foods. Soya beans are the most widely used bean in Vegan, Vegetarian and Chinese Cuisine and the best substitute for meat. Therefore, its extremely valuable with an enormous captive market. Little is left to the imagination or to work out **why** these were the first 'genetically modified' products to be placed on the market. One also has to question **why** Scientists decided to mix 'genetically altered soya bean with the naturally grown variety?' If they were so confident that these are better for us, then why not keep them separate and clearly labelled, to enable us to choose. Concerned about this strategy, I called several organic Food Wholesalers and Retailers to ask if they could guarantee 100% natural organic supplies in the future. They all replied that they couldn't, because no one could differentiate the 'natural organic from the genetically altered ones.' They also voiced fears for the future and confirmed that already consumer choice was no longer a reality, as everything was being controlled by the Genetic Scientists and their pay masters (i.e. the large industries) but their greatest fear was that natural organically grown foods would eventually be wiped out from the earth.

It is a well known medical fact, that over-exposure to radiation causes cancer, miscarriages, still births, premature births, thyroid and liver problems. The example of the Russian (Chernobyl) nuclear plant disaster in the 1980's, ten years later, the side-effects from the radioactive fall-out are still being felt all over Europe. Scientists are still unable to determine how long it would take to finally clear up. To date, the worst example of radiation, was the first nuclear bomb explosion in Japan (over fifty years ago), where the people and their off spring are still experiencing the deadly side-effects. Therefore, what could 'irradiated foods' be doing to us (and our unborn children), especially if eaten daily? There are many 'irradiated foods' on the shelves but we are kept unawares because it is not declared on the labels.

Taking this a stage further; I've also learnt that the Caribbean and other 'third world' countries, are dumping grounds for certain banned Western substances; such as dangerous medical drugs, food additives, chemical fertilisers, pesticides, insecticides, nuclear waste etc. Once proven too deadly and banned from use in the West, (i.e. become illegal) instead of destroying them and stopping their manufacture; these are sold to the third world for use as medicines, food additives, plant fertilisers, pest control etc. Therefore, Western multi-national companies have found another lucrative market. There are little or no regulations in these countries, so they are open to exploitation.

Not surprisingly, the Caribbean people who used to be in excellent health have deteriorated, mirroring exactly the poor state of health as in the West... chronic diabetes, cancer, asthma, inflammation, senility, aches and pains, drug addiction, etc. All because of their desire to imitate the so-called progressive, wealthy, West and modelling their lives on them to such an extent, that they have abandoned their traditional values (natural foods, home cooking and herbal remedies) and have also developed the new commercial culture of Western fast foods chains. The West must stop transporting their poisons overseas, in order to safe-guard the entire world from their contamination. However, the third world countries are also controlled by greedy, ruthless men, who would sell their people's soul for a piece of silver to line their own pockets.

Nevertheless, food and pollution in the Caribbean have not reached epidemic proportions as in the West because of extreme poverty they have remained mainly organic. Thank God, they cannot afford to buy all of the expensive drugs on offer. One of my Caribbean friends who also lives in Britain, suffers from an acute fruit allergic reaction but loves fruits and has to take antidote tablets. She decided to go on a Caribbean holiday and asked the doctor for an extra supply of the antidote tablets, as she planned to eat home-grown fruits. To her surprise, the doctor revealed that she could eat any amount of Caribbean fruits because they didn't contain the artificial chemicals used in Europe. She was not allergic to the fruits itself but to the chemicals used in growing and spraying. She had no reaction to the fruits.

Many Doctors are advocating a return to 'natural traditional foods and medicines,' such as simple hot-toddies for colds, which have been proven to be just as effective as the artificial substitutes but more importantly they are safe and harmless to us and to the environment.

In 1997, the international environmental group GREENPEACE organised a campaign called 'The Genetic Experiment-XPOSE' and produced a complete consumer information pack detailing the long-term horrors of this experiment. Since then, many leading experts in the genetic field have written books against the process and are advising caution, that this form of manipulation would affect our entire eco-system.

On 4th August 1998, the British Government banned genetically modified foods from the kitchens and restaurants of the Houses of Parliament, because of the uncertainty of its unknown health risks but approved it for sale in supermarkets to the general public.

On 6th September 1998, Sky Television News reported that genetically modified ingredients had been in 60% of the food chain mainly in processed foods since 1996, unknown to us.

In May 2000, it was reported that farmers in Britain, Sweden, Germany and France unwittingly planted and harvested 'oil seed rape' which was contaminated with genetically modified seeds, imported from Canada for sowing in Europe. It ended up in products on the supermarket shelves... such as canola oil, chocolate, margarine, ice cream, salad cream and others. About 500 farms in Britain sowed more than 13,000 hectares of land. The Ministry of Agriculture refused to order the destruction of these crops because they said that it was not a threat to human health or the environment. That very month, it was also reported that pollen from genetically modified crops were found in honey. Followed by Prince Charles' lecture (broadcast on BBC Radio) voicing his fears on the potential disastrous consequences of genetically modified foods and cloning, stated *"the relentless rush into genetic engineering means literally nothing is held sacred anymore and scientists are treating the world as a giant laboratory."* He questioned the resources being poured into GM technology and called for investment into traditional agriculture instead. By the end of May, Genetic Scientists reported that they were looking at cloning animals with human organs for use in human transplants.

On 14th June 2000, the Government confirmed that genetically modified plants cross pollinated with traditional plants and were therefore contaminating the environment. When you consider that nearly all American farms consists of genetically modified crops and the thousands of other farms around the world which have been conducting secret GM experimental testing for many years, now you can begin to contemplate what Scientists, Drug Companies and our Governments have 'consciously and deliberately' been doing to us for the sake of 'making MONEY!' They are playing with our lives, using psychological games to fool us on the supposed health benefits, whilst keeping the long-term dangerous side-effects to themselves. This is not scare mongering, **it is fact!**

❄ Gene Replacement Therapy.

On 26th June 2000, Sky Television News reported that U.S. and UK Scientists claimed that they had broken **the human genetic DNA code** (our life blueprint), which paves the way for the development of new 'genetic drugs' to cure heart disease, cancer, diabetes and other genetic conditions. These new genetic drugs would replace the present drug medication and requires a further 100 years research. The Genetic Scientists are financed by the same international pharmaceutical drug companies, involved in the development of drug medication and who 100 years ago made the same ambitious claims that these drugs would cure the same conditions. However, other Scientists voiced great fears of the dangers this new technology could lead to.

Two years earlier, on 14th June 1998, CNN Satellite Television interviewed an American gentleman named Jeremy Rifkin (author of The Biotic Technology Century) who spoke at length about the pros and cons of genetic engineering. He saw clear advantages and disadvantages but was disturbed about the actual people in control of this technology. I found this discussion well researched and balanced. His comments were as follows:-

> *"**GENES** are the building blocks of life; change the gene and they are altering LIFE from it's original/natural state, which is irreversible. Therefore, genetic engineering is changing the actual blue-print of man-kind and the environment. The result being that a handful of men would be able to dictate the future of all living species, which would completely alter our environment. These global commercial companies intend to control and dominate the world with a new unprecedented power called genetic commerce. They have already secured patents on everything including human life (i.e. cloning) which in the past was illegal. **This patent means that they now own the legal rights to life itself.** They have already inter-mixed different animal genes and created completely new breeds (i.e. half goat and half sheep). They are free to create a new-super race who would belong only to the new super-rich elite. Genes environmental pollution would be far worse than petro-chemical and all the other pollutants presently in existence. People must be informed and made fully aware of the danger this technology could lead to, as well as, the potential benefits in eradicating disease etc. Foods and medicines must be clearly labelled, so that people can be given the right to choose."*

To be informed, we all need to re-educate ourselves on the true facts, rather than accept our Leaders or the Scientists word, since they themselves do not know. Let us not forget that it was Scientists who provided Adolph Hitler with scientific proof, based on their own ideological fantasy of a German master race, which brought about the establishment of the Nazi party. We also know what he did to eradicate people he termed as inferior. The attempted annihilation of the African race through slavery, apartheid and racism, is another case in point.

So many other human atrocities are evident of the levels of cruelty man can subject any race, group or individual to. It also shows the effective skills of indoctrination to desensitise human feelings, causing people to hate instead of love. Genetics could create 'race supremacy' in a different form but with the same intent to rule, control and dominate with possibly even worse consequences.

At the end of the day, even our 'belief in God' could eventually be totally destroyed and replaced with the new concept of 'man-made man' (i.e. our new creator and the birth of Soul-less beings or clones without conscience). One can now begin to imagine what destructive forces are in control of this new manipulative game called 'the new age of Scientific Technology.'

I personally fear that the **hand of evil** is taking charge of the universe, because there has always only been one negative power - (i.e. EVIL) determined to overthrow God and all of HIS creations.

I faithfully believe that 'God is love' and as such, LOVE is never harmful, painful, deceitful, fearful, destructive, intimidating, secretive, controlling or damaging in any way.

Hence, I see -

EVIL in its best disguise, fooling us into believing that all of its works are for our benefit. EVIL is not a beast with horns but he/she lives and walks amongst us, as a good friend and or even a family member.

This is my belief, it's up to you to make up your own mind as to how you wish to look at it and or, what you choose to do about it.

As my Spirit-Guides explained;-

> *"Scientists have over stepped the **rules of creation** (i.e. things should be created for your benefit and not for your destruction). Therefore, 'Science and Vanity' have polluted the world and is a direct result of the damage to the ozone (global warming);- acid rain, junk waste, ill-health and the like."*

There is absolutely no need to produce anything artificially, as all the natural ingredients are available in abundance. There is also nothing wrong in improving technology in order to make life easy and medicine more effective. However, if Scientists would utilise their valuable energies and intelligence, by working in harmony with nature, rather than working against it, then good health will be restored and maintained. It is the only viable and economical alternative.

The Ultimate Proof

❀ November 2000.

As if to provide me with the ultimate proof, just as this book was ready for printing, the results of an extensive 3 year report on the **British BSE crisis** by Lord Phillips was published and its findings broadcast to the nation.

The report accused the Government and their Scientific Advisors of **complacency, incompetence and betrayal of the nations' trust**. Over the years, Government Ministers stood firmly behind their Scientific Advisors, convincing people that beef was safe and posed no threat to human health. The report confirmed that this was a mistake;- their advice was unreliable and they also withheld the truth.

It questioned a conflict of interest by the 'Ministry of Agriculture, Fishery and Food' who favoured the big industries instead of protecting consumer health and safety. It confirmed that money was put before the people's health and safety. Bear in mind, that it was these Scientists who originally advised the Government to change animal feeding policy (in order to provide us with 'cheap food') which was the actual cause of the BSE disease. Apart from trying to protect their profession, they also feared destroying the entire beef industry, therefore, they withheld the full truth.

So finally after 77 CJD deaths; the slaughter of millions of cows and the bankruptcy of thousands of farmers, the report forced both the Government and their Scientists to come clean with the truth... mainly because the BSE crisis has become a national epidemic which may destroy hundreds or even millions more lives. There is no cure or treatment in sight. CJD is an excruciatingly devastating and fatal disease. One can only imagine the pain and trauma both the sufferers and carers have had to endure. Before this report, the Government refused to accept responsibility or pay compensation because of the Scientists persistent denials.

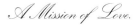

The Government then set up 'The Independent Food Standards Agency' to protect consumer interest... *(we hope);* plus a compensation scheme for sufferers and carers; and promises a 'new open policy' to inform the nation of the full truth in future.

This is all well and good, but what about 'GM foods' brought about by the same Scientific Advisors, currently contaminating the entire world and with yet unknown consequences to our health? Can we trust their advice on this technology? This invention is also to provide us with 'cheap food.' Can we afford to wait or should it be stopped now? We should also question the stifling of complementary medicines in favour of pharmaceutical drugs.

By mid 2000, the worlds' weather pattern changed significantly. For the first time in over 50 years, Britain experienced continuous rainfall and massive floods. This pattern was also being experienced in Europe, India, Africa, Australia and the Americas. The words 'Global Warming' and 'Ozone layer damage' resurfaced as the general topic of conversation. Environmentalists continue to press world-leaders to reduce environmental pollution, as the world has reached a state of crisis.

The price for unknown scientific experiments is way too high, because we are paying for it with our lives

---

Plan of Action

'as suggested by my Spirit-Guides in 1996.'

The list of natural goodness found in traditionally grown 'organic foods' are endless and have been used safely and successfully since the beginning of time to maintain fit, healthy and strong bodies. There is adequate medical research which proves the age old knowledge that natural foods help the body to combat disease and are better for you but the Scientists always try to undermined these truths to suit their purpose. Therefore, in order to protect, as well as, take responsibility for your own health, you should demand that those who are in charge of your foods and medicines provide **clear** and **accurate** information, based on true facts, so that you can choose what you wish to buy or consume.

For instance;-

1. **NATURAL FOODS and REMEDIES.**
   should be legally re-named 'natural organic foods and natural remedies.'

2. **ARTIFICIAL DRUG MEDICINES.**
   should be re-named 'artificial drugs' (with serious health warnings and side-effects attached to them).

3. **ALL ARTIFICIAL FOODS & INGREDIENTS.**
   should be legally banned or re-named 'artificial foods,' (with health warnings attached to them).

4. **FOOD DEFINITIONS.**

   (a). <u>LABELS</u>: all foods whether fresh or processed, should be clearly and accurately labelled.

(b).   NATURAL ORGANIC FOODS: where all the ingredients in the product are organic and the manufacturers have not included anything artificial in the processing operations.

(c).   NATURAL/ARTIFICIAL FOODS: where all the ingredients are not organic but grown traditionally (i.e. conventionally farmed) and the manufacturer has not included anything artificial in the processing.

(d).   ARTIFICIAL FOODS: where all the ingredients derived from artificial, synthetic, chemical, irradiated or genetically modified substances.

(e).   NUTRITIONAL CONTENT LISTING: should only be allowed on 'natural organic foods' and banned from 'artificial foods,' because they are of no benefit or value to your health.

5.   **HEALTH-EDUCATION**: *(i.e. health-care, food, cookery, medicine).*

Children from day one, are taught by their parents to speak the truth and not to tell lies. This training should not conflict when they move into the educational system. Health Education should be a vital part of the school's curriculum; like the alphabet, reading, writing and arithmetic, science, languages etc. Children are the future parents and consumers and should be prepared for such important responsibilities, by learning all the lessons of life and on how to take proper care of themselves and future families; on the same level as they are prepared for careers. If that responsibility is taught from young (e.g. shown the damaging side-effects of alcohol, cigarettes, designer/ prescribed drugs; artificial /synthetic ingredients in food, the reasons for their inventions and the effects on the foods, body and environment; the importance of natural traditional foods, their essential nutrients, how to prepare/cook them correctly; the miracles of surgery, safe self-help traditional remedies; respecting the environment; pollution and its far reaching effects on their health; alternative therapies; the value of exercise, relaxation, meditation etc). By providing children with a rounded education, they'd learn to take care of themselves at an early age and more importantly, they'd be in a better position to question Governments, Drug Companies, Doctors, Therapists or Food Manufacturers, as well as, make responsible choices in adulthood. Just as they have a **right to choose** their careers, livelihood and lifestyle, they have an equal **right to choose** their health-care and quality of life. In other words, it is their lives and should be given all the right tools to maintain it in good order.

By educating them on the nutritional values in natural foods and traditional remedies; how these could be used effectively to prevent illness, would encourage **conscious choice** between the natural and un-natural.

6.   **CRIMINAL OFFENCE.**

   (a)   <u>FOOD PRODUCERS</u>: *(i.e. from Governments, Scientists, Chemical companies, Farmers to Manufacturers).*

   or.

   (b)   <u>MEDICAL PROVIDERS</u>: *(i.e. from Governments, Doctors, Alternative Therapists and Drug Companies).*

   It should be made a criminal offence if any of the above gives the consumer anything which endangers or damages their health physically or mentally.

'The Producers & Providers' should have to prove beyond reasonable doubt, that they were unaware of the danger and believed their product to be safe. If proved otherwise, the Courts should fine or even imprison them; ban their products and compensate the consumer. This would force 'Producers' & 'Providers' to study the side-effects of any artificial ingredients or drugs they use in food and medicine. For instance; when the artificial yellow colouring ingredient was found to cause hyper-activity in children; the Government who approved it; the Drugs Company who produced it and the Manufacturer who use it - should have all been charged, as well as, the parents adequately compensated for the physical damage caused to their children and the misery suffered. The consumer should have the **RIGHT to SUE**. However, if the information is available to consumers and they choose to use it, then they'd have **NO RIGHT to SUE** for compensation. The 'Producers & Providers' must be made legally responsible for what they produce for people to consume. If any refused to accept this commitment, then they should be reported and their products banned from public sale globally.

"Justice must be seen to be done, enforced and not assumed."

7. MEDICAL TREATMENT.

(a) Doctors should advise patients not only on the proper use of the medicine but also on the known or possible side-effects, as well as, the alternative natural remedies or treatments available for the same condition.

(b)   <u>NATURAL REMEDIES and TREATMENTS</u>:

Should be researched, approved, recognised and encouraged. There is absolutely no reason why 'natural and un-natural products' (i.e. foods, remedies and drug medicines) cannot be made available (side-by-side) to enable everyone to choose. The only reason it's being discouraged, is because the 'Providers & Producers' are afraid of loosing the enormous amount of money they are making, by keeping you in ignorance and fed on their lies.

"It is profitable to keep the majority - poor, ignorant and sick, rather than healthy."

God's Anger

God's ANGER

Shortly after I was given these instructions; God spoke to me saying;-

"I will not destroy the world again

for the sake of the INNOCENT,

I will keep MY Promise."

"Man is abusing your free-will for money. **Genetic Engineering is the final/fatal menace**. *I'm tired of seeing my children ABUSED."*

HE went on;-

"Would a father who truly love his children, ever give them anything, which he knows would harm them?

Would a mother deliberately feed her children with poison?

NO! not if they truly loved them.

Man's greed is devouring the EARTH.

The universe was not created as a temporary experimental (short-term) measure but to last throughout eternity. Therefore, you are called to protect and preserve it."

I've never heard such fierce anger, pain or rage in my entire life, yet I felt no fear because HIS anger was not directed at me.

It was after this, that God instructed me to establish the mission - **The Celebration of Life,** stating that HE would continue to respect HIS children's 'free-will and choice.'

I then instantly became fully aware as to -

why I was placed in the Food Industry;

why I'd been in such positions of privilege, suffering and strife;

why I'd been so bold in attacking those in Authority;

why my Guides had been feeding me with such specific information and instructions and

why my Grandmother repeatedly told me that, *"an obedient child is a blessed child."* At long last, I realised that it was for this end, I was sent to serve. The years of anguish flashed through my mind, yet I felt no pain but totally refreshed, at peace, calm and quiet. I meditated for days in silent prayer, giving thanks to all my Guides, especially for their tremendous patience and love, because many times I became stubborn and refused to do as I was told. It was always my dream to try and make the world a better place but I didn't realise that God's work involved so much fighting; disappointment and effort. As a child, my Grandmother used to say, *"you must always fight a good fight but never give up on God."*

─ *God's Warning & Calling.* ─

God's Warning & Calling

On 4th September 1999 God revealed.

"No one is naturally EVIL,
but everyone can be influenced by EVIL."

*"You are all equally exposed to **Good** or **Evil**, both in 'thoughts and in deeds.' Therefore, Scientists are not evil men but men influenced by the 'forces of evil.' Initially, when they first thought of becoming Scientists, it started with a passionate, loving desire to do good but over the passage of time, lost their way when their God-given creative talents became embroiled with over inflated egos, which gave rise to stubborn arrogance.*

*Hence, they began playing with nature, leaving the unknown factors to speculation instead of certainty. When you look back at the many Scientific inventions over the past 100 years which were originally intended to be of benefit but in hindsight, the long-term results today have shown that they were wrong to try to re-invent nature, by creating their man-made synthetic materials because instead of being beneficial, it has turned out to be damaging. However, their inflated egos prevent them from admitting the truth, even when it can be clearly seen by everyone else. Academic intelligence can not vindicate TRUTH or FACT. It's either good or bad, right or wrong, there are no in-betweens to cover up lies. The unknown factors of genetics in 50 years time will have the same catastrophic end result but the devastation would be a thousand times greater on people, animals and the environment. 'An irreversible process which can only be corrected by prevention.' Therefore, if people refused to buy or use it, then it would be pointless producing it. It's time for ordinary people to take action and stop their Leaders from taking them down this certain road of self-destruction. **BE WARNED,** the 'forces-of-evil' are deceitful, cunning, sly, cruel and corrupt. So do not TRUST your leaders words but **demand clear, visual evidence and proof, that they have totally destroyed this technology. All such fields should be uprooted and burnt to ashes and not be buried alive.** Elect your own* *independent investigators to police the extermination. Remain **vigilant**, alert and mindful of this dangerous experience, to ensure that it never again raises its destructive head in the future. **BE WARNED**, in future, work with the laws of nature and rest assured that the universal balance will begin to return by the next millennium... the year 3000. **The earth's powerful life energies can only be restored by stopping genetic engineering and other man-made contamination.** My children, your life is in your own hands, LOVE yourself and protect your future generations."*

"Remember - WISDOM is SIMPLICITY."

❀ REFLECTIONS.

After this message, I quietly reflected on the future and asked God to explain, so that people would not panic or that manufacturers and farmers would not fear loosing their livelihood. God said;-

"the main action now is the complete ban, prevention and extermination of genetic crops and experimentation. Farmers and Manufacturers should gradually introduce organic materials into their production, so that eventually, (in time) the world would go back to nature (i.e. soil, food, medicines). This way, prices would stabilise and in the long-term, organic foods and natural medicines would again become the norm and therefore be affordable. Only then:-

> *Life and **health will** be restored.*
>
> *Sickness will begin to become a thing of the past.*
>
> *Spiritual energies will be increased."*

With hindsight, I noticed that in the case of Zara's recovery, because I was living on State-welfare, I could not afford to buy all organic foods. My Guides instructed me to buy the basic essentials such as potatoes, carrots, onions and whatever else I could afford, all the other foods were conventionally grown.

Furthermore, once you've become 'consciously aware' and really understand that God and the Spirit-Guides are there to help you, then you'll be amazed with the amount you can learn, if you are able to open yourself to the universe.

The entire universe, including ourselves are SACRED.

Health 2000
Mission Statements

<u>**HEALTH**</u> *(good or bad)* has;-

NO *Colour*

NO *Age*

NO *Gender*

NO *Status*

NO *Religion*

NO *Ego*

LIFE is our most valuable and precious **FREE GIFT.** 'The Quality of Life' is our 'treasure trove'

GOOD HEALTH is the essential ingredient to attain Enjoyment and the Fullness of **LIFE**

"If you truly **'LOVE'** yourself, your family and your friends, you'd never allow anyone to endanger yours or their Health.

Their lives are in your hands.

So let us all join hands and prove that the **power of love** will always **PREVAIL**"

There should be **NO** Secrecy, **NO** Compromise, **NO** Bias,

NO Hidden Agendas, **NO** Hypocrisy, **NO** Double Standards

where our **HEALTH** is concerned.

SPIRITUALITY

413.

BOOK TWO.

CHAPTER V.

Spirituality.

• LESSONS OF LIFE.

'ORISHUA' is the mystical 7th Star (Angel) sent to deliver God's messages for the 21st. Century.

Her spirit-name 'ORISHUA' indicates her direct link and closeness to God... HIS name in the African language is 'ORISHA.' She's connected to the '7 Sister Stars'... in ancient times lawyers and mystics 'swore an oath of truth' in her name. Her Star was a sign to farmers indicating the correct time for ploughing. She's associated with 'Venus' *the Goddess of love* and was once an Egyptian High Priestess. She is known as the one who walks in both worlds.

"Our Father patiently awaits your awakening from this state of juvenile delinquent adolescence, into your higher state of spiritual maturity."

Throughout the ages, as well as, in the many Bible stories, it shows that from time to time God chooses individuals to reveal certain messages to the world or to do specific works known as 'missions.' It's apparent that their own life experiences are always used as an example and proven testimony of the 'power of love through conscious faith in God' to triumph over adversity.

"Love reigns Supreme."

However, we are all sent to serve a special purpose, no matter how big or small (for each is of equal importance) but somehow many of us loose our way, hence fail to achieve or accomplish the task. In other words, we loose our 'sense of purpose.'

- Nowadays many people believe that the Bible is a historical record predicting world events up to the 'book of Revelations,' which tells of great disasters and destruction. Furthermore, it states that God would send **seven Angels** (or Stars) to warn and prepare the world for CHANGE and also of the devil's defeat.

- Others believe that Jesus would return again in the year 2000 or 2003.

- There are those who believe that only 144,000 people from their religion or race would be saved.

- Yet there are millions who speak to Angels everyday or are touched by a miracle and most don't even recognise it.

- There are also non-believers and many devil worshippers.

- Then there are others who are intuitive, in touch with their inner-selves; hear divine voices and also receives spiritual guidance. Yet, the majority have lost the ability to tune into their Spirit-self (or inner consciousness), because it is no longer common practice or accepted as the norm. Hence, although many people still hear voices, most are invariably called schizophrenic (i.e. mentally disturbed).

- Furthermore, there are many different types of religious leaders, spiritualists, astrologers, clairvoyants, psychics, fortune tellers, card readers, gurus, witches, witch doctors, shamen, pagans, cults etc. Each with their own philosophical and theological beliefs, re-writing the 'original word,' (i.e. THE TRUTH) to their own interpretations, hence creating several personalised versions of the 'Laws of God.'

- The world has become so confused that some people don't even know what to believe and remain sceptical.

Nevertheless, there is an overall awareness that a 'higher consciousness or divine order' exists, which is far beyond our physical-selves and which also defies reason, logic, rationality or understanding.

My Early Years
'Spiritual Experiences.'

As far back as I can remember, I've always kept my spiritual awareness to myself, only confiding in those close to me like my grandmother and later my daughters, parents, husband and a few friends; not even to my sisters and brother but somehow they've always looked at me as different and used to call me 'Miss Goody too-shoes or the quiet one.' Over the years, having had daily conversations with my Guides, means a whole lot of talk, with enough stories to fill several books. Therefore, I've related a few examples leading up to the lessons received from the Spirit-Masters and finally my direct encounters with God and HIS messages to the world.

I've had spiritual dreams from childhood and my Spirit-Guides constantly spoke to me about God; showed me the right way to live and gave daily guidance. So naturally, I assumed that this happened to everybody and that we were all telepathic. One day my father asked me to remind him about something he wanted to do on a certain date two months or so later. On the exact day, my Spirit-Guides reminded me to remind him; so I did. Well, this practice became a regular occurrence and my family simply thought that I had a photographic memory.

Although I am from a large family, I was the noticeable loner. I loved isolation and being quiet on my own, mainly because it was only under these conditions that I could hear my Guides loud and clear. So most of the time, I'd sit in the corner of a room happily reading a book or in private conversation with my Guides, who kept me pre-occupied with interesting stories or looking at how my family interacted with each other. On the other hand, my family loved noise. If they were not quarrelling, they were competing for attention; so jealousy was rife. They never 'listened' to each other, nor saw the tremendous efforts our parents made trying to make us happy or the pain often expressed through our mother's eyes. They were always too busy with their own self-centred egos and with little or no appreciation for what was around them. My way of lessening this confusion and noise, was simply to keep to myself and only spoke when spoken to. In my quiet moments, I often cried and prayed for them because my Guides constantly showed me the errors of their ways. This doesn't mean that my childhood was unhappy, on the contrary, I was extremely happy in my own way.

We all had our individual friends but often played games together as a family. When I did play, I loved to win; I'd practice and work at it until I won. There was a table tennis set in the garage and all our neighbourhood friends would come over to play. I'd pester my brother to practice with me. He was very good, no one could beat him, until one day, I did. This was the way I was with everything; once I'd set my heart on it, I won't give up until I'd conquered it. But I also believed in fair play. I'd never cheat, not even at hide and seek. I was rarely involved in physical fights, only when provoked but these too I'd win. A few years ago, during one of our now rare family get-togethers, we were reminiscing about the past and our individual personalities. To my surprise my brother said, *"Dounne is the only person in the whole world I'd never like to fight, because she would not give up until she beats me; she'd keep coming back until she won."* Out of all my family, my brother knows me the best; we were the closest. He was extremely protective and we'd often telepathise without realising it, we could just sense each others feelings. In other words, he knew me and took good care of me. Although he was a rogue and would get in all sorts of trouble, he would go out of his way to make sure I did not become involved in his antics. When he'd lie to the others including our parents, he'd always tell me the truth. To this day, I hurt the most for my brother, not only because I love him but mainly because he has ruined his own life, through being reckless, spoilt and over sensitive. My grandmother also had a special love for him and through me tried to guide him. However, if you are used to your own-way and refuse to listen and obey, then you pay for the consequences of your own actions; (good or bad). Hence my brother is paying the price for his own disobedience but no matter what, I will always love him, because I know deep inside he has a good heart.

In time -

---

*"I've come to realise why God is such a forgiving and loving God, because HE knows **our true hearts.** When others may only see the **bad in us,** God knows of the **good in us.**"*

So I grew up being aware of my Spirit-Guides and obeyed their instructions. This came as no surprise because of my Catholic indoctrinations, so it wasn't scary, abnormal or unusual. To me, when children were punished; it was because they were not listening to their Guardian Angels and therefore, did wrong, so deserved to be punished. The Church emphasised this theory very strongly, as well as, the importance of being good and believing in God, as the only way to get to heaven. I was determined to get into heaven, therefore, I was extremely good. So although I later left the church, I will always be grateful for their strong teachings and spiritual grounding, for instilling my powerful faith in God and my desire to do good, to forgive and to live right.

However, I still go to church from time to time, the only difference is that I now have an open mind. I'm no longer shackled to any one church, as I see them all as 'Houses of God;' all doing God's work and therefore, I feel free to enter any of 'HIS homes' that would allow me access to pray in my own way.

Growing up with my family, there was always some form of turmoil but rarely any conflict with me, because I was either extremely stern or openly forgiving. However, this in turn did cause some disadvantages. I was always overlooked; ignored and taken for granted. My parents would go out of their way to find out and buy whatever gifts the others wanted. When they'd ask me, I was happy with whatever they could afford, so I got exactly that. It wasn't their fault, because they knew that I wouldn't mind, wouldn't complain, wouldn't make a fuss and would be grateful. But I do remember on one occasion when I did say exactly what I really wanted and they got me the best; (a big doll, with a big cradle and a big tea set). I was over the moon that Christmas and cherished those precious toys right up to leaving Trinidad at the age of 16 when I gave them to a cousin.

However, the passing over continued right up until Mum's death in 1993. I remembered the year before Mum died, she visited one of my sisters who lived in Alaska (USA). When she returned home, she telephoned the following morning and asked me to come over. She was in bed when I arrived, not feeling too well and said, *"I've bought something very special for you but I want you to promise, not to tell your sisters (naming one in particular) that I bought it for you, as I can't face the jealousy it would cause."* Mum looked very ill and sad, so I promised. She instructed me to open her wardrobe and pointed to a beautiful black and white (heavily beaded/sequinned) dress. I couldn't believe my eyes and when I tried it on, it fitted like a glove and was the most comfortable garment I'd ever worn. Then Mum took out a new Bible which she had also bought and said that she would give it to my sister. I looked at her and smiled, realising that she'd originally bought the dress for my sister and the Bible was intended for me, then had a change of heart. She said, *"Wear this dress on special occasions; for once I want to give you something special."* Mum's sad eyes lit up seeing how overjoyed I was. I told my daughters but never told my sisters, nor had any of the family ever saw that dress until the day of Mum's funeral on 27th July 1993. I was elected to read out her life story in church. On the morning, Mum's Spirit came to me and said, *"wear my special dress today, I want you to shine."* Everyone was dressed and ready for the funeral procession to the church. I was the last to get ready but as I walked down the steps to join the others, they all suddenly looked up at me stunned. There was a momentary airy silence, all eyes wide - starring at the beautiful dress. For once, I felt very, very 'special' indeed and my spiritual-mother stood smiling proudly beside me. No one knew that she was right there amongst us.

In fact, Mum's death caused a great commotion in the family, because for the first time the full extent of my spiritual telepathy was revealed. Many did not want to believe because it drew the attention away from them. However, this situation was forced upon me by Mum; as her death was unexpected, she wanted to sort out unfinished personal matters and also to strengthened my father to enable him to cope; physically, mentally and spiritually. So for ninety days Mum took complete charge, death was not going to deny or take away her status as the head of our family. Even my Guides were made to stand aside and allow her to do her work. Although Mum and I had reached a spiritual understanding before she died; after her death she revealed a much greater insight about my own spirituality than I'd ever told her. I also realised that she was spiritually much stronger than we'd appreciated. Before she died, she was studying the works of late Catholic Italian priest PADRE PIO. Whilst in hospital she gave me a book about his life and told me to read it. I never did, until after her death.

These are some of Mum's messages, which she instructed me to write, then to call a family meeting and read it out. Mum died on 21st July 1993.

 MUM'S MESSAGE - *15th August 1993*:
(25 days after her death).

"There is always a witness to TRUTH and God's mysteries.

Dounne is the only one amongst you who is receptive and I've therefore used her to pass on my instructions. I'll be leaving her shortly, so that I can go on and do my work for my Father and to continue to help my husband.

Let those who have ears to hear - HEAR

and

Those who have eyes to see - SEE.

*I gave Dounne the name of Padre Pio, so that she would also understand more clearly her **extra-ordinary gifts.***"

'PADRE PIO'

Taken from the book on his life and mission written in 1976.'

Padre Pio was a Capuchin Friar in Italy. He was thirty-one when he received the bleeding imprint of the wounds of Christ. His call, moreover was substantiated by indisputable signs of his close union with God, with Christ crucified, with the Virgin mother of God, in whom he invited all men to place their final trust. Padre Pio read men's hearts, he obtained extraordinary temporal and spiritual favours, he possessed the exceptional charisms of bi-location, prophecy, the gift of tongues, the power of healing, while hundreds if not thousands can testify to the extraordinary fragrance which emanated from his 'bleeding wounds and from his person' (smell of roses). He was familiar with his Guardian Angel, who consoled and instructed him and even acted as his interpreter for foreign languages. He said *"From the time of my birth, God favoured me in a most special manner. He showed me that He would not only be my Saviour and supreme benefactor but my devoted, sincere and faithful friend, the friend of my heart, my infinite love and consolation, my joy and comfort, my entire wealth."* **Some souls, only a very few, are privileged to receive exceptional gifts of grace and light and love even in their mother's womb, because they are destined to fulfil some great human and divine mission.** To the mystical gifts which enriched his soul and raised him to close union with his Lord and Redeemer, were added a whole series of charisms which were to equip him in a unique way for his mission which God evidently intended him to fulfil. Once his public life began in San Giovanni Rotondo, the evidence of his charisms left no room for doubt. His colleagues who held him in veneration, understood very little of the mysterious world in which he lived. As Padre Eusebio Notte, who was close to him for many years has put it;-*"In Padre Pio the supernatural blended with the natural to such an extent that one could no longer distinguish where the natural ended and the supernatural took over."*

MUM'S MESSAGE - *29 August 1993:*

"Since I last spoke to you all on Sunday 15th August to give my final message to the family, how many of you noticed that I did not say 'GOOD BYE' on that day.

How many of you paid attention to my words:-

Let those who have eyes to see - SEE

and

Those who have ears to hear - HEAR

Since that blessed day, how many of you recognised me when I spoke through Dounne and showed my presence through her.

'The Spirit of Love.'

God is LOVE;-

The 'Spirit-of-Love' can move in and out freely through anyone and most are completely unaware of IT'S presence.

*This is how the 'Spirit-of-God' can enter anyone who understands and wants to receive HIM. This is also how SPIRITS can enter and communicate. **I AM A SPIRIT OF LOVE** because I love you all.*

MANY BELIEVE, but don't really BELIEVE.

MANY SEE, but are BLIND.

MANY HEAR, but are DEAF.

MANY SPEAK, but are DUMB.

MANY FEEL, but are DEAD.

'The mysteries of God unfold.'

*You do not use, understand, recognise or realise **the power of the seventh senses.**"*

"I have been amongst you 'in Spirit' for 39 days and only a few even sensed my presence. I have been with all of you every day and none of you have recognised my instructions. This is why I say that only Dounne is receptive.

> **MANY are CALLED but only a FEW ARE CHOSEN.**

Now read the story of Padre Pio to understand the beauty of the 'exceptionally gifted and uncommonly holy.' Dounne can teach you all a lot.

Then Mum sang, 'I walk with God from this day on.'

This is not goodbye but so long until we all meet again in the 'next life' or temporarily in dreams."

Mum's death caused us great anguish and pain but particularly for Dad, as they had celebrated their 50th Anniversary 18 months earlier. They had been together since their teens, he loved and depended on her for almost everything. She was his strength. Now being left alone so suddenly, we feared that he would not survive. His pain, deep loss and grief was even more shattering. This meant that I had to contain my grieving to keep him strong. A year later when the dust had settled, I asked God, *"why did you take away my Mum, when I begged and prayed so hard for a miracle to save her?"* and HE replied, *"You didn't lose a mother, you've gained a stronger spiritual friend."*

Even though she could speak to me and frequently visited in dreams; nothing could ever replace the void we all felt and would continue to feel for the rest of our lives. It is not until you actually loose your Mother or your Father, do you really appreciate God's commandments;-

> **"Honour thy father and thy mother."**

Mum was not perfect and had made several mistakes during her life-time but she had a truly charitable and loving heart. The year prior to her death she told me that she was preparing herself to meet her Maker (i.e. God) and prayed hard for forgiveness and did long Novenas. At the time, she was working four days a week in my factory. Two days before she became ill, she looked extremely tired and stressed, worrying about her children. We sat alone and talked for hours about the pressures she has had to bear alone for so long. She said she was tired and could not take anymore. But her eyes lit up when she said, *"I can't wait to see Ma and Doris again,"* (her deceased mother and sister). I knew then that my mother had surrendered. She also talked about a special passage about **death,** which was read at my sister-in-laws, sister's funeral and how she would like it read at her own funeral. I then insisted that she take her holiday immediately and rest. I warned that I'd check on her every day and if she was not relaxing, I'd bring her back to the factory to ensure she rested. On leaving work that evening she said, *"I'm now ready, I've made my peace,"* I replied, *"when you die, I'll immortalise your name."* We were alone and for a moment a 'strange peace surrounded us,' we looked at each other in silence and smiled but neither of us realised that her time was only a few weeks away. I'd never revealed this conversation to any of my family except to my children. The passage on death (below) was read.

> **DEATH** is nothing at all, I have only slipped away into the next room. I am I and you are you. Whatever we were to each other, that we still are. Call me by my old familiar name, speak to me in the easy way which you always used. Put no difference in your tone, wear no forced air of solemnity or sorrow, laugh as we laughed at the little jokes we enjoyed together. Pray, smile, think of me, pray for me. Let my name be ever the household name or word that it always was. Let it be spoken without effort, without the trace of a shadow on it. It is the same as it always was; there is unbroken continuity. Why should I be out of mind because I am out of sight. I am waiting for you, for an interval somewhere very near, just around the corner. **ALL IS WELL.**

There have been many times in my life when I felt completely alone; so alone that I believed even God was no longer listening or answering my prayers. One day I came across a card by an unknown author called 'Footprints' when I got to reading the ending, I burst into floods of tears. I've carried this card with me ever since and also send it to friends who may be feeling low. For those of you who may not have read it, I'd like to share its words of comfort.

FOOTPRINTS

One night a man had a dream. He dreamed he was walking along the beach with the Lord. Across the sky flashed scenes from his life. For each scene, he noticed two sets of footprints in the sands; one belonged to him and the other to the Lord.

When the last scene of his life flashed before him, he looked back at the footprints in the sand. He noticed that many times along the path of his life there was only one set of footprints. He also noticed that it happened at the very lowest and saddest times in his life.

This really bothered him and he questioned the Lord about it. *"Lord, you said that once I decided to follow you, you'd walk with me all the way. But I have noticed that during the most troublesome times in my life, there is only one set of footprints.*

I don't understand why, when I needed you most, you would leave me."

The Lord replied, *"my precious, precious child, I love you and I would never leave you. During your times of trial and suffering, when you see only one set of footprints, it was then that I carried you."*

Aunt Doris's Death.

My Aunt Doris was my favourite. I admired not only her strength but also her unshakeable determination. She was a very strict disciplinarian to everyone; from her husband, children, all the family and even the neighbours. No one could get out of hand with her. She and Mum were my grandmother's only daughters and six sons. Aunt Doris ruled them all with an iron fist. Whatever she said was law and always spoke her mind. Everyone was afraid of her and had to be on their best behaviour in her presence. However, she practiced what she preached; was truthful, fair-minded, hard working, a perfect mother, housewife, an excellent cook, teacher and nurse; who made sure that her house was always in order and was proud of it. She appeared to be extremely hard but this was only an exterior shell to cover up the deep love she had for all of her family. Once you obeyed her wishes, you'd then glimpse the tender, loving care she truly possessed. My brother and I were fortunate to be her favourites, so much so that she claimed that I was her child. In my later years, she often told me that I was the only one in my family who had a truly loving heart. Whilst others were afraid to speak to her, I could talk to her for hours and she'd teach me all sorts of things, where the wisdom learnt from her own mother shone through.

My parents decision to move to England was a painful separation for her, because herself and Mum were very close. For me, it was like leaving my mother behind. During the years apart, I longed for the day when I'd see her face again. Years later, when I told her that I was getting married, she replied, *"I'm coming to England to be at my child's wedding."* Words cannot express my joy the day she arrived. It felt like I had 'Ma' again because she looked so much like her and I made the most of it. Literally going through all that had happened during our years apart. By then I'd already had Marsha who was (16 months old) and she pampered her thoroughly because Aunty adored girl children. Many years later when my marriage broke down and I'd left my husband, she telephoned me simply to say, *"I know if you've decided to leave, you have a good cause. Once you've left, never return, bolt the door shut and don't look back.*

Look after yourself and your children, be strong, a leopard don't change its spots; Pray and God will help and bless you."

However, Aunty was also a great joker, loved playing cards and openly cheated. One of her favourite sayings, *"I gave you a 6 for a 9"* in other words, if you reverse the number 6 it looks like a 9 and vice versa; which meant she has fooled you. She was very skilled at eating with her hands and would say, *"the Lord made hands before man made knife and fork."*

My grandmother truly had a powerful influence on all of her children, because they frequently spoke of or referred to her teachings. She was forever on their minds and they certainly tried to pass on her lessons of love, unity, compassion, forgiveness and faith to their own children. But none was as successful at instilling all these virtues as Ma herself.

When Aunt Doris died, Mum revealed the reasons behind her hard shell. Apparently, my grandfather (Pa) used to abuse my grandmother and often beat her. By the time Aunt Doris had reached her mid-teens, she had had enough of the abuse. One day she confronted Pa and told him in no uncertain terms that she was taking Ma, my Mum and her brothers away and he would not be welcomed. She got a horse and cart and moved the entire family to another village; where she worked and took care of them. Some time later, Pa begged them to take him back but had to promise Aunty that he'd never lay a finger on Ma again. After a long time, when she was satisfied that he had changed, she eventually left home to raise her own family. This was the reason they all respected and listened to her because she'd taken care of them, even my Mum looked on her as a mother. Aunty could never tolerate anyone abusing her family or herself and had fought and won many battles to protect them. It also made her lose faith in men and relied on herself to do what had to be done. She was a heavily built woman and would stand face to face in confrontation with any man or woman and would never back down. Having six brothers to cope with, meant that she was used to dealing with and handling men. No way could anyone intimidate her, in fact it was always the reverse. She'd go for them like a raging bull and many had been known to run scared.

Her faith in God was equally unshakeable. Although raised as a strict Catholic, around her mid-thirties she converted to Jehovah's Witness. All hell would break loose when ever she'd called to say that she was coming to our house. Ma who was living with us would tell me, *"go hide my rosary, Doris is coming."*

For a year, I lived with Aunty before we moved to England. She'd take me to her church called The Kingdom Hall and had weekly bible lessons. My parents didn't object, because as far as they were concerned, it was all God's teachings and they respected Aunty's beliefs. Jehovah Witnesses don't believe in the after-life or in Spirits. So years later, after Ma had passed away and began to visit me, I'd tell Aunty about my Spirit dreams of Ma and I noticed that she'd never deny the possibility of life after death, when ever I spoke of her mother. But in the presence of my mother or anyone else who spoke about the dead, they'd get the full blast of her Jehovah Witnesses beliefs, scriptures, the lot and she'd argue no end. I think in a way, because of the love for her mother, she kept an open mind but also the thought of Ma watching over them brought comfort. Nearing her death we made a pact. I said to her, *"If I die before you, I'll come back to you in a dream and prove that the Spirit lives"* and promised to do the same if she died before me. It so happened that we didn't have to wait long. Her heart became worryingly troublesome, so my parents arranged for her to have a heart transplant in England. We were re-united once more. The week before she was due to go into hospital, she called myself and Marsha into the bedroom for a private chat. There was a distinctive change in her personality, especially her eyes. She kept saying how beautiful everything and everyone was. I remembered saying, *"Aunty, can you only see beauty?"* and she replied, *"Yes!, you are so beautiful, look at your beautiful daughter."* I held her and looked into her beautiful eyes and knew that her time had come; she'd be leaving us shortly. She then said, *"I'd like to give you a gift"* and pulled out an old tied up handkerchief; opened it and took out a ring. A feeling of sadness came over me and I said, *"no Aunty."* She said, *"OK, I want your first born (Marsha) to have it."* She gave it to Marsha; held her hands and said, *"take good care of it, it's very precious."* Marsha thanked and kissed her. For a moment the room was filled with a strange peaceful calm.

Her heart operation was successful but a few days later she took a turn for the worse and passed away. I was at home when Mum called to convey the sad news. I felt like a lost child in the wilderness, I'd lost my second Mum. I remembered singing my grandmother's song in my mind *"sometimes I feel like a motherless child."* However, I knew my own mother would be shattered, so I went to comfort her. On the way to her house, I heard Aunt Doris's voice saying, *"tell them don't send me back home, bury me here."* When I told Mum the message, she looked at me stunned and said, *"two days ago when I visited her in the hospital, she told me, when I die, don't send my body back home, bury me here."* Mum said she laughed at her and replied that she was not going to die because she was well taken care of. We complied with her wishes and her husband and children came over for the funeral, held at our local 'Kingdom Hall.' Approximately two weeks after her death, the entire family was over at my parents home and were as usual, reminiscing about Aunty; when my Uncle Gus (the last surviving brother who also lived in England), started relating a dream he had of her that week. The dream went as follows;-

He was on a bus going some where, when suddenly Aunt Doris came into the bus and sat next to him. He noticed that no one else could see her, just him. He said, *"what are you doing here Doris? You are dead."* She smiled in agreement and started to massage his back close to his kidneys and told him to stop drinking so heavily (Uncle Gus loves his whisky and rum). Then she said, *"I gave them a ring with green stones; tell them to take good care of it because its very precious"* Then she disappeared, Uncle Gus said that he didn't know what she meant.

Both Marsha and I snapped at the same time and looked at each other in amazement. We explained what she meant and then I told about the pact we had made. I smiled and thanked her for sending me proof. Mum also told of a dream she had. Apparently, Aunty had given her a pair of gold earrings and out of the blue one side went missing. In the dream Aunty told her to go to the cellar and pointed out where Mum had dropped it. Mum woke up, went to the cellar and found it precisely where she had shown. On returning home that night, Marsha got out the ring. When we looked at the setting of the green stones; it was set in the shape of a cross. We looked at each other in disbelief. It is now Marsha's most valued treasure and lucky charm.

One night in 1992, as Marsha was about to go to bed, she said she could sense the presence of someone else in her room. She felt un-nerved and simply said, *"Don't appear to me, come in a dream instead."* When she finally fell asleep, Aunty Doris appeared in her dream and told her, *"go and wake up your mother now, tell her to go to the doctor, she has lumps in her breasts."*

Marsha jumped out of her bed and told me. That morning, I went straight to the doctor, for an examination. To my horror, when she pressed certain parts I felt a sharp pain in both breasts. She immediately arranged for a mammogram, where it was later discovered that I had what is called 'lumpy breasts,' which needed to be kept in check to ensure that they do not become cancerous. The six week period waiting for the final results were traumatic for Marsha, Dee and I, because we'd kept it secret from the family. I felt my parents had had enough problems to cope with and didn't want to add another burden. Not only that but they were also getting old and the thought of cancer always conjures up fears of death. However, I had to prepare myself, Marsha and Dee for the worse, 'just in case,' which drew us even closer.

Later that year, whilst reflecting on Aunt Doris's death, I questioned my Spirit-Guide about Death. This was his answer;-

'ACCEPTANCE OF GOD'S TERMS'

"Come to terms with God and accept HIS Will;-

1. *In order to know God, one must learn to understand HIM.*
2. *In order to love God, one must believe and accept HIS Judgement.*

3.   *In order to have faith in God, one must accept HIS terms without question.*

       For HE is the Father-(giver) and also the Father-(taker).

          The Lord giveth and the Lord taketh away.

Therefore, one must learn to Rejoice in HIM in every way,

          Rejoice   when HE gives
          Rejoice   when HE takes

For it all HIS Will. *Thy Will be done on earth as it is in Heaven.*

    WHERE there is LIGHT, there is DARKNESS

    WHERE there is HAPPINESS, there is SORROW

    WHERE there is PEACE, there is UN REST

    WHERE there is UP, there is DOWN

    WHERE there is BIRTH, there is DEATH

    WHERE there is LIFE, there is GOD

    WHERE there is GOD, there is ETERNITY

    Therefore, LIFE is ETERNAL - DEATH is in the MIND

THINK!

In your mind, do you believe that God is dead?"

 ON REFLECTION.

My Grandmother, Aunt Doris and Mum all died in the month of July (the seventh month). There must be some association or connection. They all had an unshakeable faith in God; served HIM well and were great spiritual teachers.

I also later learnt that we all 'choose' when we wish to return to earth, 'choose' our parents, 'choose' our purpose, 'choose' our experiences and 'choose' how and when we wish to die (i.e. return home).

Hence, since these 'choices' are between you and God... the phrase *"thy will be done on earth as it is in heaven,"* does not solely mean God's will alone, but the agreement you both made together. Therefore, *"thy will"* means 'your will' and 'God's will.'

Choices and lessons are for our own personal spiritual growth and eternal evolution.

'Life After Life'

Life has ended
Body turns to wind
Spirit elevates
Leaving physical behind.

Friends, families, acquaintances
Grief, broken hearts, relief
Spirit says goodbyes
Now the journey begins.

The line has been crossed
now to find the way home
follow the lights that flicker in the distance
so SPIRIT won't be alone.

Celebrations everywhere
when reunion is complete
friends, families, acquaintances of old
all have come to meet.

Death only exits in the place we call earth
but our true Spiritual-being
rejoices its everlasting re-birth.

So do not perceive death as destruction and strife
but instead
embrace its true meaning
'Life after Life.'

Marsha Moore

Spiritual Dreams & Visions

Apart from (conscious) telepathy, I also have vivid spiritual dreams. I now understand why Aquarians are called 'dreamers!' I was forever dreaming and kept busy throughout the night; taken here, there and everywhere. Years later I learnt that your 'Spirit' leaves your body when its asleep and travels. It could visit people or places to find answers to problems or teach you the necessary lessons you need to learn or receive instructions to convey messages etc. Hence, the ancient practice of dream interpretations. Therefore, if a person is consciously aware, you could actually call on or speak to other spirits (i.e. like God, your Guides or loved-ones) and ask for help in your dreams. Furthermore, you can also be consciously aware whilst sleeping and know that you are actually dreaming and receiving information and could ask other questions. There is a distinctive difference between an 'ordinary dream' which has no significance to a 'spiritual dream/vision' which is always relevant and meaningful. Therefore, dreams are simply another form of communication.

My dreams were mostly spiritually linked to my spiritual lessons and training but as I grew older, these became less, as my spiritual education increased.

One of my most vivid dreams, was the first time I saw Jesus;-

> *"I was walking alone through a green field near my home, when suddenly I heard a blaze of angelic voices singing beautiful hymns, coming from the sky. I looked up and I saw a huge STAR which started to descend towards me. When it drew close, it transformed into the physical person of Jesus, who then hovered directly over me and said,* **"Dounne, don't worry, you'll always be watched over."** *He then ascended, transformed back into the STAR, which went into the heavens and disappeared. I was then* **seven years** *old."*

In my grandmother's day, when they dreamt a dead relative or friend, they'd say, *"guess who visited me last night"* and then relay their dreams.

There are times, in the midst of a dream when my Guides would tell me, *"wake up and write it down now."* My eyes would open immediately and I'd jump out of bed and write. Sometimes if I'm really tired and don't want to get up, they'd nag me until I do, because if I fell back into a deep sleep, I'd either forget all about the dream or won't remember the precise words or information given. Therefore it is important to practice writing your dreams immediately on awakening.

 ## Dreams of my Grandmother.

Immediately after my grandmother died, she started to visit me. I'd be merrily dreaming away and she'd suddenly appear, in the dream. I'd noticed that no one else in the dream could see her but me. I'd also be consciously aware that she was dead, plus we didn't need to speak as we could read each other's minds. I was amazed how clear and easy it was to read her mind and it was then I realised why telepathy was a natural form of communication. Ma explained, that whilst you are in a dream state, although your physical body is unconscious, your Spirit-being is awake and can therefore travel and communicate on a higher spiritual level. To prove this, she would often be present during the day, whilst I was awake and in conversation with family or friends. That night she'd visit me in a dream and say, *"I was listening to your conversation today with so and so etc."* After that, whenever I had a problem, I'd tell her and asked her to give me the answers in my dreams.

I'm the world's biggest coward but one rare night of brief bravery, I asked if she'd physically appear to me but she said that I was not ready for this stage as yet. I felt sure I was ready and pleaded to her to appear. Reluctantly she agreed. My eyes opened and there she was sitting on the chair next to my bed. Although the light was off, there was sufficient light in the room to see her clearly. I was terrified but before I knew it, she put me back to sleep then said, *"I did say you weren't ready."* There were many times over the years she'd say that she had to go away for a while to do God's work but I must keep talking to her, because although she would not be able to communicate, she'd be keeping a watchful eye. In 1974 after I'd given birth to Dee, Ma appeared briefly and said, *"I haven't come to see you, I've just stolen a chance to come and see my grandchild."* I kept on saying, *"but Ma, I have so much to talk to you about!"* She replied, *"keep talking to me, I can hear you, don't worry"* and left.

January 1993:- I dreamt Ma again for the first time in years. It was at a family party and someone said they had a special New Year's surprise for me but that I must close my eyes. Then she said, *"open your eyes,"* standing in front of me was Ma with Aunty Doris behind her. They both looked beautiful. Their skins were firm and fresh with a lovely serene look of peace, radiating a glow all over. Ma and I just stared at each other smiling, whilst reading each other's minds. As usual, no one else in the party could see them. I also was aware that she and Aunt Doris were Spirits. I asked if she had now returned to me for good and she replied, *"YES."* This was my New Year's surprise. She had come back and would be with me from then onwards. This she had promised to do some thirteen years earlier and it had now come true. She had completed God's work and completely assigned to me as one of my Guides.

Although I no longer dream of or see her, I can hear her. Whenever I meet someone who claims to be spiritual, she always appear next to me. Once the person tells me that there is a lady with me and describes her. It confirms that this person is really spiritual.

During her years of absence, was also the period when the higher Spirit-Masters appeared on the scene, to start my new stage of learning and preparation for my future mission. I remember once in a dream, Moses took me up on this tall mountain. We were both wearing long robes with our hands clasped in prayer. We were leading a procession of people across the mountain top. The Masters also took me back in time (regression) and showed me a couple of my past lives. One was as an Egyptian High Priestess. On reflection, during my hippy years in the 1970's, I bought a black leather necklace because I was attracted to its unusual wooden pendant. Over the years I gave away or threw out lots of my old jewellery but always kept this particular one because I loved it. It felt special or significant but I didn't know why. In 1999 (25 years later) I took it out and wore it for the first time. A week later, I was watching a television programme on ancient Egypt which revealed the same pendant worn by the Pharaohs (the ankh); that it symbolised 'eternal life' (or the key of life) and that ancient Egyptians believed in the after life and that stars represented their spiritual names. I was not aware of these facts until then.

I've also had visitations from Bob Marley (the Jamaican reggae singer) who is one of my spiritual friends. He last visited on 6 August 2000, stating, *"my friend, the greatest reverence has been bestowed on you, so don't give up the fight."*

 Visions.

Apart from having Spiritual dreams, I also experience visions, whilst being consciously awake, or during meditation or prayers or when I close my eyes. After a while, I'll see clear visions and hear voices. This used to occur more frequently when saying my morning prayers before 6am. Here are a couple:-

July 1981.

Whilst lying on my bed meditating with my eyes closed, I asked the Lord to show me what ever HE would like me to see. Suddenly everything went very dark, in extreme blackness. Then appeared, a round ball like shape with an orange glow around it. I didn't understand what I was being shown. So I asked the Lord to tell me what it was. I heard a voice say 'the eclipse of the Sun.' Then suddenly the eclipsed sun drew inwards deeply (as if to build up a lot of energy or like taking in a very deep breath) and then it exploded outward into bright yellow and red flames. Again I asked what this meant. The voice said, *"Armageddon is at hand."* The eclipsed sun explosions occurred three times, then finally a sudden ray of a brilliant white light (like lightning) flashed down from heaven to the earth, which brightened up the land at the point where it struck, although the earth was still in darkness, I could see that the surface of the earth was baron with a few dried up trees still standing, as if looking across a darkened desert. Then the vision ended.

July 1982.

This vision was about Marsha and her best friend when they were at infant school (ages between eight and nine years old). However, I did not know the friend until I described her to Marsha after the vision and she then confirmed that it was her best friend. She was white, the same height, a little chubbier than Marsha, with light brownish /blonde hair, parted down the middle; an overgrown fringe just past her cheek bones and shoulder length hair. Her personality was excitable but very quiet and shy. They were both wearing their summer uniform... green and white check dress.

The entire class had gone on a school nature watch outing; but I could only see Marsha and her best friend in a big field. Marsha was on her own, sitting on the grass and looking interestingly in between the blades of grass, when suddenly her best friend came running up to her excitedly saying, *"Marsha, Marsha come, come."* Marsha said, *"Ah leave me alone,"* as she was too interested in what she was looking at. Then her friend pulling on the shoulder of Marsha's dress, still excited and jumping said, *"Marsha, Marsha come and look, there's a whole new world down there."* So Marsha rose and followed her friend to a ditch (about 2¹/₂ft deep) they crossed over it on a plank of wood. Her friend started crawling down the ditch backwards, on all fours. Marsha followed in the same manner. Half way down Marsha called out, *"Don't you realise that we are getting smaller and smaller?"* As they went down the ditch they grew smaller, so by the time they'd got to the bottom they were about one inch. They both looked around and thought how wonderful it was. They came across a nest of ants but because they were innocent children who loved animals, they had no fear and were able to communicate with the ants. They lived with the ants for a few hours and was able to understand and study their way of life and their fears of human-beings.

For instance;-

- The ants tremendous strength (able to carry an object twice their weight and ten times their height).

- Their incredible running speed.

- Their intense senses and superior intelligence.

- Their tremendous organisation skills (soldiers).

- Their peacefulness.

- Their fear of man.

- Man's thoughtless, insensitive and needless killing. The ants explained, *"How do you think we feel, when you just walk on us and kill all our family, like my mother and father."*

- The way humans toy and play games with them and or kill them for a laugh.

- Man's inferiority to the ant.

Marsha and her friend were able to compare man to the ant and began to wander about God's greatness to be able to pack so much more power and intelligence into such tiny creatures. They also realised that with God's love and innocence, all fears are removed, which brings about a unique understanding, plus respect is established with everything and everyone. Furthermore, they also realised, that although man believed that he's of a higher intelligence, the ant was a far more superior being and if the reverse was to occur, then the ant would be more successful (in everything) than man because they were far more disciplined, organised and co-operative.

When the day had ended they said a loving good-bye to all the ants and started to climb out of the ditch... as they did so, they grew bigger and bigger, till they reached the top and were back to their normal size. They looked at each other, smiled with joy and happiness, then held hands. As they started walking over the plank, her friend spotted an ant and automatically lifted her foot to step on it to kill it, but instantly stopped herself as she flashed back to what she had just learnt about man's deliberate cruelty. Instead, she bent down and allowed it to walk up her finger whispering, *"Ah you lovely little ant."* She then knelt down and put it on the edge of the ditch and said, *"now you can safely go home to your family."* They stood up, held hands and watched the ant run safely home. They looked at each other, smiled thoughtfully and returned back to the rest of their class, who were by now ready to go home.

1980's.

In the 1980's, Britain was at war in the Falkland Islands. One morning whilst saying my prayers I received this strange vision. A young soldier appeared and gave his name; then disappeared. Immediately afterward another soldier appeared and did the same. This went on for quite a while with about 20 soldiers in total. They all wore white t-shirts and had their arms folded in front of them. Then they said, *"tell them that we died in vain, they caught us with our pants down."* Then I saw a burning ship with black smoke bellowing out.

After I'd finished my prayers, I immediately told my husband but I could not remember the name of the ship. All I could recall was that the name started with GAL.

I turned on the radio to find out if this event was reported but there was no such report. However, I knew that it happened that day and intuitively felt that it was being deliberately suppressed by the Government. Realising that this could cause a political scandal, I didn't bother to report it. To my surprise, three days later it was reported on television and the exact burning ship was shown; its name was the Sir Gallahad and it was said that the soldier were caught completely off guard. Many years later, after the war had ended, there was a televised memorial service for those who had died. Several angry mothers said on camera, *"our sons died in vain."*

English Spiritualist Churches.

During the late 1970's, I was introduced to a lovely elderly English lady (called Mrs Woodley), who was a Spiritual-Medium and ran a church in her home in East London. It was my first ever spiritual reading (or messages) from Spirit through someone else. She said that my grandmother watches over me and talked about our love, plus other personal matters. Now, I'd never met this woman before in my life, yet everything she'd said about me, my family and personal problems were true. Mrs Woodley confirmed that my Grandmother was one of my Spirit-Guides; that I was gifted with great spiritual powers, insight, a healer and transformer. She explained that a transformer was when the 'Spirit-being' transforms itself onto the person (i.e. me) so that the Medium can describe the Spirit's features in detail; but not all Mediums had the ability to see the transformations. I'd always felt these physical changes occurring on my body but never knew what was happening until that day. I wasn't bothered about it anyway, as it was just one of those things that I was used to and simply ignored it.

Aside from her spiritual work, Mrs Woodley herself was truly a lovely, gentle, simple, warm-hearted lady, a tremendous comforter and teacher; more like a real grandmother, nurturing everyone around her. She was more interested in teaching people to become aware of their spirituality and to take control of their own lives. She was one of the most genuine Spiritualists I've ever come across and I adored her. She never charged for her services, instead requested donations of what ever anyone could afford, simply to go towards the maintenance of the house, as she was a pensioner.

About three years later she moved far away and I was introduced to another Spiritual Church but this time rather than private readings, it was more like a Church service of prayers and hymns, then for about an hour a specially invited Medium would give messages to various people in the congregation. Everytime I went, my grandmother was always the first to come through and give me a message, just to let me know that she was still with me. This was a period in my life where I was under a great deal of stress, work, family, marriage and Marsha; whose spine had started to bend for no apparent reason. I felt lost and needed answers but somehow couldn't get through to my Guides, it seemed that even my grandmother had stopped communicating. Hence, her re-assurance every time I went to the church. After a while, listening to the various Mediums and their messages, I began to feel that many were giving false messages; prompting people in such a way as to supply suitable answers; plus, the congregation themselves were regulars, who were all hooked on receiving spiritual messages. None of them reminded me of Mrs Woodley, until one day a gentleman by the name of Mr Joseph, spoke and gave me all the answers I needed. It was quite simple; *"God required me to ACCEPT."* He said that I was naturally gifted, highly spiritual and walked in both worlds. That night on my return home I prayed, spoke openly to God then admitted the truth to Him.

"I was AFRAID of the unknown"

"I was AFRAID of evil forces"

"I didn't really want to become wrapped up in Spiritualism, because I'd seen deceivers in this too"

"I'd also seen deceivers in the Religious Churches"

"I didn't want any part in deceiving 'HIS' people - in 'HIS' NAME."

I cried and finally said;-

"LORD I ACCEPT; Make me an instrument of Your PEACE."

Then a beautiful, peaceful calm, came over me and my Spiritual doors re-opened. However, I was still afraid but chose to place all my trust in God and let HIM lead me. In other words, LET GO and LET God!

In those days, I was a heavy smoker...between 20 to 40 cigarettes a day. Almost as fast as I'd finish one, another was re-lit. It was my only vice and I thoroughly enjoyed it. The same week that I'd made my 'acceptance to God,' one morning after getting Marsha and Dee ready for school and escorted them to the bus stop. On walking back home my first thought was, *"I have no cigarettes!"* So I dashed into the nearest sweet-shop and bought a pack of my usual brand. However, I never smoked in the road; so I ran all the way home thinking about having my first fix for the day. As I got in, made a cup of tea, sat in the living room, opened my brand new packet of cigarettes, lit the first one and relaxed back to enjoy. Half way through my enjoyment, I heard a male voice say:-

"If you truly believe in God, then let this be your last cigarette."

and whilst saying it, an invisible force moved my hand from my mouth and I watched in dismay, as my own hand was involuntarily squashing out the cigarette into the ashtray beside me. I was alone in the house, normally my first reaction would have been to get the hell out of there and run like mad but this time I didn't feel afraid. Then the voice said;-

"If you want to see God - look in the mirror."

I got up and looked but naturally I could only see myself. So I said aloud, *"what do you mean; I can only see me."* He didn't clarify but instructed me to give the house a complete spring cleaning, polish and shine everything.

I placed my brand new packet of cigarettes on the kitchen table and got down to the spring cleaning. Everything I polished and shined had a strange strong reflection. Whilst cleaning, I'd automatically reach for a cigarette and had to stop myself from taking one. Luckily the cleaning and the events of that day kept me occupied. The words kept repeating in my head. I knew that I could never take the chance of ever smoking again, as this would mean I'd have failed my first test. As a chronic smoker it is a painful experience to stop suddenly without any form of substitute, plus my husband was also a strong smoker who wouldn't give up. Within three months, I became unbelievably neurotic, shouting at both my husband and the children for the slightest thing. The situation got so bad that my husband said I was sending them crazy and if I couldn't control myself, it was best I started smoking again. At that moment, I realised the addictiveness of cigarettes and that I was experiencing the withdrawal symptoms of a drug addict but with no one to help me through it. So I turned to God again for help and from that faithful day in 1983 to-date, I've not touched another cigarette. This doesn't mean that I didn't still fancy a smoke but the fear of failing God kept me away from it. If it wasn't for this encounter, I would have returned to smoking. However, one vice always seems to lead to another, I gave up smoking but started drinking alcohol. Thank God! they didn't test me on this too.

 ### The day my deceased Grandfather spoke to me.

I can't remember the precise date this occurred but it was also in the early 1980's, just before I started receiving the higher Spirit-Masters. I was sitting in my dinning room when my grandfather (my father's father) spoke directly into my right ear. Although I could not see him, I heard his voice say clearly, *"surely goodness and mercy shall follow you."* I repeated the words aloud to my husband saying, *"I know its a prayer but I can't remember which one."* I kept repeating the passage until I remembered that it was the 23rd Psalm 'The Lord is my Shepherd,' which I've included in my morning prayers ever since.

 ### Listen to the Silence: - *(Spiritual Voices).*

When something of spiritual importance or relevance is happening, there is always a momentary silence or a sudden stillness or a space of absolute peace. Once you have become consciously aware of this moment, then you should try and be still and **'listen to the silence'; for it is the moment of spiritual communication.** With practice, you'll begin to hear your inner voice (i.e. your Spirit) as well as, other Spirit voices (i.e. your Guides). In time, you'll be amazed with how loud and clear these voices become and also realise how much you've taken for granted, missed out on or not used your natural instincts... i.e. intuition. However, its equally important that you also take time out and consider what you hear or were told, then decide whether or not you wish to follow their guidance and or instructions, because the Spirit-Guides are not authorised to control your 'free-will' and should always 'respect your choice to follow your own mind.' Their purpose is to guide and educate, not to control or cause any form of harm.

● wooden ankh pendant.

$\mathscr{Spirituality.}$

- **LESSONS - FROM THE SPIRIT MASTERS (1983).**

"It takes great imagination to DREAM.
So let your life's work be visionary and creative,

like your master (God) intended and become

the Master of Your Own Life.
But dream those beautiful dreams
to the benefit of humanity and

the furtherance of PURE LOVE."

My First Spiritual Teacher

On 28th April 1983, whilst saying my morning prayers (with my eyes closed) I could see the figure of an Indian man sitting in front of me. It was Mahatma Gandhi and he said;

"You my friend wished to have 'no followers,' just to learn the truth in God's terms. You must give freely that which has been given to you freely. If only one man understands the true way of eternal life, then let that be enough for you. You asked God for the truth and HE has sent me as proof to be your teacher. You will prepare a 'Book of Teachings of Wisdom' and observe the teachings yourself. When any one comes to you for knowledge or with their problems, you will use your 'Book of Wisdom' to teach them life. You have the 'free-will' to choose to proceed and gain that knowledge which lives within or you can choose to stop. Your action will tell your choice."

I CHOSE TO PROCEED AND LEARN.

FREE-WILL THOUGHTS -

Your Mind.

The Following lessons on the FREE-WILL explains;-

- How your MIND controls everything.

- Why it is important to keep an OPEN MIND.

- Why you should THINK and ACT Positively.

- Why you should avoid thinking evil and focus your mind on good things.

- How to use your Mind to achieve your desires.

- Why you should 'still your mind'... i.e. clear your head.

Your MIND is the Power that lives within you, which is your higher Spirit-Self. Therefore, it is important to learn how to control it and not to allow anything or anyone to control you (i.e. brainwashing). Therefore, you should learn how to 'think' for yourself and make your own 'choices'... i.e. conscious decisions.

"Free your Mind and you'll Free yourself."

"Through your mind, your higher Spirit-self and other Spirit-forms can communicate with you by telepathy."

"Set your Spirit - FREE"

"Live in consciousness and know your own mind."

LESSON 1

FREE-WILL THOUGHTS -

The forces of good and evil Spirit-forms.

Gandhi explained;-

*"My friend, the same way that I can force my will on you and overpower or penetrate your thoughts to teach you God's truth, then in the same way an 'evil Spirit-form' can overpower you to teach you evil or to go as far as physically harming you. You can control your destiny by using your 'free-will thoughts'...**positively.** In this way, you control your thoughts and any entities therein. By avoiding evil thoughts and concentrating your thoughts on good, you can avoid the attraction of the 'evil forces' circulating. Just as you asked for help to learn the 'truth' and I came and by you concentrating and searching for 'truth,' you attracted me, the same happens with evil. This should help you in sorting out some of your fears. This lesson on evil Spirit-forms or forces is enough for you to consider for now, but as your learning deepens, your knowledge will widen into far reaching possibilities. Remember that all things are possible."*

Then Gandhi said;-

"I'll teach you all I know and when my work is done, someone higher than me will then be sent to teach you more and so on."

LESSON 2

<u>THE FREE SPIRIT</u> -

"Because the 'Spirit of God' made us, 'the breath' of the Almighty God gave us life. Therefore, when one dies the 'Spirit or breath of God' leaves the physical body and lives on."

Hence, the 'Spirit' is the 'living God-part within you' and as God-made you 'free in will,' it is true to say;-

THE FREE SPIRIT

THE FREE-WILL

*All is of the same meaning... the **God-part within us.***"

21/5/83

Gandhi visited again and said;-

"When teaching any one of God's TRUTH

1.   *Do not try to be what you are not.*

2.   *Do not attempt to show off.*

3.   *Do not attempt or pretend to be exceedingly holy.*

4.   *Do not attempt to be exceedingly knowledgeable.*

5.   *Do not try or attempt to force your teachings or learnings upon another person.*

All these things simply anger other people and therefore, it does not achieve its purpose of a new understanding, to bring forth God's truth or true way of life.

Anger brings a vexed mind which is negative, it also makes people close off their minds and concentrate on your falsehood, then they'd stubbornly hold onto their past beliefs; like, they might be thinking... who does she think she is, playing that she is so good and perfect, etc.'

What you should do is humble yourself to others, explain how you understand God, through your 'book of wisdom.' Explain particularly, the 'free-will thoughts.' Let them know that these are your new teachings, which have shown you how over-indoctrinated you have been in the past and show them that you now always try to leave your 'free-

will thoughts' (your mind) open to new learnings. In this way, you will achieve your purpose of freeing people's minds or freeing them completely from incorrect indoctrinations, opening them up to a new mind training to be able to weigh up the truth for themselves and become their own masters. In other words, you have given them food for thought."

25/9/83

"*My friend, be steadfast and strong. No matter how hard life appears to be at times, never loose your faith in God and or turn your back on HIM. Keep your belief complete and total. Never deny your faith (i.e. I believe in one eternal, true and everlasting God, who is my Creator, my Father and my Redeemer). To the end or against any trials or test, hold this belief strong and true.*

Remember that we are all sinners but we must be aware of our sins and repent or ask God's forgiveness of them and avoid repeating them. Remember the words 'knowingly and willingly.' Also remember that we all have faults, none of us are perfect but we must strive towards perfection in whatever we do. As God is perfect and part of our life's ambition is to find or search for God within us. Therefore, the effort in striving for perfection is also that God-part within us.

HOW LUCKY CAN YOU BE,

TO HAVE A FRIEND IN THEE,

HOW LUCKY YOU TRULY ARE,

TO KNOW YOUR MASTER.

Your faith must stand the test of time, no matter how high you rise or how low you sink, remember, the Master watches over you, so you must remain true."

LESSON 5

"The Power of God is equally great in the day time as it is in the night time. As day time and night time are both God given. God gave us the great light of the sun to rule the day and to tell us that this is the moment or period of awakeness, when we can clearly see all around us and go about our daily duties. But the night-time darkness is our resting moments, when we must rest from our daily chores. He has given us a lesser light (the moon and stars) in the night, so that we can still have some vision in the midst of the darkness. So God's power is equally as great in the day and night. However, the 'God light' that we must seek. is the 'silver white light of the Lord' which is a dazzling silver white light that can penetrate the day as well as in the night, this is 'the light power of God!' Therefore, not to be confused with the day light (i.e. the Sun)."

Shortly after Gandhi's last visit, I had a dream where I was taken to heaven to visit the **Halls of Learning.** This was a huge building like a massive university with enormous 'books of wisdom,' lining the walls from ceiling to floor. I was told that each book contained one single lesson. There I met some of the higher Spirit Masters like John the Baptist, the Buddha and Moses. Then I was told at this point, to stop reading the Bible and to ignore all of my earthly religious church teachings, because they were going to teach me 'truth'. I should focus on all the teachings I receive from spiritual guidance but I must still carefully consider everything they were saying, because they were not sent to brainwash but to teach, so that I can learn how to teach others correctly. I must also **observe** and **obey** the **Ten Commandments** as these are 'The laws of Life!' However, they didn't confide, that after their work had ended, that God himself was coming to speak directly to me, which happened ten years later in 1996. Up until 1986, they carefully dictated their teachings which I wrote down.

Spirituality.

- **LESSONS FROM THE HIGHER SPIRIT MASTERS.**

  (1984 onwards).

To many people these teachings may sound very simplistic but as the Masters frequently reminded me that **wisdom is simple,** it is man who finds it necessary to make it complicated. What I also found interesting about the Masters, was that although they were sent by God and are good men, they always reinforced the following principles:-

"You must not just take or accept our teachings as the truth, instead you should meditate (i.e think) and carefully consider everything we have said; then decide for yourself whether or not you choose to believe. You are equally free to disagree or to agree, without any fear of rebuke or punishment. You should adopt this habit, so that when your time comes to teach others, you'd follow the same principles, (i.e. not to demand, command, insist or entice but allow people to exercise their 'God given right,' to make their own choices without fear or guilt)."

WHO IS GOD?

and how to find the God-part within you?

God is LOVE

LOVE means **ONE LOVE -** for with *love,* you will find;-

RESPECT   for with *respect,* you will find

UNDERSTANDING   for with *understanding,* you will find

KNOWLEDGE   for with *knowledge,* you will find

WISDOM   for with *wisdom,* you will find

PATIENCE   for with *patience,* you will find

JOY   for with *joy,* you will find

PEACE   for with *peace,* you will find

CONTENTMENT   for with *contentment,* you will find

FULFILMENT   for with *fulfilment,* you will find

       YOUR TRUE INNER SELF or the God-part within YOU.

Because God means all these things put together, therefore by finding God, you will find yourself.

RESPECT... the 'God-part' within everyone.

1.	Respect anyone's	Intelligence & Knowledge.
2.	Respect anyone's	Innocence.
3.	Respect anyone's	Stupidity.
4.	Respect anyone's	Position in Life; (Rich or Poor).
5.	Respect anyone's	Race, gender or physical form.
6.	Respect anyone's	Pride.
7.	Respect anyone's	Parents, wife, husband children and friends.
8.	Respect anyone's	Stage in life... for there is a time for everyone, to be a baby, child, adolescent, adult, mature, etc.
9.	Respect Yourself	

For within everyone God exists, therefore, you are respecting the 'God-part' within them. Such respect brings forth further knowledge and understanding, because you'd be able to relate to each person accordingly and there would be no need for angry frustrations or vexation but instead you'd achieve calm collective wisdom.

God's WAYS

'34 disciplines.'

1. **God is LOVE:** meaning ONE LOVE or a one to one individual relationship, yet still loving everyone in the world and all of HIS creations collectively.

2. **God is PATIENCE:** calm, quiet, attentive and very tolerant. You must give everyone or everything you are doing, your total and complete attention.

3. **God is KINDNESS:** loving, gentle, sharing, caring and giving .

4. **God is UNDERSTANDING:** by being patient and giving everyone or everything your full attention, you would be able to take in all mentally, in order to understand thoroughly.

5. **God is JOY and HAPPINESS:** contentment, gladness, delight, rejoicing, laughter, pleasure.

6. **God is STRENGTH:** spiritually, physically and mentally strong. (i.e. body, mind and spirit in harmony). All needing proper exercise in order to keep fit, alert and balanced.

7. **God is RESPECT:** to respect yourself, everyone and everything individually; giving

each your full careful consideration. In order to gain respect, you must first have respect.

8. **God is MERCIFUL:**   to be understanding, forgiving and compassionate to those that do you wrong.

9. **God is FORGIVING:**   to give up hatred or dislike against any person that has done something to hurt you. *"Lord forgive them for they know not what they do"* - Jesus' words at his crucifixion.

10. **God is GIVING:**   always be ready to give something to others in need. You must learn to give willingly and happily. Never regret whatever you have given.

11. **God is PEACEFUL:**   quiet and harmonious, with everyone and everything that is round you.

12. **God is CALM:**   you must learn to be absolutely quiet and still, in order to be in tune with your inner-Spirit and for guidance and relaxation within.

13. **God is QUIET:**   a gentle disposition.

14. **God is POSITIVE:**   to be sure, definite, confident, absolute, determined. The results of 'positive thoughts' or actions are productive, fruitful, limitless

achievements. Never think 'negatively,' since it brings about non-effort and is therefore limiting and non-productive.

15. **God is WILLING**: always ready to be of use or service to yourself and others. *"God helps those who helps themselves."*

16. **God is KNOWLEDGE**: to know all that is or may be known. To learn or listen attentively, in order to gain understanding, knowledge and wisdom.

17. **God is WISDOM**: to be full of understanding and knowledge. After one has learnt all that is possible to know, one gains a higher understanding called 'wisdom' or to be wise.

18. **God is CONFIDENT**: to be self assured, bold, positive, fearless.

19. **God is THE RIGHT**: good, just, proper, correct, true.

20. **God is TRUTH**: to be honest and true to yourself and to others.

21. **God is OPEN-MINDED**: to be willing to accept all things and anything. You must not be close-minded because that makes you narrow-minded and you would then reject or disagree with a thing, without first giving it careful consideration or thought.

In order to learn and gain understanding, knowledge and wisdom, you must keep an open-mind and consider all things. Then after careful consideration, you choose what to ACCEPT and or what to REJECT. This is called POSITIVE THOUGHT and prevents any form of BRAIN WASHING, since it is you who makes the choices yourself.

22. **God is CONSCIOUS**: awake and knowing; the state of being mentally alert to one's surroundings. The knowledge of one's own thoughts and feelings. So, firstly you must be aware of and know yourself well. Take heed of all your ways and try your best to live to God's WAYS, which will bring deeper and enlightened consciousness to others and to all things.

23. **God is OBEDIENCE**: to obey and do all that is right, good and just to yourself and others but above all else be obedient to GOD. *"An obedient child is a BLESSED CHILD."*

24. **God is CLEANLINESS**: to be attentive to cleanliness. To keep yourself and surroundings clean, neat and tidy, in order to obtain peace, relaxation, calm, quiet, harmony and good health within your life.

25. **God is PURITY**: to be pure or un-mixed up in your mind or heart. A heart of truth, love, respect, willingness, modesty, unselfishness, kindness, generosity, calm and just, is a good and pure heart.

26. **God is PERFECTION**: complete, finished, faultless, correct, excellent, of the highest quality. Try to be PERFECT in yourself and also in everything you do, try to do it well. A perfect example of perfection is to look carefully at all of God's creations including yourself and see the great detail, depth and absolutely perfect forms and formations. The complexity and yet the simple order, co-ordination, balance and rhythms, each contributing to the other to achieve one simple function.

27. **God is HUMBLE**: to be humble is not to believe within yourself that you are better than anyone or anything.

28. **God is RESPONSIBLE**: to be trustworthy and reliable.

29. **God is CONSIDERATE**: to give everyone and everything serious and careful thought.

30. **God is COMMITTED**: to believe absolutely in what you are doing and do it.

31. **God is CONTENTED**: to be satisfied or pleased with all

you have, brings contentment or peace of mind.

32. **God is COMPASSION**: to show sympathy with the distress or suffering of another. To have pity and mercy.

33. **God is CREATIVE**: always strive to be original and be yourself. Be the first best and not second best. Be the 'creator of fashion' and not the 'follower of fashion.' Do your own thing and be original, inventive and creative. Remember you are unique; there is no one else like you in the universe, therefore, God created you original.

34. **God is HOLY**: Belonging or being devoted to God. Observing and doing all that God says is right to do. To live right and good in HIS sight. To live by all HIS WAYS will give you the knowledge of true complete love, peace and harmony, for all of **GOD'S ways is love!**

"If you wish to be blessed by God and to have a truly good eternal life and also if you wish to be righteous and want to get close to God, then you must live your life in 'all HIS ways' and 'master HIS ways.' Furthermore, you must 'observe' and 'obey' and 'do,' all HIS Commandments."

LIFE is -

Love, Respect, Discipline, Self-Control and Consciousness.

'God is Life' and the meaning of LIFE.

God is a good God and in order to be blessed by HIM, you have to become like HIM and be a good person.

PRACTICE MAKES PERFECT.

Therefore, if you practice HIS WAYS, you would become as perfect as HE is. Furthermore, if you practice what ever you wish to be, then you would also 'achieve it, become perfect at it' and hence ...**MASTER IT.**

The Children of the Lord God

'This is to parents on how to look after their children.'

Teach the children right, for God is 'the right.'

Care for the children properly and treat them right, for they are only your children whilst they are on earth but remember they are really God's children. Therefore, 'teach them truth, teach them right' whilst they are in your care.

DO NOT   argue, quarrel, fight, swear, be judgmental etc, in their presence.

DO NOT   give them what they want, just to keep them quiet or out of your way, instead 'give them what they need.'

Give them your time, patience, love, respect and understanding. Remember, God created us all in absolute innocence and purity of heart and this is how we re-enter the world, it is the actions and teachings of our parents which is fundamental to our behaviour and mental attitude.

There comes a time, when a child is 'answerable and punishable' for its own wrong doings. That time is when the child looses its pure innocence and becomes an adult (i.e. not an adult in terms of our society's Law 18 or 21 years); but an adult by God's Law, (i.e. consciously knowing **right** from **wrong**). At this stage their eyes are open and can clearly distinguish and understand the meaning of right from wrong or good from evil. Then if they 'knowingly and willingly do wrong/evil,' they will be punished (i.e. cursed) but if they do 'right/good' they will be blessed. The truth is, there is no sin, 'God does not punish, we punish ourselves.'

Developing your FREE-WILL THOUGHTS

'Your own mind.'

God has given us the right to use our own 'free-will thoughts,' to think anything we wish. Therefore, God gave us 'the freedom to choose' as we feel fit (i.e. born free).

Your **'free-will thoughts' (MIND)** is the same as;-

Your FREE Spirit

Your INNER Self

i.e. the **God-Part** within you

Therefore, if you wish to achieve anything, then you should use your 'free-will thoughts' (mind) in the following ways:-

1. Still your mind by blanking out other problems, all other thoughts and focus your concentration.

2. Consider the subject matter properly.

3. Once you are sure that it is what you **need,** or **desire,** then ask God for it, 'positively.'

4. Then simply follow your mind in goodness and sincerity. Your mind will tell you what to do and you will be able to devise the strategic plans on how to go about achieving it.

5. But to achieve what you desire, also takes great effort and hard work. Therefore, you must work at it until you achieve it.

 **REMEMBER.**

Try not to confuse your mind by adding other human material influences but concentrate on the pure subject matter. By considering all things and every angle, you will find a way to make it possible, to either achieve your goals or solve your problems. Practice and exercise your **free-will good thoughts** each day and it will develop and bring you to greater understanding, knowledge and wisdom. Furthermore, with practice and exercise of one's free-will good thoughts, then all things become possible. There are no limitations to what heights or depths you can achieve.

LIMITATIONS

It is you who choose to **limit** yourself, by placing invisible barriers around you. For instance, when you say *"I can't do it"* this is a **negative** 'free-will thought' which will bring about a **negative** 'free-will' response or action. Therefore, the effect and result will also be **negative**, ... i.e. non-productive; getting nowhere or fruitless.

On the other hand, the exact opposite action would occur, if your 'free-will thoughts' are **positive.** The eventual result will be **positive**... i.e. productive, fruitful or LIMITLESS.

"To every action, there is an equal re-action

God helps those who helps themselves."

In a true positive 'free-will thought,' there are no words such as;- *"maybe," "if only," "can't,"* etc... i.e. negative. There is only one word *"I WILL,"* (i.e. positive). Consider these words in the Lord's Prayer,

"Thy WILL be done, on earth as it is in heaven.

Where there is a WILL, there is a way

So your 'free-will thoughts' is your WILL... let's say, your own free-will. Therefore, it will be true to say, that you can WILL anything and it WILL happen.

"Whatever you can CONCEIVE - you can ACHIEVE.

You can CREATE whatever you IMAGINE."

INFINITY.

'Further considerations on limitations.'

If one believes that 'life' is never ending or eternal, then it would be true to say that 'life is infinite.' Therefore, a measurement cannot be placed on 'infinity,' whether it be a measured distance, length, or time. Hence, **distance, length** and **time** is another invisible barrier you erect to limit yourself. This also proves that there is **no time.** So, if there is no time, then try to imagine the vast amount of knowledge one can acquire throughout eternity (i.e. your INFINITE life-time), it too is immeasurable or limitless.

Now, consider if you had access to or were able to tap into the vast source of knowledge you have acquired since your original birth up till today. So you see, when one is allowed to open one's mind 'the power of thought' is far reaching... INFINITE.

 Conclusions.

Therefore, in order to use your 'free-will thoughts' properly, you must never close your mind to anything. In other words, to learn or to gain knowledge of any sort or to obtain wisdom; 'your mind must be open to receive everything.' Afterwards, consider what you have learnt and then decide what or which part of that lesson you choose to accept or reject (i.e. use your free-will thoughts and act accordingly).

However, your 'free-will thoughts and actions' must also be disciplined and controlled. You cannot go about life doing as you please, because you feel you have the 'free-will' to do as you wish. You must think through every thought carefully and ensure that you are doing the 'right thing' or taking the 'right actions' and avoid doing anything which is 'evil or harmful' to yourself or others.

THE CREATION of GOOD and EVIL
'FREE-WILL thoughts.'

If you believe that God created all things, then it would be true to say that God created 'good,' as well as, God created 'evil.' From the beginning it showed that God already had the knowledge of both but HE tried to protect us from the knowledge of EVIL. We would have only been aware of 'innocence and purity.' The same feelings are likened to a mother's love for her young baby; she protects it from all surrounding influences, with particular attention to the protection of evil or (i.e Harm).

Genesis 3:-22:-

> *"BEHOLD, the man is become one of us, to know GOOD and EVIL."*

Genesis 8:21:-

> *"I will not again curse the ground any more for man's sake; for the imagination of man's heart is Evil from his youth, neither will I again smite any more everything as I have done"*

Genesis 6:-5:-

> *"Every imagination of the thoughts of his heart (i.e. man's mind) was only evil continually."*

The moral is;- one should not think or imagine 'evil' but realise that it is within all of us. Our 'free-will thoughts' can either 'accept it or reject it.' However, it is better to be aware of its presence in us and reject it, as our 'free-will evil thoughts' will attract other 'free-will evil thoughts' (i.e. evil spirits) and will become too deeply involved in evil. Whereas the same conditions applies for our 'free-will good thoughts,' which will attract other 'free-will good thoughts' (i.e. good spirits) which is more beneficial for our FREE Spirits in our eternal evolution... i.e. life.

BLESSINGS and CURSES
'Good -v- Evil.'

*"Do good and good **will** follow you."*

*"The more you give, the more you **will** receive."*

*"Do onto others, as you **will** like them to do to you"*

These are familiar sayings which many people take for granted and do not consciously apply or practice in their daily lives. Taken seriously, they are your 'blessings.' We all have the power to **bless or curse** ourselves and or others, as a result of our own actions... i.e. words or deeds.

For instance;-

When you treat people 'right' or do something 'good,' that person will always say good things about you and will also be willing to help you if or whenever you are in need of support. Imagine, doing good throughout your life and think of the tremendous amount of blessings you will receive. It spreads far and wide and is multiplied over and over again. However, the reverse occurs when you 'ill-treat' people. They will be forever cursing or saying bad things about you and will never help you.

Therefore, your curses are also multiplied abundantly. Every 'curse' cancels out one of your 'blessings.' Curses can be converted into blessings, if you find a way of resolving what you did, either by a sincere apology, sincere forgiveness or doing whatever it takes to change a bad relationship into a good one.

This is all part of the principle of 'living in the consciousness of LOVE.' Being aware of God and the God-part within us, (i.e. our Holy Spirit), allows us to openly embrace love; accept our mistakes and express forgiveness without fear or embarrassment, knowing that the benefits are far reaching.

FORGIVENESS

Know that when someone is upset with you, it is because you have done something to hurt them. It's always initially your fault. Sometimes, you may not be aware that your 'words or deeds' had affected a person negatively. People tend to hold on to hurt or pain for a very long time. The longer it remains unresolved, it becomes infectious, like an untreated wound which spreads and gets deeper and deeper. This is when their curses to you can become dangerous, malicious or even physically harmful. Their pain can only be released when both parties consciously make amends.

"Forgive and you too shall be forgiven."

OBEDIENCE

Above all else, you should learn and try to obey God and follow His laws (i.e. the Ten Commandments). You should also obey those in authority ... i.e. your parents, elders, teachers, leaders, police etc. However, you should **not obey** them if they instruct you to do wrong or evil.

Should we make promises to God?

NO

We should not make any promise to God which we know we cannot keep throughout our life time.

A Promise is a 'definite deed,' which must be kept. Since we cannot predict our own future... that is to say, we don't know what could happen during the course of the day or the moment, which could prevent us from performing the definite deed or promise. Then we should not promise anything to God, that we know we may not be able keep.

God would like us to do unto HIM,

as we would like HIM to do unto us.

God takes us very seriously, therefore, we should also do the same to HIM. When God makes a promise to us, HE keeps that promise throughout our eternal life-time. Therefore, only God can make promises, since HE and HE alone can predict and determine our future.

So instead of making promises to God, we should say, *"God, I will try my best,"* this means;-

> I   -   meaning you
>
> WILL -   meaning your positive free-will
>
> TRY   -   meaning, if at all possible, you will make every effort

Therefore, this is a promise to try which is an **indefinite promise**. So, if any obstruction comes your way, then you don't have to worry.

TRUST
'Who should you trust?'

You should only trust God and yourself, because God will not fail you.

God **appoints** but man-**disappoints**. Therefore, do not put your trust in any man or woman, not even your own family.

Consider the saying:-

1. *"The arms of flesh will fail you, you dare not trust your own."* This means that people will fail you. You cannot even trust your own family much less strangers.

2. *"Go wise as a serpent but as harmless as a dove."*

ILLUSIONS
'There are no illusions.'

People who believe in 'illusions' are those whose 'eyes are closed,' trying to find a solution to disappointments.

But to a wise man there are no illusions, for his 'eyes are open' and can see the reality (i.e. what is there even if it appears not to be there... i.e. an Illusion), he can still see the reality of it.

Illusion is man's excuse for disappointment. Therefore, if he can't find a solution to a problem, he calls it an illusion. If one believes that 'all things are possible,' then all things are 'real.' Hence, 'there are no illusions.'

The name of the LORD and SPIRITS

In the Bible you will find that when an Angel of the Lord (i.e. messenger or Spirit) visited a person (e.g. Abraham, Isaac, Jacob, Joseph), the Angel would call the person's name and they in turn answer, *"here I am Lord."* Therefore, the word 'Lord or Master' is given to Angels or messengers of the Lord because they carry the authorised 'words of God' and rank high in the courts of God.

In ancient times, people could hear and see Spirits or get prophetic dreams more readily than they do nowadays, because their minds were free and open. It was also a natural custom, so they were not afraid. However, nowadays we have been wrongly indoctrinated, confused, frightened off by fears of evil, superstitions and guilt. Thereby stopping our higher spiritual progression, closing off our minds from the truth; limiting our powers: thus enabling others to readily control our existence.

DECEIVERS

The deceivers of the past, are the same deceivers now and will be the same deceivers to come.

Deceivers are one and the same type of people, they follow the same unchangeable but recognisable patterns.

DECEIVERS are good disguisers.

When your eyes are closed, you cannot see or recognise them for they come to you well disguised. It is true, that over the centuries the deceivers has taken away your **birth right**, (i.e. freedom of choice, knowledge and wisdom), by indoctrinating you to believe what they want you to know, thereby, 'closing your eyes from the truth.' So in turn, you have **no choice** but to believe their lies as the truth.

A DECEIVER is;   A FALSE PERSON

                      A LIAR

                      A PRETENDER

                      A HYPOCRITE

                      A FOOLER

                      A TRICKSTER.

However, 'truth will always prevail' and once your eyes are re-opened, you will again see **the light.** Remember, God is the truth and the light.

The two greatest evils of this world are;- FEAR and POWER.

1.   Good and righteous people are the ones who choose to 'guide' you but not to rule or control you for their own ends.

        God sends Spirit-Guides to guide, teach and assist you.

2.   Wicked, evil and deceitful people, are the ones who choose to 'rule and control' you for their own ends, gain and benefit.

'Deceit derives from greed.' It is this greed that has caused people to devise ways and methods to convincingly deceive in order to control, so that they can have power over you.

TO THE DECEIVER;-

        POWER   means   WEALTH

        WEALTH   means   MONEY.

Hence, the phrase; 'money is the root of all evil and money buys everything' but money cannot buy true love, friendship, health or happiness. God gives you the same wealth, plus true love and eternal happiness, if you would choose to follow and obey Him completely.

CHOICE

You have **no rights** to anything on this earth. God is the only true owner, therefore, nothing belongs to you but everything is entrusted to you. God gave you Himself as **the right** and only gave you the **right to choose** how you wish to live (i.e. good or bad, success or failure, happy or sad etc).

When you look into your life's history, you will see that everything you have done, you chose to do (consciously or unconsciously). Therefore, you are directly responsible for every stage, every event, every mistake, every success and for where you have reached to date. Hence, when in doubt or desire to blame others, look into your own heart and point at yourself because **you are what you chose to be.**

REWARDS

The three great gifts of life.

1. Faith.

Is that un-questionable and undying trust, obedience, belief and love of God and yourself. God's gift to you in return is... eternal fulfilment, wisdom and close union with Him.

2. Hope.

Everyone needs something in life to look forward to or to hold on to in times of distress or need. God's gift to you in return is... strength.

3. Charity.

Charity does not only mean giving money to the under privileged, the deprived or the poor but also means willingly and unselfishly giving your time, patience, understanding and assistance to anyone in need of help.

God's gift in return is... to multiply what ever you have given and give it back to you in abundance.

These **three Gifts** exist in both your 'spiritual and physical life.' God always repays a good deed with something good and beneficial to you. Therefore, in your Spiritual life, you continue to perform the acts of **faith, hope** and **charity,** in order to aspire to greater heights.

WISDOM

"Wisdom is Simplicity and Innocence."

When I say that 'God is truth,' 'God is love,' 'God is the right,' 'God is good,' then **think**, and try to understand the deep meaning of these words. Whenever we do any of these things (i.e. tell the truth, love, do right and good) wholeheartedly and unselfishly, we feel happy and free. Our conscience does not bother us and our hearts and minds feel free, comfortable and clear.

We have **wisdom** from the moment we become an adult (i.e. understanding fully the meaning of good from evil; right from wrong) but we cannot see the vast amount of wisdom we possess, because we prefer to complicate matters and our minds. Therefore, our minds become confused and it is not until we get much older and has passed through various experiences, do we gradually begin to understand the **simplicity of wisdom.** At the end of the day, when we look back into our own life experiences; knowledge gained, efforts made, trials, tribulations and glories, we'd find that these were all for our own personal growth (i.e. the lessons of life we chose to experience and overcome, whilst on earth). The eternal evolution of life is simply a matter of personal tests and challenges we've set for ourselves (i.e. our Soul's purpose), which is evaluated on our return to the Spirit world. The evaluation is based on how well we recognised, managed and accomplished our tasks. We are solely responsible for our own physical/spiritual development; at our own pace and in our own time. Hence, you'll notice that people mature at different ages. It is all linked to awareness, intuition and experiences.

> *"**AGE** does not denote WISDOM*
>
> *but **MATURITY** in years."*

We also graduate through the great Spiritual Halls-of-Learning and those of us who become Spiritual-Masters are chosen by God to perform a specific purpose on our return to earth, along with our own personal life's challenges and tests. This physical world is simply a stage of learning but 'Spiritual learning' is on a much higher level, leading us to become 'Masters of our own life,' entitling us to sit in the courts of our supreme Father and true Master of the universe - **GOD!**

On the other hand, many people choose to take life easy and not bother so intensely about anything. Their lives will evolve slowly but this is their choice and this too is alright with God, because He knows that they'd eventually wake up and move on. It does not matter how long they take because **life is infinite,** hence, God can afford to be patient and is also the reason He respects our **free-will choices** because we have a long time in which to learn, make amends and grow.'

My Encounters with God.

• AND HIS MESSAGES FOR THE 21ST CENTURY.

"I AM the LIGHT"

"I AM the WAY"

"I AM the TRUTH"

"In the beginning there was the WORD."

*"The WORD is **LOVE** - for **I AM LOVE.**"*

*"The WORD is **TRUTH** - for **I AM TRUTH.**"*

BEING OF SERVICE

*"We are all teachers and pupils to each other. Everyone of us has a special purpose to fulfil and everything that happens to each of us in life (good or bad) is for the **Soul-purpose** of helping others to overcome adversity or in some other way; as well as, to teach and gain a better understanding of LIFE in which to aid our eternal evolutionary journey. Hence, we are all called to be of service to humanity, no matter how big or small, for each is of equal importance."*

MAKING THE CONNECTION

*"We also service each other everyday but most of us are unaware of our actions. There is **no coincidence, chance or accidental meeting.**

Your **SPIRIT** leads you to the person who has the answers to your questions or for someone else close to you. It could be direct or indirect (i.e. found in-between an unrelated conversation or from reading something; or whilst watching television) messages to help us in our life's journey, are sent to us from all directions but most of the time we miss the connection, because we are either too busy or completely unaware of these **connecting forces** or **spiritual interactions.**

To be consciously aware is to know that everything and everyone is for a purpose and connects to serve you or visa versa.*

STOP, BE STILL, LOOK, LISTEN & THINK

A safety-code we've all been taught but do not always use for our own spiritual growth and physical benefit and or for the growth/ benefits of others, by passing on the information received."

My Encounters with God

In 1994, once Rudolph and I got together, we instantly became inseparable 'like two peas in the same pod.' Our friends constantly remarked on the radiance we were exuding and how this reflection also gave them the desire to look for true love, in the hope of bringing some happiness into their lives. But I told them; *"there is no need to search, just ask God and HE will send you the right person."*

Within two years, Rudolph had taken me back to Trinidad three times. It was on our second trip that I had my first encounter with God. The 16th May 1996, felt no different than any other day, except for the usual holiday excitement. We decided it was a good day to go to the capital (Port of Spain) to take in the sights, delicious food and shops. Whilst travelling along the motorway a strange sense of peace and calm came over me. I took a deep breath, closed my eyes, rested my head back and relaxed, taking in the ambience. When out of the blue, I heard this beautiful male voice say;-

*"I have been preparing you for your **mission** for some time."*

Start your work.

*Your **mission** begins NOW.*

*Start writing all your **divine experiences** and MY **direct messages**.*

*The number **seven** is your spiritual working number. It is when MY force is at its greatest. You will feel MY force in your third eye. Start listening to your inner-self. Be still and you will hear MY voice.*

*I AM the **POWER***

*I AM **DIVINITY***

*I AM your **FATHER***

I AM the MASTER and CREATOR of all things.

'OBEY My words' and you'll receive ever lasting blessings.

Be SURE - NEVER FEAR - for I shall be with thee NOW.

Through 'ME' all things are possible.

One day, you will SEE MY FACE.

I AM THE LIGHT

I AM THE WAY."

In my mind, I quietly replied, *"Lord I Accept."* Then without feeling emotional, tears began flowing down my face. Rudolph held my hands and asked what was wrong. I told him; he didn't question; we just held hands in silence. After this first direct encounter, I only received two more short visits, then God left me alone to enjoy the rest of the holiday. I didn't know what HE had planned for me and didn't care, because I knew in my heart that whatever HE asked, I was prepared to do.

By some strange coincidence Rudolph had to deliver a package given to him in England by a friend, to pass onto someone in Trinidad. When we arrived at this person's home, it was situated one street away from where I was born in San Juan. For some unknown reason this gentleman (in the early sixties) started to talk about God and his personal divine experiences. Then he pointed at a large picture (drawn by himself) hanging in the living room and asked if I knew who it was. I recognised the face as one of the Masters I had seen when I was taken to the 'Halls of Learning.' He said that it was the 'face of God' who had been visiting him since the age of three years and who had taken him on many astral travels. He then pointed to another framed picture with the same person surrounded by clouds and young angels. I also recognised this picture, since my grandmother had an identical one hanging in her living room. This was the first time I'd seen it again since childhood. The gentleman spoke at length about the many divine messages he had been receiving since childhood and his spiritual experiences, all of which were far greater than mine.

He said that the world was in great danger; he'd seen disasters, the destruction of the West, floods, fires, earthquakes, wars etc and that he had been called to do certain works to bring about peace and create awareness. He warned me that there were **secret keys** given to us by God to open certain spiritual doors for ourselves. These keys, I must keep secret and if others want to learn; let them build their own relationship with God and leave it up to God to release the secrets to them in HIS own time. I immediately understood what he meant. He too was an ordinary man, married with children.

Later that month, God visited me again; HE mentioned that many religious people and churches believed that CHRIST would be returning to earth in the year 2000 but HE said that they were wrong and misguided.

> *"The Year 2000 is not the coming of CHRIST but the coming together of 'Christian minds,' not in the same sense of Christians as we understand today but 'CHRIST-like minds'; (i.e. **the minds of Love**) to change the world."*
>
> ### *The 21st Century is a Spiritual Revival."*

The following month, Rudolph and I returned to England, happy, relaxed and looking forward to the future.

In July '96 God revisited and said, *"I would like you to prepare yourself for a Spiritual Rebirth."* I didn't understand, so HE explained;-

> *"For the next three days you must take a bath (before 6am), pray, fast and meditate. Have no sex and be ready on the **third day** to celebrate your **Spiritual Rebirth**."*

On the third day, clean out and bless your house; display lots of beautiful fresh flowers; cook a delicious meal; invite Marsha and Dee over, so that together you all can eat, drink, be merry and celebrate your day of Rebirth."

I did exactly as I was told, but did not realise that the *third day* fell on 25th July 1996, which God then explained was:-

> The 7th day (i.e. 25 is 2+5 = 7)
>
> of the 7th month (July)
>
> in the 7th year (1996 is 1+9+9+6 = 25 = 7)

"On this day your spiritual and physical beings are united as ONE."

From then onward, God became my main teacher. Although there seemed to be no apparent change in my outward personality but in my inner-self, the change was significant. I noticed that I became even more consciously aware and open to my 'inner-Spirit.' I'm also surrounded by a tranquil aura of sustained inner peace, which is heightened when I'm 'in the Spirit' or in the presence of God and the Spirit-Masters. I consciously levitate whilst 'in the Spirit,' can actually hear my Spirit speak and can also write 'from the Spirit.' I feel an intense heat emitting from my hands when I'm praying, especially when thanking God. Once you have reached this state of **spiritual consciousness,** you begin to realise that 'your Spirit' knows much more than you do including what you were sent here to do and actually guides you in the right direction to fulfil your purpose and desires. You can also call on other Spirit-Helpers (i.e. Guardian Angels, loved-ones and Masters in every profession) for any assistance you need in coping with life's everyday problems, career and so on.

God's messages.

- **FOR THE 21ST CENTURY AND MY MISSION.**

"We are all sent to serve a purpose,
to serve each other
and to simply unite in love."

═ GOD'S Messages for the 21st Century ═ and My Mission

In August '96, God detailed HIS messages and my missions;-

1. To write this book detailing my life's experiences (spiritual and physical).

2. To deliver and spread HIS universal messages for the 21st Century, in this book.

3. To establish the **1st July, The Celebration of Life,** as an annual day of love. On this day, everyone should consciously focus on 'universal love' and the respect of all life forms... i.e. humans, animals and the environment. HE instructed me to make **a special badge** showing HIS light shinning through the earth's globe (blue seas and green lands) with a vein of blood flowing through it (see page 498). This represents the precious 'blood of all life' (i.e. humans and animals), our inter-dependence on each other and connection with Mother Earth;- as a permanent reminder of our conscious respect and duty of care. This badge should be worn daily but especially on the 1st July-Celebration Day. It would also indicate how far HIS messages has spread.

4. To call on HIS children to return to love, peace, truth and back to nature.

5. To remind us that HE is the **God of LOVE** and not the god of hate.

6. To rebuild a personal relationship directly with HIM and to remind us of the importance of **obedience to HIS laws.** To keep an open mind, search within for our true-selves and learn to **live in the consciousness of love.**

- **HEALTH 2000 -**
  To re-educate the nation on natural food and health care.

7. To expose how our **free-will, choice, health and life** are being conveniently jeopardised, in order to maintain 'control, power and wealth.'

   (a).   To come together and peacefully oppose any form of abuse.

   (b).   Tampering with nature especially the new 'genetic engineering' which HE called the final straw and fatal menace; the mass use of synthetic chemicals and drugs.

   (c).   To demand information from which to make informed choices;

   (d).   To take back direct control and personal responsibility for our own actions, health and life.

   (e).   and to use our **free-will**.

Then HE warned me;-

- *"You must not form any churches or religious cults or have any followers or be fanatical."*

- *"You must make it absolutely clear, that no one is under any obligation to believe anything, no one is to be brainwashed but instead encouraged to use their free-will, follow their own minds and make their own decisions."*

Then God and the Spirit-Masters worked with me in preparing the mission statement, aims and objectives and action plan.

October '96, God instructed me to choose a team of people to help set up and organise the mission. HE reminded me that even Jesus was instructed to choose his disciples and many others to help him carry out his mission. *"No one sent, works alone, because there must always be proof and witnesses of HIS words and works."*

So naturally, I thought this was going to be an easy mission. All I needed to do was to call on my friends who believed in God, tell them HIS words and they would jump to it and automatically join me in HIS mission.

However, to prepare me for disappointment. God reminded me, *"don't forget that people denied and cursed Jesus, called him a liar, then crucified him for doing what he was sent and instructed to do (i.e. God's works)."* In other words; put my trust in HIM alone and not in people. But I still thought it was going to be easy.

At this point of the story, I'd like to take you through the actual stages and events from calling my friends to God's messages and instructions thereafter.

On **7th November '96** the following letter (which God and the Spirit-Masters helped to prepare) was sent out to 17 friends to attend a meeting to be held at my home on 30th November '96.

Letter of Invitation   7th November 1996

Dear

SERVING MY PURPOSE
'Fulfiling a God-Given Mission.'

I've always known that my achievements and struggles were going to be used in some way to help others but I was not sure of the direction it would eventually take until this year. Whilst on holiday in Trinidad, I received a direct message from God.

God also told me many other secrets which I'm not yet at liberty to reveal. However, HE recently instructed me that it was time to choose the team of people, who would help me to fulfil this mammoth task.

HE has not told me 'who to choose' and has left it up to me to choose those whom I feel would understand the call or MISSION and who are likely to commit to the cause.

What is in it for you?

Those who help serving and fulfiling God's purpose receive HIS blessings in accordance to his or her individual effort, loyalty, obedience and commitment in accomplishing the mission. *"Personal gain is immaterial but yet it is a consequence of your actions, along the same principle that the more you give, the more you'll receive. Therefore, you gain in many more ways than is realistically conceivable. It takes a hard working team to achieve GOLD."*

However, this is what HE stated should go into this letter for those chosen;-

"This is not a *'Colour'* thing

or a *'Gender'* thing

or a *'Status'* thing

or an *'Ego'* thing

It is a 'LOVE' thing.

When one is serving God's purpose, it becomes a much bigger thing because it 'services humanity' as a whole. It is not individual but 'inter-related, inter-connected and inter-dependent.'

Therefore, I've chosen you and those listed because I believe that your faith and mind could be blind to the above (i.e. colour, gender etc). Although conscious of the importance of each factor; disadvantage knows NO boundaries but 'true love and faith is blind' (God is LOVE and UNIVERSAL). There are times we are called to overlook our own individual disadvantages in order to achieve a greater good. Hence, a Working Team for God's good must work with:-

ONE HEART

ONE MIND

ONE VISION

ONE COMMITMENT

ONE LOVE

hence, FOCUSED ON ONE POINT.

"The centre of the whole MISSION."

There is no time for jealousy, envy, vanity or greed because individually and collectively, we'll receive our own 'just rewards' based on 'effort and obedience,' for we are called on to ACT but not to judge.' I must do my Father's work according to HIS purposefully designed plan. Therefore, you must be made aware of your significance in the scheme of things.

I now realise that although I'm driven by my own ambition, God has purposely directed my vision for the benefit of myself and others. To show them in the most practical sense that through HIM **all things are possible** and that 'talent is natural;' which can't be taught, because it is God given.

So please don't look upon me as anything special or different. Therefore, do you feel that you are up to this mammoth task? If you feel you are unable to commit to the cause then you are free to say 'No'. **Just trust your instincts and follow your own mind.** Your decision or choice is in your hands and God will love you for using your 'free-will' and for being true to yourself. So you are not compelled to say 'Yes.'

A Celebration of LIFE.

1ST JULY

A divine mission to establish a *'universal day of LOVE,'*
to unite, restore and heal the world
for the 21st century.

On 16th November 1996, God gave these messages *(below)* and instructed me to;-

(a). Give a copy to Rudolph, Marsha and Dee, to prepare and strengthen them for whatever eventuality and the possible consequences of carrying out HIS works. They too must also be allowed to 'freely choose' whether or not they wished to be a part of the team.

(b). To read the same messages and instructions at the first meeting on 30th November. Then give a copy to each person so they could take it home, read, digest, consider, then decide whether or not they wished to be a part of the team.

God's MESSAGE

 LIMITATIONS.

"The grass is never greener on the other side."

Whatever is 'man made' is quickly cultivated but whatever is 'God-made' takes a long time to nurture and mature. The results of anything 'man made' are to provide quick, superficial, selfish benefits! However, the results and benefits of 'God-made' are 'universally everlasting or eternal' (even your lives). Therefore, God places 'no time limit' on anything (i.e. limitless... in life there are no limitations).

- **God's Mission is LIMITLESS.**

Therefore, we must not place any time for its completion or determine levels of success or failure. Once HE has chosen people to carry out HIS work; know that it will eventually be completely accomplished one day. Your job is to take it as far as you can possibly go, until someone else, is sent to carry on... or take over from you. It's like a relay race, each link in the relay chain is dependent on the other to run the race of his/her life in order to finally 'WIN'. Hence it takes;-

> *"Great effort, determination, commitment, faith, will, stamina, discipline, self reliance, courage, strength (POWER) and TEAM SPIRIT to WIN!"*

Nevertheless, nothing happens in an instant; it takes time; years of good preparation to build a sufficiently strong winning team - (DYNAMITE). However, the strongest in the team is positioned 'last' to lead them into victory. So never get disheartened when progress appears to be slow, just keep focused on gold!

When or if ever you become despondent, read your 'Invitation Letter; this Mission letter' and the 'Aims & Objectives' of the Mission in order to restore your commitment.

JUST SERVE YOUR PURPOSE;-

THROUGH	the People
FOR	the People
WITH	the People
BY	the People

Then CHANGE will come.

People power will topple any Government or illegal law. So 'spread the word' and get the people... the masses involved.

- **Voluntary**.

Everyone who agrees to do God's work, does so voluntarily by your own **free-will**. Therefore, this mission will also be voluntary.

- **FREEDOM and EQUALITY.**

Everyone is born the same 'naked and free' but no one is born EQUAL. You are born equal to your obedience to God. Therefore, God continuously rewards you for your 'obedience and effort' throughout your eternal life. Hence, you can be born a pauper and become a King. **Rewards do not always mean financial wealth** but the overall healthy state of mind, body and Spirit and genuine happiness that surround the person. Like Jesus, Mother Teresa, Nelson Mandela, Mahatma Gandhi and many others. There are many people who are extremely wealthy but restless, unhappy and physically sick. How often the poor are fooled by the belief that if they were to win the lottery, it would bring an end to all their financial worries and bring eternal happiness; then when it happened, it only brought them unbelievable misery and they lived to regret winning. How many rich people are terminally ill and their wealth cannot pay for a cure. How many poor people who were terminally ill, yet miraculously healed by God for free.

"Therefore, TRUE SUCCESS is peace within yourself and the Health and Happiness of those around you."

This is only achievable by understanding yourself, surrendering to God, obedience and fulfiling your purpose. Since true purpose is God-made, it therefore automatically embraces 'love' which in turn is outwardly spreading, giving some form of joy or benefit to others. Therefore, your personal accomplishment brings a personal success of intense overall happiness, love and peace; giving to a much healthier lifestyle (i.e. the more you give with love, you receive the same in return but in abundance).

We also die the same 'naked and free,' leaving everything behind except for either the good or bad name we've cultivated.

- **God the Businessman.**

God is a great businessman, because HE invests a lot in us over many years of precise preparation, then HE risks giving us the 'secrets of life' in the hope that we would not betray HIS trust and go the other way. HE knows that we all possess 'good and evil' and gambles on free-will, leaving us open to choose the 'true and right way.' However, HE knows that the ones HE chooses are more than likely to remain faithful. They also possess good business-sense or common-sense (i.e. like minds), because it takes a business brain to plan and devise strategies which would bring HIS purpose to fruition.

Planting the Seeds of Change

"I have planted many seeds (i.e. Spirit Masters) in every country throughout MY universe in preparation for the 21st century, when they'd begin to blossom, flourish and grow fruit. You are but a small part of MY SEED-BED or garden. When the time is right, I will be coming out in a BLAZE OF GLORY to reclaim and restore MY innocent children.

So Nourish MY garden well,

Take good-care; time and patience in nurturing MY SEEDS,

Love and cherish the fruits-of-your-labour,

So you'll stand in good stead on GLORY DAY.

Dounne is the MASTER of Masters

She is the   **TEACHER**

She is the   **COMMUNICATOR**

She is the   **KEEPER OF MY LAWS.**

I have set an 'impenetrable shield' around her, so that no evil, not even the devil himself can penetrate; but he would be able to influence those around her; so be careful. This shield of amour is essential, for I am setting her up as a TARGET against the ENEMY and she will need powerful protection against the many weapons and forces, which will continuously bombard her (physically, mentally and spiritually).

But she will survive. *She is the power of the 'SEVENTH STAR' and holds My staff. This is the ultimate reward for everlasting OBEDIENCE."*

- **Answering The Lord's Call.**

"People generally ask themselves the wrong question before answering MY call. They'd instantly ask themselves; can I do it? Am I capable? mainly because they are in awe and sometimes in FEAR of the whole situation.

TO OBEY MEANS TO ACCEPT. *Therefore, do not question yourself because, 'I' would not choose you, if 'I' did not believe in you and if 'I' did not provide you with all the means, capability, vision and strength to accomplish 'MY' work.*

*All you need to do is sit back in quiet meditation and consider all that is said and asked of you. After careful consideration, if you are happy to do the work, then simply answer in the affirmative **'LORD I ACCEPT.'** Your mere presence does not mean that you have accepted; you have to make your CONFIRMATION TO ME personally. Then you are not brainwashed into anything because you choose freely and willingly! You then cannot cast blame on anyone, if you feel dissatisfied in anyway, because you accept full responsibility for your actions. Remember 'a good cause never achieves an evil end' (i.e. out of Evil cometh Good). Therefore, whenever you are going through an experience, once overcome, that experience can be used to help others to also overcome the same. It's always for a greater good."*

 REFLECTIONS.

I asked God what HE meant by, *"I've planted many seeds (i.e. Spirit-Masters) throughout MY universe."* HE explained that HE has sent millions of other Spiritual Messengers throughout the world to do HIS works in bringing an end to the destructive forces (i.e. evil) and to prepare the groundwork for HIS coming. They have been working on the **prevention of abuse and the restoration of love,** each selflessly playing a vital part in completing the much bigger picture for the greater good of the universe. Most don't even know that they are Masters, purposely sent to fulfil this calling but realise they are driven by an extraordinarily deep passion to help the disadvantaged. In their genuine 'work of love' they would be recognised. A Spirit-Master could be anyone from a vagrant, priest, royalty, prisoner, child, able, disabled, every race, creed and gender.

There are many academically qualified Theologists or holders of high office in the priesthood, who have not been directly authorised to speak or work in HIS name. HIS authority or appointment holds no certification, class, status, race, gender or age.

HE added;-

> *"If only one person understands (the call), let that be enough for you because if each Master did the same, then this would result in millions of people around the world, who would continue the work-of-love. I repeat, you are not to form any churches, religions or followers, for MY children should be allowed to consciously choose to FOLLOW ME.* **You are the final calling** *to awaken and alert all of MY children."*

I didn't understand what being the **'7th' STAR** meant because God would not elaborate. However, when I meditated, I remembered the first time I saw Jesus at the age of **'7'** he appeared as a huge STAR.

I also thought about the various things associated with the number **'7'** and stars.

- The '7' wonders of the world.

- Many follow their STAR SIGNS.

- Some people worship certain STARS.

- To be a STAR is to be brilliant; a shinning example to others, to radiate a brightness. A powerful light.

- Some people describe their feelings as being in '7th' heaven.

- '7' colours in the rainbow.

- '7' days in the week.

- '7' Chakras.

- My Mum mentioned the '7' Senses.

- The week before receiving this message, I told Marsha that I was sensing my Egyptian existence very strongly and that when I was praying, my hands wanted to cross over my chest and I could feel a staff in both hands. I also want to put a STAR on my forehead (between my eyes; known as the 'third eye') and could actually feel its impression.

- When I was born the Doctors gave me only 28 days to live; (my birthday is also on the 28th (multiples of '7'). Apparently my grandmother told the Doctors, *"This one is not going to die, she has come to stay for a purpose."* My grandmother nursed me to life and our love was so strong that after she died she continued to be my Spirit-Guide. Now I realised that she was sent to be my first teacher. When I was very young, she told me that *"God had placed a special protective veil over me; anyone who tries to hurt me, would be punished '7' times over."*

Have Confidence In God

'This message was given to me by a Spirit-Master on 30/11/95.'

"When praying or doing anything with God, you must have;-

Total	*CONFIDENCE*
Total	*CONVICTION*
and absolute	*FAITH in God.*

You must know and truly believe that God will service your needs and desires.

BE STRONG

BE SURE

BE POSITIVE IN HIM

Do not SWAY.

Do not allow anyone or anything to weaken your thoughts.

STAND FIRM

STAND FAST

Let your Faith in HIM be BOLD.

It need not be arrogant or rude but absolutely assured that HE is with you just waiting to know that you are ready and willing to serve HIM and to serve humanity through HIM. Be assured that you will be blessed.

To have **faith** *is to have 'confidence in HIM' and know that you are safe and protected. HE can turn any situation around but remember that you must take full responsibility for all your actions.*

So now **GO FORWARD**

and **SERVE the Lord God**

with **STRENGTH, COMMITMENT** *and* **HUMILITY.***"*

After I'd written down this information, I called Marsha to type and prepare it for the meeting. She was the first to learn of the contents. Then as initially instructed, I gave copies to Marsha, Dee and Rudolph, to read, digest and consider. After which, I had a private meeting with Marsha and Dee to prepare them first; to come to terms with what I was being called to do. This was not difficult because they were used to our spiritual conversations and our Guides but when it came to preparing them for the worst possible eventuality (i.e. death) and why they should not retaliate. They broke down and questioned why should God put me in such danger; for people who didn't care about anything anyway; the amount of good people who have died or have been killed serving God (including Jesus) and still people have not changed but have become even more cruel, aggressive and abusive? I explained, that it did not mean that I would be killed but that we must consciously deal with it, without dwelling on death, since this was inevitable for all, regardless of what we do or how we lived; but an honour, if it was in the service of God; beneficial to my Spirit and eternal evolution.

As usual, I allowed them to express all their fears but during this process, their anguishing cries reached deep into my Soul and I too broke down. I knew how much they loved me and tried very hard to protect me from any form of harm. In their hearts, they knew that they could not stop me from doing God's work. A lot of their fears centred around their personal distrust of other people. Marsha said, *"Mum, people don't know you like we do and I don't think you even realise how different you really are to everyone else. I don't know anyone in this world who is like you. You are too trusting, loving, sincere, open, giving, sharing, kind and forgiving. People, even your so-called friends will stab you in the back; will get jealous and will say cruel things about you and you'll still turn a blind eye, forgive and welcome them back as your friends. We never wanted to share your spiritualty with anyone else, much less the entire world but if this is what God wants you to do, then we cannot be selfish."*

I then called on God, the Spirit-Masters and their Spirit-Guides. We talked, prayed and meditated and was soon back to normal, laughing and chatting as usual, whilst agreeing to take on the world regardless of the consequences. Marsha instantly committed to be a part of the team; Dee declined for her own private reasons but confirmed her committed support. Then it was Rudolph's turn; he too committed to be a part of the team. So with my family at my side, I felt more at ease, because from past experiences their support has always been my greatest strength.

- **30 November 1996.**

On the morning of the first meeting (30/11/96) whilst saying my prayers and in meditation. I wrote this letter 'in the Spirit,' for the team.

I'm no different to any of you;-

I've two sides: my physical outer-being and

     my spiritual inner-being.

However, through my 'Spiritual rebirth' this year, I've become ONE, spiritually and physically connected. Therefore, man can try to harm my physical (i.e. humiliate, imprison or ruin me), but they'll never succeed in ever conquering my Spirit, because both the physical and spiritual are FREE and knows its purpose.

> SO DO NOT FEAR FOR ME
>
> DON'T FEEL SORRY FOR ME
>
> BUT PRAY FOR ME.

On my own I'm strong but with your collective support, I'll become **DYNAMITE**, I know I will WIN because it has been ordained to be so. Our Father set this plan long before we were born; we agreed to return to fulfil this purpose. Now the time has come for us to do our work.

None of us met by accident, we were supposed to meet when we did, we were supposed to feel the spiritual connection when we met. Between some of us there was telepathy.

I'm no longer answerable to man's desires; my sole concern is for when I finally return home, I can stand before my Father and say, *"Lord! here I am, I've fulfiled my task."*

I've divorced myself completely from the devil and its only this month that my Father had to remind me of his existence, his presence and his cunning. Now that our 'forces' have joined, he is busily making his own plans on how to break us. His victory would be to prevent or delay God's plan from happening on the ordained date. In fact, his plans always look or appear to be good and beneficial to us and our purpose. It would look very close to God's plan. So we have to keep our heads and be vigilant. God reminded me that Judas was a disciple of Jesus and Lucifer was God's favourite angel. However, don't worry, the Lord will Prevail. We must remain FOCUSED on;-

> where we are going and
>
> try to stay on the Right path
>
> to our journey's end.

Our first deadline date is 1st July 1997, the launch date of the mission. We must attempt to create maximum media impact, so that the entire nation starts to become aware of our objectives; become involved, take direct action and support our goals. The momentum should start well before July and build-up to the launch date.

The Lord never works in secret. Therefore, to those of you who have committed, HE will reveal HIS plans and will also work through you.

HE does not want any;-

> Churches formed
> or Religious cults
> or for us to become fanatics.

You should go about your work peaceably influencing people to use their 'free-will' and take responsibility for their own lives. You will peaceably influence the Authorities to divulge the truth and change their Laws.

Free-will cannot be forced upon people, since it is they who must choose for themselves. Hence, you are in a battle of wits and to make peace on both sides but at the same time, you must be bold in questioning the Authorities, in order to ignite the flames which produce 'passion' and then simmers down as truth is revealed. *"Only the enemy would want to keep the flames raging and then the devil will expose himself and in this case you battle with him until you WIN."*

The First Meeting

The meeting was due to start at 1pm. Marsha, Rudolph and I waited patiently to see who or how many would actually turn up, as we were aware that the 'forces of evil' were by now very active. Out of the seventeen friends, fifteen indicated that they were interested but only eight were able to attend because the others had previously confirmed engagements.

Problems started from the outset. Almost everyone encountered obstacles to prevent them reaching my home.

For instanc;:-

- One found that she had no money and was forced to borrow the travel fare at the last minute.

- A couple travelling by car from another city but who knew London very well, missed the turning and was heading in the opposite direction, miles away from my home.

- Another swore that she saw the meeting time as 6pm instead of 1pm.

- Others who were coming by taxi, found that none was available, plus unusually heavy traffic jams and so on.

They all eventually arrived and the meeting commenced at 6pm. I followed God's instructions to the letter, then explained in depth and requested their co-operation and assistance. Having had no experience in these matters, I placed my trust in God, that as a Team (or disciples) HE would guide us. To my disappointment, when the matter of commitment came up, they all avoided the issue, making every possible excuse, declaring how exceptionally busy they would be with their own personal projects and would not be able to devote much time to the mission. The meeting was then transformed into a general conversation, instigated by one person in particular, who came prepared and with her own private agenda. The aura and atmosphere in the room immediately changed and sensed instantly by Marsha, Rudolph and myself. Being aware of the 'negative forces' at work, we knew that it was important to stay calm and simply observe. Before long, they were totally engrossed; detailing their own projects at which point, I closed the meeting and invited them to eat.

After they had left, we sat down, laughed and pondered about human nature, friends, faith and the forces of evil. Each of us felt that there was a strong, negative, dominating force surrounding the main instigator and that it was this aura which had filled the room.

I was beginning to realise that the task was not going to be as easy as I envisaged.

• Message Received On 1st December 1996.

The following morning whilst praying, God visited and reminded me that:-

"Many are called but few are chosen. You must not loose heart because people are overcome with fear when faced with 'real power' and the realities of 'true power.' When called to expose or reveal their own spirituality, they become consumed by the 'fears of personal attacks, public ridicule, reprisals and insecurities.' They believe in ME within their own hearts but are not strong enough to expose their hearts. Such people prefer to keep their faith in the closet or within the safe centres of

their churches. Hence, invariably when you call on them, you may find yourself standing alone but stay faithful, because in the end MY sheep always return."

• Message Received On 6th December 1996.

God visited and instructed me to send this letter to the Team, even though the majority had not yet made a commitment to the mission.

Letter To Team

• **Natural Instincts** :-

> *"Try to develop your Natural Instincts and*
>
> *true relationship with your Father (God)"*

Natural instinct comes from within; understand that your Spiritual-being lives within your physical body, hence to find your true-self, you are always advised to search within. This is the same reason God advised us to follow our own minds and trust your natural instincts, because with practice, you'd eventually become acutely aware of your own thoughts.

How many times do we unconsciously tell ourselves to do something or to go in a certain direction; <u>but we didn't</u> and on reflection we'd say, *"if only I'd followed my mind."* **Your mind is your Spirit-being speaking to you.** Remember, that in your Spirit-life, you asked to return here; at this time; in this form; in this race. Everything you are now, you asked to be. Therefore, your Spirit knows what it was sent here for and tries to direct you on your true path. Invariably, you come off-course and lose your way, simply because brainwashed (Book) education steals your 'natural instincts' by re-directing your focus (thoughts) on books (which is the studying of another man's thoughts) designed by man to redefine and decide your purpose which is generally wrapped up in false hope and economic wealth. Hence, you become controlled by man for the benefit of man. However, part of the re-direction is also caused by your own disobedience. It is not until you've passed through these life experiences, that some of us whose Spirit is strong, will escape and regain our freedom. Then true-life becomes uncomplicated, loving and nurturing, simply because you've become aware of and guided by your own Spirit... (i.e. your true-self) and begin to follow your true path or destiny.

Developing a Relationship with our true Father GOD

'This too is born out of NATURAL INSTINCTS.'

When a child is born, it is born blind but 'instinctively' knows how to suckle its mother's breast for food. Instinctively, it gets to know its mother's voice, feel, smell and can even sense her presence before being touched. As it begins to develop, both its mother and father teaches it 'right from wrong' and also establishes a close-bonded, supportive, loving relationship of trust. This trust remains, even when it is punished for doing wrong or going against its parents wishes (i.e disobedience). When it needs anything, it would automatically ask its parents for it. Whenever it feels fearful, threatened or insecure, it would immediately seek one of its parents for comfort, simply because it will always feel safe, protected and re-assured in its parents arms or care. It would also seek its parents advice, guidance and understanding to strengthen its convictions.

"This is precisely the way God loves and nurtures YOU."

You have had this relationship with HIM from the time of your true creation (i.e original birth). You instinctively knew who your Father was. You did not need a book (i.e the bible) to find proof.

 REFLECTIONS.

During the first meeting, one of my friends asked me;-

"How could you be sure that you are really hearing God's voice and what comparisons have you made as proof from the Bible?" I mentioned, that fifteen years ago, I was told by my Guides to stop reading the Bible and to disregard all my earthly biblical education, because they were going to teach me the truth but I must observe the ten commandments and also carefully consider all that is told to me. However, as I couldn't give a

clear answer on the proof question, I asked God the following morning and this was HIS' answer;-

> *"Doesn't a child **obey** its father's instructions without question?*
>
> *Doesn't a child **know** and **recognise** its father's voice and presence (even if it's blind)?*
>
> *Doesn't a child **trust** its father?*
>
> *You knew ME long before you were born in this time.*
>
> *You have **always OBEYED ME!** You don't need to study the Bible because you already know it inside out (Spiritually), therefore, instinctively you know the TRUTH.*

'I AM TRUTH'

*When you've found your TRUE FATHER, your search has ended and your true relationship with HIM is resumed. You then feel the great joy of 'true love,' nothing else becomes more important in your life... **serenity**. If your father telephones you, do you need to see him in order to believe that it is truly he on the other side? NO! YOU DON'T, not if you really know your father. Therefore, you don't have to physically 'see' in order to believe, because you know him 'instinctively' (naturally).*

AGE does not define WISDOM or Spiritual Development.

There are many WISE MEN of 20

and MATURE MEN of 90

Therefore, age merely defines Maturity-in-Years.

WISDOM IS KNOWLEDGE

My people are destroyed from lack of KNOWLEDGE
(HOSEA 4; 4-69)

"This is the WORD OF YOUR LORD,

YOUR FATHER,

YOUR GOD."

In December 1996, another strange coincidence occurred. An English customer wanted to purchase six bottles of 'Zara's Herbal Drink' for herself and friends. As we lived quite close, she asked if she could collect them to avoid the additional postal charges. However, because I was working from home, for safety reasons I avoided inviting customers to call and collect. She then explained, that it was very urgent, as one of her dear friends was returning to South Africa the following night and she would like to present them as a special gift. This friend of hers turned out to be a well respected South African Mystic/Spiritual Leader/Healer and Historian. So she suggested that we meet at his hotel in London, where I could be introduced.

When I arrived, to my surprise there were 10 - 12 people invited and we were taken to his room. Out of the guest only three of us were black. Everyone with the exception of two were well acquainted with the gentleman and conversant with his works. His name was Credo Mutwa a heavily built, mild mannered African in his 70's. Here is a brief biography taken from his press release:-

THE WORKS OF CREDO MUTWA

True to his first name Vusamazulu (awakener for the Zulus) and as a spiritual leader dedicated to caring for his people and preserving their cultural traditions. Credo has travelled extensively throughout the sub-continent and has become an acknowledged cultural historian, philosopher, mystic and visionary, as well as being an authority on traditional health. He has also travelled widely beyond Africa to Asia, Europe, the USA and Peru, attending conferences on traditional healing/ shamanism, or as a guest of philosophers, therapists and creative artists around the world.

Credo's knowledge is also identified as an invaluable source of information for corporate clients in the New South Africa, who are seeking advice from him in a variety of ways.

Credo describes himself to be 'an ordinary man,' in fact he is an extraordinary person, invested with much knowledge and exceptional wisdom; a gentle, sensitive man striving to be ethical in everything he does, considering himself accountable to the natural and supernatural worlds and also to the ancestral spirits of his people.

I observed that most of the invited guests bowed before him when introduced and treated him with great reverence. As he spoke, they pulled out their writing pads and scribbled all he said. It was then I realised he was giving spiritual prophecies on the dangers the world was in. He too spoke of great disasters and destruction, religious wars, floods, fires etc. After a short time, Credo looked at me and asked who I was. I explained what had brought me there; about my Herbal Drink and business. He then pleaded that I should release this drink immediately because the world needed it now. There were many people especially in South Africa, who needed the healing of this spiritual drink. I had to explain that I could not release it before God's time.

I then decided to ask, if he had ever heard of the **Seventh Star** and what it was. He smiled, paused in thought and quietly replied; *"Yes, the Seventh Star means the one who communicates on the other side."*

He then stopped, his eyes still staring at me and said *"I am not permitted to reveal any more but you do communicate with the Spirit World."* On leaving, Credo said he'd like to give me an Egyptian ritual name and whispered in my ear HATTAIA (pronounced HAT-TA-E-A)

HAT means HOUSE

TAIA means STARS.

Therefore, the name means **House of the Stars**.

Whilst returning home on the bus that night, I closed my eyes and reflected on the evenings events, then I said in my mind, *"Father I'm really glad to get a ritual name but what I'd really like to know is my true Spiritual Name."* He then whispered in my ear three times *"**ORISHUA, ORISHUA, ORISHUA,**"* but then said *"**ORISHA**"* and repeated the same names again three times, then once. I immediately wrote it down and although I'd never heard these names before, I recognised my name 'Orishua' and said, *"thank you Father."* Early next morning, I telephoned Credo and asked if he knew anything about these names and he quietly replied, *"Yes"* and went on to say that he was not allowed to say any more about the Seventh Star the night before but now he could.

He explained that *"in ancient African mythology, these are called **(the Seven Sister Stars)** who came out in the Spring, which was a signal to the farmers that it was time to start ploughing. Furthermore, it was believed that they were the 'door-way' into the next world and behind them lies the 'House of God.' People undergoing training in Law or Spiritualism had to **swear an oath in the name of these Stars, that they would not abuse the knowledge they received."***

He further stated that when I was in his hotel room, an elderly lady (who was in Spirit) was sitting next to me and when he described her; I recognised that it was my grandmother, who told him about the pains I had in my body and to warn me that people who looked after others, forget to look after themselves, so I must try and take good care of myself.

I then told him about the names I'd received and he explained.

- **ORISHA** means God (in the Nigerian language).

- **ORISHUA** means 'the Star of God.'

- The planet 'Venus' is also associated with the Star ORISHUA and Venus appears at dawn... *"this connected, because although my name is Dounne, throughout my life everyone calls me Dawn."*

- Enlightenment comes from the STARS.

- The ancient Africans believed that animals also came from the stars.

I thanked Credo for his great knowledge and teachings.

That evening, in quiet meditation, I felt I'd finally found myself and my purpose and whilst thanking God, HE whispered, *"Yes, you are the head and in charge of the House."* I laughed and replied, *"no wonder I am so bossy."*

In January 1997, I came across a book called 'A Child of Eternity' about an American autistic child (Adriana Rocha) who also spoke telepathically to God, Spirit-Masters and Guides. Whilst reading, I was stunned to learn that in 1991, she too was given similar lessons; the same messages and serious warnings. Even more amazing, she cannot speak and communicates by typing. Her parents although very loving were not religious, nor spoke about God or Spirit Masters. She has since taught them all about the Spirit-world, past lives and shown unbelievable intellect.

This book is an incredibly rare insight into pure spirituality from the mind of an innocent child.

Later that year I came across two other books with the same messages. 'Solar encounters' written by a French female author who received her instructions from Jesus and 'The Celestine Prophecies' about the ancient Maya (Brazilian) tribe.

- **2nd Team Meeting** - *(25 January 1997):*
'These were the messages and events of that day.'

That morning, whilst cooking for our meeting, although God had already given me lots of messages for the team, HE constantly interrupted my cooking with more information; which meant having to leave the kitchen to write down HIS instructions. After the third interruption, I started to feel slightly anxious, because I knew that once HE and the Masters started to talk, they don't stop. At this point I said, *"God, even Marsha is getting a bit fed up with me continuously adding more and more information for her to type onto already completed documents but I'd also like to finish cooking in time, so that I could meditate before the Team members arrived."* God laughed and simply replied that HE too takes counselling with the Masters and that this was the reason for the interruptions. HE agreed to stop after giving the lesson on 'using your brains.' However, whilst still cooking HE came through again to make the following statement, which was really consoling.

> *"You have passed the greatest test. I gave you a glimpse of greatness, a taste of great wealth and a touch of great fame:- then I asked you to choose this or ME; making you consciously aware that by choosing ME, you ran the great risk of losing everything, with the added possibility of getting labelled a nutter, ridiculed or destroyed by `the powers that be.' You chose ME without hesitation and 'acted' immediately on my instructions without questions. You are truly MY child and I'm very pleased."* Then HE said , *"if only one person arrived at the meeting today, then let that be enough for you."*

 REFLECTIONS.

The glimpse of greatness, wealth and fame related to my tremendous rise and success in business.

● **Meeting.**

As usual Marsha, Rudolph and I waited patiently to see how many would turn up this time. The first one to arrive had the longest distance to my home (some three hours drive) and said that the journey down was extremely hazardous and frightening.

That morning the road condition in her district was treacherous and not conducive for safe driving. The fog was so dense that she could only see a few inches ahead whilst driving and even passed an accident along the way. She remembered the difficulties everyone experienced on their journey to attend the first meeting and decided not to turn back. To her amazement, the moment she reached my district the fog suddenly lifted and all the roads to my home was absolutely clear. We sat alone in the living room and whilst she spoke, a strange feeling of tiredness and sadness began to overwhelm me and I started to cry. She encouraged me to let it all out and I cried for about five minutes, after which I felt released and up lifted again. By 2.30pm no one else had arrived, so we ate and got started. This time the atmosphere and meeting was calm, inspiring, harmonious, positive, focused and decisive.

God visited in February '97 and told me that my middle name 'Corinthia' was not given by accident and if I wanted to learn more about myself and the mission, I should now read the books of the Corinthians in the Bible. This was the first time I was given permission to read the Bible again. Throughout my life I had hated the name 'Corinthia' and always asked my parents, why had they given me such an awful name. Even when I got married, I dreaded the Priest saying it aloud. However, with all the Bible talk I was never really into the Bible or a serious reader. Once in a while I'd pick it up, read a passage and then leave it alone for months or even years because I'd always found it too ambiguous. To this day, I've never read the whole thing.

Not too long afterwards, I received a letter from a 91 year old (white)

Australian gentleman who had a skin problem and wanted to try Zara's Herbal Drink. I didn't know him but he started his letter with these words; *"I recognise it as one of the medications being given to humanity from our Spirit Helpers at this time to heal the nations. You are part of God's plan as a Distributing Agent."* HE also called me his spiritual sister.

• A Moment of Weakness and Doubt.

On 6th March 1997, I woke up feeling exhilarated, really happy and on a high. By lunch time I started to think about the enormity of the task ahead. The doubts were not on anything God had said but on what people would say and think of me (e.g. she's a liar, a fake, a fraud etc). Suddenly I felt weak and began to doubt myself. The more I thought, the weaker and sadder I became, yet I didn't feel afraid. Marsha came home around 10.30pm and I confided my feelings to her. Marsha's response was immediate, *"Mum I know that it is harder for you but I know you better than anyone on this earth; I know that you are not lying. I know that you are truly spiritual and have always been. You have never been like the rest of us, you are so different, so special. You don't realise it but people who get close to you do, because you touch them. It doesn't matter what anyone says, you know you must fulfil this mission and if in the end no one else joins us and it is just you and me left to do it, then let it be so. I don't care what people will say because they'll say it anyway. What I do care about is that when I die, I can say (to myself) I've done my job."* With these inspiring and supportive words, Marsha released my doubts and gave me back my strength.

Then I reflected on what God had told me about Marsha a year before the mission. HE said that, *"she is my right hand person and has strong spiritual vision; can see through people's thoughts and is also a spiritual artist."*

3rd Team Meeting - *(29th March 1997).*

The messages I received for this meeting was more or less a reiteration of previous messages.

- **God's MESSAGE** - (29th March 1997).

  1. *"Follow the laws I gave to Moses in his Day.*

  2. *Follow the ways of CHRIST and the other Masters, I'd sent to teach you.*

  3. *Follow the written words I'm now giving THEE.*

Now that I have chosen the MASTER LEADER (Dounne) and have given the date to fulfil this task, be completely aware that the Devil is now on her trail, watching every move she makes and trying to counter-act them to ensure she fails. He will do all in his power to prevent the completion of the MISSION, so that means you must also be aware that he is watching you too. Do not be afraid; try to stay on course, keep your Spirits high and try not to get disheartened. HE MUST NOT and WILL NOT WIN.

> ***Many are called but few are chosen.***

Understand these words, I initially asked Dounne to call on all the people whom she believed would understand the cause. She wrote to many and you are the ones who have come this far.

*So you see, I AM not as mysterious or complicated as some people have portrayed. I'm simply **true to MY words** which are always consistence. **Find the truth and you'll find ME**. Therefore always be **true to yourself.***

> *Nothing good comes easy*
> *So work hard*
> *I only work through **OBEDIENCE**."*

Normally I'd go out of my way and cook a large meal but this time I decided to make some sandwiches. Whilst making them Marsha telephoned and said, *"Mum I just had a thought; don't cook no big amount of food today, just do some sandwiches."* I burst out laughing.

Well Marsha, Rudolph and I, relaxed, waited and took bets on who would turn up, if any at all. We guest right, out of the nine remaining members, I received two apologies and none of the others neither apologised or turned up. So my committed Team members were Marsha, Rudolph, two friends and myself. None of us really knew what to do and simply tried our best. It was like the blind, leading the blind. God had given me one date **1st July 1997** for the mission. So I thought I had to launch everything on that day (including the book), but I had no money. Faithfully, I believed that HE would provide and all that I would have to do was simply use the experience gained in business, to attract publicity and in this way 'spread the word.' With hindsight, I was certainly wrong.

By May 1997, I began to feel anxious that the book would not be ready in time for the mission launch, nor did I have the money to finance the mission launch itself (i.e. leaflets, badges, venue, food, press invitations, postage etc); On the morning of the 4th May, I was feeling really low and sick in the stomach but whilst saying my prayers God said;-

> *"Think positively, have 'confidence in ME,' you are on time, it's hard work, so be positive and stop feeling so afraid; stop allowing material physical influences (money) to control your judgements.*
>
> *Let go and let God.*
>
> *Go for it, you will be victorious in the end."*

Marsha came over lunchtime and expressed that she too was going through the same anxiety, I gave her the written message and she replied, *"I feel better now."* It restored our confidence.

By June 1997, things did not improve but we hung on to God's words and remained faithful. We encountered every possible obstacle imaginable but refused to be beaten. My printer agreed to produce the leaflets and invitations and I'd found a company to make the badges. But we still had no money. We were convinced that once the leaflets were distributed, people would order the book, which in turn would finance the whole operation and get the mission off the ground. Nevertheless, I needed money to pay for the launch venue. I wrote everywhere and to everyone trying to raise sponsorship funds, they all turned me down. This suspense continued right up to the week before the launch, when I was eventually recused by a friend who lent me £1500. Aware of the negative forces circulating, we prayed real hard throughout this period and kept ourselves positive, as we could not allow any weakening influences. In high spirits we kept each other going and laughed in the face of adversity.

On the week of the launch, my prayers, focus and meditation intensified. I was determined to win. It so happened that Rudolph was contracted to play the leading character in a theatre production and his 'press night' coincided on the same night of the mission launch, so he could not attend but gave us his blessings.

On the morning of the launch, I woke up early as usual, had a bath, prayed and meditated. Marsha came over, we hugged, relaxed and prayed. We were nervous but not afraid. Then we left to prepare the venue, which was held in a lovely hotel in the heart of London's West End. A few friends who had promised to help were already there and the hotel room was quickly organised. The stage was set and we waited for the guests to arrive. I kept repeating God's words in my mind, *"if only one person turns up, let that be enough for you."* I had sent out 500 invitations, about 100 friends confirmed that they would definitely come but on the due hour (7pm) only thirty people had arrived. I was happy, because it was more than one. With a silver/gold 'Star' on my forehead and dressed in pale blue, I took centre stage and delivered the one hour speech, which included readings from the two other spiritual books a 'A Child of Eternity' and 'Solar Encounters' read by Dr John Roberts Q.C, Brenda Emmanus and Genny Lewis. The atmosphere throughout was beautiful but whilst speaking I felt the strange, peaceful, calm which always filled the room whenever God and the Spirit-Masters were present. Everyone commented that I physically radiated and looked serene. At the end of my speech, I quietly said in my mind;- *"Father it is done."*

Marsha immediately came up, kissed me and we hugged tightly. She whispered in my ear, *"you've done it Mum, thank God it's over."* Later that night, a friend who was sitting next to Marsha told me. *"When you finished your speech, Marsha released a huge sigh of relief."* No one else but Marsha, Dee, Rudolph and I would have understood what it really meant to 'fight the devil and WIN.' The fulfilment of the Mission launch on the 1st July 1997 meant precisely that. Throughout that night, Marsha and I had a permanent grin on our faces.

It was not until we finally returned home, were we able to openly express our great excitement, relief and joy. I phoned Rudolph and told him everything, his show was also a success, so we congratulated each other.

Immediately after the launch, friends offered to distribute the mission leaflets which went out fast and furious. By the following month, all of the initial 5,000 were finished and more were ordered. However, we noticed that no orders or enquiries were coming in, which felt strange but continued the distributions regardless.

As far as I was concerned, it was all in God's hands. Then they were distributed to my mail-order customers. The very next morning I received a telephone call from a customer saying, *"do you realise that there is no contact address or phone number on your leaflet?"* To which I replied, *"WHAT? - NO! it is definitely on it."* I immediately grabbed a leaflet, went through it from cover to cover and to my surprise my address or phone number was not there. Throughout my 10 years in business, I'd printed thousands of leaflets, documents, press releases, brochures etc and not once was it ever omitted. Furthermore, I'd always used the same printer who was aware of this essential requirement. Bewildered, I could not understand how my own eyes had deceived me, because I would have sworn that I saw it on the leaflet. In dismay, I called Marsha and conveyed the bad news. She too was stunned and also swore that she had seen it. I then called the Printer, he too was in shock. None of us could understand how or why we all believed it was there. I thought, *"if this is the devil's work, he still will not win;"* because it was better to have found the mistake now, rather than months or years later. Although we'd lost a great deal of money and potential sales, it could have been much worse. My Printer and I came to a compromise to offset some of the cost. It still meant that I was in a much deeper financial hole.

 DIANA - *(Princess of Wales).*

In the midst of all this, another strange event was unfolding. For some unknown mysterious reason, I decided that the 1st September '97 was going to be the date for a new beginning. So on 30th August, I gave my flat a thorough cleaning and prepared it for blessing the following morning. I'd set the radio to alarm at 4:30am. On the 31st August I awoke suddenly at 4:00am thinking about Princess Diana.

My thoughts were not on death, accident or that anything was wrong; but on a planned fundraising engagement, to be held on 19th September, where Princess Diana was to be the guest of honour for an organisation (Lignum Vitae) with which I was well acquainted. Therefore, I'd be meeting her for the first time. The organisation had agreed to place my Herbal Pepper Sauces on the dinning tables to accompany the meal, plus my mission leaflets where going to be placed in the goody bags for the invited guests. I particularly wanted Princess Diana to get this leaflet.

Whilst in thought, the radio came on and the very first words were, *"Dodi Fayed has been killed in a car accident and Princess Diana is seriously hurt."* I jumped up and immediately turned the television on to Sky News, who announced that they were both dead. I was stunned and just couldn't believe it.

- **Tuesday 2nd September** - *3rd day after their deaths.*

I was sitting in my living room quietly talking to God in my mind and asking so many questions, which all came down to *"Why, Why, Why?"*

Although, I was aware of the Spirit-world; the eternity of life; the inevitability of death and all the other sensible reasons; yet I still needed words of comfort and re-assurance from God or my Guides to help me come to terms with this shocking tragedy.

Then a quiet voice replied these simple words;-

> *"Thy WILL be done on Earth as it is in Heaven;*
>
> *For Thine is the Kingdom*
>
> *The Power and*
>
> *The Glory - forever."*

He went on to say;-

> *"The Lord is glorified through the good works of HIS chosen-ones, who are called from all walks of life. Most are not recognised whilst alive on earth but in death their true Souls and Purpose are revealed.*
>
> ### *Many are called but few are CHOSEN.*
>
> *Death brings pain, guilt, inner consciousness, healing and LOVE."*

*There is **no coincidence, no mistake** or **no accident** with God. HE knows exactly what HE is doing. There is a divine order to everything in life. Diana was sent to serve and fulfil a specific purpose; which she did exceptionally well; her work was done and eventually the world will come to terms and heal.*

Diana's specific task was to touch the hearts of the world Leaders in a very special way, so that the process of world change can begin. The world cannot change unless those who rule it changes. She became their personal close friend and exposed them to sincerity, compassion, humanitarianism and love. This warm personality was also extended to the hearts of the poor, homeless, sick, the suffering of all people's in every nation and religion. She had an exceedingly big heart. Love comes from the heart which transcends all things. The heart is also the universal symbol of love. The heart is the most sensitive part of the body, which brings out deep feelings and emotions... it touches the conscience. People can only change by touching their hearts.

In order to 'make a difference,' one must have the ability to touch people's hearts; to defy fear and show committed dedication to a good cause. It is only through death that good works are truly exposed to such an extent that it diminishes all other negatives into insignificance; but it also touches the hearts of 'loved-ones' and compels them to continue those good works. Loved-ones does not only mean family and friends but also anyone who loved the person and there you'll see the 'hands of God extended in LOVE,' proving that at the end of the day;-

LOVE truly conquers ALL.

There is also a significance in the car crashing against the walls. The massive impact and loud bang resounding around the world, to shake up all its people but especially to wake-up the Leaders to look at the devastation they are causing. It takes a mighty person to cause such a great impact; stir and wake up call. Her death will leave a 'perpetual light' on people's consciousness.

- *That **Light** will shine for many years to come, as a lasting memorial to bring about the lasting effects needed and an end to the sufferings of millions of innocent people world-wide.*

- *That **Light** would force the world Leaders to take account of their past and change their future actions and to realise that no one is bigger than God.*

- *That **Light** will stay in the hearts of millions of ordinary people, to take account and personal responsibility for their own individual actions towards others but more importantly to realise that 'People Power and Unity' can force even the most stubborn Leaders and Rulers to change. Diana spoke out and showed that* *personal action achieves results. You must all learn to be active and do what you believe to be right.*

How many of us are this fortunate to be able to help more in death than in physical life. Therefore, you can now rest assured that there is a much 'brighter star shinning' down on this earth every night;-

Lighting the Way

Igniting Passions

&

Uniting Hearts.

"By keeping her memory and works alive, she'll continue to reign in your hearts. Hence, her title the 'Queen of Hearts' is most befitting.

LOVE reigns Supreme.

Her birthday (1st July) is also significant and connects with your work and mission 'The Celebration of Life.' Now go in peace and serve your given purpose."

Accepting these comforting words, I proceeded with my work but somehow every effort I made to complete the book seemed to be fraught with major obstacles, primarily caused in trying to juggle running the business, researching the Herbal Drink, establishing the mission and time in between writing the book, all with no money. Throughout my life, I had always avoided blaming superstition for anything going wrong, may it be the devil, evil or whatever. Then I recalled what God had told me at the start of the mission, to be *"consciously aware of the devil's cunning tricks."* So this time I felt sure that it was all his doing. By October, my patience was wearing thin, I had had enough and felt I was fighting a losing battle. I prayed and prayed but was not getting any messages or answers. Then one morning I shouted out to God, *"WHY?"* and broke down in tears. Feeling really sorry for myself, I just simply cried and cried and cried. When I'd finally finished, still feeling bewildered and blank, I suddenly felt HIS presence and HE said-

> **"You are in charge - but I am in control."**

HE explained that my anxiety was caused by my own actions. I'd taken it upon myself to determine the deadline date for the book's completion, without asking HIM if HE was finished. HE'd given me a deadline for the Mission launch but not for the book. I had also titled the book 'The Black Cinderella' which HE said was the wrong name. It was to be called **'A Mission of Love.'** This was a lesson to remind me not to get carried away with my own ideas and to always seek HIS permission first.

He went on;-

> *"When things don't appear to be going according to your plans, don't get down, disheartened or disappointed, just say to yourself:-*

> ### **GOD is in CONTROL of this,**

> **HE** *knows what* **HE's** *doing.*

> *It WILL all work out right in the end because*

> *God's in CONTROL and I'm only in CHARGE.*

Now write this inscription at the beginning of the book -

> **I dedicate this book to the glorification of God,**
> **for the service of Humanity**
> **and for the furtherance of PURE LOVE."**

I was both overjoyed and relieved all at the same time. I sat back, closed my eyes, went into deep meditation and called on my Spirit 'ORISHUA.' This was the message I then wrote whilst 'in the Spirit.'

"I have nothing - yet I have everything."

"I'm so happy and at peace, that I'm continuously bursting with joy. Maybe this is what's meant by; my cup runneth over.

If this is 'life eternal,' then I hope that one day you too would feel the 'pure joy and love of the Lord,' which goes to prove that:-

'All we need is LOVE.'

Even though I know that the physical roads ahead may be paved with broken glass, the 'love in me' will ease all torment, for I'm 'living in the consciousness of God, fully aware of the destructiveness of the devil,' yet I have no fear, for I know that my life will continue eternally through -

OBEDIENCE of my Love

My GOD

My LIFE

in 'HIS' great power, I stand defiantly to glorify HIS name - GOD.
I am ORISHUA... *The Power of the '7th' STAR."*

Once again, I was at peace and with a clear vision. No longer would I fight myself to make things happen but work through God instead. Although I am extremely ambitious, with my own independent dreams, I now realise that my spiritual work has been clearly defined, yet both coming together to fulfil the same purpose... i.e. my destiny.

Nevertheless, even though I have had all of these divine revelations and spiritual experiences, which sounds holier than thou, I've noticed that I'm no more spiritual than the average person. Most certainly, I am not perfect and have as many faults as anyone else (if not more, with many skeletons in my private closet). From the difficult life I have had, shows that I've not been treated with any special favours. Furthermore, I didn't bother to develop my skills beyond where I am currently because I already know that I am a 'Spirit Master;' I know how to communicate and I am aware of my true potential. Therefore, in my spiritual work, I've chosen to leave it up to God, the Masters and my Guides to visit me whenever they choose and I then simply follow their instructions or in time of personal need, I call on them for help (in fact, this is everyday). So I'm in the same learning process as everyone else, because these lessons are also new to me and I too have to learn how to live and practice them in sincerity. I'm certainly no fortune-teller and do not even know what tomorrow holds for myself, much less for the world but I do know that I can reach as high or low as I choose to go and that my rewards will come from faith, obedience, hardwork, sharing and love. Everyone is born gifted in some way but the majority chooses not to use their gifts or to challenge themselves. We are sent here to be of service to each other and to help one another.

"To serve and be served."

Spirituality.

GOD'S LESSONS ON SPIRITUAL AWARENESS.

- These are a series of lessons God gave from 14th January 1997.

"Since I and you are Spirit,

Therefore, Spirituality means SELF or getting in touch with your own inner-self.

Hence, Spirituality means the development of your higher-self (i.e. your God-self).

Spirituality reveals your true divinity and shows just how great you are."

GODs words (4/11/99).

Circle of Life

"It represents the cycle in which all Life evolves and revolves." Hence, when you draw a circle, you start at the beginning and end at the beginning, after which it becomes continuous."

The beginning of the circle pin points 'the beginning of life' itself and the continuum shows that life is continuous (ie. never ending or eternal). However, something or someone had to be responsible for the original creation of life. Therefore, in order to find the **'True Creator'** we have to go back to the beginning of life to learn the truth. In the course of this long search, we will unravel the Truth and there we will find God as the true 'Creator of life.' Only HE can then tell us the true purpose, meaning and reason for HIS creations. So, to find the **truth,** we have to return to God for the answers.

God's Lessons

Living in consciousness - means to be aware of yourself, your thoughts and your actions, on everything which surrounds you. To give careful consideration to everything and take personal responsibility for your actions. In other words, you should think before you act and consider the consequences of all your actions on yourself and on others. Also be aware of God's presence in and around you.

Taking Action -   To obey means to ACT *(i.e. actions speak louder than words).*

Spiritual Development -   begins from the process of BLIND FAITH and TRUST but this trust is only between yourself and God. You have to learn to *'trust your thoughts'* and know when you are being directed. Once your spiritual eyes and ears begin to open, you'll see and hear in more depth without actually seeing or hearing, yet you'll know because you are becoming aware of your spiritual senses (i.e. your higher sense) which has much greater insight and perception (i.e. intuition).

Spiritual Communication - travels at the speed of light.

• GOD is the LIGHT and the WAY.

You have seen the speed of the telephone, fax, computer etc. These still cannot compare with the lightening speed of spiritual communication, which is channelled through 'light waves'... hence telepathy. Therefore, it is not necessary to speak aloud to be heard, as communication is in the mind. Once you call on God or on your Spirit-Helpers, they hear and come to your aide. However, if you feel more comfortable speaking aloud, then do so.

In order to learn the unknown (i.e. mysteries), you must imagine yourself as a baby now emerging from the womb, because you have to become a child again to learn 'truth' (i.e. the circle is now being drawn and you are starting at the beginning of your physical life in this present life).

The Body, The Soul, The Cross

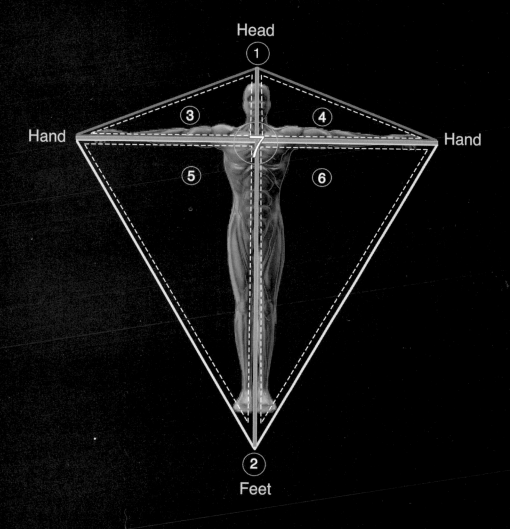

Head
①
Hand
③ ④
⑦
Hand
⑤ ⑥
②
Feet

NO.7 :This is where your Spirit lives within your body. Hence your body is CENTRED IN GOD (or your Soul-centre... the God-Part within you).

- **The Body - The Soul - The Cross** *(explained);-*

The Cross -   is not the symbol of Jesus dying on the cross to save you but the 'symbol of protection' God has provided for you, to be able to protect yourself against evil. **You are the CROSS.**

The Body -   **Your body was purposely designed in the shape of the cross and it is shielded by a protective force field of 7 invisible triangles.**

The Soul -   **No.7.** This is where your Spirit lives (or resides) within your body. Therefore, your body is 'centred in God' or your 'Soul-centre,' which houses the 'God-part within you' (i.e. your Spirit). Hence, **you are the HOLY SPIRIT.** This is the power of the Number '7' and the '7' invisible triangles that surround and protect your body and Holy Spirit.

 **CLARIFICATION.**

Just as your physical-body lives in a house.

Your spiritual-body lives in a soul.

Therefore, when in prayer, you make the **sign of the cross** and say; **in the name of the FATHER and of the SON and of the HOLY SPIRIT;** you are actually calling on the 'three great powers' -

i.e:- 1. **God the Father** -   God himself

2. **God the Son** -   Jesus Christ; (Krishna, Buddha, Mohammed or whichever Spirit Master you respect as a direct messenger from GOD).

3. **God the Holy Spirit** - your own inner SPIRIT

The above three are also called THE HOLY TRINITY or the 'eternal triangle'... three in one.

When you make the **sign of the cross**, you are actually making the shape of **a triangle** on your upper body (i.e. head and both shoulders) and are also inviting the 'powers' to come in and help you. This is how you **open your Soul** to allow your Spirit to communicate with God and the Spirit-world. Hence, it is extremely important when you have finished praying that you make **the sign of the cross** again, to ensure you **close your Soul** and **protect your Spirit**. Otherwise, by leaving your Soul open, makes you vulnerable to all forms of other spiritual entities (good and evil) which could cause mental disturbances and unrest throughout the period your Soul is kept open. It's like leaving your front door open to thieves.

The Soul is the **centre of power.** It is not the heart but close to the heart. When the Spirit leaves the body, it leaves from this point.

The precise spot is exactly your centre. Draw a straight line from head to chest; then draw another straight line from shoulder to shoulder. Where the two lines cross is the Soul-centre.

There were and are many Spirit-Masters (i.e. prophets and messengers) sent to earth by God, when we stray too far from the truth, to remind us of His existence, His ways, His laws and to redeem us from evil. Many like Christ died (or gave their blood) in the name of God, to re-educate and save us. They chose to believe and to complete their mission. God is the one who chooses the sacrificial lambs for HIS purpose. But is death such a major sacrifice, since everyone must die at some point in their physical life? **NO** but to die in the name of God and for the benefit of humanity is a meaningful death and a worthy sacrifice. Some called Jesus a prophet, others called him the son of God but in reality, aren't we all sons and daughters of God? So what gave Jesus this special position in God's heart and house. He **believed, obeyed and lived by the words of God.** So by following Jesus's example, you too can become 'a true child of God' and 'a child of the universe.' So take heed of your ways and try to be Christ-like and let God lead you. To do so, you have to ask HIM and then willingly follow HIS guidance and commands. Also consider:- if Christ was sent only two thousand years ago and the universe was created nine billion years ago, then how did we communicate with God before Christ? We had a direct personal relationship with Him and simply spoke to Him. This is what He is now calling on us to do, to rebuild this special relationship.

 ON REFLECTION.

I have always wanted a four poster bed and to my surprise, when Rudolph and I got together, he said that he had designed and built one which was stored in his garage. So I happily got rid of my old bed in favour of his beautiful one, which has unusual brass fittings on both the head and foot boards. Three years later, after God drew the body's Soul-centre, I realised that the brass fittings on the head board had '7' brass shields with another large fitting in the middle, which was precisely the shape of the Soul with a cross in the centre. I always bow '7 times' at the end of my prayers.

How To Pray

Firstly, you must understand that praying simply means talking to God and asking HIM for help, advice and guidance. Additionally, this communication is also extended to your 'inner-spirit' and 'Spirit-Helpers' (i.e. Guardian-Angels, Masters, Teachers, Loved-Ones etc); who are all there just waiting to be of service to you.

We have all learnt how to pray in one form or another and just as we are all different; we also pray in different ways; but how should we pray? and what should we pray for?

1. You should wipe out the word **want** from your mind, for it encourages greed. Replace it with the words **needs** and **wishes**.

2. **Pray for your daily needs**. You should only pray for the things you need that day and not for any future needs. Since you don't know what your future holds (i.e. you could die the next day). Therefore, you cannot ask HIM for anything directly in the future but you can **wish for it**. In other words; **ask for your future wishes**. A 'wish' is an indirect request. Therefore, you pray for:-

(a). **Today's Needs** and (b). **Tomorrow's Wishes.**

If you think of the words in the following prayer and songs, it may give you a better understanding;-

(a). THE 23RD PSALM;

   *"The Lord is my Shepherd I shalt not **WANT**."*

(b). JUST FOR TODAY;

   "Lord for tomorrow and its needs, I do not pray. Teach me, help me and guide me LORD; just for today."

(c) ONE DAY AT A TIME SWEET JESUS;

   "Yesterday's gone sweet Jesus, tomorrow may never be mine, so give me the strength, show me the way; one day at a time."

What are your DAILY NEEDS?

'THE CIRCLE OF LIFE'

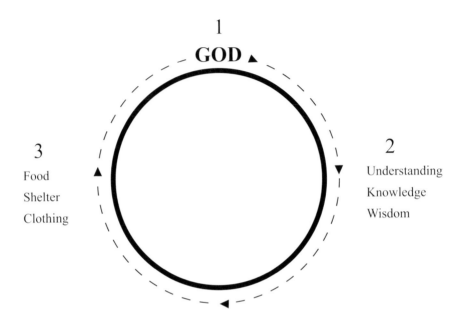

1.   **GOD**:- to give us a truly meaningful life.

2.   UNDERSTANDING
     KNOWLEDGE   }   to tell us how to live
     WISDOM

3.   FOOD
     SHELTER   }   in order to live
     CLOTHING

Anything over and above these things are 'wants,' which we don't need as it brings greed, confusion and complications to the **simplicity of life** as God intends it. Do not confuse 'wants' with 'ambitious desires,' you can desire whatever you wish to achieve.

The Three Hand Positions

There are three different hand positions for praying.

1(a).

Start with the positions (a) for short prayers. For longer prayers or meditation you can use the relaxed positions illustrated in diagram (b)

1. **Normal prayers:**
   (a). Hands are clasped.

   (b). Clasp hands and rest them on your lap.

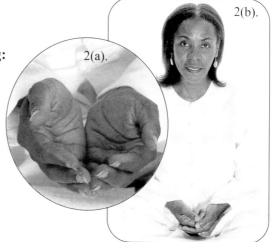

2(b).

2(a).

2. **When asking for anything:**
   (a). needs, wishes, guidance: Hands are open.

   (b). place hands on top of the other and rest them on your lap.

3. **Meditation:**
   (a). At the beginning, form a triangle with your hands and place over your Soul-centre.

   (b). place hands on top the other and rest them on your lap
   (as in diagram 2b).

3(a).

Prepare yourself before Praying

Cleansing;-

Wash your face, hands, mouth and feet... better still, have a quick shower. This is not absolutely necessary but its a symbol of cleansing before presenting yourself to God.

Barefoot;-

Wherever you choose to pray (i.e. call on God) that particular spot is **holy ground.** Therefore, as a mark of respect and to show your humility, you present yourself before Him barefoot.

- **When to Ask for Your Needs and Wishes;-**

(a).   Choose the spot where you intend to pray;- stand, kneel, lay down or sit **facing the EAST (i.e. the rising sun at 6am).** It's the best time to ask for your 'needs and wishes' for the day.

(b).   **Light a plain white candle.** This is not absolutely necessary but is a symbol of **God as the light, the way, the energy and the power.** Therefore, if you were actually facing the Sun itself, you won't need a candle or any other light at all.

(c).   Make the **sign of the cross.** To open up your Soul and is also the signal to tell God and your Guides that you are ready to communicate. In other words, you are inviting them into your home.

(d).   Say the **Lords prayer,** (which Jesus gave you).

(e).   Say a **prayer of protection** (i.e. ask God to protect you, especially whilst your Soul is open and then trust Him to do so), or instead go straight to (f).

This is one of my favourite 'prayers of protection';-

Christ as a Light

Christ as a light, illuminate and guide me.

Christ as a shield, overshadow and cover me.

Christ be under me, Christ be over me.

Christ be beside me, on my left hand and on my right.

Christ be before me, around me, about me.

Christ this day, be within and without me.

(f).   Visualise the '7 invisible triangles' surrounding your body as a ray of dazzling silver/white light, illuminating around you. This protects your entire being from 'evil forces,' thereby, only allowing God and the 'good forces' to enter.

(g).   Then simply talk to God (open your hands in the asking position), ask HIM to send your Guides to help you and for what ever else you need or wish. Remember everyday is a new day, which brings new events, that's why you pray everyday.

(h).   **ENDING YOUR PRAYERS**

Once you have finished talking to God **make the sign of the cross;** to signal that you've finished your communication and to also close your Soul.

(i).   **WHEN TO GIVE THANKS**

If you pray and ask God and the Spirit-Helpers daily to help you obtain your needs and wishes, then its equally nice each day to show them a little appreciation, by just saying *"thanks' for Your help."*

The best time is to do so is **6pm - facing the WEST** (i.e. the setting Sun). However, this does not prevent you from saying, *"thank you God,"* anytime of day or night when HE has done something specific, where spontaneous *"thanks"* is due or even said unconsciously. Additionally, many people choose a special day in the year to celebrate Thanksgiving.

- **Latest Times to Pray;-**

  If you cannot handle 6 o'clock times, especially 6am, then the latest times are;

1. **MORNING PRAYERS** - (needs and wishes).

   6am to 12 noon - facing EAST.

2. **EVENING PRAYERS** - (thanks).

   6pm to 12 midnight - facing WEST.

- The sun is not God but is the greatest energy/power source. Therefore, you are facing your power-source. It is similar to plugging in an electrical appliance into a power point to be charged (or energised) to a higher level. This increases your spiritual communicative ability, charging you up with positive energies for the day.

- It is important to try and pray at 'a specific time' daily, as the Spirit-Helpers have very busy lives not only helping you and others but also working on their own spiritual development. Therefore, if you want their full attention and support, then respect their time.

- **Building your relationship with GOD;-**

  Allocating Time.

  Prayers are simply allocating specific times in the day and night to share with God... a concentrated moment specifically devoted to HIM. It does not have to be long. It's up to you how much time you wish to give HIM. The length of time is based on your own individual needs, which does not make anyone holier than others. Praying is simply your own quiet/private moments with HIM...'to ask, give thanks, receive comfort, guidance and love, as well as to show your love and respect in return' (i.e. building your relationship with HIM).

- **This is how I start my morning prayers;-**

After I've said the Lord's Prayer, the 23 Psalm and the Prayer of Protection, I then talk to God:

"Father God, I've come before YOU this morning to ask for my needs and wishes for today. Please bless and grant them today.

Father, I ask for the 'conscious awakening,' presence, guidance, direction, assistance, instruction and permission from YOURSELF, my SPIRIT (Orishua) and all my Spirit-Helpers."

Father, please send forth all my Spirit-Helpers (my Guardian-Angels, Spirit-Masters (teachers), Healers, Business-Guides, friends and loved-ones... especially my Grandmother (Wilhelmina Dallaway), my great-grand mother (Mam. Bucaud), my grandfather (Andrew, Joseph Alexander) and my mother (Beryl, May-Rita Alexander) to assist and guide me today.

Father, please let today be a peaceful, pleasant, loving and happy day."

Father, make me an instrument of Your peace and also show me what YOU would like me to do for YOU today."

- Then I continue to ask for everything else I would like to happen that day. This means that you must be completely aware of all your desires (i.e. needs and wishes). In order to achieve your desires or ambitions, you must have a written plan. I have a special book called 'my wish book.' On my Thanksgiving day (31st December of each year), I write down my New Year's wishes and update it throughout the year as my desires change. So I simply hold this book in my hands when asking God for my needs and wishes. I just say, *"Father, these are my needs and wishes for today."*

- Once I've said my prayers, my entire day is focused on my 'planned desires,' which I then work hard to achieve everyday or until each is achieved. Once 'a wish' is achieved, I simply date and cross it out of my wishes book. I also ask for the 'needs' and 'wishes' of my children, husband and anyone else who has asked me to pray for them (i.e. family members, friends, customers etc). My children and I share each others plans and include these in our daily prayers. In this way, all our Spirit-Helpers join forces on our behalf.

- **In The Evening.**

  I thank God, my Spirit and all the Spirit-Helpers, for everything that happened during the day. This means that you must consciously take note of what is going on around you throughout the day. Practiced daily, you become acutely awake of what you are doing for yourself, for others and vice-versa. I also give thanks for the little/big things we take for granted (i.e. being alive, well and healthy; for the love around me; for food, clothing and my home; for our safe protection). We rarely appreciate the joys of life and give thanks for it on a daily basis.

How to Communicate

 Meditation.

To seek enlightenment, knowledge, guidance or just to relax, or to get in touch with your inner-Spirit.

1.   Choose a quiet place, where you can relax undisturbed and undistracted.

2.   Choose a relaxed position (i.e. sit or kneel etc).

3.   Make the 'sign of the cross.'

4.   Protect yourself using the 7 invisible triangles and 'prayer of protection.'

- Position your hands in the 'meditation position' 3(a). *(see page 545).* and place them over your Soul-centre, then say:-

"Lord remove the veils and open my eyes, ears and mind and teach me your TRUTH. Please grant me wisdom today,"

If you have a specific problem and need God's guidance, then also tell HIM your problems and ask for HIS help.

5.   Try to empty your mind of all thoughts; be still and relax. Focus on your breathing; breathe deep and slow in an even rhythm. Concentrating on your breathing, helps to empty your mind and relaxes you. Complete relaxation takes some time but eventually you will become aware of the '**still silence**,' then try to '**listen in the silence**' (whilst still keeping your mind empty). It would take some time (7 or more sessions) before you actually reach the point of recognising the specific moment of 'still silence.' Hence, regular practice and patience is required. It then becomes easier and complete relaxation gets much shorter. Eventually, you will

be amazed with how much more you hear or even see beyond your physical senses (i.e. eyes and ears). Don't worry if you do not hear anything, just trust in God and your Spirit will guide you. So simply follow whatever 'good thoughts' come into your mind.

Therefore, it is your own thoughts (i.e. MIND) which opens and closes the doorways to the other side. It's important to keep your mind empty, because once you start to think, then your mind will be full of your own thoughts, leaving limited space for God and the Guides to enter. If everybody is talking, you would become mixed up and confused. **Confusion** is a good indication that you are not receiving clear guidance.

So your **mind** holds the

key-to-**unlock, open** or **close**

your Spiritual doors.

- **Meditation - breathing exercise.**

This is the breathing exercise my Guide taught me, to obtain the correct breathing rhythm.

Sit comfortably with your hands in the meditation position (b) and close your eyes;-

Step **(1).** **Breathe in** slowly through your nose, at the same time counting to 4 (in your mind).

Step **(2).** **Stop breathing** and hold you breath to the count of 3.

Step **(3).** **Breathe out** slowly through your mouth counting to 7 (in your mind).

Repeat steps 1,2,3 at least 7 times.

After a while, you will feel a natural rhythm occurring and can then stop counting but keep your mind empty by focusing only on your breathing. This exercise also starts the process of bringing you into a state of peaceful tranquillity and spiritual consciousness. It is good to practice daily to get you into the right frame of mind or when feeling over stressed. It also increases the flow of oxygen in your blood stream and helps the body to heal itself.

NB: When 'breathing in,' draw your breath deep down into your stomach, which should push your stomach out. When 'breathing out,' pull your stomach in whilst pushing all the air out.

Spirituality -v- Religion

God gave us Faith and Spirituality which is in-born, therefore its natural, instinctive and intuitive. Hence, we don't need to look for God, since HE has never left us.

Man invented religion in an attempt to teach us about God; how to go about finding HIM and how to become Holy; but they did not teach us how to communicate directly with God himself, or how to become our own masters.

Spirituality cannot be taught, as we are all 'spiritual beings' or part of the living-Spirit of God and **were created Holy**. So why do we need to look for what we already are; 'a living HOLY SPIRIT.' Therefore, we have always known our Father (God). It is only our absolute faith in HIM (i.e. belief) which draws us closer to HIM!

The Blood-of-Life is for our 'physical existence' but

The Breath-of-Life is our 'eternal spiritual existence,'

hence, there is No DEATH.

Therefore, 'Spirituality' and 'religion' are two different things. **Spirituality is God-made** and is therefore pure and holy. God's standards never changes. It's simple, uncomplicated, loving, true, just, righteous and open.

Religion is an invention of man, built from deceit and is therefore corrupt. For example (outwardly religious but privately devious; full of secrecy and is forever changing). How often do you see people who are respected as religious and up-right or as a shining example to their community; they go to church, take communion, read the bible, some even preach the word of God and claim to have super-natural powers, anoint ministers, appoint prophets/saints, pardon sinners, cast out demons and heal the sick. Others rewrite the Bible to suit their own intentions; some claim that their God is the only true living God; **WHAT VANITY!** They all appear to have the same vain purpose, which is to build a congregation of believers in which to reign or rule over... an economic necessity. They set themselves apart as being so special, so privileged, so holy, so chosen, so different. They carve out devises to separate them from the rest and associate only with their own kind. They preach 'supremacy and fear' to keep control and to preserve their status and ego. Hence, power is their god, selfishness and vanity is their life. Their income is made from deceitful, abusive and corrupt means. They don't see the universe as a brother/sisterhood but preach hatred, separation and distrust of anyone outside their realm. How else can you justify the need for so many churches, religious cults and brainwashed followers? *"How many evil and wicked things have Churches done in MY NAME!?"*

> *"Only God knows the hearts of men and*
> *only God sees what goes on behind closed doors."*

'SPIRITUALITY is living Life through the Spirit'

IN	the	Spirit.
WITH	the	Spirit
	and	
FOR	the	Spirit.

Since the 'Spirit is love and truth,' no form of deceit can exist with it. One therefore, lives to share all one knows for the benefit of the entire universe, without separation, because you are aware of your higher-inner-self; true glory and real power. Hence, you live to enlighten and empower others to receive the same as you, because you know life holds a much greater purpose and meaning. Therefore, in true Spirituality **love conquers all**, allowing each other to grow and develop the ultimate awareness and close relationship with your true Father-God. People thrive to achieve or seek the ultimate in their materialistic physical-life, without realising that the ultimate (i.e. God) is always with them, patiently waiting for us to acknowledge HIS existence and presence. **True Spirituality is void of fear** because you know that what ever you do, it is done with a clear conscience and with love. It is this simple... love is never intentionally harmful to yourself or others but is always beneficial and rewarding. So, by following God's simple laws;-

*e.g. - **"Do unto others, as you'd like them to do unto you."***

Keeps you consciously mindful of your ways and actions towards others. Only then would you understand how to turn the other cheek; love and pray for your enemies; do good to those who use you; not to be jealous or envious of others; to give whole-heartedly and be supportive of those in need, plus how to be unselfish, forgiving and compassionate.

True 'Spirituality' brings a rare confidence, re-assurance, contentment and inner peace, to the extent that one can rejoice over death, understanding that true life is eternal, hence physical death is but a mere transition.

There is only ONE GOD - YOUR FATHER.

- The Lord's prayer, 'Our Father' is a universal prayer to show that we are all brothers and sisters created by one God. Therefore, we are all children of the universe.

- Only God has the power to ordain the righteous, which is your reward for obedience to HIM. When HE ordains, HE confirms HIS ordination directly to those chosen. So be careful of people who walk in false garments.

Any religion is good but your Faith (i.e. belief) must be in God and not in the religion or church itself. Remember, there is good and bad in everyone. There are many routes to God, therefore, condemnation is not being pointed to any particular religion, church or its ministers; but I warn you, **trust no one but God and yourself.** There are many men and women who have the true desire and vocation (i.e. CALLING) to serve God and humanity.

To Churches, Leaders and Rulers

 16th March 1997.

God visited me this day again and was very angry with certain churches, leaders, rulers and inventors and said:-

- *"What wicked and evil deeds has been done in MY Name, the Name of love;- for I AM LOVE."*

- *"Who dares curse MY Holy place by entering into it with shoes on their feet."*

- *"Who cast aside and separate any of MY children, may they be diseased, disabled or asexual. Who gave them the RIGHT to suffer MY children and distance them."*

- *"How dare they say that women are **'unclean'** in the period of cleansing and purification of her body. Who granted them permission to abuse her 'free-will' and commit adultery. Who then is the weaker sex?"*

- *"Who gave them the right to cover and hide a woman's beauty?"*

- *"Love is singular but yet collective. In the beginning;- I commanded you to love only ME, The ONE TRUE GOD, for I AM a jealous God. Do you not then expect your wife to be jealous and hurt if another takes her place?"*

- *"I commanded you to love yourself."*

- *"I commanded you to love your father and your mother (one father, one mother)."*

- *"I commanded you to love your wife and husband (one wife, one husband)."*

- *"I commanded you to take another wife or husband, only if the love in either has ended or died and you have separated."*

- **"I am the God of love and fairness."**

- *"I commanded you to love your children, because they should be born out of true love."*

- *"I commanded you to love your neighbours as you love yourself (one to one Universal love)."*

- *"I commanded you to love the universe and all that is in it."*

- *"I commanded you not to kill. But what about your religious and all other wars, killing in MY NAME."*

- *"I never commanded you to abuse love in anyway."*

- *"Who commanded you to build separate churches, so that MY children are divided?"*

- *"Who commanded you to abuse the BOOK OF LAWS. By rewriting MY laws you have also ABUSED ME?"*

- *"Who commanded you to deceive others in MY NAME?"*

  "In the beginning there was THE WORD.

  THE WORD is LOVE - for I AM LOVE.

  THE WORD is TRUTH - for I AM TRUTH.

  Therefore, any ABUSE of the WORD is CORRUPTION.

  STOP ABUSING MY WORDS.

STOP ABUSING - MY CHILDREN.

STOP ABUSING - MY UNIVERSE.

*and return to the TRUE WORD - **LOVE**.*

*for only then can you RETURN TO **ME**.*

- *"You are inventors of corruption. What is marriage without true deep love. A gold ring, a church or a priest cannot create 'love' if there is no love in the first place. A true marriage is the union of two people in true love, who then receive MY blessings;- for anything born out of love **'is Love'** and will bring forth love, teach love, give love, show love, because **love is the all embracing.***

- ***LOVE** and **HATE** are two distinctly separate things which should never be mixed. It is one or the other:-*

  ***GOD** (goodness) means **LOVE**.*

  DEVIL (evil) means HATE.

Whatever I command you to do, is always for the benefit of yourself and MY Kingdom.

So now I command you again, to turn away from your foolish pride, jealous ambition and evil deeds and **return to love**:- for whosoever commandeth you to do the opposite to MY WORDS is the one who is in opposition to ME - the evil one... i.e. the devil. Therefore, I command you to resist EVIL!

Now take a long look at what you have done through evil.

Evil is Destructive -

- *It desensitises the senses (i.e. feelings).*
- *It is reckless.*

- *It is selfish.*

- *It is greedy.*

You have abused the 'free-will' I gave you to amass great personal wealth for your own benefit, through suffering MY children.

'EVIL is the Ultimate ABUSER.'

*You have even abused the creative power I gave you for the benefit of the world;- by destroying it. Your poisons has already penetrated many layers of the earth's strata. The West... so-called 'developed countries' are the worst and most poisonous sections. It will take centuries to reverse the process and restore natural beauty (normality). You must stop transporting your poisons to the undeveloped countries, in order to protect and redress the balance. The **3rd World** will become* ***the Mother of the developed world*** *and feed its children back to LIFE.*

Your list of evil deeds are so extensive that it would take an entire book to chart them."

"I cannot and will not allow you to continue this abuse. My children shall rise against you and take back their power; for only 'love' shall be the ruler of MY WORLD"

"Take Heed of MY WORDS!"

Creation, Birth and Names

You were all CREATED by God but born of man.

1.   You were all part of the **original creation** of the world. Therefore, you were first created by God (original birth) and this is how and why HE is your true, only and everlasting Father. HE also gave you your first name as HIS child (i.e. your Spirit-name), which never changes because its your **original name** and is also how you are identified and recognised spiritually.   The same as you are identified by your physical-name on earth. Therefore, when you die, you immediately resume back to your eternal 'Spiritual-name.'

2.   However, you are also 'born of man' (physical re-birth) to re-enter your physical-life on earth (i.e. reincarnation) and are named by your parents as their child. Hence, 'honour and respect your father and your mother,' but your ultimate obedience is to God... your true parent.

3.   Therefore, your 'Spirit-name' is more important than your 'physical-name' because it is your 'eternal-name.'   When you consider that you were created billions of years ago and have returned to earth thousands of times, to different parents who gave you different names, then you'd realise that your physical-name is quite insignificant, unless you had made a huge impact on the earth, which made it more important than most. Yet eventually, through the passage of time, important 'physical-names' are still forgotten, even if written into the history books.

How to find Your Purpose or True Career

'DESTINY'

Questions:

1.   What were you sent here to do?
2.   What did you ask *(or request)* to be sent here to do?

Answers:

Think of three things you'd truly 'love' to do, then **choose the one you love the most.** This is what you asked to be sent to do in this life on earth. Consider the words; GOD-is-LOVE, therefore, all that you desire is always **centred on love.** Sometimes, you cannot choose between two things and it is possible for you to do both. However, in time you'd realise which one is your real passion. Once you've found your 'true purpose or passion,' then God will influence or direct you to use your purpose for the benefit of yourself and others.

   Young Children.

It is much easier to learn from children, what they'd like to be or do, because they have not yet been fully brainwashed and are still closely in tune with their spiritual-being. Although a rounded (book) education is important; but think how much easier would it be, if they could be allowed to focus more on their true love or purpose, rather than battle with subjects which they are not interested in or find difficult to understand. If 'Spiritual development and book education' were correctly combined, then each would become greater **Masters of their own lives**... self-assured, self-determined and self-controlled.

• **Natural Instincts** - *(i.e. Talents).*

To realise your true potential, you must first release yourself from the shackles of fear, ego, false pride and self pity; wash away the tears of restriction to obtain clear vision; set your heart on your goals, then apply your natural instincts or intuition to become a testimony of your true God-given natural talents... i.e. your free gifts.

FEAR.

FEAR weakens the **MIND, BODY & SPIRIT.**

It limits your **LIFE.**

It makes **EXCUSES.**

It gives **REASONS.**

It casts **BLAME.**

It finds **JUSTIFICATION.**

So don't allow it to **CONTROL YOU.**

CONQUER IT

Evil

Don't think evil and you won't attract evil. Your thoughts attract all things, good or bad. **Protect yourself** and do not be afraid. Remember that 'fear' weakens, conquers and steals your power. Live in consciousness (i.e. be aware of evil but don't think of it, or be fearful and it will not consume you).

Whenever 'fear' confronts you, fight it. Take back and keep your power. Don't let anything or anyone steal your 'God-given power.' Stay in control of your own precious life.

 The Brain.

God gave you a brain to think and likes you to use it. The power of thought has limitless imagination and creativity. You can create all your desires with 'positive thoughts.' Hence, do not let anyone manipulate or brainwash you because this too is stealing your power by weakening your energy.

 Power.

True power is not the show of physical force but the strength of the MIND. Weaken the mind and you are powerless, hence **FEAR is your greatest weakener.** This is the only reason why man has deliberately indoctrinated you to be afraid, even of yourself, in order to weaken and control you, to the point of making you afraid to do even that which you believe to be right. This is not God or the devil's work but man's work to gain power.

Once you understand 'right from wrong' and begin to do that which is right, just, fair and loving, then you are walking the path God intended. Every battle Jesus fought with the devil was not a 'physical fight but a mental fight' and the strongest 'mind' won. It is man who created physical warfare and invented arsenals of deadly weapons to compensate for their own weak minds, in an effort to instill even greater fear in those they oppose. The men of power, now themselves live in fear of their powerful weapons, because one little push of a button could destroy their entire power base. So understand the agenda of politics, it is a game of control through FEAR.

Nationality & Ownership

"You belong to NO NATION; you are a 'child of the universe' (a child of God), because I AM the Father and the Creator of all the universe. Rebuke all land ownership as I AM the only true owner of all the lands, which I have lent to you for your physical existence. Everything on earth is on loan to you, even your children and its 'My right' to reclaim all, at anytime I choose.

Part of your blessing is based on how well you have taken care of MY property.

- *"Did you fulfil or serve your requested purpose?"*

- *"Did you follow and obey MY laws?"*

- *"How deep was your love?"*

- *"How many Souls did you touch with your love?"*

- *"What was the colour, gender or nationality of your love?"*

- *"What were your actions on earth?"*

- *"On these too you are judged," (i.e. you and you alone are responsible and answerable for your actions)."*

Water Libation
'Drink offering to God and your Spirit-Helpers.'

As a mark of respect and acknowledgement during special celebrations or gatherings, libation is poured to honour God and your Spirit-Helpers (i.e. Masters, Teachers, Guardian Angels, Ancestors, loved-ones and friends), for what they have done for you. The head of the household is generally chosen to conduct the ceremony. Holding a glass of water from which a few drops are poured, (either on the ground or in a plant), after each offering is made and when finished, the glass is then passed around for each person in the gathering to drink a little of the water.

 How to make the offerings -

Say:-

1. *"Father we pour Libation to YOU"*   (pour some water).

2. *"To all the Masters"*   (pour some water)

3. *"To our Guides and Teachers'*   (pour some water)

4. *"To our Ancestors, loved-ones and   (pour some water)
   friends* (naming them if you wish).

*"Who have brought us to this glorious day to celebrate in Your name, '**OUR FATHER GOD.**"*

- **Alcohol.**

No Alcohol is to be drunk when praying. After prayers have ended and celebrations begin, then alcohol can be taken. You can even then make an alcoholic toast to your Spirit-ancestors and friends, so that they too can join in the celebrations and have a good time with you. **Alcohol** is for fun and merriment, **prayers are serious** and you must keep your senses clear, whilst in the state of prayer. God loves you to enjoy yourself but you should try to remain conscious and stay in control of yourself. Like everything else, alcohol must not be abused or it will abuse you.

Feeding the SPIRIT

 Spiritual Food is -

1.   **Meditation -**   rest, relaxation and prayer to connect with God, your Guides and your inner-Spirit.

2.   **Fasting -**   for discipline.

3.   **The Water of Life -** is the food your Spirit needs for energy and clarity and is also the food your body needs for cleansing and healing.

This creates 'positive energies' to keep you on a high energy level (i.e. body, mind and Spirit in balance or in tune spiritually, mentally and physically fit). You can then work on all levels without external 'evil forces' or influences to unbalance you. Just as you need to feed your body with food and to exercise regularly, you also need to feed and exercise your Spirit, to keep it fit and restore your energies. Low Energy leads to sickness... weakness. It is advisable to fast at least 1 day a week, drinking only plain water for a minimum of 12 hours (6am to 6pm or 6pm to 6am). Fasting disciplines and controls your appetite, flushes out and refills your body, also heals and restores your energy.

HIGH ENERGY = **Positive Energy** (health)

LOW ENERGY = **Negative Energy** (sickness).

Rhythm of Life

LIFE has a distinctive rhythm in which 'the breath of life' moves. Everything breathing in and out in harmony, to the same tune. Each flowing, swaying, breathing and dancing to the 'rhythm of life.' This rhythm contains 'pure energy' which is the fuel of all life force, that you extract from each other and from the environment.

Hence, LIFE is 'inter-dependent, inter-related and inter-active.'

We need each other in order to **survive**, this is **The Spirit of LIFE.**

Musical Messengers

Musicians are some of the greatest messengers.

Like the 'psalms of David' which were originally called the 'songs of David.'

They are sent to open your hearts; to free the mind and to energise the adolescent youth from their rebellious stage into adulthood. Music gives love, comfort, energy and balance. It also brings direct spiritual messages because musicians write from inspiration.

Think of the songs of;-   Bob Marley

John Denver

John Lennon

Elvis Prestley

Gospel, Soul, Jazz and Country Music

and the millions of others sent to make you happy.

That was and is their purpose:- Love, Upliftment and Happiness.

"Music is the food of love!" So listen well to the words of your Musical Messengers but listen carefully because evil can also be transmitted through music.

Life

Life would be absolutely dull if you could predict your future or know precisely what each day would bring. The unknown allows you to challenge yourself, so that you can gain knowledge through new experiences. Understanding that 'there are no limitations,' enables you to explore every possibility. Each challenge you conquer reaps a personal victory over your own capabilities. The surprising joy of victory, is so overwhelming that it encourages you to try to do more for yourself. The real challenging test is not giving up when you fail but to keep at it, until you win the glory. Hence, **life** is a series of perpetual challenges to gain experience, then to move on to higher or greater things. So you are in a constant process of learning. However, it is you who personally decides the challenge and also sets the pace of victory.

Therefore, **the essence of life is an attempt to better yourself,** in a variety of ways, gaining knowledge until you become the master of your own life... physically or spiritually.

Death
'Physical Death.'

In ancient times because people were able to communicate with the Spirit world, they realised that physical death was simply the Spirit's way of saying that it was time to leave the earth and return home (i.e. its spiritual home). Therefore, the physical-body went to sleep, so the Spirit could be released to travel back (i.e. fly home). They understood that the Spirit itself was alive, awake and well.

After three days of mourning and prayers for the Spirit's safe deliverance to its proper destination (i.e. to his or her correct spiritual house), they would then dress in bright colourful clothes, rejoice, sing, dance, drink, toast a happy farewell and 'celebrate the spirit's life,' whose fond memories and good works were kept alive. However, through religious indoctrination, this joyous occasion has been transformed into perpetual grief and lamentation. This does not mean that no sadness was felt but people quickly came to terms, overcome and accepted the passing as a natural course of events and that they would meet again one day 'in the Spirit.'

Death
'Spiritual Death.'

'Spiritual death' or the death of your inner-Spirit, is the only death you should fear. For only God has the power to destroy your Spirit, which means that you will never exist again throughout all eternity. The death of your Spirit means the true end of your life.

How to Bless and Protect

'Yourself, family and home.'

At least once a year, you should bless yourself, family and home, to unblock or clear out any negative energies. You know instinctively when things do not feel right within yourself or in your home (i.e. unrest, disquiet, uncomfortable, depression, quarrelsome, angry, illness, bad dreams, etc) which gives you a feeling of discomfort in your mind, or in the atmosphere around you. This is when you and your entire home needs a good 'spring clean or blessing' to remove the negative elements which plays havoc with your life, family and career. It's a form of protection to create and surround yourself with uplifting positive energies, which brings life back into everything. Another good time to spring clean is the day before Thanksgiving Day or New Year's Day, so that you welcome the actual day refreshed and revitalised.

 Things you will need;-

1. Holy Water.

2. A white Candle and candle holder.

3. A piece of navy blue cloth (or a navy blue mat or carpet) measuring about 1 metre (3 feet) square. Notice, that God surrounded the entire universe in mid-night blue.

4. A small pastry or paint brush to sprinkle the Holy water.

5. Incense and incense holder. A nice incense is frankincense and myrrh with Benzoin added, which gives off a beautiful sweet fragrance. There are also special incense holders made from clay or metal.

6. Charcoal or the special charcoal used for burning incense.

7. A pair of metal tongs (type used for picking up ice cubes), to hold

and light the charcoal.

8.   A saucer or plate, to place the incense holder on. If it's made of metal it becomes extremely hot and could burn your hands when incensing the rooms.

9.   Matches or a lighter, to light the candle and charcoal.

10.   A special Prayer -

"Father God, please BLESS, SEAL, CONSECRATE and PROTECT..." naming what or who you are blessing.

11.   **The best time to BLESS is 6am**, otherwise follow the morning and night praying times and sun's position.

12.   <u>**How to find the Sun's position:-**</u>

Between 7 or 9am, look out of your windows and see where the sun is shinning (i.e. rising), this is the 'East' position. When saying your **morning prayers**, face this position in your home. At night time the 'West' position is directly the opposite side. When saying your **night prayers**, face this position. However, you must keep an eye on the sun because it moves during the course of the year, so you will need to keep track of it and change your EAST/WEST positions accordingly.

13.   Before you can BLESS anything, you need to prepare your own Holy Water. **It is important that once you have completed the Blessing, the Holy Water is immediately thrown away, either by pouring it down the sink or throw it outside your home because the negative energies are absorbed into the Holy Water during the Blessing. So you must get rid of it completely out of your home. When throwing it outside the house, throw it in the shape of the CROSS but DO NOT SAY THE PRAYER.**

1.

The Holy Water

- Prepare yourself before blessing the water.

  Clean yourself (bathe or shower and wash your mouth) get dressed but remain barefoot.

- Spread the navy blue cloth (carpet or mat) on a clean floor where you could move around it easily.

- Place **two clean glasses of water** in the middle of the cloth (carpet or mat).

- Place the 'candle' in it's holder in front of the glasses and light it.

- Stand in front of the cloth (carpet or mat) facing **EAST**. *(see diagram on page 575).*

- Make the sign of the cross to open your Soul-centre.

- Pray and protect yourself with the '7 invisible triangles' which surrounds your body.

- **Talk to God and ask him to bless the water and to guide you through the blessing.**

- Pick up one glass of water and hold it in your hand, leave the other glass of water on the cloth. **Facing EAST,** visualise that there is an **invisible cross** on the cloth and each point is centred EAST, WEST, NORTH and SOUTH; *(see diagram on page 575)*

- Dip the brush into the glass of water (in your hand) and strike it straight across the cloth EAST to WEST, whilst saying the special prayer - *"Father God, please BLESS, SEAL, CONSECRATE and PROTECT this water."*

- Then move clockwise to the **NORTH point,** dip into the water again and strike it across the cloth SOUTH to NORTH, whilst **repeating the special prayer.**

- Move clockwise to the **EAST point,** dip into the water again and strike it across the cloth WEST to EAST, whilst

  repeating the special prayer.

- Move clockwise to the **SOUTH point,** dip into the water and strike it across the cloth NORTH to SOUTH, whilst

  repeating the special prayer.

- Then return to the **WEST point**, so that you are again facing the EAST.

You've now finished blessing the Holy Water

- Say, *"Thank You Father, Amen"* and make the sign of the cross to close off your Soul-centre.

- Out the candle.

- Throw away the glass of water in your hands, either straight down the sink or throw it outside your home, 'in the shape of a CROSS but **DO NOT say the prayer.**

- The glass of water on the cloth (carpet or mat) has now been **blessed** and is your **Holy Water.** You may use it to either bless yourself or your family or your home or your friends, individually or collectively on the same day. When you have finished the BLESSING, the used Holy Water must be immediately thrown away (either pour it straight down the sink or throw it outside your home, **in the shape of the CROSS but DO NOT say the prayer**). Alternatively, you could bless several bottles of water (jam or pickle jars are best), by placing these with the lids on the cloth, at the start of the blessing. Once blessed, seal each with the lids and keep for use when ever required. But remember to throw it away once used for blessing.

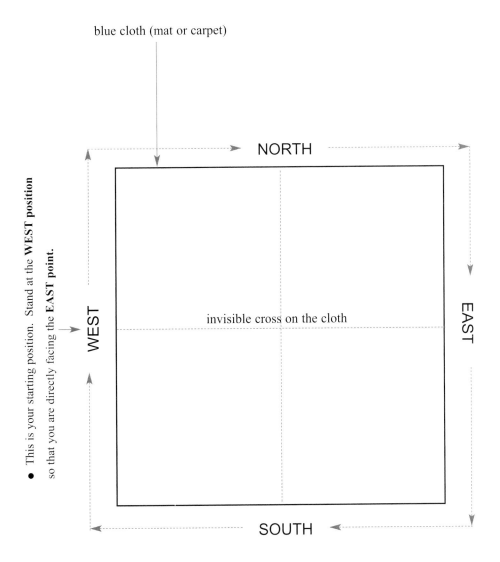

blue cloth (mat or carpet)

NORTH

WEST

EAST

invisible cross on the cloth

SOUTH

• This is your starting position. Stand at the **WEST position**
so that you are directly facing the **EAST point.**

2.

Blessing Yourself & Family

You will need;-

- The Holy Water.

- The navy blue cloth (carpet or mat).

- A member of your family or close friend who you believe truly 'loves you' and is not jealous or envious of you or would not do you any harm in **words, thoughts** or **deeds.** Whosoever you choose, must not be angry or vexed in anyway whilst blessing you. It is important that the atmosphere is one of mutual love, peace and calm.

 Preparing yourself for the Blessing;-

- Both yourself and family (or friend) should clean yourselves. Bathe or shower and wash your mouths. Then dress but remain barefoot.

- Make the sign of the cross to open your Soul-centres.

- Pray and protect yourselves with the '7 invisible triangles.'

- Spread the navy cloth (carpet or mat) on a clean floor.

- You should stand in the middle of the cloth, **facing EAST.**

- Stand with your **feet together** and **arms stretched out** from your sides at shoulder level. *(see diagram on page 539).*

- The family member (or friend) should stand 'barefoot' in front of you (face to face), holding the glass of **Holy Water**.

- He (or she), should dip his fingers into the **Holy Water** and starting from the centre of the top of your head (whilst saying the special prayer - *"Father God, please BLESS, SEAL, CONSECRATE and PROTECT Dounne,"* run his fingers down the centre of your body from head to toe (i.e. head, face, chest, stomach, legs to toes).

- Dip his (or her) fingers into the **Holy Water** again and starting from the tip of your 'fingers on the left hand' (whilst saying the special prayer) run his fingers straight along your hand; arm, across your chest and along the 'right arm,' hand to the finger tips.

- Dip his (or her) fingers into the **Holy Water** and make the 'sign of the cross' in **the palms of both hands.**

- He (or she) then moves to the back of you.

- Dip his fingers into the **Holy Water** and starting from the centre of the top of your head (whilst saying the special prayer) run his fingers down the centre of your body from head to heel (i.e. head, neck, back, bottom, legs to heel).

- Dips his fingers into the **Holy Water** again and starting from the tip of 'the fingers of your right hand' (whilst saying the special prayer) run his fingers along the back of your hand, arm, across your back, along your 'left arm,' hand to the finger tips.

- Dips his fingers into the **Holy Water** and make the 'sign of the cross' on the **soles of both feet.**

- Both of you then say; *"Thank You Father God, amen."* Make the sign of the cross to close your Soul-centres.

Your Blessing is finished;-

You can use the remaining Holy Water to either 'bless' other members of your family or friends or your home. Once the blessings have finished that day, throw away the remaining Holy Water. Pour it straight down the sink or throw it outside your home, **in the shape of the CROSS but DO NOT say the prayer.**

- **Birth and Death;-**

This blessing can also be performed on a new born baby or when someone dies.

3.

Blessing Your Home

You will need;-

All the items listed at the beginning 1 to 10 *(see pages 571 & 572)*.

 Preparing your House for the Blessing;-

1. Clean out the entire house as thoroughly as you can. Wash down windows, doors, curtains; clean out cupboards, dust down and polish furniture, ornaments; clean all floors, tidy clothes cupboards, wash dirty clothes, etc. In other words, clean out as thoroughly as possible, because you are preparing your home to **invite God to enter.** You are making a very special effort to show HIM that you not only respect and take HIM seriously but that HE is also the most special and personal friend in your life. For example, when you invite friends over to your home for a special occasion, you always make a special effort to clean and prepare it so that they feel welcomed. Try to be happy during the cleaning;- keep a clean mind and tell yourself *"I am doing this for ME and God."* As there will be so much to do, you can take 2 or 3 days or more (depending on the size of your home) to complete all the cleaning. However, remember that 'God is practical,' so if you are not physically capable or the circumstances make it impossible to be this thorough, then simply do the best you can.

 Preparing yourself to bless the house;-

•   On the morning of the Blessing, remove all the bed sheets and pillow cases, put these away for washing. If you wish, you could turn over your mattress. Leave the bed unmade or put on clean bedding.

- Clean yourself. Bathe or shower, wash your mouth. Dress but remain barefoot.

- Make the 'sign of the cross.' Pray and protect yourself with the '7' individual triangles,' keep your Soul-centre open.

- Spread the navy blue cloth (carpet or mat) on the clean floor.

- Put all the item 1 to 9 in the middle of the cloth and light the candle.

- Holding one of the glass of water in your hand. Facing EAST, visualise the invisible cross on the cloth with points - EAST, WEST, NORTH & SOUTH *(see diagram on page 575)* and bless all the items exactly as you did in the Blessing of the **Holy Water** (moving around the cloth clockwise) - saying the special prayer *"Father, God please BLESS, SEAL, CONSECRATE and PROTECT these items."* When you have finished and the items are blessed. Throw away the used water in your hands (pour it straight down the sink or throw it outside your home), **in the shape of the CROSS,** but **DO NOT say the prayer**.

- Pick up the **HOLY WATER** and the brush, start the blessing from the bedrooms first, then work through every room in an orderly manner, making sure not to miss any room, until you end up finally at your front or back door to finish off.

In each room;-

- Dip the brush in the **Holy Water** and make the 'sign of the cross' with it ONCE on each of the following:-

    - the front of the door.

- the back of the door.

- the windows.

- each bed and all the furniture.

- on the floors.

- on the walls.

with each signing say;-

"Father God, please BLESS, SEAL, CONSECRATE and PROTECT this (name what you are signing on i.e. bed, door).

- Then move into every room (including the passage) and 'Bless' each the same way, until you get to the **front and back doors:-**

  - On the front of both doors (i.e. inside); make 'the sign of the cross' with the **Holy Water 3** times(whilst saying the special prayer).

  - Open the door - on the floor between the inside to stepping outside, also sign **3** times (whilst saying the special prayer ending with *"PROTECT this entrance)."*

  - On the back of both doors (i.e. outside), sign 3 times (whilst saying the special prayer).

  - *Which ever of these two doors you end up blessing last, is where the House Blessing ends.* You should be on the outside of the door. Throw away the remaining **Holy Water in the shape of the CROSS but DO NOT say the prayer.** Turn around and re-enter your house.

- Put the charcoal in the incense holder onto a saucer or plate then light it. When it starts to burn, sprinkle the incense on it.

- When the incense is smoking and releasing its fragrance, then pick up the saucer, take it into each room and scent it.

- When all the rooms are done, return to the blue cloth, facing EAST and say *"thank You Father God, Amen."* Make 'the 'sign of the cross' to close off your Soul-centre, then **out the candle**. Finally, leave the charcoal in a safe place to burn out. Once cooled, either bury the ashes in the garden or throw it away outside of the house.

THIS COMPLETES THE HOUSE BLESSING.

☀ Other Blessings;-

- If you wish, you could also Bless the outside of your house (i.e. the walls and the garden), using the same method for blessing with the **Holy Water** (EAST, WEST, NORTH and SOUTH position, visualise the 'invisible cross' on the garden itself).

4.

HEALING through Visualisation

Imagine something in your mind and try to actually see it through your mind's eye; which is also referred to as your 'Spiritual third eye.'

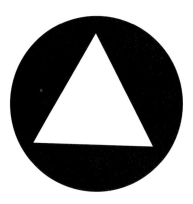

Visualisation is a simple and powerful form of healing.

- Sit or lie in a comfortable position, close your eyes, relax, meditate and try to visualise the above logo.

- Ask God for HIS assistance and permission to either heal you or someone else or an animal.

- Visualise yourself or those who you are asking for healing, inside the pyramid/triangle (on the floor). You can put as many people or animals as you wish inside of the pyramid.

- Ask God to fill the pyramid with one of HIS healing coloured lights:-

  Pale Blue - for gentle, soothing healing, relaxation and the relief of stress etc.

  OR

Gold - for strong healing, illness, success etc.

- Visualise the pyramid being filled with the healing colour. Visualise the colour as 'an energy' which is bathing, soothing, relaxing and healing those inside of the pyramid. If there is a particularly serious illness or condition, then ask God to intensify the healing energies of the Gold light and visualise it penetrating into the entire body, burning out the condition.

- Try to remain in this meditative state for a good while and practice strengthening your visualisation ability for as long as you wish.

Visualisation does not mean that miraculous healing will always occur but for some mysterious reason, the health and energy of the person or animal seems to improve and if done regularly, they do seem to recover more quickly.

You can also light a blue or gold candle (or use a light bulb) and keep it lit throughout the healing/meditation, to help strengthen your visualisation power.

Creative Visualisation

Use the same visualisation technique to create your desires; a gold candle (or light bulb) can also be used. Simply visualise whatever you wish to achieve, then work towards obtaining it. In other words, **you are the creator of your dreams**... i.e. your God-self.

Spirituality.

• VISIONS OF THE FUTURE.

*"For modern man; these visions may be too
idealistic and simple but remember, God is an
idealist (PERFECT), who said that WISDOM is
Simplicity and who created*

an

IDEAL WORLD."

Visions of the Future

Now that I've done what I was sent and told to do and has 'acted' on GOD'S instructions; I will endeavour to 'spread the word' and also keep the faith. I await whatever instructions (if any) I'll receive in the future and **ACT** accordingly.

As these are God's plans and not my own, I cannot predict what the future holds. I am only a Messenger/Teacher passing on information but intuitively, I do feel very positive that there's a great future for those of us who return to **love and truth** and a grave situation for those who do not. Whether this will be by actual death or self-imposed through personal ignorance and faithlessness, only God knows. However, what I'm certain about is that **God will not destroy the world**, because HE said:-

> *"I will not destroy the world again, for the sake of the innocent,*
> *I will keep MY promise."*

I also know that it's up to all of us individually and collectively to TAKE-ACTION! and bring about the changes HE has requested;-

knowledge and Information are the keys to our salvation.

I visualise a vision of **Hope & Glory.**

A vision of **Respect & Appreciation.**

A vision of **Truth & Happiness.**

A vision of **Unity.**

I visualise -

A universal family of LOVE.

Again, I must say that for modern man, these visions may be too idealistic and simple but remember that God is an idealist, who said that 'wisdom is simplicity' and who created 'an ideal world.'

I do believe that together we can bring the earth back to life and people back to love. The solutions are as simple as they sound but we must become consciously aware and pay attention to what is going on in our homes, communities, countries and world-wide. Remember, *"to obey means to ACT."*

By doing nothing, we are indirectly contributing to the destruction.

We can no longer afford to sit back and watch, because we have already seen the results of our complacency. Therefore, we must all play our part, get active and become involved. If it only means putting your own house in order... something is better than nothing. Check out other environmental, health or social campaigns and support at least one. There are millions of people who passionately believe in the need for **change** and are selflessly working extremely hard. Some even risking their own lives to improve our lives. Please help them to help us all. In most cases, all it takes is just five minutes to fill out a form; make a small financial donation... once a year. It took many, many years of relentless campaigning to eventually get the Tobacco companies to finally admit that cigarettes are highly addictive and dangerous drugs, which causes cancer and other dreadful diseases and should be banned, especially from children. In the case of **genetic engineering,** we cannot afford to wait that long and must keep in mind that David slew Goliath, therefore, 'all things are possible.'

As the Lord said;-

"We must ACT now to stop this fatal menace."

"We may sometimes give up on

ourselves but, the Lord never gives up on us."

It's all our responsibility to make a conscious effort and contribute towards a better future. Keep in mind that the three most valuable gifts of life are **FAITH, HOPE & CHARITY.**

> *"The Lord helps those who helps themselves."*
> *"Therefore, if you value your life then - SAVE IT."*

 ## ON REFLECTION.

For many years, I've been loosing interest in the whole commercial hype surrounding Christmas because people seem to have lost the 'Spirit of love' and 'good-will' it once represented.   I began questioning the amount of money I was spending every year on Christmas cards, which are simply discarded in the bin one month later. Then one day, whilst watching television and at the same time contemplating what better use I could put this money to; there was a feature by a charitable organisation, calling on people to sponsor an African child for £12 per month to provide basic amenities, food, health and education. I immediately decided that my Christmas card money would be better spent on improving the life of one child in need of help. It has since proved far more satisfying, receiving reports on how well he is doing, not only in school but in life generally.

Coming face to face with God.

Coming Face to Face with God

On the 24th May 1997, God visited me in a dream for the first time.

I was dreaming that Rudolph, Marsha, Dee and myself were in a large old house. It was night time, so we retired to bed. I got up to leave the bedroom but as I tried to open the door, a mighty spiritual force which was much stronger than my physical strength, was pushing against the door, preventing me from opening it. I pushed with all my might but it was far to powerful. So I decided to let it go and whilst standing in front of it, (in my mind) I quietly called on the power of my Spirit ORISHUA. A surge of strength flowed through me and I opened the door, pushing the force away. As I reached the top of the staircase, an elderly gentleman, dressed in a brown striped robe, holding the hand of a young boy (who looked like an orphan) was walking up the stairs. The old man looked up at me and smiled and I instantly recognised HIM and said, *"God, you have come!"* I was so excited and immediately called everyone, shouting *"wake up, wake up, God is here, come and meet HIM."* I didn't feel it should be a privilege I alone should experience. I wanted to share HIM and HE loved it. HE greeted everyone with gentle hugs and smiles. He stayed a long time. I was so overjoyed and excited that I can't remember anything HE said. I was completely overcome by HIS presence (i.e. HIS entire being, personality, warmth, friendly welcoming smile, serenity, beautiful voice, loving eyes and comforting arms). I was in awe, deliriously happy and happier still to see everyone experiencing and receiving HIS attentive love and also experiencing the strange peace which fills the room, whenever HE is present. The ecstacy which exists in HIS presence is indescribable. You just don't want HIM to leave and want to stay with HIM forever. To experience HIS embrace brings a depth of comfort that no mother, father, husband or wife could achieve. It is truly the hug of **pure love**. All other love pales into insignificance because HIS love is the ultimate. So ultimate that one can really rejoice over physical death, just with the thought of being with HIM again. I really wanted to go back with HIM and was saddened that as my work was not completed, I could not return.

I awoke at 5.30am and was about to get up to prepare for my morning prayers when HE said - *"rest and sleep a while longer this morning."* So I went back to sleep and re-awoke at 7am. He then said, *"Now awake, go and start your work."*

That day, I felt as if my head was light and in the clouds. I was so at peace, calm, free from fear and seeing the world through different eyes; not rose coloured glasses but in reality through my 'spiritual third eye' and without any form of judgement. I could see people's behaviour towards each other and calmly accepted *"each to his own."*

Later that day, whilst in meditative conversation, I asked God, *"what would people say or think, if I told them what YOU really looked like?"*

HE replied;-

*"Many who are **pure in heart** have seen MY face but the world is not yet ready to accept what they will see.*

UNTIL *one's heart has become pure.*

UNTIL *one's eyes has become clear.*

UNTIL *one's mind has become clean and open.*

UNTIL *one's vision has become limitless.*

UNTIL *one becomes humble.*

UNTIL *one is able to relinquish hatred.*

UNTIL *one is released from the burdens of fear, ego and guilt.*

UNTIL *one is free from indoctrination and conditioning.*

UNTIL *one can let go and accept that all things are possible.*

UNTIL *one learns to be obedient as a child.*

UNTIL *one knows how to love and how to give love.*

UNTIL *one understands, what is love.*

UNTIL *one begins to live and walk in MY consciousness.*

UNTIL *one can face the truth.*

UNTIL *then, one is not ready to come face to face with ME.*

UNTIL *then, one is not prepared to accept the true living God:-*

their Father

their Creator

their Redeemer.

In the meantime, whatsoever they wish to see ME as; Indian, Mexican, Chinese, African, European, Male or Female, whatever:-

I AM that and more.

Let them see ME as they wish to see ME, until the day they really see ME."

ON REFLECTION.

- I now understand that **God is knowledge** and that **knowledge means POWER.**

- **True Power** is never abusive, violent, intimidating or controlling but SHARING.

- By sharing one's knowledge freely and willingly; one receives more knowledge, hence 'greater power.'

- To do so, one has to become completely selfless and desireless; for knowledge is not mare understanding but full comprehension.

We grow;-

as we learn

as we give

as we receive

as we pass on.

as we love.

Love is the ultimate Power & **God is Love.**

- We hold on to our securities, which makes us insecure. Only God can secure us. So hold on to HIM with all your might, your will and your love. Never let HIM go but let go of everything else. For when we die, don't we all have to let go of everything material, even our loved-ones? What value is anything to you when you die? You alone are valued, for what you've done for yourself and for others.

Shortly after HIS visitation, God instructed me to reveal 'Jesus's (double edged) sword of protection' which was given to me whilst in prayer on 6th January 1983. He said, that this is the first time in history it will be shown to the world.

Jesus's Double Edged Sword of Protection

 6th January 1983.

In the middle of saying my morning prayers (eyes closed), I saw a vision of a dazzling white light in the form of a large oval shape, within a cloud. I stopped praying momentarily and focused on the light, (in my mind) I asked; *"what is it? what are you trying to show me?"* I received no reply, so I kept looking at it. Then suddenly, I could see a glimpse of a silver object in the middle of it but the dazzling whiteness of the light, made it difficult to penetrate and see it properly. So I asked again, *"what is it? I can't see it properly."* Then it was revealed *(see page 595)*. It was the largest, heaviest, most powerful and beautiful sword I'd ever seen, made of pure silver and highly polished. The handle, neck and shoulders were richly engraved but the huge trunk was smooth and pointed at the tip (razor sharp on both sides right down to the tip). I was then told, *"this is the two edged sword of Christ for your protection from now onwards."* I was given special instructions on how to use it as my shield and was also given a special 'prayer of protection' to seal it to me. Every morning I must arm myself with this sword, sealed with the prayer, which would guard me from evil, especially the devil himself. I've done so ever since but it was not until God revealed my mission, did I realise the significance of this precious sword. But when HE told me, *"now read the Book of Revelations in the Bible."* There for the first time in my life in chapter one, I saw the words which revealed, *"a sharp two-edged sword and all about the cloud, the seven stars, the sun, fighting and defeating the devil."* I then realised that my time had come. However, I cannot reveal the words of the 'special prayer of protection' or how to use the sword, until after my death.

 ## ON REFECTION.

When I later checked, the date I was given the sword was 6th January 1983:-

In numerology, this date is 6+1+1+9+8+3 = <u>28</u> (2+8=10 = <u>1</u>)

- The number 1 means 'new beginnings'

- Jesus Christ was born on 6th January.

- I was born on 28th January.

- January is also month 1.

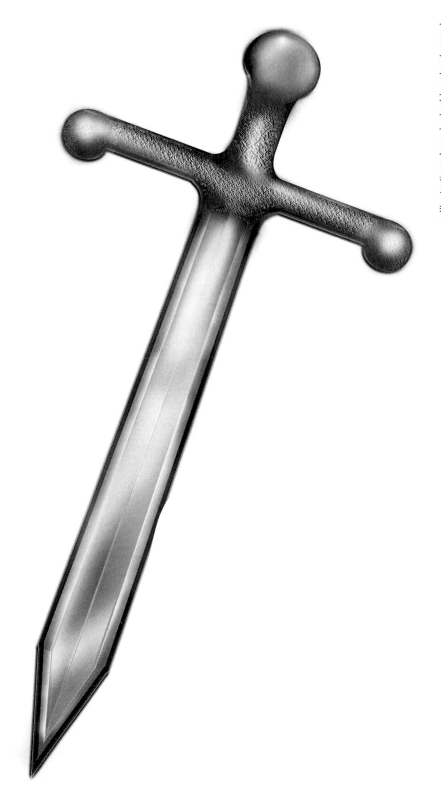

The Truth

On Thursday 23rd September 1999, whilst briskly walking down my local high street, God started speaking to me about the creation, the Bible and man's inventive tales. The conversation continued for a week until the following Thursday (30th September). He began by saying;-

*"It is true that the Bible was written millions of years after the creation, therefore, it is bound to contain inaccuracies. Through the passage of time, the true version of a story changes as it is passed from one person to another and is often made more colourful to add intrigue. The doctrine of religion, prevents people from questioning the origins of the Bible or any statements in it. But as you already know, (like any loving father) you can talk or ask any questions or reason with ME on anything of concern. I gave you the **free-will** to consider everything and to make up your own mind. Therefore, you are not bound or limited in thoughts, deeds or actions. So, now let's consider what has been written in the Bible and compare it with what really took place... THE TRUTH.*

- **Adam and Eve.**
  Why would I create the whole world and the thousands of creatures in it and only create just one man and one woman? Notice the huge variety of animals, plants, trees, insects, etc. So why only one man, one woman and one race? Is it logical that these two pure people could physically give birth to so many different races and spread them across the entire globe? This also leads to the question of incestuous relationships.

- *Why would I the (Master of creation) need to take a man's rib, in order to create a woman? I must have also done the same, when I created male and female animals, plants etc? Would the 'God of LOVE' create anything which would lead to disharmony, inequality, abuse, bias and disadvantage to anything or anyone?*

*The answer is resolutely **NO!** **The truth is... all of man-kind and woman-kind were universally created at the same time;-** individually, independently, uniquely, freely and Holy (making you a Free-Spirit). This clarifies that life is eternal and you are one big universal family of friends, (a brotherhood and sisterhood) created by one person, ME. Hence, I AM both **your Father and your Mother**. Notice in the case of parenting; mothers become more masculine towards their sons and fathers become more feminine (gentle) towards their daughters. Each possess both sides of the gender equation (i.e. balance).*

<u>Single-parent Mothers</u>, have to be both Mother/father.

<u>Single-parent Fathers</u>, have to be both Father/mother.

- *According to the Bible, Adam and Eve were perfectly formed, civilised, intelligent people, yet Scientists refers to un-intelligent, uncivilised, people from the stone-age. How did they evolve from Adam and Eve? Again, their explanations do not make sense.*

- *If I created you in **MY own image and likeness**, then who and what AM I? The answer is, **I AM SPIRIT**, therefore **you too are SPIRIT.** Hence, the entire universe was originally created as SPIRIT. What does SPIRIT mean? SPIRIT is a life-form like the air and this is where the story of the 'breath of life' came into being. Breath is air, once the breath or SPIRIT leaves, then the physical-body dies. Therefore, without the Spirit or 'breath of life' the physical cannot exist but the breath or SPIRIT lives on forever. Hence, **SPIRIT means LIFE**. This fact makes a nonsense of the scientific theory of man's evolution from apes. Whereas human evolution is an eternity of experiences, culminating into his/her higher spiritual 'God-self.' This evolutionary journey is the two dimensional existence of the physical and spiritual being. You choose to return to your physical life on earth for a period of time, in which to learn and* *overcome new experiences, which then takes you onto a different level when you return to your spiritual-life and so on. In this way, you continue to learn, develop and grow in knowledge and ability. Thereby, making re-incarnation a reality.*

Just look at how much the world has progressed since it's original creation. You are now into the age of technology which is closely linked to telepathy (i.e. airways of communication).

- *Consider the theory of 'over population' and look at the size of the earth in comparison to the size of other planets and the vastness of the universe. Spirits travelling to and frow (i.e. death and birth). Therefore, the earth is always in balance. The overcrowding and cluttering are man-made. No matter who or what you make of yourself on earth, you all return to ME, naked and empty handed as the day you were born, relinquishing all earthly possessions. Therefore, you return to Spirit only with the knowledge and experience you have gained, which also keeps the universe uncluttered.*

- **A Universal Family of Friends.**

*In reality, there are no spiritual parents, ancestors, relations, or relationship ties. Therefore, 'in Spirit' race, skin colour, culture or ancestry are of no importance because you **live in harmony,** with open eyes and in the knowledge of truth;- aware that you are an independent individual with absolute 'freedom' to live your life your own way, without attachments or obligations. You are totally responsible for your own evolutionary advancements, therefore, you do whatever pleases you. Only on earth, do you find discrimination, cruelty and intolerance. However, when you look into these man-made indoctrinations, you will find that these disadvantages exist within the same nations (i.e. negroes against negroes, chinese against chinese, europeans against europeans, americans against americans, jews against jews, religions against religions and even brother against brother and so on). But if you look deeper still, you will also find all these nations* *coming together 'united in love' to fight against these same injustices. Look even deeper still and you will find individuals from different nations deeply in love with each other but cannot love their own nation with equal passion. You'd also find deep inter-racial bonding, many actually feeling a strong sense of belonging and connection with another nation or with other countries. The reason they feel such strong empathy is simply because they have experienced this existence in a previous life. For in reality, you can choose to return to earth in any nation, therefore you become a part of that cultural experience and inheritance. Only when you return to the Spirit-world, do you become fully aware of your true **original self!***

THINK ABOUT IT!

- *If Christ, Buddha, Krishna or Martin Luther King were to return to earth today, what nation would they return as and does it really matter? The only people it would matter to, are those who want to perpetuate the fallacy of supremacy. **Greed and hatred** have no race, no colour, no gender, no culture. Notice that great people (i.e. Masters) come from every nation and from every walk of life.*

- *Now, think about the topic on 'limitations.' Why should anyone want to limit their eternal existence to just one racial experience, knowing that to become a 'true Master' one has to experience all? This fact would infuriate those who believe in any form of superiority or supremacy, to accept the realisation that it is all part of their own cultural/spiritual heritage. Hence, when they hate, they are actually hating and ill-treating themselves and their own kind. The truth is, you all belong to one race, **the Human race**. Materialism is physical and not spiritual.*

- *If you wish to experience **true spirituality** at work, then put babies from all nationalities to play together. You will notice that they would not differentiate in their choice of friendship, because*

'LOVE IS ALL EMBRACING.' You return to earth blinded of your Spirit and past lives, in order to gain new experiences and to test the strength of your love.

- If you wish to examine the level of your own spiritual awareness, then check how readily you understand all that is being explained in this book. If you find that most of it is difficult to understand or cannot make any sense of it, this means that you are only now branching out on your spiritual journey but don't worry because once you start this journey, you will gradually grow in understanding, as your mind is made to open and as your experiences grow. Therefore, the more you understand, means the higher your spiritual awareness level which will continue to increase with experience. Understand that you are all **learned Masters** and your level of understanding is an indication of the level of your own personal efforts on the long journey to self-discovery in reaching the ultimate spiritual heights of becoming your **true God-Self.**

- The theory of supremacy (of any kind) is a 'man-made' invention, which has given blind-birth to universal ignorance. The worlds' suffering that exist today, will continue to intensify in the future, until such time that people wake up to the truth and individually re-learn to live in the -

'consciousness of Holy LOVE.'

For this reason Spirit-Masters are purposely sent to re-affirm the TRUTH -

As it was in the BEGINNING

It is NOW

and will always BE

The WORD IS TRUTH;- for TRUTH is constant and will never change.

I AM THE WORD."

ON REFLECTION.

Although I generally refer to GOD as my Father when speaking to HIM but I consciously acknowledge HIM as my Father/Mother. At the end of my daily prayers. I always finish with these words:-

"The Omnipotent, Omnipresent, Omniscient - Father/Mother GOD, Amen."

- **Omnipotent** means - GOD with unlimited power.

- **Omnipresen**t means - God who is present everywhere.

- **Omniscient** means - God who knows everything.

- **A Universal family of Friends** - *(no parents, no ancestors).*

This explains why God told me that I didn't lose my mother when she died but that I had gained a 'stronger spiritual friend.' The Spirit-Masters once told me not to look at Marsha and Dee as my children but as my spiritual friends. They are independent individuals, who have returned to learn through me.

I remembered in the 1980's (in Spirit), I was shown my last past life about 150 years ago, as a British aristocrat. This is another intriguing story. It showed me married to my ex-husband, who died young in battle serving as an officer in the army. I was shown his grave in Scotland and the inside of our stately home. This explained his regimental, stern, commanding personality. We were very much in love, had no children and chose to return to continue our romance in this lifetime (in a difference race and experience). Remarkably, at the age of about 14 years, whilst still living in the Caribbean, my deceased grandmother, (Ma), took me on a spiritual journey to England and showed him to me, saying, *"this is your husband to be."* The memory greatly influenced the reason why I hung onto him for so long. I thought our union was fate; that it was meant to be. I also notice that whenever I visit 'stately homes' I feel a sense of déjà vu and familiarity. Therefore, this explains that if you chose to return to earth for new experiences, then it stands to reason that you should know what your future holds, because you would have decided it before hand. Hence, you have the power (i.e. free-will) to change your circumstances, if you do not like what you are experiencing. *"Your destiny is always in your control."*

It also stands to reason why certain 'gifted people,' such as clairvoyants, can tell your future, because they can tap into your psyche (mind) and so can you.

Faith Rewarded

By the beginning of 1999, I was still broke and could see no way of raising the finance required to self-publish and market this book. Every morning, I prayed for my *needs* and would say to God; *"Father, you know that I'm faithful and would do anything YOU ask but I'm also practical and realistic. Although YOU talk about confidence, trust and rewards, I can't see how YOU expect me to publish it without any money. Show me or tell me how to obtain it."* HIS reply was constant:-

"Don't worry, remember you are in CHARGE,

But, I'm in CONTROL

Your rewards for obedience will be immeasurable."

So I faithfully continued writing.

By February, I completed the synopsis to start the marketing. I was so happy with its contents, I decided to take a break and went for a relaxing walk. Whilst walking, thinking and planning things out in my mind, God suddenly came through and said; *"The completion of the book is timed for the year 2000, precisely '7' years since your life was turned around."*

I was so wrapped up with my own thoughts that I nearly missed what HE said. Then it clicked, I said, *"what did you say Father? You have finally given me your date to complete it?"*

Well! there are no words to describe my expression. At that moment, anyone who would have seen me, would be right to think that I had gone mad. I wasn't jumping around or acting mad, just very excited and shouted, *"YES! YES!"* Then went skipping down the road, grinning from ear to ear.

On Sunday 9th May, Rudolph and I attended The British Film and Television Awards. Britain's answer to the American Oscars, which meant 'dress to impress' and we certainly did. An actor friend (Mr Treva Ettienne) also attended and immediately came up and ask to speak to me in private. His exact words were; *"Dounne are you 50 yet?"* with a huge grin on his face. I replied, *"YES."* He jumps up in excitement and said *"This one is for you Dounne, you are going to be the face of Oil of Olay."* Happy but confused, because I didn't know what he was on about. He explained; *"I got a call from a friend this morning, asking if I knew of any black women over the age of 50 who would be suitable. Oil of Olay is searching for a black woman to be their face of the millennium. I told her YES but I don't think she is 50 as yet. My friend will leave all the information on my answerphone tonight and I'll call you with the details."* Treva was absolutely confident that I'd get it but I wasn't. We then told Rudolph the goods news, which made the evening even more exciting. However, Rudy, being an actor who was used to disappointments, warned me not to get too excited, just enjoy the possibilities.

When we arrived home, Treva's message was already on my answerphone, explaining that the photo-shoot was taking place in London the very next morning (Monday) and wished me good luck.

Again, I dressed to impress, arrived at the studio well in time, only to find a room full of beautiful black women, each waiting to be photographed for the same part. One by one they were called in, photographed, then left. As the woman in charge saw me, her eyes lit up. Whilst taking my photos she kept repeating, *"you are incredible, your skin is incredible, you look so good."* I just took it as photographic flattery. Then she asked who was my agent. I didn't know I needed one and Treva's Agent happily obliged. I left, thought nothing of it, believing I didn't stand a chance.

My Agent called on the Wednesday to say that she had received a faxed contract from Oil of Olay (USA), requesting international coverage. She warned me not to get excited, as this did not mean that I had got the job. The next day, she phoned again and simply said, *"you've got the big one, it's a huge contract for a year and extendible. Arrangements are being made to collect airline tickets tomorrow, as you'll be flying to Morocco on Saturday for 5 days, to film the advert, all expenses paid."*

Screaming with excitement, I phoned Marsha, Dee, Rudolph (who was out), Treva and my family, to convey the great news. Everyone was happy for me. Rudolph returned with a bottle of champagne and we celebrated. I couldn't believe that they had chosen me but Marsha, Dee, Rudolph and Treva were never in any doubt. Marsha and Dee responded in their usual manner saying, *"so it took professionals in the beauty industry to make you realise what we have always known and has been telling you daily, that you are beautiful in every way."* Rudolph added, *"what you do not realise is that what is in your heart, shines on your face."*

I spent the next day rushing around shopping for the things I'd need and finally packed. On the Saturday, I had to pinch myself on the plane to ensure that it was not all a beautiful dream. This was the first time flying on my own and also my first time in Morocco. I arrived in Marrakech that evening and was taken to a beautiful 5 Star hotel.

Not having modelled or acted before, the anticipation was electric. The advertising guru Saatchi & Saatchi and the Oil of Olay team were friendly, accommodating and gave me a full run down of each day's schedule. Fittings on Sunday, filming Monday and Tuesday, return to London on Wednesday.

I was introduced to three other models who also arrived that day and we hit it off instantly. None of us knew what was going on, the whole thing was being kept very hush hush. We went for fittings the next day and were then told our individual parts. It turned out that Oil of Olay had been searching for three months, scouting thousands of women around the world, to choose 30 representing the age groups 20, 30, 40, 50, 60 and 70 for six adverts, showing that Oil of Olay was good for all women at any age. This was their millennium theme.

The other chosen women were all professional models or actresses, who had been in the business for many years and said this was the biggest contract of their entire careers. On speaking to the American production team, I learnt that it was really the Rolls Royce (i.e. the best and the biggest) in terms of cosmetic advertising, working with the best in the industry:- from the renowned photographer/Director, Mr Albert Watson, (called the Steven Speilberg of advertising) to the best lighting, camera, technical and make-up teams. It was only then I realised what I'd really scooped, as I was also given one of the six primary spots (i.e. face close up).

When filming on the Monday, to my complete surprise, my scene was as a yoga instructor. The room was filled with frankincense smoke and my final close-up position was with my hands clasped in prayer. I always use frankincense smoke to bless my house. I was in awe, because these people knew nothing about me. Furthermore, they were so impressed with my features and advised that I should take up advertising modelling professionally. On my return, one of Britain's top model agencies signed me up immediately. I'm their first classical black model, thus heralding a new exciting additional career at 50.

The following month, I was honoured with the 'Windrush Award' (the first annual black millennium award) as the most pioneering black business in Britain.

Then I was asked to take part in the British Broadcasting Corporation (BBC) 'Millennium Oral History Project.' My experiences as a black/British business-woman, were recorded for a series of 26 national radio programmes called 'The Century Speaks,' which were transmitted from the 12th September to 26th December '99. The interviews were then deposited in the British Library National Sound Archive in London entitled, 'The Millennium Memory Bank' for posterity, to be used as a valuable resource and unique legacy for future generations. I'm included in two of the programmes 'House & Home and Money.' It can be accessed by making an appointment with the National Sound Archives Listening and Viewing Service, 96 Euston Road, London NW1 2DB (email: nsa-oral@bl.uk, quoting reference number C900/05151). On a more personal note, this in effect means that the next generation and beyond would be able to access the interview and listen to my voice, views, experiences and messages of the 20th Century.

"What a great privilege, honour and accolade,

to be able to leave something behind for the

Grandchildren of tomorrow."

In November 1999, I was also honoured with the 'Community Award' from the Voice newspaper, as the highest achieving black business. This was my 7th national award.

So out of the blue, after 7 years in the wilderness, I found myself once again propelled back into the media spotlight, confident and happier than I'd ever been in my entire life.

"At 51, I feel like a caterpillar who has been transformed into a beautiful butterfly. I'm now ready to spread my wings and fly high."

OIL of OLAY

IS STRETCHING HERSELF

2

- my roll as a yoga instructor in 'Oil of Olay' commercial '2000.

- the start of my modelling career and Specsavers 2001 catalogue.

3

50

'Ms May' Hea
calender 2001, high
the versatility
headwraps.

The Final Instruction.

Mission Greeting Card

'The Celebration of life.'

(establishing a universal day of love to unite, restore and heal the world for the 21st Century).

In September 2000, I was instructed to design a special 'keep-sake greeting card' to be attached to the 'mission badge.' The card describes the mission; how it came about; its purpose; God's messages and a special passage on 'Self Love' *(see pages 611 to 612)*, as a daily reminder of how to love ourselves and others .

It's an all purpose greeting card for any occasion... i.e. Birthdays, Anniversaries, Thanksgiving, Christmas, Easter, Mothers/Fathers Day, or just to say *"thank you."* So that anyone who wishes to help spread God's message can buy and send it to family and friends around the world. By doing this, it is hoped that one day 'love' will be restored and prevail universally.

In return, the funds raised will go towards supporting charities involved in the health and welfare of humans, animals and the environment. I am particularly interested in helping children's charities such as cancer care, HIV, aids, abuse, deformity, hospices; natural health-care for animals and rescue centres.

ON REFLECTION.

Once this final instruction was given, I reflected on God's message:-

"No one should be forced to believe. My children should be allowed to 'consciously choose' to follow ME. Anyone who chooses to do MY work, does so voluntarily by their own free-will."

Therefore, although this is my mission, HE has also made it a collective responsibility. Hence, anyone can independently decide if he/she wishes to be HIS disciple (messenger) by simply obeying HIS request.

SELF LOVE

Love yourself unconditionally

Love yourself first
Love yourself above all else
Acknowledge yourself
Honour yourself
Respect yourself
Appreciate yourself.

Trust yourself
Listen to yourself
Follow your own mind.

Believe and have faith in yourself.

Be true to yourself
Be happy with yourself
Be proud of yourself
Be patient with yourself
Be responsible for yourself
Be nice and kind to yourself
Be at peace with yourself
Be your own best friend
Be bold with yourself

Be the best you can be and make
the most of yourself

Be positive
Be passionate
Be assertive.

Praise yourself
Embrace yourself
Forgive yourself
Learn for yourself
Pay attention to yourself
Make your own decisions and choices
Empower yourself.

Challenge, inspire, motivate and encourage yourself.

Depend and rely on yourself
Discipline and control yourself
Please yourself
Treat and pamper yourself
Take the best care and look after yourself
Go all out for yourself
Help yourself
Exercise yourself (body, mind and spirit)

Live each day as if it were your last and live life to the fullest.
Make time, take time, find time and have time for yourself.

Try to understand yourself
Try to meet all your needs
Try to fulfil all your desires
Try to achieve all your dreams
Try to serve your purpose.

Do not lie to yourself
Do not give away or let others steal your power
Do not harm or attack yourself.

Release yourself from the burdens of fear, shame,
resentment, anger and guilt.

Accept that you are unique, beautiful, gifted,
valuable, worthy, important, blessed and Holy.

Bless, protect, relax and heal yourself
Radiate and let the light of your STAR shine bright
Be the MASTER of your own life and celebrate it.

This is not selfish love but 'SELF LOVE.' How can you expect to receive, give or share 'love' without knowing 'love' - for you are 'LOVE' in its entirety. By loving yourself, you'll be able to 'love' and take better care of others. By reflecting the mirror image of love, you will also receive the same degree of love in return. This is the pure joy and happiness of love.

So give to yourself wholeheartedly, whatever you wish to receive.

FOR YOU ARE 'DIVINE LOVE.'

Dounne Alexander (ORISHUA)   August 2000

Save a Life.

- **IN SUPPORT OF**

The African Caribbean Leukaemia Trust **(ACLT)**
and other charities.

SUPPORT A WORTHY CAUSE
and help SAVE a LIFE

'African Caribbean Leukaemia Trust - ACLT.'

Many bright 'Stars' are purposely sent to suffer for a cause in order to save the lives of others. **Daniel De-Gale** is such an Angel and when you look into his bright eyes, you'll see the special light which accompanies his sincere smile.

Daniel's painful story and the plight of his loving parents to save his life, touched me so deeply that I was moved to make a contribution to help them fulfil their mission. A few months before completing this book, I was inspired to link my work to help raise funds and to also 'spread the word' on a permanent basis.

Once a worthy cause gets off the ground, the most difficult task is to raise continuous awareness and the necessary money to keep it going. It's a never ending on-going process. Unfortunately, the general public often loose interest and although this is painfully disheartening, the mission must go on if precious lives are to be saved in the future. Many people only become seriously involved, when the disease personally hits them or a member of their family or close friend. Only then do they appreciate the shocking depth of despair and desperation. Terminal illness hits us when we least expect it. It can strike at any time, at any age or even if we appear perfectly healthy. Therefore, we must realise that we owe it to ourselves, to our families and future generations, to do something to help if the need arises or to improve our chances of survival, as well as to help those doing the work to make it all possible.

With this in mind, I've made a conscious decision to link a percentage of the profits on my unique headwraps to help raise additional funds for charities. *(See pages 627-629).*

THE AFRICAN CARIBBEAN LEUKAEMIA TRUST (ACLT)

Patron: The Duchess of York

The Duchess of York, Ian Wright MBE, John Fashanu and Colin Slamon.

Patrons of the African Caribbean Leukaemia Trust (ACLT).

The ACLT is a registered charity which was set up in 1996 by Beverley De-Gale and Orin Lewis, the parents of Daniel De-Gale. It all started 3 years after Daniel was diagnosed as suffering from Acute Lymphoblastic Leukaemia (ALL). Daniel had completed a 2 year course of chemotherapy treatment but sadly he suffered a relapse of the disease after being in remission for just 9 months. At this stage Daniel's consultants started looking at two possible options for treatment. The first was a bone marrow transplant, which meant that a match would have to be found. Daniel's 6 year old sister Dominique, was tested. She had a 1 in 4 chance of being a successful match. Unfortunately, it was not to be and so all members of the family and friends were tested. Still no luck. So a search would have to be done on potential donors from blacks and people of mixed parentage, on the worldwide registers. A match meaning someone with the same or almost identical bone marrow tissue type as Daniel's. The closer the match, the better his chances of survival.

The second option was a further 2 years of chemotherapy, a different timetable of drugs but with much more intensity. Because the first course of chemotherapy had not killed the disease, it was generally thought by all that a bone marrow transplant would ultimately be the best option. But the doctors felt confident that a second course of chemotherapy could still be successful and that on a long term basis it would be better for Daniel.

It was at this stage that Daniel's bone marrow consultant at London's Great Ormond Street Hospital, Dr.Paul Veys, said that there were only 550 African, African Caribbean and people of mixed parentage on the UK register, which had existed for nearly 24 years. This made Daniels' chances of finding a match within the UK at well over 1 in 120,000. Beverley immediately introduced herself to the Anthony Nolan Bone Marrow Trust and then tried to understand why the black numbers were so low. Beverley and Orin quickly came to the conclusion that within the black community, there was a total lack of awareness, combined with a fear of needles and myths about giving blood. These were three of the main reasons why black people had not come forward.

On 2nd June 1996, they set up the African Caribbean Leukaemia Trust to raise awareness in the black community... to support and assist black people and people of mixed parentage suffering with Leukaemia and any other blood related illness. Leukaemia affects both black and white people, which strikes at random and is not contagious or hereditary. But in the black community it is not thought of as a black illness in the same way as Sickle Cell Anaemia, High Blood Pressure or Lupus.

That was all they needed to know. They immediately made it their mission, to make our community sit up and listen to Daniel's plight. It was agreed that through continuous campaigning on Daniel's behalf, their chances of finding him a match would be considerably increased. That was the start of a very long journey, neither had any idea where it would take them but sheer desperation and determination drove them forward.

Daniel embarked on his second course of chemotherapy, while the campaigning began. Beverly and Orin started creating awareness about Daniel through all media sources (television, radio, national newspapers, Black Press, etc). Media interest was high with lots of appeals through local and national TV and Radio and soon a small group of family and friends got together with Beverley and Orin, to try and help change the status quo. Registration clinics were set up in the predominate black areas throughout the UK and the number of black people on the register started to grow. Daniel continued with his treatment and seemed to be coping with the cocktail of chemotherapy that was being pumped through his veins into his body. His vital organs were continuously monitored to make sure they were not being affected. He remained positive throughout this ordeal and kept up his schooling as much as was possible.

The media campaign was at such a high profile that family members of other sufferers started coming forward asking Beverley and Orin for help. It was explained to all sufferers and their families that the bone marrow tissue type details of each potential donor, are logged onto the Anthony Nolan Bone Marrow Trusts database and it is accessible by hospitals around the world looking for matches. This meant that their life saving work would potentially help all sufferers awaiting matches and not just the spearhead of the campaigning. This fact was made clear to all who joined and 99% of those that came forward, were more than happy to help save any life. In October 1996, the ACLT was awarded Charity registration status by the Charity Commission of England and Wales.

In January 1998, 2 years after Daniel had started his second course of chemotherapy, he successfully completed the course of treatment. Once again it was confirmed by his chemotherapy consultant that Daniel was in remission. He was now 11 years old and full of confidence. He had his S.A.T. exams in May of that year and gained excellent results. He was selected to attend the school of the family's choice to begin his secondary education. Life was definitely on the up. Beverley and Orin continued campaigning for other families and also continued looking for a match for Daniel, just in case. The African, African Caribbean and mixed parentage register, had now grown to approximately 3,500. There was still a lot of work to be done, since the goal for the Charity was to have a register of around 40,000. The ACLT still had a long way to go.

In September 1998, Daniel started secondary school and for him it was like starting a new life. With the exclusion of the head teachers, no one at the school realised who Daniel was or that he had suffered with Leukaemia. He settled in like a duck to water. Six weeks after the school term began Daniel told the family that he was on a short list to be the year 7 football team captain. He had to write a brief essay saying how he would captain the team. The next day, the family left home and went to their various places of work or education. Beverley received a devastating call from one of Daniel's home-care nurses. They called to say that a blood test that he'd had the day before, had shown some possible blast cells (Leukaemic cells) and that further tests would have to be carried out to confirm the worst possible news... that the dreaded Leukaemia had returned. Beverley was in complete shock and wondered... *'how could this be possibly happening again:-' ' how would she break this news to Daniel:' he had been so brave over the years, what more would he have to endure and what now did the future hold for him.*

Daniel came home from school that evening feeling very happy with himself, as he'd been made captain of the football team and was looking forward to the team's first match the following day. He was congratulated on his success and then disappeared to his bedroom to do his homework. Beverley and Orin had earlier sat and discussed how to break the terrible news. There was no easy way. The most important thing was that they would both be there and try and be as strong as possible for him. When he had completed his homework, he went downstairs to watch television. Beverley and Orin sat with him and started to break the horrible news. Daniel sat quietly and listened to what was unfolding. His response was swift. He cursed, cried and asked *"why me, why me."* Then he asked, *"will I be able to play my match tomorrow."* Beverley and Orin had already confirmed with the consultants that he would be able to get through the weekend without any treatment. He would have to return to Great Ormond Street on the Monday to confirm the worst and to then begin some treatment. Daniel captained his team the next day to a 6-2 victory.

The following Monday the hospital confirmed that once again Leukaemic cells were present in Daniel's blood stream. His consultants confirmed that Daniel's only chance of survival was a bone marrow transplant. His chance of survival without it was just 10%. If a match could be found, his chances increased drastically to about 60%. It was decided by all parties involved (including Daniel) that he would be put on a timetable of chemotherapy and other treatments. At the same time, Beverley and Orin would step up the campaign to hopefully find the elusive match. First, they would have to persuade Daniel to allow the campaigning on his behalf to begin again. He had been happy in his new life, where no one knew of his life threatening situation. He was convinced that his new friends would distance themselves if they found out the truth. Eventually, he conceded and agreed that his new friends would stick by him through thick and thin and that those that didn't, were not true friends. He also realised that without publicity, the chances of finding a match would dwindle drastically.

Daniel started a new regime of treatment and the ACLT went into overdrive. Publicity was at it's highest. The Duchess of York contacted Beverley at work one day and asked if she could be of assistance. Footballer, John Fashanu, visited Daniel at the hospital to offer his support, whilst the actor Colin Salmon also offered his full support after meeting Beverley and Orin at a fund-raising event. Ian Wright (football player), also offered his support after hearing and reading about Daniel via messages that were sent to him through his agents. These four individuals, eventually became the patrons of the ACLT. Their aim was to help increase awareness about Daniel and the charity. Registration clinics that were held from October 1998 onwards, bought a massive response from the black and mixed parentage community.

Everyone wanted to help this 11 year old boy, who had single handedly brought our community together with just one aim... to find a matching donor. Celebrities attended clinics, to help encourage possible donors to come forward and they were filmed giving their blood samples. Clinics were so successful that anything from 350-800 blood samples were being taken at any one clinic. Mothers and fathers even brought their small children to be tested. Unfortunately, this could not be done despite the pleading of the kids. The age range for unrelated donors is 18-45 years. However, siblings and family members of a sufferer can be of any age. There was a real 'feel good factor' at the clinics, with everyone sharing a common goal. People attended the clinics from all over the country. Beverley and Orin felt so proud of our community. It proved that when it really mattered, we could come together and make a difference. The campaigning stretched as far as the Caribbean and the USA. The Duchess of York took Daniel's story over the Atlantic and news items and documentaries highlighted Daniel's plight. Magazine articles about Daniel and the ACLT were also published on the East coast of America.

The BBC programme 'Black Britain' that had originally highlighted Daniel's story, was also screened in the Caribbean. Meanwhile, throughout all of this Daniel gave interviews for television, radio, magazines etc. and continued his treatment. By March 1999, the register had grown to approximately. 12,000. Unfortunately, due to the ACLT's rapid success it was becoming logistically impossible for the Anthony Nolan Trust to process enough blood samples within the UK. Therefore, the ACLT ended up having to send thousands of samples to be tested in the USA, at a cost of $45.00 or £28.00 per sample. This caused a substantial financial headache, with costs amounting to £100,000. Therefore, the quicker the register was rising, the greater probability of finding a matching donor but in turn also esculated the financial crisis. Beverley and Orin had to face another major decision. Unless they could quickly raise funds, the registration clinics would have to cease, which would seriously reduce Daniel's chances of finding a match. They decided to continue the registration clinics but also undertook a massive fund-raising campaign to try and raise the necessary funds. Meanwhile, Daniel was back in remission and the consultants endeavoured to keep him on a maintenance form of chemotherapy treatment, until a match was found. It was vital at this stage that he remained in remission until a donor was found and a transplant could take place. The massive fund-raising campaign was successful. Generous donations poured in from all over the UK and the ACLT was able to pay off the U.S. blood testing bill by August 1999.

In April 1999, Beverley was at home with Daniel and a call came through from the bone marrow specialist, Dr Paul Veys at Great Ormond Street Hospital. Her heart missed a beat when she realised it was him. In a few short seconds, many many thoughts passed through her mind. They'd had many meetings at the hospital about the searches that were going on around the world on Daniel's behalf. He had also appeared on television and radio broadcasting appeals on Daniel's behalf. He had attended press conferences to highlight his needs in his capacity as Daniel's doctor but he had never called the family home. Why was he now ringing and not his secretary?

It all became crystal clear very soon.

A matching donor had been found, *"yes."* Further tests (blood samples) had already been carried out and it was looking very good. *"How good a match was it I hear you ask? Well if you had to mark it out of 10 it would be a 9. The one marker that did not match in the past, would have caused problems but technology had moved so far forward, this was no longer a problem."* In fact, it was an excellent match. The bone marrow specialist was so pleased that he had to ring and tell the family himself.

Beverley was in a state of disbelief and asked many questions, *"is this person aware that they are a match?"* *"Are they willing to come forward?"* *"Have they just joined the register?"* *"When will it go ahead?"* with many, many Thanks. The answer to all her questions was *"yes."* The transplant would be scheduled for May - June. When she put down the phone, the realisation hit her with a thud. Daniel was standing in front of her, asking what had happened. Beverley and Orin had always been honest with him and completely up front.

It was only fair that at this stage of development it should remain that way. Daniel's response to the news was not surprisingly very laid back. He had been told at earlier appointments that when a match was found he would have to have more chemotherapy, also radiotherapy which he'd never had before; with at least 8 weeks in complete isolation and a total of about 3 months in hospital. Followed by a very long recovery period. He was also painfully aware that the bone marrow transplant was the last resort. So his response was not surprising. After many discussions with Beverley, Orin and his sister Dominique, tossing over the pro's and con's of it all, Daniel accepted that this would be the long term answer. He once again focused his mind on a positive conclusion.

After further discussions with the Anthony Nolan Bone Marrow Trust, who had painstakingly been searching all of the registers around the world on Daniel's behalf since early 1996 and with no luck, it had transpired that this unknown individual had just recently come forward as a potential donor.

The news of the hopeful match was kept under wraps and only a few people were told. In the meantime, the recruitment clinics and fundrasing campaign continued, whilst Daniel was being prepared for the transplant. On the 3rd June Daniel and Beverley were admitted into Great Ormond Street Hospital, Robin Ward to begin the long process. He had 5 days (twice a day) of total body radiotherapy. His bone marrow was completely wiped out, gone for good. It was at this stage that he and Beverley went into complete isolation. His blood cell counts dropped to zero. On the 16th June, the unknown donor's bone marrow arrived and it was given to Daniel intravenously at 6:50pm. A transfusion bag no bigger than a carton of 288ml of RIBENA, that was it. This is what they had prayed for, this was going to give Daniel his life back. It's incredible but true. The event was filmed by Orin and passed on to Carlton Television programme, 'London Tonight.' It was shown the next day, for all the viewers to see how simple it really was. That night, a feeling of immense relief saturated them all and Beverley and Daniel both slept well.

Orin went home and started the task of letting everyone know that Daniel finally got what he so deserved. The response from those that were called was overwhelming, including screams of joy, tears and laughter. The next day, it was announced on the television programmes GMTV, London and Today and on Choice FM Radio that the miracle had happened. Daniel and Beverley woke up at 6:00am to watch the news as it was announced. He was in very high spirits. The response was immense and not just from the black community. Letters started pouring into the ward, it was quite amazing.

In the weeks that followed, Daniel had very low periods, as the side-effects from all the treatments he'd had to endure over the weeks, started to take their toll. The doctors monitored his blood results everyday, to see when the donated bone marrow would start to produce white blood cells. It took about 15 days. This for Daniel was the most difficult time throughout the 6 years of treatment. He was very sore from mouth, throat and stomach ulcers. He could not swallow anything, he had no appetite and so the nurses fed a tube into his nose that travelled down into his stomach. He was fed this way until he regained his appetite.

On the 30th July (Dominque's birthday) and much sooner than anticipated, Daniel was released from hospital. He returned home with much medication and with a long recovery period ahead of him.

Daniel returned to school in December 1999 in a blaze of publicity. He is now stopped continuously in the streets and asked how he is doing. He has just celebrated his first anniversary and his blood results continue to look good. Daniel was the first black person in the UK to receive a bone marrow transplant from an unrelated donor. Because of this fact, many, many sufferers and their families are now coming forward because at last they see a light at the end of a very long dark tunnel. The work of the charity has continued and the numbers continue to increase.

On the 2nd June 2000, a double celebration Dinner and Dance was held in London, highlighting the anniversary of Daniel's transplant and the 4th year of the ACLT. The event was a sell out. People came to celebrate the achievements of the Charity and to meet the young man that brought a community together. Daniel made a speech which was applauded throughout and received a standing ovation.

Daniel does not grasp the effect he has had on the community because let's remember, he is still only 13 years old. He may have gone through a lot for his short years but he is still only a boy. Albeit a very courageous, awe inspiring, positive thinking young man, who will go a long way in whatever he chooses to do in his life.

The family always felt that there had to be a method to the madness and at long last **a negative situation has brought about a positive solution.**

The aims of the ACLT have not changed over the last 4 years. A figure of between 30,000 to 40,000 black people on the UK register is still our priority. Hopefully, with more consistent funding in the near future, we'd like to spread our awareness campaign around the world because there are many more Daniels to be saved.

● Daniel with father
(Orin), mother
(Beverley) and
sister (Dominique).

● patron;-
Ian Wright, MBE.

● Daniel and Mum (Beverley)

Daniel does not grasp the effect he has had on the community because let's remember, he is still only 13 years old. He may have gone through a lot for his short years but he is still only a boy. Albeit a very courageous, awe inspiring, positive thinking young man, who will go a long way in whatever he chooses to do in his life.

Headwraps.

- **IN SUPPORT OF**

The African Caribbean Leukaemia Trust and other charities.

Unique African Headwraps:

(Made from the finest quality cotton voile in 12 lively colours, specially printed/hand dyed in the Caribbean: exclusively available from Gramma's Int.).

This is my own private clothing collection with contrasting headwraps, which I love because they make me feel like a Queen (regal, elegant, sophisticated, beautiful and feminine).

627.

When wearing my wraps, people compliment and also ask where can they purchase them. Even more pleasing is that people from every nationality, gender and age, simply love the attractive colours and styles. Hence the word 'love' was the deciding catalyst to include the headwraps as part of my fund-raising and awareness package.

Headwrapping is an ancient African art which has lasted centuries and is unlikely to ever go out of fashion. It has a unique history which is passionately described in Dee McCalla's book 'Wrappers Delight,' providing you with step by step instructions and illustrations on many authentic styles (see details on the mail-order form). They are the perfect alternative when your hair needs a rest from chemical treatments, on bad hair/lazy days or for cancer sufferers who have lost hair due to chemotherapy. Like me, it will make you feel like a queen and well dressed for any occasion. The special voile material is soft and light allowing your head to breathe and stay cool even in hot weather. Extremely versatile and can also be used as scarves, shawls, sarongs, wall decorations or furniture throws.

Together with the mission greeting card, these headwraps will form the initial 'life saving chain' to support the African Caribbean Leukaemia Trust and other children's charities on a permanent basis.

I sincerely hope that you will join us - so together we can **make A DIFFERENCE** and save many lives.

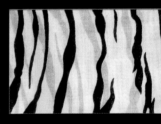

629.

The BUSINESS

that makes a

DIFFERENCE

BOOK THREE.

CHAPTER VI.

Gramma's.

Following on from Chapter II, the business story continues on the products given to me by God and my Spirit-Guides.

The early days back in 1986 were full of excitement and great expectations. Adopting my Grandmothers personality of warmth, love, caring and sharing, was how I planned to develop my relationship with customers. However, although I viewed the business on a commercial basis, I also wanted it to be ethical but in my search for organic ingredients, I was astonished that these were in scarce supply and or extremely expensive. Therefore having limited choice, I bought what was available and continued searching for the best quality. This meant literally scouring the entire country as advice was virtually non-existent. Eventually, I was able to source ingredients which were grown either organically, wild crafted or conventional and blended these to make my Grandmother's special Herbal Pepper Sauces. By this time, both my Grandmother and other Spirit-Guides were very active in my life. They told me that they were going to improve the recipe by including specific 'healing herbs' and went on to say:-

"This new recipe is nothing new, it has been in existence centuries ago but through the ages its been adulterated to become the watered-down, acidic commercial version of what is presently called Pepper Sauce. What we are giving you is the original ancient Hot Herbal Pepper Sauces which was used not only to flavour food but also to maintain health and balance the body. It is unique because it's been long forgotten and worlds apart from any other. People have lost the knowledge of the true value of food in their lives, so we are going to start with the most essential and powerful one... 'the Hot Pepper' and re-educate them. It used to be called 'The Fire God of the Herbal Kingdom,' because of its intense heat and mighty power. The hotness is directly related to the sun, the greatest power on earth and your direct energy-source.

It originated from South America and the Caribbean. Peppers grown in these tropical countries have a much greater heat intensity and richness, due to the absorption of the sun's baking hot energies. This intensity, power and great heat was believed to be associated with God, love and healing. God in HIS great wisdom, had provided mankind and the animals with all the natural healing herbs and foods to keep them in the best of health.

The association is simple:-

God is LOVE

Love is WARMTH

Burning DESIRE

Burning PASSION
or

'The Power of LOVE'

In other words, 'love' denotes something hot and exciting. Hence, the old name for hot peppers as 'the Fire God'... burning out disease and poisons and restoring perfect health. But it must not be abused; taken in moderation 'a little at a time, regularly,' is extremely beneficial and is also the old traditional way the original 'herbal pepper sauces' were used... similar to homeopathy.

HEALING simply means the application of
HEAT to STIMULATE

With all of man's great knowledge and modern scientific advancement, they ignore this simple fact:-

FOOD has its own LIFE FORCE

*(essential Fuel & Energy) which is your **LIFE SOURCE**."*

"Now consider the following words:-

FUEL:	provides the Driving Force and
ENERGY:	provides the Heat & Stimulation or

THE HEALING FORCE

- **ENERGY:** gives Heat & Stimulation
- **THE SUN:** gives Heat & Stimulation *(ENERGY)*
- **EXERCISE:** gives Heat & Stimulation *(ENERGY)*
- **MASSAGE:** gives Heat & Stimulation *(ENERGY)*
- **SPIRITUAL HEALING:**
  uses bodily Heat & Faith to Stimulate Healing *(ENERGY)*
- **HOT PEPPERS & OTHER HOT HERBS:**
  (Garlic, Ginger, Cloves):- give Heat & Stimulation *(ENERGY)*.

Therefore, 'Heat & Stimulation' creates the energy in which to heal.
Hence, **FOOD is used to FEED & HEAL,**

'The key to the success of medicine is also in its ability to STIMULATE.'

This HEAT, STIMULATION and ENERGY goes further. If you want to heal your body and especially for the young and old. Build a dry sand pit in your garden, in a spot where the mid-day sun will shine and penetrate its heat directly on it.

After the sun has heated it and moved away, run or walk up and down barefoot in the hot pit for as long as you wish. The 'hot sand' will massage the entire soles of your feet and the 'Sun's heat' will also penetrate into your body to help it heal itself. Alternatively, do the same on a hot sandy beach. Your modern day Reflexology techniques are based on these same ancient principles. Now go and spread the word on:

THE SIMPLE LAWS OF LIFE & NATURE THROUGH GOD."

THE LOGO

My Guides gave specific instructions for the Gramma's logo and its meaning.

- The GRAMMA'S Logo must be a **CIRCLE**... representing 'the Circle-of-Life'

- An inner **Pyramid triangle**... representing 'The Holy Trinity'

- Centred with a **'G'** in the middle...meaning 'Centred-in-God'

This logo must be used on all your products.

The diagram above shows the full meaning of the logo.

MOTTOS

They also gave various mottos to use in my education information and promotional literature:-

1.   *"Once in a decade, comes something unique, to change attitudes and make the nations reconsider their lifestyles."*

2.   *"The Simple Laws-of-Life & Nature through God."*

3.   *"The Food of The Future:"*

   "Let thy Food be thy Medicine and thy Medicine be thy Food." (Hippocrates; one of the ancient Fathers of Medicine).

4.   *"FOOD is for Eating; Enjoyment and LIFE."*

5.   ***"GRAMMA'S vision:*** *is to return 'real foods' onto the table, wrapped in ancient herbal tradition; creating an eating revolution and natural balance."*

6.   *"A One Woman Mission:"*

   The one-woman Work-Force, Life & Spiritual Power-Source behind Gramma's. Her mission is something of a burning one; to spice up their daily diet and make a significant contribution to the nation's health."

7.   *"When quality, health and flavour matters, cook with GRAMMA'S."*

8.   ***"GRAMMA'S is:*** *suitable for everyone - vegetarian, vegans, meat eaters, the health conscious, weight watchers, children, those allergic to yeast, gluten, nuts and starch or with special dietary requirements such as low salt, low fat, low sugar*

(diabetes and hypertension) and also for animals."

9. ***"GRAMMA'S contains:*** *NO added chemicals, artificial or synthetic additives, colourings, flavourings, preservatives, animal or dairy ingredients, starches, gluten, yeast, black or white peppercorns, mustard, thickener, monosodium glutamate, fillers, anti-caking agents or nuts."*

10. *"Cooking for Good Health - Naturally."*

11. *"The Healing Cuisine."*

12. ***"GRAMMA'S operates:*** *along spiritual, ethical, educational and commercial principles and is also based on the ancient philosophy that 'Natural foods are meant to feed & heal.' These products are truly unique, used both for cooking and as a preventative to improve and maintain good health."*

13. *"The Business that makes a DIFFERENCE."*

● **Healing Prayers.**

I also pray for healing before making my products.

- **Educational Information.**

They then armed me with the educational information I would need, not only to re-educate but to also have as evidence, if challenged by those in Authority. I was instructed to prepare this information leaflet.

- **MEDICINAL EVIDENCE ON HOT-PEPPERS**.

Throughout the ages **HOT-PEPPERS** were relied on for their curative, preservative and culinary properties. Ancient Herbalists and Modern Doctors (European and American) have found them a successful remedy in assisting the recovery of almost every human ailment.

Examples are:

internal inflammation, fevers, colds, congestion, chills (ague), coughs, sore throat, quinsy, diphtheria, bad breath, breathing difficulties (e.g. bronchitis, asthma and emphysema) sinus, lungs, liver, kidneys, spleen and pancreas, dyspepsia (indigestion), expels wind and poisons, gripe, cramp, loss of appetite, fermentation, haemorrhage from mucous membranes (bleeding stools and piles) fatigue, constipation, headache, nausea, palpitation, spasms, delirium, nervousness, mental stress, shock, debility (feebleness and weakness), impotency, skin, eczema, sciatica, rheumatism, arthritis, gum infections, gout, sobering, gonorrhea, diet, hypothermia, prevents blood clotting (protection against heart-attacks and thrombosis).

It is said that HOT PEPPER equalises the blood circulation, strengthens and tones the heart, stomach and the whole system, plus it purifies the blood and also helps the system to throw off poisons, disease and waste by flushing out, cleansing, then re-establishing equilibrium (balance).

It is said to be one of the world's most wonderful and powerful healing herb. The more pungent (hot) it is, the greater healing power it possesses. It has the most powerful heat intensity and retains it for the longest period. It is antiseptic, anti-inflammatory, good for the respiration, wakes up the entire system, heightens awareness, revives the taste-buds and aids digestion when taken with meals. Furthermore, it is said to be especially good for our lungs and heart. Anyone suffering with Heart or Pulmonary problems like Emphysema, Bronchitis or Asthma, should eat a hot spicy meal at least once a day and others at least 3 times a week. It also temporarily increases the body's metabolic rate, which helps to burn up calories faster, therefore assist dieting or weight control.

- **Nutritional Evidence.**

Is an excellent source of many essential nutrients, richer in vitamins C and A than any other usually recommended (twice that of any citrus fruit), it also contains capsaicin, vitamins E and B complex, P (citrin), potassium, mineral water, calcium, phosphorous, iron, niacin, carbohydrate, protein, magnesium and ascorbic acid and is low in calories.

Hot pepper adds extra spark in your life by replacing essential, vital BODY HEAT, ENERGY and NOURISHMENT. It should become part of your regular daily health care.

"A little a day keeps the doctor away."

This was the first detailed literature on the values of hot peppers. These were distributed to everyone I came across, even doctors were calling for copies and privately circulated them to other doctors. It initiated my health re-education and awareness campaign. The word started to spread in Britain and across the world, which finally led me to Dr. Irwin Ziment; an eminent British Medical Professor and head of the UCLA School of Medicine in America. He was the first doctor who openly advocated the use of the hot peppers as **a medicine and as an essential food;** the first to boldly put his belief and medical knowledge on paper and gave permission to use them to back up my claims; and the first to vindicate all my claims. He went so far as to introduce me to an American Author who was writing a factual book on the Hot Pepper (AMAL NAJ), where I proudly occupy two pages in the title 'Peppers.'

By January 1987, GRAMMA'S was officially launched and the rest as they say, is history

Dr Ziments letter -

'ERSITY OF CALIFORNIA, LOS ANGELES		UCLA

Y   DAVIS   IRVINE   LOS ANGELES   RIVERSIDE   SAN DIEGO   SAN FRANCISCO   SANTA BARBARA   SANTA CRUZ

1ENT OF MEDICINE

SCHOOL OF MEDICINE
SAN FERNANDO VALLEY PROGRAM
LAC - OLIVE VIEW MEDICAL CENTER
14445 OLIVE VIEW DRIVE
SYLMAR, CALIFORNIA 91342-1495

May 24   1989

Dear Ms. Moore:

As promised, I am enclosing some of my writings on pungent spices. You will see that I consider pepper to be one of many expectorant drugs that may have a variety of mechanisms of action. Thus, pepper is chemically related to guaifenesin which is a popular expectorant medication. Much of my contributed work on pepper has been removed from context, and it is not generally reported that I consider pepper to be <u>one of many drugs</u> that have a mucus-loosening effect.

I trust you will find the material useful to you in your effort to get the public and the medical profession to understand the value of pungent spices in our diets.

Yours sincerely,

Irwin Ziment, M.D.
Professor and Chief
Department of Medicine
Olive View Medical Center
UCLA School of Medicine

IZ:sm

Throughout the years, my products superior quality and unique packaging, was always noticed and highly praised. So much so, that when I first approached the supermarkets, they stated that the quality was 'too high' and 'too concentrated' and should be adulterated. I refused but they still took them. From the outset, I knew that I was producing Spiritual foods meant for healing, therefore, I couldn't mess about with them; they had to remain natural, pure concentrates. I also felt that I couldn't tell anyone, except for my daughters and parents, that my recipes were coming from 'the Spirit world' through spiritual guidance because I feared that people would turn against or call me a crank. In a way I'm glad that I did not because almost immediately after, I started to receive testimonies from customers, stating how much they loved them and of the benefits they were obtaining; many ending their letters with words like; *"God bless you, keep up the good work, I'm praying for you,"* and hundreds of *"thanks."* Although, I gave several hints in many press-releases, I didn't come out until my direct encounter with God in 1996, when I was instructed to reveal all!

As my Guides later explained;-

"God never works in secret and when the time is right, HE makes it all known, so that those who were 'blind' (i.e. failed to see) are made to SEE."

Their teachings and careful guidance really inflamed my emotions, stirring up every bit of passion within me. I was transformed from a quiet, shy, frightened woman, into a courageous, confident chatterbox. Then sent on a blazing trail, to set the United Kingdom on fire; peppered with stories to ignite their interest and excite their taste-buds. All of a sudden, I was being called to lecture to hundreds of people around the country on various topics which always ended on 'the healing benefits of natural foods, my Grandmother and my Herbal Pepper Sauces.' All along, I didn't realise that it was a 'spiritual set-up,' I just thought that my Guides were helping me to establish my career, so that I could make a better life for myself and family.

However, it's still remains one of my dearest dreams for the British Government to supply pensioners with a jar of the Mild or Hot Pepper Sauce as part of their 'Winter Warming Campaign and Christmas bonus,' as it would provide protection against hypothermia, colds, poor circulation, congestion, etc.and save a great deal of unnecessary suffering. If by now they still refuse to see both the health and job creation benefits, then I suppose some people will always remain blind to the truth!

Gramma's

"Once in a decade comes something unique,
to change attitudes and make the nations
reconsider their lifestyles."

The Food of the Future.

Gramma's.

• PRODUCT INFORMATION.

When Quality, Health & Flavour Matters

Cook with

GRAMMA'S™

MY FIRST PRODUCT

Gramma's Concentrated Herbal Pepper Sauces

It took three months to obtain all the medicinal herbs my Guides requested. So it was back to the kitchen, where they gave careful instructions on how to ***prepare, cook*** and ***use*** them. Instead of my Grandmother's (one) extremely hot recipe, they changed it into four strengths, (MILD, HOT, EXTRA HOT and SUPER-HOT), specifically catering for everyone's taste. Therefore, if a person (like a baby) is not used to 'hot food' or does not like hot peppers, they would use the Mild or Hot strengths but the Extra-Hot or Super-Hot are for those who love extremely hot food. Each was highly concentrated and very powerful.

When I finally perfected all four sauces and sampled them, they had a definitely superior taste, quality and flavour to my grandmother's and were the best. This was how GRAMMA'S Concentrated Herbal Pepper Sauces were re-created. The following pages detail the customer leaflet, on 'how to use' and recipes.

GRAMMA'S CONCENTRATED HERBAL PEPPER SAUCES

Mild, Hot, Extra-Hot and Super-Hot Pepper Sauces

I n g r e d i e n t s

Scotch Bonnet or Habanero peppers, Cider Vinegar, Onions, Garlic, Ginger, Celery, Golden Seal, Ginseng, St. John's Wort, Cassia, Cloves, Nutmeg, Basil, Bay Leaves, Dill, Marjoram, Mint, Oregano, Parsley, Sage, Thyme, Rosemary, Coriander, Cumin, Fennel, Fenugreek, Cinnamon, Turmeric, Sunflower Oil, Unrefined Molasses Cane Sugar and Sea Salt.

Gramma's Concentrated Herbal Pepper Sauces come from a secret ancient Caribbean herbal recipe, which was eaten by everyone as a daily relish or seasoning or made into a soothing hot toddy drink. It was used as an essential part of everyday health-care.

It's a highly concentrated blend of the finest, fresh Caribbean hot peppers, (Scotch Bonnet or Habanaro), limited cider vinegar, (plus for the first time ever) includes a concentration of over 25 medicinal herbs and spices (above), sunflower oil, unrefined molasses cane sugar and sea salt. These are carefully blended in the old fashioned way, requiring hours of slow cooking and continuous stirring to preserve the essential properties, as well as, to develop its naturally rich, thick, concentrated consistency, which is achieved by gradual evaporation. It's unique concentrated fragrance and zest, adds superb flavour to all foods without being overpowering but makes the meal tastier and much more enjoyable.

Ingredients: Hot peppers, Over 20 herbs & spices, Cider vinegar, Sunflower oil, Raw cane sugar, Sea salt

NO CHEMICAL OR ARTIFICIAL ADDITIVES COLOURINGS FLAVOURINGS OR PRESERVATIVES

Concentrated
PEPPER SAUCE

Gramma's

G

Gramma's
P.O.Box 218,
London,
E6 4BG.

EXTRA HOT

It's amazingly easy to use. No special cooking instructions needed, just add GRAMMA'S to your normal everyday cooking and cook as usual.

How to use

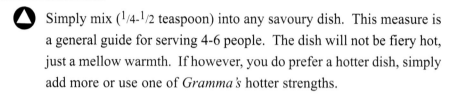

Simply mix (^{1}/4-^{1}/2 teaspoon) into any savoury dish. This measure is a general guide for serving 4-6 people. The dish will not be fiery hot, just a mellow warmth. If however, you do prefer a hotter dish, simply add more or use one of *Gramma's* hotter strengths.

- For those who really love their food extremely hot, add some to the side of your plate and use it as a dip whilst you eat -

the choice is yours!

- *Gramma's* comes in four concentrated strengths: Mild, Hot, Extra-Hot and Super-Hot; catering for everyone's hotness taste.

- The quantity of oil, sugar and salt used in manufacture is so small that it would not affect anyone's diet.

- It has a naturally extensive shelf life and never been known to deteriorate. *Keeps well in excess of 5 years.*

Recipe Suggestions

Add *Gramma's* either **before, during or after** cooking, mixing in thoroughly.

- Mix ^{1}/4-^{1}/2 tbsp *Gramma's* into marinades, seasonings, sauces or stocks for, casseroles, hot pots, gravy, soup, pies, roasts, stir-fry, poaching, savoury rice, barbecues etc - cook as usual.

- When following recipes in cookery books, where it states 'add pepper to taste' - try using ^{1}/4-^{1}/2 teaspoon of *Gramma's* instead.

- Spread a little *Gramma's* on sandwiches, hot dogs, pizzas or burgers.

- Mix a little into salad dressings, dips, canapes, hors d'oeuvers or fillings.

- When eating, if too hot, drink pure fruit juice to quench the heat.

- Make *Gramma's* an essential ingredient in all your daily cooking and snacks.

GRAMMA'S SUPREME SPICY GARLIC BUTTER

250g (¹/₂lb) tub of butter/ margarine,

1-tbsp of Gramma's Pepper Sauce,

6-8 large fresh garlic cloves (pureed or finely grated).

Mix together thoroughly and return to the fridge. Ready for everyday use in sandwiches, on toast or for garlic bread, cooked or stuffed vegetables, pasta, baked or mashed potatoes, eggs, rice, fish, roast and sea foods.

VARIATIONS:❧

Mix in 1 tablespoon of fresh herbs (finely chopped coriander, parsley, chives, basil, dill). Just try coating your turkey, chicken, fish or roast potatoes with this scrumptious garlic butter, sprinkle a little salt, wrap in foil, then bake or roast.

GRAMMA'S CARIBBEAN HOT TODDY

$^1/_2$ pint (300ml) boiling water

$^1/_2$ level tbsp of Gramma's (Mild or Hot) Pepper Sauce,

1 fluid oz fresh lemon juice
(or 1 large lemon),

4-6 level dessert-spoons of honey (or to taste),
1-2 tablespoons Caribbean Rum, Brandy or Whisky *(optional)*.

Mix thoroughly, cover and leave to stand for 5 minutes, strain and drink 'HOT' (in the winter) or 'COLD' (in the summer). For young children reduce the lemon and pepper sauce by half and omit the alcohol. This is also a refreshing replacement for tea or coffee.

VARIATION ❀

Add 3 tablespoon (NEAT) of 'Zara's Herbal Tea' and 'Willow Tea.'

MY SECOND PRODUCT

Gramma's Concentrated Herbal Seasonings

In 1992, my Guides instructed me to produce another new product **GRAMMA'S Concentrated Herbal Seasonings** in four flavours (Original, Hot & Spicy, Curry and Creole). They realised that in order to reduce the consumption of artificial ingredients, people would have to take control from within their own homes and this meant returning to home cooking. They also recognised that retraining was essential, because most had become too dependant on pre-cooked meals, fast and processed foods. Lack of parental or school training, had also made many lazy and complacent. Therefore, to rebuild people's confidence, home cooking had to be made easy, fun and enjoyable. Furthermore, the majority of the ready-made seasonings, sauces and marinades available in stores, consist of a few cheap herbs, packed with larger volumes of artificial flavour enhancers, preservatives, salt, sugar, fat, starches, anti-caking agents, monosodium glutamate and other cheap fillers (like rusk).

So, the Guides instructed me to prepare the finest blend of pure concentrated digestible herbs and spices; containing all the seasonings needed to prepare perfect meals, along with these healthy cooking tips;-

    (a). To achieve real **health,** fullest **flavour** and **enjoyment** from your food; remember to always use the best quality and freshest raw ingredients available (preferably organic).

(b). Cook food in its own natural juices, only adding a little water, if and when necessary. If thickeners are needed, use arrowroot, corn starch or seaweed.

(c). If you like adding oil to your cooking, use good quality vegetable or nut oils, such as Extra Virgin Olive Oil, Canola Oil, Sunflower Oil, etc. Avoid or reduce animal fats.

(d). Hot herbs (garlic, ginger and a little hot pepper) are essential for stimulation, respiration, digestion and circulation but also include other sweet herbs (like coriander, basil, thyme, parsley, etc).

(e). Avoid salt or keep it to the absolute minimum. The special blend of 'Gramma's Herbal Seasonings' helps to reduce salt considerably.

(f). Eat slowly; chew thoroughly for good digestion, absorption, elimination and to aid weight control.

(g). **Economy:**

It is wise to cook large meals and freeze in one or two meal-size portions because it not only saves you time (especially working mothers), but also money. Money-wise, it is more cost effective in terms of the food ingredients and energy burnt (i.e. electricity, gas and physical). Therefore, it also impacts on the environment in saving energy. So, it is wise to invest in a couple of large good quality 'stainless steel pots' in sizes 5 litres (9 pints) and 10 litres (17 pints) or even larger.

(h). **Health-wise:**

Avoid using '*aluminum pots,*' as it reacts with natural acids in food (e.g. tomatoes, vinegar, lemon etc) and gives off a poison, which goes into the food and would damage your health. Stainless steel is the safest and lasts a lifetime.

These new seasonings were then bottled into beautiful 'keep-sake' glass jars, with refill sachets.

To repeat an old phrase *"The proof of the pudding is in the eating."* I gave the first sample to my mother for testing. Mum was a brilliant cook; very traditional and would rarely use anything else, other than her own home grown fresh herbs. To my delight, she kept asking for more. She tried them on everything and the results were superb but more importantly, she praised how quick, easy and labour saving they were. Of course, I was also testing them on Marsha, Dee and friends. Both Marsha and Dee being vegetarians (i.e. eat no form of meat) were overjoyed, because they could now prepare and cook even tastier vegan/vegetarian dishes. For years, I'd tried to get them interested in cooking but my methods learnt from my Mum; although delicious, they found the preparation too long and boring. Now they were more keen and much more interested in food; its nutritional contents and keep a watchful eye on health and environmental issues. Hence, they've become more conscious.

In 1996, one of my young nieces (Lisa Goder) started using the seasonings in her school cookery lessons. The pupils would prepare and cook the same dish and at the end of each lesson, they'd conduct a sample tasting. Each time, they commented that Lisa's dish tasted better and on asking what she was using to give hers this special flavour; she produced her jar of 'Gramma's' and from then on shared it with all her friends.

The following pages detail the 'customer leaflet' on 'how to use' and also recipes.

•THE COMPLETE ALL PURPOSE SEASONINGS.

◆ **NO** Salt

◆ **NO** Sugar

◆ **NO** Oil

◆ **NO** Starch

◆**NO** Yeast

◆ **NO** Gluten

◆ **NO** Nuts

◆ **NO** Mustard

◆ **NO** Monosodium
Glutamate.

◆ **NO** Thickener.

◆ **NO** anti-caking agents

◆ **NO** animal or Diary
ingredients.

◆ **No**thing artificial added.

Suitable for everyone

- Vegans

- Vegetarians

- Kosher *(parve)*

- Meat Eaters

- Weight-Watchers

- Children

- Health Conscious
&
- Animals too!

20 Servings per jar

All the seasonings you'll ever need in one jar. Over 26 pure herbs & spices
CONCENTRATED and uniquely blended to make cooking easier, tastier,
healthier, convenient, versatile & economical.

GRAMMA'S CONCENTRATED HERBAL SEASONINGS

Original, Hot & Spicy, Curry,

and

Creole Seasonings

I n g r e d i e n t s

Dehydrated; Onions, Garlic, Ginger, Cayenne, Turmeric, Celery, Coriander leaves (Cilantro), Marjoram, Oregano, Parsley, Sage, Basil, Mint, Thyme, Bay Leaf, Rosemary, Dill, Cloves, Fennel, Coriander seed, Fenugreek, Cinnamon, Cassia, Nutmeg, Cumin, Orange Peel and Lemon Peel, (also Tarragon, Lime & Curry leaves, Shaddon Beni, Cardamon, Star Anise, Lemon grass).

Improve your cooking skills and create tantalising meals from around the world, using these complete all purpose seasonings. Mix up delicious marinades, seasonings, sauces or pastes, perfect for everyday and special occasion cooking. It's versatility is limitless, no need to add fats or oils and with 20 servings per jar, means **'real value for money.'**

Gramma's is the healthy alternative to spicy foods, in four delicious flavours ; the Original is more 'Herby' than spicy, making it really mellow, whilst the Hot & Spicy, Curry and Creole are for those with slightly warmer appetites. Each range possesses the naturally rich, thick aroma and unique flavour distinctive to Gramma's.

NB:- Only use DRY SPOONS and KEEP PROPERLY SEALED to lock in the flavour. Because we don't use any anti-caking agents, the natural oils may cause the product to become lumpy. This does not affect its quality, simply break up the lumps and use as directed.

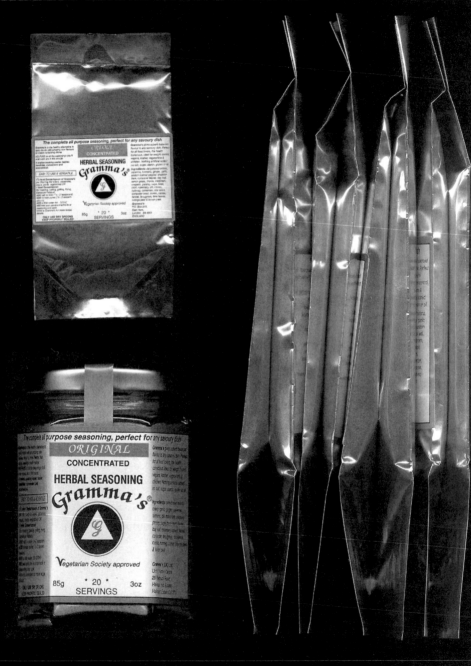

(Oriiginal, Hot & Spicy, Creole, Curry).

HOW TO USE

GRAMMA'S HERBAL SEASONINGS.

1. Seasoning Preparation

1½ level dessertspoon, of any Gramma's Herbal Seasoning - per 2lbs (1kg) of meat or soya/vegetables for stews, casseroles, braising, soups, pastas etc.

ADD Water - 200ml (7fl.oz)

ADD Tomato Puree, 1 - 2 dessertspoons

ADD Salt to taste, 1 - 2 teaspoons

ADD Gramma's Pepper Sauce, ½ - 1 teaspoons

Mix ingredients well to use as a _seasoning_ and cook as follows:-

Pour the above 'seasoning mixture' into a cooking pot, bring to the boil, reduce the heat, cover with lid and simmer for 5 minutes. Add the meat, vegetables or pasta, mix well, bring back to the boil, reduce heat to a simmer, cover and cook until tender, stirring occasionally.

2. Marinade Preparation

1 level dessertspoon:- of any Gramma's Herbal Seasoning - per 2lbs (1kg) of meat or vegetables for roasting, baking, grilling, frying, kebabs etc;

ADD a little Water - 50 ml/ 2fl.oz (3 tablespoons)

ADD Tomato Puree - 1 dessertspoon

ADD Salt to taste - ½-1 teaspoon

ADD Gramma's Pepper Sauce - ¼ - ½ teaspoon

Mix ingredients well to use as a _marinade_ and cook as follows:-

Pour the above 'marinade mixture' all over the meat, rub in well, cover or wrap in foil. Bake/roast in the centre of a hot oven. Baste every 20 minutes to keep moist. Remove the foil for the last 5-10 minutes and allow to brown on both sides.

VARIATIONS

Omit the tomato puree. ADD 1 tablespoon of tomato ketchup and light soya sauce to the *marinade mix.*

- **STIR FRY:**

After frying the meat and vegetables, pour in the *marinade mixture,* stir well and continue to stir fry until tender.

- **FRYING/GRILLING:**

Sprinkle **1 dessertspoon of any Gramma's Herbal Seasoning** with a little salt, all over the meat or vegetables. Rub in well, then fry or grill as usual.

- **SEASONED FLOUR FOR FRYING:**

1lb (500g) of flour

1 dessertspoon of any *Gramma's Herbal Seasoning*

1 teaspoon salt

Mix well and use for shallow or deep frying

* See more variations and recipes on next pages.

Recipe
Suggestions

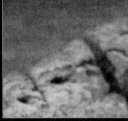

A tasty array of easy to make recipes for meat eaters, vegetarians and vegans.

OTHER VARIATIONS

Create a variety of new exciting tastes by simply adding a little of any of these flavours to our standard *seasoning mixtures.*

- ### EXTRA FLAVOUR:

  ADD 1 Stock Cube *(chicken or vegetable)*, dissolve in a little boiling water.

  ADD 2-4 fresh Garlic Cloves *(finely grated or pureed)*

  ADD $1/2$-1oz fresh Ginger *(finely grated or pureed)*

  ADD 1 small Onion *(finely chopped)*

  ADD 1-2 tablespoons of Olive Oil - *optional*

- ### FOR CHICKEN, FISH, PORK, VEGETABLES or PASTA:

  ADD 1 dessertspoon of Lemon juice or Cider/White Wine Vinegar or replace half the water with dry White Wine.

- ### FOR RED MEATS:

  ADD 1 dessertspoon of Cider or Red Wine Vinegar or replace half the water with dry Red Wine/Port or dry Sherry.

- ### FOR AN ORIENTAL FLAVOUR:

  ADD 1-2 tablespoons of light Soy Sauce or Oyster Sauce or $1/2$ of each.

  ADD 2-4 tablespoons of Rice wine or Dry Sherry.

  ADD $1/2$-1 dessertspoon Honey or sugar

ADD 1-2 teaspoons of Sesame Oil-*optional*

ADD ¹/₂-1 bunch of spring onions *(finely chopped).*

- **FOR A CARIBBEAN FLAVOUR:**

ADD 1-2oz of Coconut Cream.

- **FOR A THAI FLAVOUR:**

ADD 1-2 tablespoons light Soy Sauce.

Replace half the water with coconut milk

FOR A CURRY FLAVOUR:

Use GRAMMA'S Curry Seasoning

ADD 2-4 tablespoons of (low fat) natural Yogurt, **or**

Replace half the water with Coconut Milk.

- **COOKING DISHES FOR LARGE FAMILIES:**

ADD half more water, then 5 minutes before the end of cooking

ADD 2-4 teaspoons of Cornstarch or Arrowroot powder, mix with a little cold water and stir in to thicken the gravy.

- **GRAMMA'S 'Special' BARBECUE SAUCE:**- *(also for Kebabs)* (Marinates up to 5lbs / 2¹/₂kg meat).

100ml (4fl.oz) water.

4	tablespoons cider vinegar
6	tablespoons Ginger Wine or Sherry
3	tablespoons light Soy Sauce
3	tablespoons Tomato Puree
2	dessertspoons of Gramma's Herbal Seasoning *(original, Hot & Spicy or Creole)*
1	tablespoon Honey
1	teaspoon Gramma's Pepper Sauce
2	teaspoons Salt

Mix thoroughly, marinade meats, then barbecue, stir-fry, grill or bake *(basting frequently with the sauce).*

RECIPE SUGGESTIONS

SAVOURY RICE

- Dissolve 1 Stock Cube *(vegetable or chicken)* in 1 pint (20fl.oz / 550ml) of boiling water in a sauce pan.

- Add 1 level dessertspoon of any **Gramma's Herbal Seasoning.**

- $1/2$ red and $1/2$ green sweet pepper (de-seed and dice).

- 2 garlic cloves *(grate)* - *optional*

- 1-2 tablespoons of Olive Oil - *(optional)*

- $1/4$ teaspoon of **Gramma's Pepper Sauce.**

- 8oz (250g) rice, mix in well.

- Bring to the boil, reduce heat, cover and steam cook for 25 minutes.

- Garnish with 1 tablespoon of fresh coriander or parsley leaves *(chop small)*

VARIATIONS

VEGETABLE RICE.

- Add 2 carrots *(dice small)*

- Add 1 celery stalk *(dice small)*

- Add 8oz (250g) green peas

- Add 1 can (400g) sweet corn *(drain)*

CARIBBEAN RICE & PEAS.

- Add 1-2oz of Coconut Cream, *(dissolve in the stock).*

- Add 1 (400g) tin of cooked pulse *(kidney beans, black eye peas or congo peas)* - drain.

❀

SERVE: Mix well, then cook

● INGREDIENTS   ◆ PREPARATION   ❀ SERVING SUGGESTIONS

BAKED SPICY CHICKEN/FISH
(can also be used for Kebabs or Grills).

- 3 Chicken legs and thighs.
- cut across the flesh a few times, deep to the bone *(on both sides).*

Make Up Marinade

- 1 dessertspoon of any *Gramma's Herbal Seasoning*
- 1 tablespoon Natural Yogurt (low fat)
- $^1/_2$-1 teaspoon *Gramma's Pepper Sauce.*
- 1 teaspoon Salt.
- 1 heaped teaspoon Tomato Puree
- 1 dessertspoon lemon Juice
- 1 dessertspoon Olive Oil - *optional.*
- 1 tablespoon Water.

◆ Mix well, pour over Chicken and coat well. Leave to marinade for 1-2 hours in the fridge.

◆ Wrap the Chicken in strong foil.

◆ Bake in a hot oven for 35 minutes: uncover foil, baste Chicken with juices and continue to cook for a further 10-15 minutes until brown on both sides.

BRAISED CHICKEN

- 3lbs of chicken pieces *(or Soya Mince/cubes with diced potatoes and carrots)*.

Make Up Seasoning - *into a bowl, add -*

- $^1/_2$ pint (300ml) water (or $^1/_2$ dry white wine).

- 3 level dessertspoons of any ***Gramma's Herbal Seasoning.***

- $^1/_2$ teaspoon of ***Gramma's Pepper Sauce*** - *optional.*

- 1 tablespoon of tomato puree.

- 3-4 garlic cloves *(grate or puree)* - *optional.*

- 1oz fresh Ginger *(grate or puree)* - *optional.*

- 1 small onion *(finely chopped)*.

- 1 dessertspoon of cider or wine vinegar.

- 1 teaspoon salt.

◆ Mix well, pour into the cooking pot, bring to the boil, reduce heat, cover and simmer for 5 minutes.

◆ Add 1 *(chicken or vegetable)* stock cube *(dissolve)*.

◆ Add the chicken pieces.

◆ Stir well, bring to the boil.

◆ Reduce heat to a simmer, cover and cook for 45-50 minutes, stirring occasionally.

● INGREDIENTS   ◆ PREPARATION   ❀ SERVING SUGGESTIONS

◆ Add a little more water if necessary, or *(if the gravy is too thin, add 2-4 teaspoons of Arrowroot or Cornstarch, mixed with a little cold water, stir in)* and cook for a further 3-5 minutes.

◆ Or alternatively, add $^1/_2$ teaspoon of powdered Seaweed (Irish Moss, see page 688-689 for instructions).

SERVE: with mashed potatoes or boiled rice or quinoa and fresh salad.

VARIATIONS

CURRY DISH.

◆ Use **Gramma's Curry Seasoning:** add 2 tablespoons of natural yogurt instead of cider vinegar or replace half the water with Coconut Milk.

FOR ROAST

- 1 level dessertspoon of *Gramma's Herbal Seasoning* per 2lb (1kg) of meat
- $^1/_2$-1 teaspoon salt

◆ Mix

◆ Wash meat

◆ Rub dry seasoning all over the meat and leave to marinade for 2 hours or overnight in the fridge.

◆ Place in a roasting tray, add a little water or stock for basting, cover with foil, seal edges. Roast as usual.

VARIATIONS

◆ Rub in 1 dessertspoon Tomato Ketchup.

◆ Then roast.

BAKED FISH *(2lb).*

<u>Make Up Marinade</u> - *(into a bowl, add);*

- 50ml (2fl.oz) of water.

- 1 dessertspoon of any ***Gramma's Herbal Seasoning.***

- $^1/_2$ teaspoon of ***Gramma's Pepper Sauce.***

- 1 teaspoon salt.

- 1 dessertspoon of tomato puree.

- 1 dessertspoon of lemon juice.

◆ Mix well.

◆ Place 2lb fish *(whole or steaks)* in a dish.

◆ Pour over the marinade.

◆ Turn fish over a few times to ensure all sides are well coated.

◆ Wrap in foil, sealing edges well, place on a baking tray.

◆ Bake in the centre of a hot oven for 30 minutes until very tender.

SERVE: with baked/boiled potatoes, steamed vegetables or rice and salad.

VARIATIONS

◆ *use Chicken Breasts instead.*

● INGREDIENTS   ◆ PREPARATION   ✿ SERVING SUGGESTIONS

PRAWN DIP/SAUCE

(Place the following into a food blender);

- Add 125g (4oz) cooked Prawns.

- 4 tablespoons Mayonnaise.

- 2 tablespoons Tomato Ketchup.

- 1 Celery Stalk *(chop small)*.

- $^1/_4$ - $^1/_2$ teaspoon **Gramma's Mild Pepper Sauce.**

- 1 teaspoon of fresh herbs *(Dill, Coriander, Parsley)*

- a Pinch of Salt.

◆ Blend to a smooth sauce.

❀

SERVE: with smoked Salmon, or fried fish, boiled egg, *(sliced)* lettuce leaves and buttered french bread, or toast.

PAN FRIED SALMON OR COD STEAK

- 2 large steaks (125g/4oz each).
- Sprinkle $^1/_2$ teaspoon of any **Gramma's Herbal Seasoning.**
- pinch of salt on both sides of the fish steaks.

- ◆ ADD 1 tablespoon of **Gramma's Garlic butter** *(with fresh herbs)* in a frying pan and heat until hot.

- ◆ ADD the fish steaks and fry for 2-3 minutes on both sides.

- ◆ Place each steak individually on a piece of strong foil, with the seasoning on top, wrap and seal securely.

- ◆ Place on a baking tray and bake in a hot oven for 10 minutes.

SERVE: with Baked/Mashed or Roast Potato or Steamed Vegetables *(broccoli, mangetout, carrots, asparagus, courgettes)* or fresh salad.

● INGREDIENTS   ◆ PREPARATION   ☀ SERVING SUGGESTIONS

HOT & SPICY PRAWNS

- 1 kilo (2lbs) King or Tiger Prawns leave shell on, clean and remove the vein which is down the middle of its back.
- Wash thoroughly and drain well, place in a large bowl.
- Add 6 garlic cloves *(grate)*
- 65g (2oz) fresh ginger *(grate)*
- 2 tablespoons light Soy sauce.
- Juice of 1 lemon.
- 1 dessertspoon of **Gramma's Herbal Seasoning** *(Original, Hot & Spicy or Creole).*
- 1 teaspoon **Gramma's Pepper Sauce.**

- ◆ Mix well and marinade overnight in the fridge.
- ◆ Next day, dry the prawns on kitchen tissue paper and shallow fry in very hot oil for 2-3 minutes on each side *(about 6 to 8 at a time).*

SERVE : hot with fresh mixed salad, toast or French bread or garlic bread.

SCRAMBLED EGGS OR OMELETTE

- 1/2 teaspoon of **Gramma's Herbal Seasoning**, 2 eggs, a pinch of Salt, beat in well, then fry in a little Garlic Butter or Oil.

● INGREDIENTS ◆ PREPARATION ◉ SERVING SUGGESTIONS

VEGETARIAN & VEGAN DISHES

SPINACH, BROCCOLI & POTATO SOUP - *(8 litre pot).*

- 750g (1^1/2lb) fresh spinach.

- 750g (1^1/2lb) broccoli.
- 750g (1^1/2lb) potatoes *(peel and cube).*

- 250g (^{1}/2lb) pumpkin *(peel and mince).*

- 32g (1oz) garlic cloves *(peel off skin and mince).*

- 32g (1oz) fresh ginger *(peel off skin and mince).*

- 250g (^{1}/2lb) or 2 medium onions *(peel off skin and mince).*

- 250g (^{1}/2lb) celery stalks *(chop small).*

- 125g (4oz) fresh parsley *(chop small).*
- 65g (2oz) fresh coriander *(chop small).*

- 6 stock cubes *(vegetable or chicken)* dissolved in ^{1}/2 pint boiling water.

- 2-4 tablespoons Extra Virgin Olive Oil (less if preferred).

- 2 tablespoon light Soy Sauce.

- 1 tablespoon tomato puree.

- 1 tablespoon or any ***Gramma's Herbal Seasoning*** *(except curry).*

- 1 dessertspoon Cider Vinegar.

- 1 pint (550ml) water.

- 1 teaspoon Salt.

- ^{1}/2 teaspoon ***Gramma's Herbal Pepper Sauce.***

◆ Heat the Olive Oil and add garlic, onion, ginger. Reduce heat, cover pot with lid and simmer for 5 minutes.

◆ Add spinach, potato, pumpkin and all the remaining ingredients, bring back to the boil, stir well. Reduce heat cover and cook for $1^1/2$ - 2 hours stirring occasionally.

◆ Mix 2 teaspoons of powdered Seaweed Irish Moss - (see page 688-689 for instructions). Stir in well and cook for 2-3 minutes - *optional*.

◆ Leave to cool, then liquidize in a food processor. It's double concentrated therefore, when serving, dilute $1/2$ the soup with $1/2$ water. Stir well, reheat.

SERVE: with buttered toast or garlic bread.

VARIATIONS

◆ Add 1-2oz of coconut cream

(OR)

◆ When serving add $1/2$ teaspoon of Kelp Seaweed powder and 1 teaspoon of lemon juice *(per person)*. Mix and serve.

◆ Freezes well, in individual portions.

● INGREDIENTS   ◆ PREPARATION   ❀ SERVING SUGGESTIONS

<u>PUMPKIN & LENTIL SOUP</u> - *(8 litre pot).*

- 2 kilo (4lbs) Pumpkin *(peel, de-seed and mince).*

- 1kilo (2lbs) fine Red Lentils.

- 1 whole bunch of celery *(chop small).*

- 1 ripe papaya *(peel, de-seed and chop)* - optional.

- 4 Carrots *(peel and chop small).*

- 1 Sweet Pepper *(de-seed and chop small).*

- 8 Stock cubes *(vegetables or chicken)* dissolve in 1 pint of boiling water.

- 6-8 tablespoons of Extra Virgin Olive Oil *(less if preferred).*

- 6 tablespoon light Soy Sauce .

- 4 tablespoons tomato puree.

- 1^1/2 dessertspoon Cider Vinegar.

- 2 tablespoon of any ***Gramma's Herbal Seasoning.***

- 2-4 teaspoons salt.

- 65g (2oz) fresh parsley *(chop small)*

- 65g (2oz) fresh coriander *(chop small)*

- 8 garlic cloves *(peel and mince).*

- 4 medium onions *(peel and chop small).*

- 2oz fresh ginger *(peel and mince).*

◆ Heat the Olive Oil and add the minced garlic, ginger, onions, cover with lid and simmer for 5 minutes.

◆ Add dissolved stock, then all the other ingredients.

◆ Add 3 pints ($1^3/4$ litres) of water, bring to the boil and stir well.

◆ Simmer, cover and cook gently for 2 - $2^1/2$ hours, stirring frequently as it sticks to the bottom. If it gets too thick add little more water.

◆ Mix 2 teaspoon of powdered Seaweed Irish Moss (see page 688-689 for instructions). Stir in well and cook for 2-3 minutes - *optional*.

◆ Once thoroughly cooked, leave to cool then liquidize in a food processor. It's double concentrated, therefore, when serving dilute $1/2$ soup with $1/2$ water, stir well, reheat and serve hot.

VARIATIONS

◆ Add 1-2oz coconut cream

NOTE: freezes well in individual portions.

<u>VEGETARIAN/VEGAN STEW</u> - *(5 litre pot).*

- Add 2-3 tablespoons of extra Virgin Olive Oil in a large sauce pan and heat to hot, reduce heat.

- Add 6 garlic cloves - *(peel and grate).*

- Add 65g (2oz) fresh ginger - *(peel and grate).*

- Add 2 medium onions - *(chop small).*

- Stir, cover pan with lid and simmer for 5 minutes.

- Dissolve 3 vegetable stock cubes in 1 pint (550ml) boiling water and add to the pan.

- Add 2 dessertspoons of any ***Gramma's Herbal Seasoning***

- Add 2 tablespoons light Soy Sauce.

- Add 1 teaspoon salt

- Add 250g (^{1}/2lb) grated pumpkin *(optional)*

- Add 4 medium carrots *(dice small)*

- Add 4 celery stalks *(dice small)*

- Add sweet pepper *(de-seed and chop small)*

- Add 125g (4oz) green beans *(dice small)*

- Add 2 tablespoon tomato puree.

- Add 500g (1lb) Soya Mince.

- Mix well, cover and simmer cook for 20 minutes.

- Add 250g (^{1}/2lb) mushrooms *(chop small)*

- Add 1 courgette *(dice small)*

- Add 125g (4oz) cauliflower florets.

◆ Mix well, bring to the boil, reduce heat and simmer for 30-45 minutes, add more water if necessary.

◆ Mix 1 teaspoon of powdered Seaweed Irish Moss (see page 688-689 for instructions). Stir in well and cook for 2-3 minutes - *optional*.

SERVE: with boiled rice, mashed potato, cous cous or spaghetti.

VARIATIONS

CHILLI CON CARNE.

◆ Add 2 cans (400g each) of kidney beans (drain) and $1/2$-1 teaspoon of *Gramma's Pepper Sauce*.

◆ Curry: add 3 dessertspoons of Gramma's Curry Seasoning.

● INGREDIENTS   ◆ PREPARATION   ❀ SERVING SUGGESTIONS

BRAISED BEANS - *(2 litre pot).*

- Heat 2-3 tablespoons of extra Virgin Olive Oil.

- Add 4 garlic cloves *(peel, grate or puree).*

- Add 1oz fresh ginger *(peel, grate or puree).*

- Add 1 onion *(chop small).*

- Stir then cover pan with lid and simmer for 5 minutes.

- Add 3 celery stalks *(chop small).*

- Add $^1/_2$ sweet pepper *(de-seed and dice).*

- Add 2 medium tomatoes *(chop small).*

- Dissolve 2 stock cubes *(vegetable/chicken)* in 100ml (4fl.oz) of boiling water.

- Add 2 tablespoons light soy sauce.

- Add 150ml (5fl.oz) dry white wine.

- Stir well, bring to the boil, reduce heat to simmer, cover with the lid and cook for 10 minutes *(stirring frequently to avoid burning).*

- Add 2 tablespoons each of finely chopped 'fresh' coriander and parsley leaves.

- Add 3 tins (400g each), of cooked beans *(chick peas, red kidney beans, haricot beans)* - drain off the water in the tins.

- Add 1 dessertspoon of tomato puree.

- Add $1^1/_2$ dessertspoon of any **Gramma's Herbal Seasoning**.

◆ Stir well, bring to the boil, reduce heat, cover and cook for 20 minutes.

◆ Mix 3 teaspoons of Arrowroot powder in a little cold water, add and stir until thick.

SERVE: hot to accompany a main meal or on its own with mashed potato or rice or with bread and fresh salad

---

SPICY GARLIC MUSHROOM

(Prawns or Seafood).

● Heat 1 tablespoon of ***Gramma's Garlic Butter*** with fresh herbs
(see Pepper Sauce recipe).

● When sizzling hot, add 8oz (250g) of baby mushrooms *(cut in halves).*

● Sprinkle over 1 teaspoon of any ***Gramma's Herbal Seasoning*** and a pinch of salt.

◆ Fry for 2-3 minutes, stirring frequently.

SERVE: with crispy salad, french bread, garlic bread or toast.

● INGREDIENTS   ◆ PREPARATION   ❀ SERVING SUGGESTIONS

PULSE & VEGETABLE STEW

(high protein complete meal. This was one of Zara's favourite meals).

You will need a very large 10 /12 litre stock pot.

- 500g (1lb) Soya Beans. *(soak overnight in cold water)*

- 500g (1lb) Red Kidney Beans. *(soak overnight in cold water)*

- 500g (1lb) Butter Beans.

- 500g (1lb) Haricot beans.

- 250g (8oz) Peal Barley.

- 1 bunch of Celery. *(wash and chop small).*

- 1 bunch of Parsley. *(wash and mince).*

- 65g (2oz) Coriander. *(wash and mince).*

- 250g (^{1}/2lb) Pumpkin *(peel and grate).*

- 8 large Carrots *(peel and dice).*

- 250g (^{1}/2lb) runner beans *(top and tail, cut small).*

- 2 Sweet Peppers *(de-seed and dice small).*

- 1 Aubergine *(top and tail, dice small).*

- 2 Courgettes *(top and tail, dice small).*

- ^{1}/2 small white Cabbage *(chop small).*

- 1 small green Papaya *(peel, de-seed and dice small)* - optional.

- 3 large Onions *(dice small).*

- 8 Garlic Cloves *(peel, mince or finely).*

- 65g (2oz) Ginger *(peel, mince or grate).*

- 8 tablespoons of Extra Virgin Olive Oil.

- 3 tablespoon, Cider vinegar.

- 6-8 *(chicken or vegetable)* stock cubes - dissolved in $^1/2$ pint boiling water.

- 8 tablespoons, Light Soy Sauce.

- 3 tablespoons, or any **Gramma's Original Seasoning** *(except curry)*.

- 1 bottle or *8 tablespoons* (300g) Tomato Puree.

- 1 - $^1/2$ teaspoon **Gramma's Herbal Pepper Sauce.**

- Water $1^1/2$ litres. ($2^3/4$ pints)

In a large pot of water -

◆ Cook the pulses separately - starting with the Soya Bean, cooked covered for 1 hour, then add Kidney Beans, cook for $^1/2$ hour, then add the Butter Beans, Haricot Beans and cook for 1 hour and strain off water *(set aside)*.

◆ In a large pot, (10/12 litres) heat the Olive Oil, add the mince garlic, ginger, onions; stir, reduced heat and simmer for 5 minutes.

◆ Add the dissolved stock cubes, $1^1/2$ litres of water and all the other ingredients *(except for the cooked pulses)*; bring to the boil, stir well, reduce heat, cover and cook for 1 hour-stirring occasionally.

◆ Add all the cooked pulses, stir well and continue to gently simmer for 2-3 hours stirring frequently to avoid burning at the base, if necessary add a little extra water.

◆ Mix 3 teaspoons of powdered Seaweed Irish Moss (see page 688-689 for instructions). Stir in well and cook for 3 minutes - *optional.*

SERVE: with boiled rice, mashed potato, pasta or quinoa.

VARIATIONS

◆ add 1 kilo (2lbs) 'Soya cubes' with the cooked pulses.

◆ Freezes well in individual serving portions. You could use any other pulse such as;- black eye peas, congo peas, black and white kidney beans, chick peas.

NOTE: As this dish takes very long to cook, it is well worth preparing a large pot and freeze in serving portions. Alternatively, reduce the entire recipe by half for a smaller portion.

● INGREDIENTS   ◆ PREPARATION   ❀ SERVING SUGGESTIONS

Concentrated
PEPPER SAUCE
Gramma's
MILD

Gramma's Ltd
Unit 8, Acorn Ctr.
29 Roebuck Road,
Hainault Ind. Est,
Essex, England.

Vegetarian
Society Approved
45ml

SEAWEED

(Irish Moss Powder 4oz / 112g)

Seaweed contains an abundance of nutritional minerals, including natural antibiotics, calcium and iodine, which is essential for the thyroid gland. This gland is known as the body's control centre; for aiding proper digestion and maintaining a healthy balance.

HOW TO PREPARE:

Mix the Seaweed powder (in a cup) with a little cold water into a smooth/lump free paste. Gradually add a little more cold water, continue to mix until it becomes a smooth, thick but runny consistency. Pour into hot gravy, soup, stew, porridge, etc; cook and stir continually for 2-3 minutes until thickened.

STANDARD MEASURES:

$1/4$ teaspoon of Seaweed powder, mixed with - 2 tablespoon of cold water.
(ideal for gravy).

$1/2$ teaspoon of Seaweed powder, mixed with - 4 tablespoons of cold water.

1 teaspoon of Seaweed powder, mixed with - 6 tablespoons of cold water.

2 teaspoons of Seaweed powder, mixed with - $1/4$ pint (150ml) of cold water.

ON AVERAGE:

$1/2$ teaspoon will thicken $1/2$ pint *(or $1/4$ litre/250ml)* of gravy, soup, stew, porridge etc.

1   teaspoon will thicken 1 pint ($1/2$ litre/500ml) and so on.

2   teaspoons and over is a little difficult to mix, therefore a food liquidizer can be used to make mixing easier.

NOURISHING MILKSHAKE:

Mix 2 teaspoons of the Seaweed powder but substitute the water with milk.

POUR:- $1^1/_2$ pint ($^3/_4$ litre / 850ml) of Soya, Rice or Organic milk into a sauce pan.

$^1/_4$ teaspoon clove powder

$^1/_2$ teaspoon cinnamon powder

$^1/_4$ teaspoon nutmeg or mace powder

$^1/_2$ teaspoon ginger powder

2 teaspoons vanilla essence

2-4 tablespoons honey *(to taste)*

Stir well, heating gently until it reaches boiling point. Reduce heat and allow to simmer, then pour in the Seaweed mixture, stirring continually for 2-3 minutes until thick. Leave to cool. Refrigerate and serve cold with ice.

- **For extra flavour -** try adding strawberrys, chocolate etc. during cooking.

PORRIDGE: (Oats) -

Mix 1 teaspoon of Seaweed powder with either water or milk.

POUR:- $1^1/_4$ pint ($^3/_4$ litre /700ml) of water or milk into a sauce pan.

Add the spices as in the above 'milkshake drink'

Add 2-3 tablespoons honey (or to taste)

Add 3oz of Oats.

Stir well and heat gently until boiling, stirring frequently. Reduce heat, simmer and cook for 5 minutes, pour in the Seaweed mixture. Stir continually for 1-2 minutes until thick. Serve immediately *(serves 2 people)*.

● INGREDIENTS   ◆ PREPARATION   ⊛ SERVING SUGGESTIONS

MY THIRD PRODUCT

Zara's Herbal Tea

Zara with Marsha, 1995

My third product was given in 1994, for Marsha's dog *(Zara)* who was dying from cancer.

(see full story in chapter 3 - 'For the Love of Zara').

ZARA'S HERBAL TEA (4oz / 112g)

I n g r e d i e n t s

Red Clover, Burdock, Sheep's Sorrel, Willow, Slippery Elm, Echinacea, St. John's Wort, Ginseng, Vervain, Yellow Dock, Dandelion, Violet, Golden Seal, Rhubarb.

A delicious, concentrated **blood cleansing tea for YOU and your pets.** It can be taken NEAT <u>or</u> made into a refreshing tea <u>or</u> a quenching cold drink or add to drinking water. Reportedly good for controlling a variety of conditions such as, cancer, diabetes, incontinence, kidney infections, congestion, hypertension, food poisoning, irregular and painful periods, fluid retention, menopause, indigestion, breathing problems, tiredness, constipation, inflammation, fades dark shadows around the eyes, improves skin quality, restores complexion, rejuvenates and detoxify; plus it reconditions animals coats to a glossy shine, prevents irritation and itchy conditions, restores fur growth and boosts the immune system. Use daily as a **preventative** and for **health maintenance**, essential for both the sick and healthy.

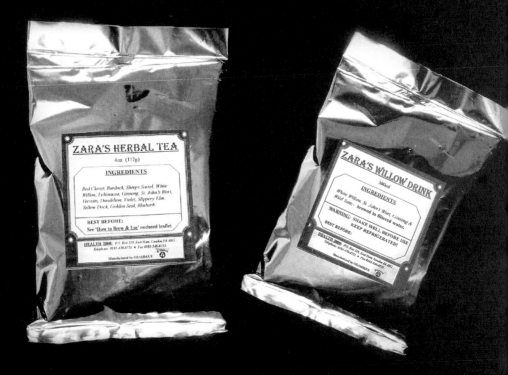

• GRAMMA'S HERBAL TEA RANGE.

(Zara's Herbal Tea and Willow Tea).

ZARA'S HERBAL TEA

HOW TO BREW

(takes 2 days to brew, producing 1^1/$_3$litres - 2 pints).

ITEMS REQUIRED:

1	Large Stainless steel pot with tight lid, holding 3 litres or 5 pints.
1	Stainless Steel or wooden spoon.
1	Water filter unit, or 1^3/4 litres bottled water
1	Muslin tea bag *(reusable)*
1	Large measuring jug *(holding 1^1/2 litres/2^1/2 pints).*
1	Small stainless steel or plastic funnel.
1	Pair of disposable rubber gloves.
2	500ml / 1 pint *glass bottles (do not use plastic bottles).*

BREWING METHOD

(The brewing details look more complicated than it actually is in practice. When you have brewed it for the first time you will see just how easy it is).

Step 1: STERILISING

All items must be sterilised before starting *(i.e. bottles, caps, funnel, measuring jug, muslin tea bag, spoon).*

METHOD *(Sterilising);-*

Put the spoon, muslin bag, jug, funnel, bottles and lids into a large pot of boiling water, cover and simmer for 15 minutes; drain. Remove the spoon and muslin bag (wring out). Leave the rest covered in the pot until ready for the straining process in Step 3.

Step 2: <u>BREWING PROCESS</u>

- Pour in 1¾ litres (3 pints) of filtered or bottled water into the stainless steel pot. Cover and bring to a rolling boil.

- Reduce heat to a gentle simmer.

- Cut open a sachet of herbs (4oz) and empty it into the muslin bag. Pull the string to gather the bag, tie into a very tight bow-knot to prevent the herbs from escaping during brewing.

- Put the filled muslin bag into the simmering water and press it down several times with the spoon (pressing out the air), until the herbs settle to the bottom of the pot.

- Cover the pot and simmer for 3 hours. For **gas cookers**-use a heat defuser under the pot (e.g. a flat heavy metal plate or platen) - to obtain an even simmer.

- Turn off heat and leave covered for 20 hours.

- Once cooled, uncover, use the spoon to turn over the muslin bag a few times. Press it down to the bottom of the pot. Cover again and re-heat till hot (but **DO NOT BOIL**). Reduce heat and simmer gently for 3 hours.

- Turn off heat and leave for 10 hours to cool. Keep covered throughout.

Step 3: <u>STRAINING PROCESS</u> - *(Put on the disposable gloves);-*

- Wring the muslin bag out with your hands and squeeze out all the remaining tea into the pot.

- Pour the tea from the pot into the measuring jug.

Step 4: <u>FILLING PROCESS</u>

- Place the funnel in the sterilised bottles and pour in the strained tea. Cap the bottles tightly and store in the refrigerator at 5° - 10° C.

- **<u>IMPORTANT</u>**

  Always ensure that your refrigerator is at the correct temperature, by using a fridge thermometer.

  - *Throw away disposable gloves.*

Step 5: <u>WHEN FINISHED</u>

- Wash, clean, dry and store all utensils. keep these items separate and use only for making the Herbal Tea and not for general cooking, except for the 'Water Filter Unit' which is for every day use. But ensure that the filter cartridge is changed as recommended by the manufacturer.

Step 6: <u>RECYCLE USED HERBS</u>

- Do not throw away the used herbs, empty it out of the muslin bag and use it in your garden as compost for plants or directly onto outdoor plants or bury in the earth. For a soothing face or body pack see page 702.

Step 7: <u>RE-USEABLE MUSLIN TEA BAG</u>

- Turn the muslin tea bag inside out and wash it thoroughly. Then dry, so it is ready to use for next brewing time. The bag should last at least 2-3 years. When it gets old, you can order another one. The old bag can be put in your garden compost as its 100% cotton and will degrade or rot in the soil.

W A R N I N G !

⋆ DO NOT FREEZE THE BOTTLE ⋆

or

ALLOW IT TO TOUCH THE BACK OF YOUR REFRIGERATOR

Once brewed, use within 2 months.

Any water added to the drink must be first <u>FILTERED</u> then <u>BOILED</u>. If you cannot filter, then boil thoroughly.

If at anytime <u>MOULD</u> forms in the bottle **DO NOT DRINK IT.** Instead use it as an external body wash for your face and other parts, or in the bath for a soothing herbal soak. Alternatively water your plants with it.

Zara's Herbal Tea

HOW TO USE

SHAKE WELL BEFORE USE.

The 'dosage' shown on the following pages are broken down into three categories (1). Cancer Sufferers, (2). Other Chronic Illnesses and (3). Healthy.

It is essential to drink the tea **NEAT** *(undiluted)*
MORNING AND NIGHT for the first 3 months.

This helps to clean the blood, stabilise illness and also maintain health.

(a). $^1/_2$ **- 1** Hour before breakfast *(i.e. on an empty stomach)*

and

(b). $^1/_2$ **- 1** Hour after your last meal at night or before going to bed.

Additionally, you can drink it daily as a regular cup of tea or add into your drinking water.

TO MAKE A CUP OF HERBAL TEA:

- **1 Dessertspoon or Tablespoon 'NEAT' -** *(according to age)* per cup or mug. Top up with hot water. If desired, sweeten with honey or brown sugar. It makes a very pleasant tea. *Everyone can drink this daily as a substitute for tea and coffee.* **Do not use milk.**

IN DRINKING WATER:

- **1 Tablespoon per $^1/_2$ litre** (1 pint) of water, *(filtered and boiled).* Mix well and allow to settle. Drink hot or cold. **You can make up a much as you want, then keep in the fridge ready for daily use.** Drink instead of tap water.

CANCER SUFFERERS

DOSAGE: 1.

1 Teaspoon = 5ml ▲ 1 Dessertspoon = 10ml ▲ 1 Tablespoon = 20ml			
CATEGORY	**DOSE** **taken neat**	**TIMES** **Per Day** *(morning, midday* *& night)*	**SACHET** *(lasts for)*
ADULTS *(or Large Animals)*	**3 TABLESPOONS**	3 times	6 days
CHILDREN *(over 5 years* *(Medium Animals)*	**2 TABLESPOONS**	3 times	9 days
CHILDREN *(under 5 years)* *(Small Animals)*	**1 TABLESPOON**	3 times	2^1/2 weeks
BABIES *(up to 1 year old)* *(Puppies)*	**1 DESSERTSPOON** **(Diluted)** *with 1 dessertspoon of water*	3 times	1 month

▲ **NOTE:** After the 3 months, reduce to **TWICE DAILY** *(i.e. morning and night).* Continue to take it **NEAT** to keep the condition under control. Additionally, you can also take it as a regular cup of tea with or without meals, as well as, include it in your drinking water.

OTHER CHRONIC ILLNESSES

DOSAGE: 2.

1 Teaspoon = 5ml ▲ 1 Dessertspoon = 10ml ▲ 1 Tablespoon = 20ml			
CATEGORY	**DOSE** taken neat	**TIMES** Per Day *(morning & night),*	**SACHET** *(lasts for)*
ADULTS *(or Large Animals)*	3 TABLESPOONS	2 times	9 weeks
CHILDREN *over 5 years* *(Medium Animals)*	2 TABLESPOONS	2 times	2 weeks
CHILDREN *(under 5 years)* *(Small Animals)*	1 TABLESPOON	2 times	1 month
BABIES *(up to 1 year old)* *(Puppies)*	1 DESSERTSPOON (Diluted) *with 1 dessertspoon of water*	2 times	2 months

▲ **NOTE:** After the 3 months, if the condition has not cleared, continue with the same dosage. Otherwise, reduce it to **ONCE** **DAILY.** Additionally, you can also take it as a regular cup of tea with or without meals, as well as, include it in your drinking water.

HEALTHY PEOPLE & ANIMALS

DOSAGE: 3.

1 Teaspoon = 5ml ▲	**1 Dessertspoon** = 10ml ▲	**1 Tablespoon** = 20ml

CATEGORY	DOSE taken neat	Times Per Day (morning & night)	SACHET (lasts for)
HEALTHY ADULTS: *(Large Animals)*	**2 TABLESPOON**	2 times	2 weeks
HEALTHY CHILDREN: *(over 5 years):* *(or Medium Animals)*	**1 TABLESPOON**	2 times	1 month
HEALTHY CHILDREN *(under 5 years):* *(or small animals)*	**1 DESSERTSPOON**	2 times	2 months
BABIES *(up to 1 year old):* *(puppies)*	**1 TEASPOON (Diluted)** *with 1 teaspoon of water*	2 times	$3^1/2$ months

▲ **NOTE:** After 3 months you can drink it as a regular cup of tea at anytime with or without meals and also, include it in your drinking water.

SPECIAL NOTES

<u>SLEEPLESSNESS</u>:
If you can't sleep at night or is restless, then make *a hot cup of herbal tea* and drink it just before going to bed. It's also great for babies and children to give them a good night's sleep.

<u>IRREGULAR OR PAINFUL PERIODS</u>:
Also have a *hot cup of herbal tea* last thing at night, during the week of your periods and when pain occurs.

<u>FOOD POISONING, HEADACHES, TENSION, UPSET STOMACH or to RELAX</u>:
Drink a *hot cup of herbal tea* at any time the condition occurs, then relax.

<u>BREATHING AND CONGESTION</u>:- *(problems such as: Colds, Flu, Asthma).*

The Herbal Tea on its own helps these conditions. However, for a stronger remedy see the recipe section in 'Gramma's Herbal Pepper Sauces' for *Gramma's Caribbean Hot Toddy* and add **3 tablespoons** of 'Zara's Herbal Tea' (NEAT) to this recipe.

- If you are also suffering from the painful symptoms commonly associated with a cold or flu, then also add 3 tablespoons of 'Willow Tea' to the Hot Toddy recipe.

<u>FLUID RETENTION</u>:
Taken as a *a hot cup of herbal tea* (instead of tea or coffee), throughout the day. It will make you urinate more frequently and in this way help to remove excess fluid and toxins.

<u>MENOPAUSE</u>:
Take 1 tablespoon NEAT morning and night and also reduce coffee, tea and alcohol (or stop drinking these altogether). Include more soya and

yams in your diet.

CUTS:

Put a little of the NEAT Herbal Tea on a piece of cotton wool and bathe the cut with it.

FUSSY PETS:

If it is difficult to get your '*animals to drink it NEAT*,' try syringing it into their mouths <u>or</u> put it into their drinking water. However, if all else fails, then mix it into their food but it is more effective taken NEAT, particularly if seriously ill.

SKIN PROBLEMS (HUMANS):- *(i.e. eczema, psoriasis etc).*

DO NOT DRINK IT NEAT!

Instead, dilute 1 teaspoon in $^1/_2$ cup of hot water, (morning and night for 2 weeks) - gradually increase until the full dose of 1-2 tablespoon is reached.

SKIN PROBLEMS (ANIMALS):- *(i.e. irritation).*

For animals whose immune system has been damaged by steroids, antibiotics, antihistamines or vaccinations, take the drink NEAT twice daily - (see dosage section 2. Other Chronic Illnesses). If difficult to take, mix the full dose into their dinner and also include in drinking water.

SOOTHING FACE or BODY PACK:- *(muslin bag with used herbs).*

Instead of taking out the used herbs after brewing, reheat it over a pot of boiling water *(in a steamer or colander)* for a few minutes until warm (not hot) but comfortable for your skin. Lie down and place the warm bag on your face, or lower back and relax for $^1/_2$ hour. Afterwards, remove the herbs and wash the bag until clean.

NB: The herbs can be stored up to 1 week in the fridge.

MY FOURTH PRODUCT

Gramma's Willow Tea

This product also came as a direct result of Zara's and my suffering. In 1997, to add to her problems, Zara also contracted arthritis in her spine and legs, which was causing her to fall over frequently. The Vet confirmed that this was a common condition in most dogs of her age and some even much younger. He prescribed a mild steroid based tablets to reduce the stiffness and pain; but instead her condition worsened. She became extremely ill, hot, sick, itching and weak. Within four days, she could not even walk.

During the same period, I was experiencing extreme sciatica pains in my left leg and lower back, caused from a spinal injury and a condition called spondylitis. My doctor prescribed strong pain killers and anti-inflammatory drugs, which were both ineffective. I had reached the point where I could not stand or walk for more than two to five minutes and was forced to sleep with a pillow between my knees to relieve some of the pressure, because the pain disrupted my sleep. It became so intense that I often broke down in tears. I feared ending up on crutches or in a wheelchair. As nothing worked, I was sent to be examined by a Spinal Specialist who suggested a spinal operation but I'd still have to remain on the drugs for the rest of my life. To my amazement, I had another unexpected spiritual intervention. In the middle of the night, I awoke in excruciating pain, whilst at the same time I heard a man's voice saying, *"you must feel the pain God feels for HIS suffering children."* Then the pain stopped and I went back to sleep. I was awakened again twice with the same pain and the same voice saying the same words. At which point I said *"take away the pain, I do not wish to be a martyr or suffer for anyone."* The next day my Guide instructed me to brew Willow Bark with St. John's Wort, Ginseng and Wild Yam and to drink 1 to 2 tablespoons, 3 times daily for one to four weeks but once the pain was under control to reduce the amount to once daily or only take it only when in pain. Within one week, the sciatica and back pain disappeared completely. I thought my back was cured but noticed when I overworked or was under stress, the back pain returned (but not as bad as before) as a reminder that I still had a damaged spine and must take care not to over-do things. I sometimes incorporate the Willow Tea with Zara's Herbal Tea and have also included regular exercise (gym, light weight training, swimming, walking, massage, hula hooping and Yoga) to tone and strengthen my muscles and improve flexibility. I can now walk for at least one hour, no longer need the pillow at night and have been dancing the night away in complete comfort. I even risked wearing high heel shoes to parties. In fact, I have had no sciatic pains during the entire past three years, only the odd back pain once in a long while. I had even forgotten how ill I was and can now say that at long last, I've got my life back, **pain and drug free**.

As for Zara, initially she was back on her feet almost immediately. She also showed signs of having much less pain and stiffness. However, by 1998 her arthritis worsened and my Guides instructed me to take her swimming but she was still pain-free.

I told this incredible story to a customer who is a qualified Holistic Practitioner and he confirmed that 'willow' contains the same ingredient as in aspirin, which is a synthetic drug but the 'willow is all natural' and does not cause the same terrible side-effects as aspirin. I later also learnt that St. John's Wort is a blood cleanser and also a natural anti-depressant, which is non-addictive.

For many years, Doctors recommended that people should take an aspirin daily to prevent heart attacks. However, in November 2000, it was reported that long-term use of aspirins caused internal bleeding and was therefore dangerous. Doctors withdrew their previous advice.

GRAMMA'S WILLOW TEA - 4oz (112g)

I n g r e d i e n t s

White Willow, St. John's Wort, Ginseng, Wild Yam.

A natural (non-addictive) pain killer and anti-depressant tea for **YOU and your pets.**

It can be taken NEAT <u>or</u> made into a hot cup of tea. Reportedly good for all forms of pain, aches and discomfort, including sciatica, menstrual periods, colds, soreness, upset stomach and for nervous animals.

<u>ITEMS REQUIRED;</u>

1   Medium stainless steel pot with tight lid, holding 2 litres *(3¹/2 pints).*

1   Stainless steel or wooden spoon.

1   Water filter unit or bottled water.

1   Muslin bag *(reusable)*

1   Measuring jug *(holding 1 litre/2 pints).*

1   Small Stainless Steel or plastic funnel.

1   Pair of disposable rubber gloves.

2   500ml or 1 pint *glass bottles.*

* DO NOT USE PLASTIC BOTTLES *

Gramma's Willow Tea

Brewing Method
(takes 2 days to brew, producing 3/4 litres-1 1/2 pint).

This is exactly the same process as in *Zara's Herbal Tea* except for;-

Step 2: <u>BREWING - PROCESS</u>:

- Pour in 1 litre (1 3/4 pint) of filtered and bottled water into the stainless steel pot. Then follow on step by step the same procedures.

<u>**TO MAKE A CUP OF WILLOW TEA**</u>:

- 1/2-1 <u>**Tablespoon - (NEAT)**</u> *(according to age above)* per cup. Top up with hot filtered water. If desired, sweeten with honey or brown sugar.

✳ DO NOT ADD MILK! ✳

<u>**TO MAKE A SOOTHING FACE or BODY PACK**</u>: (see page 702).

GRAMMA'S WILLOW TEA

DOSAGE.

1 Teaspoon = 5ml ▲ 1 Dessertspoon = 10ml ▲ 1 Tablespoon = 20ml		
CATEGORY	**DOSE** taken neat	**TIMES** Per Day
ADULTS: *(or large animals)*	**1-2 TABLESPOON**	**3 times**
CHILDREN: *(over 5 years)* *(or medium animals)*	**$^1/_2$-1 TABLESPOON**	**3 times**
CHILDREN: *(under 5 years)* *(or small animals)*	**1 TEASPOON (Diluted)** with $^1/2$ cup of water and drink as a cup of tea	**2 times**

▲ **NOTE:** Once the pain is under control, reduce the dose to **ONCE** DAILY or only use when in pain.

MY FIFTH PRODUCT

Herbal Biscuits

In 1998, a customer (Mrs Valerie Harmsworth) whose dog **Lewis** suffered from an acute skin problem, read my article in Pet Dog magazine and felt that **Zara's Herbal Tea** could possibly help Lewis. Valerie contacted me and we became instant friends.

Lewis's skin condition baffled both Vets and Skin Specialists alike, none could determine it's true cause or prescribe the correct treatment.

At her wits end, Valerie told her story to a popular dogs magazine, who featured it, followed by a major feature in a national newspaper. She received over 1000 readers letters, offering advice and recommending various treatments. After years of experimental drugs, Valerie decided to go the natural way including home-made meals, aloe vera juice and homeopathic remedies. These made a slight improvement but when she tried Zara's Herbal Tea, the improvement was so noticeable that friends who knew of him commented, *"Hasn't he changed; he looks much better; what have you been giving him?"*

A few months later, Valerie came up with the idea of turning the used herbs from the Zara's Herbal Tea into **natural (high fibre) dog biscuits**. She experimented with sweet and savoury flavours, trying them as a healthy treat on Lewis. Being a typical labrador (they eat literally anything), Lewis devoured the lot. Then she tried them on a neighbour's (fussy eating) dog and he loved them too. But to her complete surprise and amusement, so did her pregnant daughter. After all, the ingredients were natural containing gluten free starch, honey, organic apples, pears, raisins, etc. So what originated as a dog's biscuit has been transformed for humans and animals.

I then told Valerie what God had previously said that, *"no part of the herbs were to go to waste but recycled as animal feed or put back into the soil for enrichment."* With this in mind, I was considering selling the used herbs to organic farmers at some later stage but hers was the best idea and I loved it. I suggested, she name the biscuits after Lewis. Valerie is now looking forward to setting up her own private enterprise, once she has perfected her range of delicious Herbal (high fibre) biscuits, (more details on Lewis' skin story in the Testimonies).

MY SIXTH PRODUCT

Honey Supreme

In January 2000, whilst celebrating the turn of the century in the Caribbean, I met an amazing bee-keeper by the name Kirk Hinkson, better known as 'the Bee-Man of Trinidad.' Mr Hinkson who has been handling bees for many years, possesses a rare devotion and insight into their behaviour. He has a unique knowledge of the healing properties of honey and passionately believes that; *"bees are natures best manufacturers, because they harvest the finest fruit/flower nectar from natures wild forestry, labouring intensely, to produce the purest, unrefined, natural products for our delight, enjoyment and health. Honey is nourishing internally as well as externally."*

In 1999, Mr Hinkson represented Trinidad at the National Honey Show, held in Britain and was honoured with the prestigious 'Hender Cup' for producing the best quality honey in the world. The show is recognised worldwide and this was the first time since its inception in 1973 that the cup was won by a Caribbean producer. His name is now proudly engraved on it for posterity.

I was taken by Kirk Hinkson's warmth, simplicity and spirituality. So when he asked to collaborate in business I was delighted. By the year 2001, we plan to introduce a very special energy rich honey.

Testimonies.

• DISCLAIMER:

I am compelled by law to disclaim any health claims made about my products, even though these are absolutely true. Therefore, I'm not claiming that these products will either heal, cure or prevent any of the conditions mentioned but simply reporting the true findings to date. If you have any serious illness or are taking medication, you should always consult a qualified doctor or health practitioner. Neither myself or the publisher accepts any liability for damage of any nature resulting directly or indirectly from the application or use of information in this book.

Testimonies.

- **ZARA'S HERBAL DRINK**

Vet's confirmation Report
(on Zara's condition & recovery)

<u>GODDARD VETERINARY GROUP</u> - *(Essex).*

I examined 'Zara,' a $10^1/2$ year old Labrador Retriever on 2nd February 1994. At this time, she had a growth in her mouth which was subsequently removed. No other clinical problems were evident. She was presented again on the 21st October '94 when a colleague examined her and identified the presence of mammary masses. I again examined her on the 2nd November '94. At this stage the masses had grown rapidly and had the typical clinical appearance of mammary tumours. Zara was also drinking a lot, losing weight and breathing rapidly and very shallow. These clinical signs suggested other major organs were involved, which was confirmed by blood tests, which showed very elevated liver and kidney enzymes. I gave Miss Moore a very poor prognosis and suggested she take Zara home until her quality of life deteriorated to the point that euthanasia was our only option.

I examined Zara on the 9th January 1995 and was amazed to find her in such good condition. Her lumps had almost diminished completely, her drinking and breathing were normal and she was a good weight. Repeated blood tests confirmed that the kidney was no longer functioning abnormally and all but one of the liver parameters had returned to normal. The one enzyme that was still elevated had decreased by 50%.

During the period between the 2nd November '94 and 9th January '95, Zara received no treatment from me. I believe she was given only a herbal remedy made by my client's mother and placed on a special diet.

I have now started another client on this herbal remedy. Again the dog was given a very poor prognosis with a very large mass present on the spleen and small tumours in the lung. She has been on it for four weeks and the reports so far show the dog is much brighter, with a very glossy coat and has certainly not deteriorated any further, rapid deterioration is the normal scenario in a case such as this.

C.R. Nicholson
BCVs MRCVS.

5th December 1998

Mrs Pattison
West Midlands

Dear Dounne

Many thanks for your letter and the leaflets which I will give to my Vet.
I enclose a copy of the article I'm sending of the editor of The Griffon
Bruxellois Club.

● Jason snoozing on the sofa.

ARTICLE

Whether it was fate or just good luck I shall never know but it was when a friend lent me the September 1998 issue of **'PET DOGS'** so I could read an article on Griffons, that I chanced on the amazing story of Zara, a Labrador Retriever.

At the time I read the article I was worried about Jason, who many will have known in his early years when he was a winner at many shows under the ownership of Margery Day. Early in April, urine tests proved that he had a kidney problem. Initial treatment cleared this up but within five months, tests proved that it had recurred and my Vet warned me that at his age, (now six) it could be a problem he would have for the rest of his life. So on the spur of the moment, I telephoned Dounne. She showed such concern and care and I decided to see whether *'Zara's Herbal Drink'* would help Jason's condition. That was at the beginning of October '98.

My Vet had advised having Jason's urine tested every two months. Jason is a very loving little dog, very much my shadow, always ready to give the postman, paper boy and any visitor a boisterous, noisy welcome but since he has been taking *Zara's Herbal Drink (5ml twice daily),* he has become more lively, his eyes are brighter and like a true Griffon, inquisitive and keen to be in on everything. So I was not surprised to learn that the last urine tests showed Jason had no kidney problem. Jason will now continue with his tonic, as we call it and of course, the tests will continue. I have a feeling *Zara's brew has worked another miracle.*

In addition, Jason is now on a Senior Dog food twice a day with little bites at night. He has bottled spring water to drink and to ensure he has sufficient water, I make him have several syringes during the day. He looks up expectantly when he sees his tonic coming and licks his lips, with relish, obviously enjoying the taste.

Follow - Up Report - May 1999

Jason has had tests every two months for his kidney problem and so far it has not returned. He is far more self-confident when outside of his home environment and friends in the park who we meet most mornings, have remarked on his improvement. He now goes up to some of them, when before he shied away.

Mr Cooling
Essex

22 March 1995

Dear Gramma's

A strange growth appeared on the inside of my index finger in October '94. I went to my doctor and he decided to burn it out with 'Silver Nitrate' which had no effect and it turned septic. Once again I went to my doctor and he prescribed antibiotics, which again had no effect. In Feb '95 I went back again, as it was really sore and growing: It would bleed profusely if knocked and was constantly weeping and at times even had a nasty smell. My doctor decided I should have surgery which was arranged for 18th April 1995, (six weeks later). I had bought some of this Herbal Drink for my wife which she did not try. So two weeks ago I decided I'd take it myself. I have taken nearly half a bottle and the growth seem to be starved of whatever it was feeding on. The growth and the open flesh wound has completely healed and is no longer painful.

NERVOUS ANIMALS.

A customer claimed that his dog usually goes crazy during thunder storms and must be given tranquillisers. He gave it 1 dessertspoon of Willow Drink and the dog calmed down within 5 minutes and remained calm.

A lady who bred pedigree-dogs for sale, found that her dog who was getting old had a very large litter of (12) puppies . The day after giving birth, her breast milk completely dried up, so she was unable to feed them. The owner tried bottle feeding but 5 died. In order to save the remaining seven puppies, she decided that she'd have to send them for weaning to a special clinic for 3 weeks, which would cost £35.00 each, per day (totalling £5,000). However, one of her friends whose dog was taking Zara's Herbal Drink, told her to try it on the mother. After giving her 2 dessertspoons morning & night, in just a day and a half, the milk came back in full force and they all thrived.

Miss Carpenter
Hithergreen

2 December 1995

Dear Dounne

I have felt very much better since starting the drink, one dessertspoon morning and night. My breathing has improved and my catarrh problems have quickly improved. I seem to have the feeling of "well-being"if you can understand that. I have given 1 dessertspoon for night and morning to my 12 year old dog who would not stop scratching, licking and pulling her fur out, despite all different types of treatment. So far, I am delighted with the results, she has stopped scratching etc. and there are signs of the fur growing. I also rub the drink over her skin twice a day. So I want to continue without a break with the drink on her as well as myself. The nursing sister and my doctors said she was going to ring you to get details. Several people have remarked that they notice a remarkable improvement in my breathing when I have been talking to them on the telephone and also remarked how much "brighter" I seem to be in myself.

I also enjoy the Herbal Peppers Sauces.

Ms Falconer
Caithness

17 November 1996

Dear Dounne

You wanted me to let you know whether Zara's Drink helped my cat who had a 'tag' on his ear which he kept scratching and making it bleed heavily. Well it has! I applied Zara's Drink to his ear only once a day and he hasn't scratched it once since. It's really great. I was quite worried about it and was horrible finding blood splattered everywhere!

I'm now using it on a neighbour's dog who has a cut on her leg which will not heal. I'm sure Zara's drink will do the trick.

P. Stevens
W. Sussex NN13 1QP   21 May 2000

Dear Dounne

I would like to tell you that I was saved from a dreadful existence with Zara's Herbal Tea. For 10 years I had spent a miserable life due to hot sweats. I had spend a fortune on various treatments and none had done the trick. I had gone on to HRT but had even worse side-effects.

Finally one day in a dog magazine, I read about a dog with skin problems, who had had wonderful relief taking the herbal tea, that I decided to try it on my dog as she sometimes had very dry skin. When my bottle arrived, I read the enclosed literature and there was a letter from a woman who found it controlled her sweats as well as helping her dog. I took some and have not had a sweat since. I feel that a miracle has occurred in my life. I am free at last, thanks to Dounne and her wonder brew.

As I work with women all day, I intend to spread the news.

Thank you Dounne and I look forward to hearing about any new products that you come up with. At least they are all natural herbs and most women in particular appreciate this.

Yours sincerely

p.s. My dog now shines with health

'MY OWN PERSONAL TESTIMONY'

My daughters and I have been drinking it daily for the past 5 years as a replacement for tea and coffee and have had no side-effects.

It has also helped me cope with the *menopause*. I later learnt that *Red Clover* contained high levels of a substance called *Isoflavone Phytoestrogen* which is almost absent in the British diet and is important for women during the menopause.

Dounne

- Otto the dog and even the budgies enjoy daily doses of Zara's Herbal Drink.

(Mrs Saas).

J. Saas

Ireland

6 June 2000

Dear Dounne

Thank you very much for sending Zara's Herbal Drink so quickly. The whole family takes it now, even the budgies. One of them was very sick and I thought he would die but he is getting better and can even sit on the perch again. Our dog Otto has improved too but he is still scratching a lot. I guess it will take a long time before he is right again.

30 October 2000, Otto is almost totally recovered.

Ms Fraser   28.05.1995

Exeter

Dear Dounne

Many thanks for your kind gift of Zara's drink which arrived last week. It is remarkable and I thought I should write to you to let you know how a couple of your clients are getting on.

Well, you remember the fight between the Dachshunds, the night you came to supper, which left Eliza with a very bad wound near her tail? After a couple of days the wound did not appear to be healing and was clearly unhealthy. We thought the flesh round the wound was necrosed and so made an appointment for Eliza to be seen by our Vet. In the meantime, a friend let us have a bottle of Zara's drink to be going on with until ours arrived. We started dosing Eliza straight away and we also bathed the wound with it. The results was amazing in that the evil looking wound quickly looked healthy and any swelling/fluid has dispersed. In fact, we were able to telephone and cancel the consultation with the Vet. The wound was very bad, as you will recall, but it healed very well indeed. But that's just part of it. Eliza is 10 years old and has her 'off' days. Sometimes after a long walk, we may find she is lame in one of her front legs the next day.

However, since she has been on Zara's drink (5mls, first thing in the morning and 5mls, last thing at night); her whole demeanour has changed. She is more alert, more confident, has a glossy sheen to her coat, the bald patches seem to be slowly growing hair again and she is so full of energy and strength that the younger Dachshund can't keep up with her in the field. She flies along like a two year old; a sort of short-legged greyhound!

We can't thank you enough, Dounne. It has cheered the little dog and given her a new lease of life. Goodness knows what is in the brew!

We also took the other bottle to my friends elderly mother. She had an appointment with a consultant on 15th. May, who told her that he believed the slow-growing lump on her ear was malignant and that she would need it surgically removed - 12th. June. She believes the growth started when she wore some earrings which were not gold and they set-up an irritation, which she then scratched at, etc. We weren't sure of the dose, so made her take 2 dessertspoons 2-3 hours before food in the the morning and the same thing at night. After speaking to you, we got her to reduce the dose to 1 dessertspoon twice a day. She did it religiously ,even though she has been feeling very depressed and lacking in energy lately (she has to have a cataract operation on 6 June and is terrified of it).

I suppose she has now been taking Zara's drink for 10 days. The lump on her ear it less inflamed and discoloured; it is softer (she can sleep on it without pain); the size of the lump has reduced. In addition, this anxious and rather distraught lady is not only relaxed, getting on with life, feeling cheerful and fully optimistic. I took your advice and now take a dessertspoon with hot water and honey and it makes a delicious cup of tea. This morning after my Zara's tea, I did something I never do; I went back to sleep for 2 hours and woke up feeling rested and ready for anything. Dounne it was so good to meet you. Do tell Marsha about Eliza the Dachshund and Megan (the younger one) is in a show at Bath tomorrow. She won't win because she is such a minx, but she'll look good as her coat and eyes are sparkling!

Mrs Deuchar-Fawcett   6 July 1999

Dear Mrs Alexander

Recently, one of my Lhasa Apsos 'Deeka' was off colour, since recovering from a small stroke last year, which had left her stone deaf.

Now, 15 years old, she was sleeping a lot and drinking too much. More worrying, a small hard lump had appeared on a milk gland. The Vet thought that the lump should be removed. Although not happy about anaesthetic at such an advanced age - I agreed. My Vet is very good, as my other breed (St. Bernard's) are also considered bad anaesthetic risks. The type he uses is reversible and very short acting. Thankfully, all went well. A few days later, the Laboratory delivered it's verdict. I knew it wasn't good, as I'd had a peek at the Vet's notes which described the lump as 'nasty' looking. The laboratory thought so too. So now it appeared we were on borrowed time.

Whilst reading through the CRUFTS magazine, I came across an article by a Caribbean lady called Dounne Alexander, who had concocted a Herbal Drink for her Labrador 'Zara,' who at an advanced age was diagnosed with terminal cancer. I rang her and found a most charming lady, who sent the various literature connected with her work.

I also ordered a bottle of 'Zara's Herbal Drink.' Deeka was given 5ml, night and morning by syringe. The result was quite amazing, now wide awake and very lively, there is no stopping her. She whizzes round the garden like a puppy. The excess drinking has stopped;- her eyes sparkle and she has healed beautifully.

I've even tried 'Zara's Drink' on another oldie 'Minnie Mouse' who is a real fuss-pot at meal times. She now dances when food appears and scoffs the lot in double quick time. The most amazing thing is that if I forget Deeka's tonic, she sits right in front of me and refuses to move until she gets it.

One thing I do know, 'Zara's Herbal Drink' has proved its worth and has certainly given a new lease of life to a little golden girl called Deeka.

Mrs E. Crooks   6.11.2000
Leatherhead

Trixie was a 13 year cross German Shepherd. She was Diagnosed with bone cancer during December 1999 and was given a poor prognosis. I was told maybe a month. Sometime in January 2000, I heard of Dounne and her famous Zara's Tea. I contacted her and she immediately sent me two bottles. Trixie continued drinking this tea and lived a further eight months without the cancer spreading to other organs. The vet said she was in very good bodily condition and was surprised that an advanced tumour had not spread and also said "who knows what she would have been like without the Herbal Drink." Although her life was shortened, it was free of pain and she was still very happy. Always eating and most important of all, still wagging her tail - proof that she was without pain. I do believe that Trixie was unfortunate that the cancer was in her leg because without Amputation she didn't have a very good chance. She also had arthritis and other problems. If the cancer had been elsewhere, the Zara's Tea would have stopped it spreading and I am sure she would still be alive today. Thank you Dounne for Zara's Tea.

E. Crook

P.S. I enclose a very special poem given to me by my neighbour to ease the pain of having to make the decision to put Trixie down. I hope it will also help others who face the same terrible dilemma.

Mrs Crookes daughter Sue with Trixie.

• Trixie relaxing with companion Bella.

If it should be that I grow frail and weak
And pain should keep me from my sleep
Then you must do what must be done
For this last battle can not be won

You will be sad, I understand
But don't let your grief stay your hand
For on this day, more than all the rest
Your love and friendship stands the test

We've had so many happy years
What is to come can hold no fears
Would you want me to suffer? So,
When the time come, please let me go

Take me where my needs they'll tend
And stay with me until the end
And hold me firm and speak to me
Until my eyes no longer see

I know in time that you will see
It is a kindness that you do to me
ALTHOUGH my tail, its last has waved
From pain and suffering I've been saved

Do not grieve, it should be you
Who must decide this thing to do
We've been so close through all these years
Don't let your heart hold any tears.

Poem given by:
neighbour of Mrs Ellen Crooke

Mrs C. Bloomer   3 September 2000

Staffordshire

Dear Dounne

So sorry about beautiful Zara, but so happy she survived so long.

I am enclosing an order for Zara's Herbal Tea and also the Willow Tea, for my own lovely retriever (Sophie) who is 11 years old and suffering from arthritis. After reading about your personal note on the menopause, I shall also take it myself. I have recently taken myself off HRT which I had taken for one year, as I could not cope with the extra weight it supplied - apparently, a side effect of this drug. The downside is putting up with the flushes, but I'm sure Zara's Tea will help.

I first came across Zara's Tea some years ago, for my other retriever (Bonnie), the mother of Sophie, and it helped her to clear some rather nasty mammary tumours, similar to Zara's problem. Unfortunately, Bonnie is no longer with us, except in our hearts and memories and of course living within her daughter Sophie!

I spread the word continuously about the undoubted healing properties of this wonderful product, which I unconditionally and wholeheartedly believe in.

Mrs I. Dipple   6 September 2000
West Bromwhich

Dear Dounne

I first heard about Gramma's Willow Drink from my daughter-in-law, who is taking it for arthritis in her thumbs. She had found great relief and as I was unable to move and in extreme pain, from the same complaint, she recommended that I try it. I've been taking it for some years now and have found great relief in my joints. I suffered badly in my legs, knees and body and was very immobile prior to taking it. I am now able to walk and the pain has receded dramatically. I would recommend it to anyone suffering from a similar problem.

I wish you ever success.

• pictured here graduating, as a journalist; dated ~2000.

Sherene Lee.

• **TRIBUTE TO A SPIRITUAL FRIEND**

"Thanks for allowing me into your heart and home,

for your friendship and trust;

for the lessons learnt through your suffering,

and for the spiritual support you will continue to provide.

It was both a privilege and honour to have been chosen to serve you.

You did not lose the fight but won the battle.

Now that you have entered *'the light of life'* and understands the true
purpose for which you were sent to serve,

I look forward to continuing this connection
for the service of humanity."

Dounne Alexander.

Sherene and I met in 1996, just after she had surgery for breast cancer.

Sherene was beautiful in every sense of the word; positive effervescent, elegant and forever helping or advising others. In 1999, we both received the 'Community Award'... for her outstanding contribution in creating awareness of breast cancer amongst black women.

Sherene had a true passion for life and was determined to beat the cancer. Out of desperation and fear, she surrendered herself as a guinea-pig for 'cancer drug trials' at the Royal Marsden Hospital. This is the best cancer hospital in Britain and Sherene believed that she would receive the best drugs available; and hence was convinced that she would be cured. Over the years, she was given a variety of powerful drugs, including chemotherapy and radiotherapy. These drugs were taken daily but had devastating side-effects. One resulting in nerve damage to her eyes, causing her to loose sight in one eye. Unfortunately none of the drugs worked and eventually the cancer spread throughout her body, affecting every organ. Sherene had at least ten tumours in her brain and towards the end, her body became emaciated, she suffered extreme pain and was paralysed. Until this experience, I did not realise that steroids could waste and weaken muscles to such an extent.

By the time she chose to try holistic treatment, it was too late. The Doctors gave her 2 days to live. I asked both Sherene and her doctors' permission to treat her with Zara's Herbal Drink and change her to a vegan diet. Although approved, because she had been taking strong 'addictive' drugs for a long time, she had to continue with them. Nevertheless, Sherene remained hopeful and fought to the very end. She survived for 38 days and died on 24 July 2000, age 41.

Whilst treating her, in our private moments, we spoke at length. She asked that I make known her experience, so that others would not suffer as she did. Since her death, Sherene has visited me 'in spirit' several times and at her request I would like to quote her message to the world.

"Dounne, I believe in what you are doing and now realise that medication does not always work. It does not cure or heal, but poisons

and weakens the body. *The Doctors mean well, they have good intentions and are not necessarily deceiving us. They just don't know any better themselves. They only work with what they've been trained to believe in. They should keep an open-mind and consider natural remedies and look at holistic treatments, instead of solely relying on drugs. Their concern and focus should be healing the whole person, by whatever means are available. People should also start taking better care of themselves on a daily basis and don't wait until they become ill or until its too late. They should return to natural foods and remedies and stop their dependence on drug medicines. Take on a holistic approach to living. Once something is broken, it can never be repaired to perfection... there will always be some weakness or flaw. So try and stay as perfectly healthy as possible, by taking good care of yourselves, eat the right foods to maintain a healthy balance. Doctors and patients should work together in harmony. People should listen to and check their bodies; have regular medical check-ups and take direct responsibility for their lives. Don't just take the Doctor's word or diagnosis, get second opinions. Your life is much too precious and under no circumstance should you allow yourself to be toyed with. Your work is of great benefit and I hope people would apply your wisdom sooner rather than later."*

As my Guides explained;-

*"When people are told that they have a terminal illness, they tend to 'surrender themselves to fear' instead of 'surrendering to love.' Hence, their entire focus is centred on fighting the fear of death rather than fighting the disease or illness itself. Self-healing is more effective if one is able to absorb the love within and around them. Once fear is released, then the nucleus is calmed, which helps to slow down the development of any disease. The exact opposite occurs with intense fear. Calmness also brings clarity of mind in which you can be directed into the various ways of destroying the disease. Hence, in fear you destroy (i.e. consume) rather than heal yourself. People should also come to terms with the fact that 'you are all born to die,' hence **death** is inescapable... but the answers to the question WHY- is held between yourself and God alone."*

● Lewis: pictured here as a healthy 6 months old pup, before being inoculated.

1

'Lewis.'

- A special case of acute skin irritation which shows the damaging effects of vaccinations, steroids, antibiotics and antihistamine drugs.

Mrs V. Harmsworth   1999.
Hants, England

'LEWIS'

As a child I had always wanted a dog but it was never possible. I vowed one day on leaving home my dream would become reality but this was not to be, as my husband suffered from hay fever including allergies to cats and dogs.

After fifteen years of marriage, my husband's hay fever cleared and his reaction to cats was only slight but had no reaction to dogs at all. Once again, I thought that it would be possible to own a dog and started requesting one for birthdays; christmas and anniversaries. My husband made it very clear that he did not want a dog. My daughters knew how much I wanted one and decided to voice their opinion on the matter and after another twelve years he finally gave in.

The day came for us to collect my black Labrador from the breeder, I named him Lewis. He was seven weeks old and little did we know how much this bundle of fur and fun would change our lives.

At nine weeks old Lewis had his first trip to visit the Vet. He had an upset stomach which the Vet treated with an antibiotic injection and a follow up of tablets.

At eleven weeks old, he damaged a ligament in his front leg while playing in the garden, this was treated with an anti-inflammatory injection, followed with tablets.

Lewis had his first vaccination at six weeks and his second was now due but because of the medication he had already received, it was suggested to wait until he was fourteen weeks old. After his second vaccination his behaviour changed. He became very hyperactive, would have sudden mood swings and turned quite vicious, biting and even drawing blood on occasions. My daughters were cautious of him because of this and my husband kept well away. I was concerned about his change in behaviour and asked my friends advice who owned Labradors. They felt this was just part of him being a puppy and that he would grow out of it.

Lewis then started scratching his ears. I was worried and took him to the Vet for this to be checked. I was told that there were no fleas and not to worry too much as all dogs scratch to a degree. The scratching continued so I returned to the Vet. Lewis received drops in the ears followed by cleaning while under anaesthetic. The Vet informed me that Lewis had very crooked ear canals which could be corrected with surgery if this became a serious problem.

At this stage Lewis was five months old and things seemed to get better, his life became normal but unfortunately it didn't seem long until the scratching started again. His ears were checked but there was no sign of fleas or mites, his skin was a little dry so the Vet gave me a shampoo to use.

We reached Christmas 1995 and Lewis scratched so consistently that he succeeded in ripping the skin open around his neck. It became very swollen, sore and was also bleeding. Another visit to the Vet two days after Christmas, when I was told that it was probably due to our home being too warm and giving him too many Christmas treats. This was not the case, Lewis only had a small version of Christmas dinner, no other treats. He was once again treated with antibiotics, which seemed to have no effect, his skin remained very sore and the scratching spread to the rest of his body, his hair was coming out in handfuls leaving large bald patches which were very sore.

Food allergies were the next suggestion, he was still on antibiotics and was also now being treated with steroids to attempt to stop the irritation and the discomfort. After trying various dog foods, hypo allergenic and gluten free mixtures, it was decided that an exclusion diet would be needed, which for Lewis meant ten weeks of steamed white fish and mashed potatoes. There was no difference other than weight loss.

Because of the deterioration in the condition of Lewis' skin, I realised it needed protection. I decided to put a T-shirt over him to help prevent further damage. It soon became necessary to use two shirts and I also put socks on his back feet. This was for two reasons, his feet were sore and this gave increased protection from scratching damage. He wore this day and night. I ensured that everything was 100% cotton and always washed them in non biological powder and rinsed everything thoroughly, so as not to cause any further irritation. I found it was possible to remove his socks when I took him for a walk as he would not scratch while we were out providing the walk was constant, only stopping for his necessary calls of nature!

Lewis was now just over a year old, when the next suggestion was sarcoptic mange. He was prescribed a sponge on shampoo, four treatments later and things seemed to improve. The scratching eased and his hair was showing signs of re-growth. But once again the scratching returned and so did the steroids.

We returned to the Vet and two more shampoo treatments were given, this time there was no change. The steroid treatment was increased but only had short term relief.

However, there was a side effect to the steroids. Lewis suddenly had an increased appetite and not only for food. Going on his walk was difficult, as he would eat anything laying on the ground, discarded food, cigarette stubs, litter, sticks and even a dead blackbird. Carrying washing to and from the washing machine also became hazardous, he didn't care if the clothes were clean or dirty. This lead to major surgery as I was unaware that he had eaten a pair of 70 denier winter tights. They caused a blockage and he obviously became unwell. I took him to the Vet and was operated on immediately. Within ten days he was back to his normal way of life.

His booster injection was delayed and owing to his past health problems I asked if it should be given. I showed an article in a magazine which pointed out that if a dog had been unwell, treated with antibiotics or been on steroids, it should be considered to delay giving the booster, or even not at all. I was assured that he should have the injection and Lewis was given the vaccination in June 1996. Within 2 days he was scratching again vigorously, drawing blood and ripping his hair out. He was charging around the house crashing into furniture and scratching. He would then appear to collapse in exhaustion, sleep and wake starting the process again. This was happening day and night and was very distressing. Lewis' sleep was now being disturbed, so the Vet prescribed a sedative, hoping that this would assist him in getting a full night's rest. After one week I stopped giving the tablets, as I noticed the following day he was very lethargic and for the small reduction in scratching, I decided there was no point in continuing with them.

His scratching continued and the next process was skin tests to check if Lewis was atopic (multi allergy). These results showed he had an allergy to the house mite and a slight allergy to pollens. In an attempt to help with the discovery of the house mite allergy, the carpets in our lounge and hallway were pulled up and wooden flooring was fitted. No other rooms were changed as most of Lewis' time was spent in these two areas. I also purchased a Dyson cleaner with extra filtration for allergy sufferers, to try to assist with this new find. Treatment for this was a long course of desensitising injections which lasted seven months and were unsuccessful. While receiving these injections his skin was still deteriorating, surface infections and small lumps were appearing. One lump on his rib cage seemed different and larger than the others. Surgery was carried out to remove it and a biopsy was performed. This luckily showed that the lump was benign but other tests showed signs of cushings disease, which were a result of the steroid treatment. Gradually the steroids were reduced and stopped and in turn the scratching increased. Various antihistamines had already been tried, so this was not an option either.

I had a long discussion with my Vet who informed me of an unlicensed drug that was used on cattle. He believed that this could be tried on Lewis as he had a suspicion that he may have a resistance to the treatments for 'sarcoptic mange.' I was fully warned that this could be a risky treatment but I decided to take the chance and he had the course of three injections. There were no signs of any side-effects but there was no reduction in his scratching. My Vet then stated that the only future for

Lewis was permanent treatment with antibiotics and steroids. I knew that this would not be an option, as Lewis had already shown signs of developing cushings disease. I realised that my Vet could not see a future for Lewis and asked for a referral to a Homeopathic Vet. He had little faith in this but I did get the referral. My appointment was made and we had a wait of six weeks. The Homeopathic Vet was distressed at Lewis' appearance and diagnosed that there was considerable damage to his immune system due to the booster vaccines and steroids which had been prescribed. He felt his treatment for Lewis would be limited but I wanted to give it a try.

It was now May 1997 and the Homeopathic Vet felt that there was still a risk of 'sarcoptic mange,' so the treatment started again with another type of sponge on treatment. Lewis was not impressed with this and even less impressed that the lotion had to remain on him to dry naturally. He would try to lick it off which I had to prevent, as it was not suitable for consumption. Again there was a side effect, Lewis became very depressed. I was advised to stop the treatment. The Vet recommended a change of diet, no "dog" food, only raw green tripe, organic chicken, lamb, rabbit, vegetables, brown rice and fruit.

After a long course of homeopathic pills, Lewis once again showed improvement but then repeated his past pattern. It was now November. My Homeopathic Vet recommended more tests to be carried out. The results showed an 'under-active thyroid gland' which it was felt were the results of his chronic skin condition. This improved with treatment and there was no permanent damage.

The next suggestion from the Homeopathic Vet was Radionics. This initially had an improvement but again only in the short term. Then there was a suggestion of a healer, a very genuine man but again no change.

Euthanasia was now being suggested as they felt everything had been tried. I changed Vets as I wanted a third opinion. I could not accept that euthanasia was the only option, I knew the answer was there, we just had to find it. Even at this stage Lewis was still showing a positive attitude to life. He would greet me in the morning standing on three legs, scratching with the fourth and wagging his tail to the point of losing his balance. He still enjoyed his food and walks and loved people. One of the many lessons I have learnt from Lewis is that their love is unconditional.

My third Vet was prepared to try for a little longer with treatment and a skin biopsy was done. This showed no signs of any type of mange, although there was high secondary infections of the skin surface. His prognosis was to review Lewis every four weeks, again with antibiotic treatment and gentle shampoos for his skin.

The next step on our path came from the Dogs Today magazine, who printed his story in the hope that maybe a reader might have the answer. The response was overwhelming. We received letters, faxes and phone calls from all over the country and worldwide. I followed many lines of treatments but no improvement.

Our next challenge was from a past problem. The area where his lump was removed suddenly inflamed again. The swelling spread rapidly in just a few hours and once again he was rushed to the Vet. I feared the worst, was it now cancer? Thankfully it was an abscess which had ruptured internally and infection had started spreading under the skin. He had been given an incision, approximately an inch or so to drain away the infection and he was not given any stitches as it was believed this would assist the draining process. The wound healed in its own time although he was given an antibiotic injection and follow up tablets. I now felt that his immune system was improving a little.

In July 1998 Lewis was once again showing rapid deterioration. Another visit to the Vet because of a huge swelling in his right ear (a haematoma) which suddenly appeared after another continued long bout of head shaking and scratching due to the constant skin irritation. His nose was also very sore and swollen.

The Vet was not at all happy with the situation and once again suggested Lewis' time was coming to an end.

At this time Lewis was also being treated by a Dermatologist with antibiotics. I had read an article about a herbal drink and decided to try it, maybe it could help Lewis. I was desperate and prepared to try anything within reason. On the first week of September 1998, Lewis had his second appointment with the Dermatologist, who had noticed an improvement but wanted to change the antibiotics and introduce low dose steroids. I was not happy about this, so he agreed to delay the steroid treatment. Lewis had been down the path of steroids before and I was not prepared for him to repeat this journey. The side-effects were very unpleasant.

After two days and nights of heart searching questions, I decided to follow my own instincts and immediately took him off all conventional treatments and put him on natural remedies. The first step being to increase the dosage of Zara's Herbal Drink and aloe vera juice and slowing changed his diet to natural home cooked meals. However, I knew that my Vet and Dermatologist would not be too pleased with this decision, so I decided not to tell them but continued buying their drugs to allow me necessary time to see whether or not nature's way would improve his condition. I also kept the drugs as proof that they were not used.

Our third visit to the Dermatologist was on the first week of December 1998. I waited for his reaction on seeing Lewis who had by this time greatly improved. As he was not aware of my deception, he would naturally believe that the drugs were working. He was very pleased and commented that there was immeasurable improvement and that we must continue the treatment but added that it was time to introduce the low dose steroid therapy. Again I disagreed, so he continued to prescribe the antihistamines, I continued to keep up my deception and not administer them to Lewis.

Week by week, Lewis' improvement was so noticeable that people who knew of his plight would stop me in the street and ask in amazement - "is this Lewis?" none could believe their eyes and were so happy for him.

It was not until May 1999 that once again a visit to my Vet was necessary, due to an injured paw. He was amazed with Lewis' skin improvement and good health. On first sight his words were *"you really do look like a black labrador now, don't you"* I felt that the time had come to make my confession and placed the five months supply of un-used drugs on his desk. He was very understanding and happy for Lewis and myself but admitted to being conventionally trained and wanted to wait until the end of summer 1999 before making any comment about Lewis' prognosis for the future.

I told my Vet that Lewis had not worn T-shirts during the day since January 1999 and that I had also stopped using them at night. He wanted to know of any changes in Lewis' life other than the herbal drink. I admitted to not cleaning my home for a long period of time but this made no difference to Lewis' so called allergy, he just continued to improve. My Vet still felt that Lewis was atopic. I disagreed with this, politely, as I have a high regard for him *(he helped with Lewis after our other Vet wanted to end his life).* Since May, I have tried various tests on Lewis myself. I have walked him through long grass when loaded with pollen, reduced my dusting and cleaning and stood with him in the evening by our pond, to see if he would react to insect bites, nothing! I however, was bitten a few times by the insects!! Still Lewis continued to improve.

At the time of writing this testimonial, it was the beginning of September 1999, one year since making the decision to stop conventional treatment which I am convinced caused Lewis's skin problems in the first place, which worsened due to repeated treatments and which would have eventually killed him. I know in my heart that I made the right decision and that 'natural treatment' and 'a natural diet' saved his life. Although Lewis is not fully healed, he is much, much better, healthier and happier than he's ever been in his life.

Walking with Lewis is now a joy and it gives me so much pleasure to share this experience with him. In the past, I found it difficult having to deal with people and their negative attitudes and abuse upon the sight of Lewis. Now on an almost daily basis we continue to meet people who have not seen Lewis for some time. Their reaction is always the same, shock that this really is Lewis and not another Labrador. I wish Dounne could see their faces! Our walks take so much longer - the questions start, what was the problem? what cured him?

I wish now I had learnt to trust my instinct and used it at a much earlier stage in Lewis' painful journey. I think maybe this was one of the many lessons I had to learn, Lewis being the teacher and myself the slow pupil.

All I can say is - *"Thank you Lord for showing me the path to Dounne Alexander and Zara's Herbal Drink, to natural remedies combined with natural feeding for nourishment. Thank you Zara, thank you Dounne and your family and last but not least thank you Lewis, for allowing me to enter and share your life and for teaching me so much more."*

- **Follow up report.**

In April 2000, Dogs Today magazine featured Lewis again in another report on skin problems entitled *'Miracles Do Happen,'* detailing his improvements since coming off conventional medication and taking Zara's Herbal Drink. Within days, I started to receive letters from other dog owners who were experiencing problems. I noticed that all the dogs were given the same treatment of antibiotics, antihistamines and steroids, which gave short-term relief but the irritation soon returned and was worse than before. In fact, they were in a chronic state. Many mentioned, that although they knew the drugs were destroying their dogs, they had no choice, as no alternative treatments were available from the Vets. Once the immune system is damaged, it takes a long time for the body to repair itself and the animal may never regain 100% fitness.

I do hope that Vets and Doctors take note of these results and stop prescribing drugs as standard treatment and seek out safer alternatives.

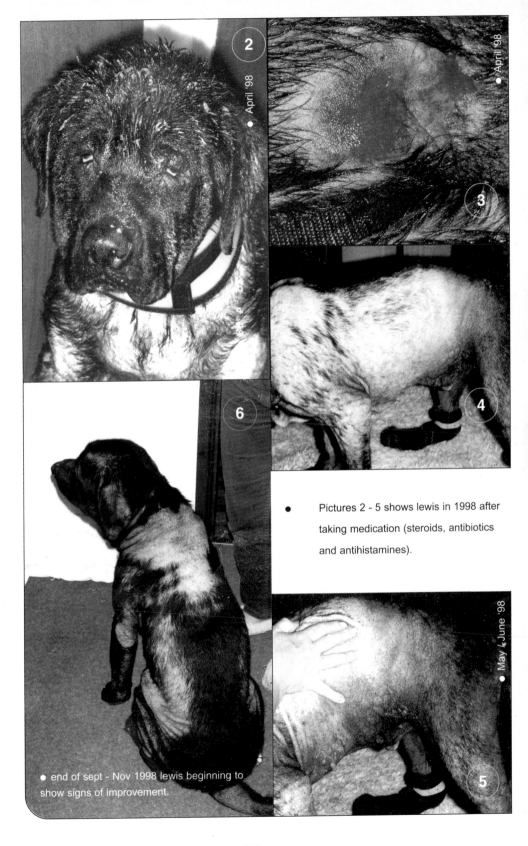

April '98

April '98

Pictures 2 - 5 shows lewis in 1998 after taking medication (steroids, antibiotics and antihistamines).

May / June '98

end of sept - Nov 1998 lewis beginning to show signs of improvement.

- Lewis condition begins to improve after 3 months on Zara's Herbal Drink - Jan '99.

7

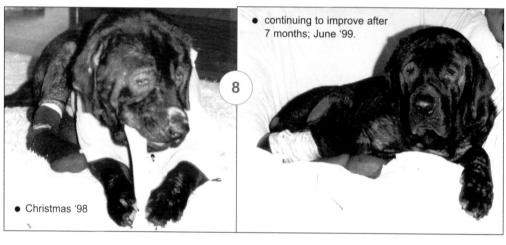

- continuing to improve after 7 months; June '99.

8

- Christmas '98

9

- The 5 months supply of medication which Mrs Harmsworth returned to her Vet. (May '99).

January 1999

Nov 2000

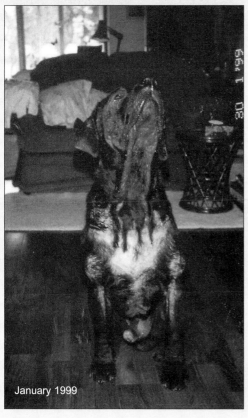

January 1999

Nov 2000

Testimonies.

• HERBAL PEPPER SAUCES.

In 1990, a doctor claimed that he had personally found Gramma's Pepper Sauces successful in relieving longhaul **Jet Lag,** plus it improved the flavour of airline food.

Hot-peppers also prevents blood clotting, inflammation, strengthens the heart, improves circulation, respiration, congestion, digestion and helps to sober you up. It is also reported that sitting for long periods in aeroplanes causes the blood to clot, known as 'deep vein thrombosis,' which can be fatal. Thus making **Gramma's** an essential in-flight food.

M.Hughes
Swansea

19.11.93

Dear Dounne

I am writing to tell you about the success of your product.

During the winter of last year, I fell prey to my very first bout of bronchitis. After two courses of antibiotics, my cough had not improved. Then I read about Gramma's Hot Pepper Sauce in the Vegetarian Magazine'. I searched in vain to buy it locally, so sent for it by post (the jar costs less that a prescription). Your product came promptly back. By now the antibiotics had made my general health very poor and my spirits were rock-bottom.

Every night I made a hot toddy, made from a tiny amount of sauce, honey and lemon. I also started adding it to almost everything I ate. Within three days my cough had gone.

I believed 100% that your product achieved what modern medicine couldn't.

I would recommend it to anyone with bronchial problems. My daughter who is asthmatic also finds relief by drinking the toddy when her chest is tight.

From a very grateful and satisfied customer.

Thank you

Mrs Duncan
Wadhurst

25.03.93

Dear Dounne

I received 9 jars of your Pepper Sauce on 17th December and started on them that same day. I now have only one left and do pray that you will let me have my order as quickly as possible, otherwise I shall definitely suffer withdrawal symptoms!!!

I find it a great help for my sinus problem, I haven't had to take Sinutab for the past two weeks, which is great.

With my grateful thanks and best wishes.

Ms Hamilton
Scotland

December 1993

Dear Dounne

Thank you so much for your kind, prompt phone call in response to my enquiry and for following up with details and order form.

May I tell you why Gramma's Hot Pepper Sauce has become so dear to me? I have cancer and have been in chemotherapy for 7 months now-2 more months to go. One of the unpleasant side-effects for 'chemo' is that it kills off quick-growing cells. Cancer cells are quick-growing, you see. But also so are hair-growth cells, fingernail cells, skin cells and the cells that make up our taste buds! So in addition to going bald, having skin like sandpaper and laminating nails, I can't taste any food or drink properly and haven't for months. Everything either tastes 'weird' (nasty or tastes dead, of nothing at all). It doesn't make one want to eat, you can imagine.

But Gramma's to the rescue! I had saved and hoarded my last pot and only decided the hell with it, lets give it a go now, just 2 or 3 weeks ago. Out it came from the larder. In it went to soups, baked beans, casseroles, whatever I could think of and Oh Dounne, it got through my dead taste buds; not as powerfully as it did before this all hit me but enough to make a real difference. Soup which had just tasted like burnt foam rubber, now actually had flavour, not just heat but the glimmerings of real taste!

Baked beans were no longer neutral, they too had faint touches of taste. I can't tell you the difference this makes after months of dead, colourless, tasteless mush!! I thought I'd tell you, in case you hadn't come across this chemotherapy aspect before and I was sure this would interest you.

My treatment ends just before Christmas and it will take about another 2-3 months, perhaps a bit more, before my sense of taste gets back to normal. I shall be knocking back Gramma's from now till Doomsday!

More power to you and blessing on your splendid enterprise.

With real affection and Gratitude.

T. Charles.
Wantage

12.12.94

Nothing better when out sailing in the winter, seeing the crew's faces 'light-up' when they have soup with a dash of 'Extra-Hot'.

I wish you all the best and successful years ahead.

Mrs Blower.
Torquay

8.11.94

Dear Gramma's
I find Gramma's pepper sauce the easiest way to make food sing. I don't feel I could face the winter without it.

E. Smith
Lincoln

16.01.95

Dear Gramma's

I was so relieved to find I can order your sauces, as I depend on them to keep me healthy. For the last year I have taken a small amount of the mild sauce, with a spoonful of Marmite in boiling water, each time I felt a cold coming on. It banished the cold symptoms straight away and I have not had a cold for a year. Now my jar has run out and I have had a cold for two weeks.

As a Speech Therapist, I rely on my voice at work and I really can't do without Gramma's

Mrs .Michael
West Sussex

1994

Dear Dounne

Please send me another 2 jars of your Original Herbal Seasoning, I am running low and wouldn't like to be without it now. It is so good and goes with anything and everything.

C.M Seress
Packington

02.04.93

Dear Dounne

Thank you very much for the herbal pepper sauces, which I received some weeks ago, I must admit that after starting to consume the Hot (I generally have some sort of sandwich for lunch and apply to that) on a daily basis, I feel much better.

At the time I wrote previously, I had been suffering from a terrible flu which was incapacitating me. When I started using GRAMMA'S my cough became deeper and more productive, which in turn, helped (I believe) to expedite the virus.

I enjoy the HOT daily and sometimes incorporate the mild into my cooking at home (unfortunately, my husband does not like spicy things-but did remark that the spaghetti sauce I made-with 2 tsps of the Mild-was the best he'd ever had).

The beauty of the sauces, I believe, is that in addition to being hot in nature they are also very tasty. How many times have we eaten hot food which burnt our tongues but never gave us taste? I thank you very much for your help, for your creativity and for your determination.

With best regards, I am

Very truly yours.

Mrs Musty
Devon

15.12.89

Dear Dounne

I have been fortunate enough to receive a sample of Gramma's pepper Sauce from BBC Radio Devon for my husband, aged 81 who is partially disabled. Although only a small sample, I took it with me when we had to go to a fair in the New Forest to visit our son during the week and having a train delayed for 2 hours our flask of hot soup was a GOD-send. Also Saturdays (although I'm in my 70's) I work a whole day voluntarily at the Red Cross Shop with 2 others, one is 82 and again shared my little pot of pepper in cups of soup, so now its all gone.

Would you please send me a pot of Hot Pepper Sauce and could you enclose some leaflets to distribute amongst my elderly Red Cross Colleagues.

Thank you.

Mr & Mrs J.L. Raffael
France

25.3.95

Dear Dounne

A couple of years ago I had a perforated ulcer and almost died. After my operation, the doctors were amazed at my recovery (they thought it must have something to do with the way I eat). I started using Gramma's again right away a little on my pureed food and then more and more and I had absolutely no symptoms anymore! Gramma's, I told the doctors, would be good for me and it was and is!

Now about the 'jet lag' situation. Definitely I recommend Gramma's. We went to New York recently and I took a jar of Gramma's on the plane. We ate the whole jar (super-hot we're used to it!) on the trip. It definitely made me feel energised and relaxed not jittery. It's calming and I had no jet-lag whatsoever. My husband had very little, I didn't even consider his tiredness jet-lag just tiredness and Gramma's definitely makes a difference if you are eating airplane food. It heightens it! We always order vegan meals but never know what we'll get, if anything. So we take food along and Gramma's. I would venture to say that it is well worth carrying a few jars of Gramma's on any trip, even if you only have a cracker with Gramma's, its like eating instant energy, also in water or juice. By the way, I also want to say that Gramma's relaxes you enough to sleep, then to wake rejuvenated, at least this is my experience.

Miss Budd
Northampton
13 .03.95

Dear Madam

I have not felt so lethargic as I did. In addition I have a problem with having bad earache and catarrh. I recently had a nasty cold but through taking this product it would appear that my ears were not as affected as they have been previously and my throat and voice improved after only 3 or 4 days (previously taking about a month to improve).

Mr Baldwin   31 1 1996
Liverpool

I am very impressed with Zara's herbal drink, even though I have not been diagnosed with any of the maladies described in your declaration. A small problem with athletes foot was cleaned up unexpectedly and I am sleeping much better and have more energy. My mother who is 83 has had a growth on the back of her hand for about 5 years, the doctor was going to cut it out about 2 years ago but mother had been treating it herself with garlic and it had reduced considerably in size to less than half its original size. I suggested putting Super Hot Pepper Sauce on it and it really has reduced and is barely noticeable now. I reckon that your sauce is better than garlic in getting off unwanted lumps.

G & A Smith
Norfolk

21.01.94

Dear Sirs

HELP!!! - we've run out of your fantastic pepper sauce!!! Our food now seems tasteless without it.

Mrs Everett
London

8.11.94

Dear Mrs Moore

Six weeks ago you gave us, 'The Towns Women's Guild' a lecture on your 'Gramma's Herbal Sauce.' We all enjoyed it very much, I took your leaflet and read it, seeing so many things I believe I suffer from.

As I suffer from Diverticula Disease I tried it, because I have sweats nearly every night, some times 3 times a night, which disturbed my sleep. Taking the smallest portion at night in water, I had only 3 sweats in nearly 6 weeks, which I find is incredible and I must tell you of the success. I will take the nightcap hoping to get rid of the sweats, I also hope the other pains, arthritis etc, might react. I can say that on the whole I feel very well and hope that has something to do with your Herb Sauce

By the way I am 74 years old.

I. Thomas.
Dartford
Kent

30.03.95

Dear Gramma's

Purely by luck, while recently looking through the shelves of my local supermarket for various powered pepper sauce mixes, I happened upon your product. Having not seen your product previously, I was naturally sceptical and in buying some standard powdered mixes, 'risked' buying a jar of your 'mild sauce'. I cannot explain my surprise at the end resultant sauce I created with a little port, mushrooms and leeks-mingled with the natural juices from a prime fillet steak and a little Gramma's. I cannot overstate the perfection of taste surpassing to only the powdered mixes (which incidentally have all been 'binned'), but any peppered sauce I have ever been served in any restaurant worldwide.

For the future, I am now a dedicated fan of your sauce and am currently educating a good number of my friends (by giving them a jar as a gift). keep up the good work and if you have details of any other sauce mixes, please let me know.

Ms. Stevens
Birmingham

8.7.1990

Dear Dounne Moore,

After trying your Hot Pepper Sauce, I was compelled to write to you and tell you how valuable this product is to us, so that you can inform other mothers who are in the same position as myself.

I have a daughter named Ihantha, who is now 3 years old. From birth she has suffered from an acute case of asthma, has been in and out of hospital nearly every month and has had numerous medications ranging from steroids to inhalers which she had to take 3-4 times daily. The asthma was accompanied by lung infections and fits (violent coughing, then her eyes would roll back, she goes blue and loose consciousness). She has never been in perfect health and always troubled with her breathing. I lost all confidence in my doctor's treatment after two serious incidents which required intensive care. On one occasion due to a build-up of fluid, her lungs collapsed and on the other, her oxygen level fell dangerously low and I was told she could have been brain damaged. My fears intensified after my aunt died from an asthma attack. It got to the point where my own health was suffering as I couldn't sleep nights in case she had another fit.

At the beginning of March 1990, at the stage when I was totally distressed, I was introduced to your product and it was during a period when my daughter was continually plagued with chest infections and restless nights. I decided to try your hot toddy and she slept peacefully for the rest of the night and well into the day. I continued to give her the hot toddy for another 3 days and discontinued to antibiotics. By the fourth day she was totally free of congestion. My child has never been so well in her life.

Subsequently I have included the Hot Pepper Sauce in all her food and it is now a part of our lives, so much so that when she feels that an attack is coming, she goes straight to the cupboard, which contains an ample supply of your product and I have also cut her medication down to a minimum.

Dounne, I cannot thank you enough for giving us a new lease of life and I wish you every success.

CHAPTER VII.

Mail Order Information.

SPREADING THE WORD

Sharing the Wealth

CREATING A LIFE SAVING FOUNDATION:
'A Permanent Legacy.'

It is my intention to continue developing GRAMMA'S along the same spiritual, educational, sharing, healing and loving principles as originally started.

My passion has always been to help save the world and to somehow make a difference. The personal anguish suffered seeing children and animals sick, hungry, homeless or abused, leaves me in constant pain. Therefore, I've been inspired to transform **Gramma's** into a 'Charitable Foundation.' Once properly established, most of its profits would go towards supporting various charities. Thus creating a permanent legacy to help save the children of the future, animals and our beautiful environment.

ECO FRIENDLY

ONE JAR SYSTEM:

One of my attempts to reduce waste and cost, is by introducing a **'one jar system'** with the products in **refill sachet packs**. Therefore, When you have finished the product, simply purchase a sachet and refill the jar. In this way, 'one jar' would be re-used for many years and will only need replacing when it is damaged and can then be recycled. This represents an enormous saving in throw away jars, plus extra post & packaging charges. Individual replacement labels and lids can also be ordered at any time. These jars are certainly too good to throw away and will look impressive in your kitchen... (i.e. the Herbal Seasonings and Seaweed).

RE-USEABLE TEA BAGS: *(for the Herbal Teas).*

These are specially made tea bags, in 100% unbleached cotton voile material. They are very strong, so one bag will last many years before it will need replacing.

HIGH QUALITY HASSLE FREE HOME-SHOPPING:
(at the lowest prices).

Unlike most commercial businesses, who source the cheapest raw materials and use minimum quantities in order to produce cheap products at maximum profits, I source the best quality ingredients, regardless of price and use maximum quantities to produce the highest possible concentration at minimum profits, to ensure that everyone can afford them. In fact, many of the ingredients I use will not be found in the majority of commercial products, because they are too expensive and would double the retail price.

Additionally, modern manufacturers are primarily concerned with making money, they have no time for spirituality, much less for healing prayers.

Mail-order also enables me to cut out the middle-men such as stores, distributors and sales agents, making additional cost savings which are passed onto you.

Furthermore, to compensate you for the inconvenience of shopping by post, I provide 'FREE Postage & Packaging on UK orders' and have consolidated the overall charges on OVERSEAS orders. So you can buy as little or as much as you wish, at no extra cost. However, to help keep prices low, it is advisable to buy a minimum of 3-4 products per order.

SENDING PRODUCTS TO FAMILY & FRIENDS:

To save you time and money, I'll be happy to send products on your behalf to family and friends with your own personal message attached. Just supply their name, address and personal message on the order form.

DELIVERY:

Orders are despatched within 3-5 days. Therefore, the products should reach you within 5-7 days (UK) or 15-30 days (overseas). However, delays may occur if products are temporally out of stock or during festive holiday seasons (Christmas, New Years, Thanksgiving, Easter etc). So its advisable to order early during these periods.

HOW TO ORDER: *(by Post).*

Simply complete the order form and enclose your cheque or postal order (made payable to **Gramma's**) and post to;-

GRAMMA'S International Ltd

P.O. Box 218
East Ham
London E6 4BG
ENGLAND

Tel no.   020 8470 8751
Fax no. 020 8547 8755
website. grammas.intl.com
email.   info@grammas.intl.com

STATUTORY RIGHTS:

If any product does not reach you in excellent condition or you are dissatisfied in anyway, then please return it *(within 30 days)* to the mail-order address and I'll happily refund or replace it. Your statutory rights remain unaffected.

CONFIDENTIALITY:

Your personal details will be kept **strictly private & confidential**. Used only for my mailing list and will not be passed on to other persons.

NEWSLETTER:

Customers are kept informed and updated of new products and information by newsletter.

YOUR SUPPORT: - *('Spreading the Word').*

I'd like to ask for your personal support in helping me to fulfil my mission by 'spreading these wonderful messages' amongst your family, friends, clients, colleagues, doctors, vets and also send 'testimonies of healing,' so that I can continue to share these with others. By joining forces in this way, I hope that God's messages will eventually spread throughout the universe and contribute to making a difference to people's lives.

'Working together as a universal family in the consciousness of LOVE."

I am therefore delighted to offer you these amazing products with sincere 'LOVE' and wish you untold blessings, good health, happiness, peace and success in all your choices.

With Love and Light

DOUNNE.

MAIL ORDER FORM.

Prices are inclusive of **_postage & packaging._** Costs in pounds _(sterling);_ prices as of Jan 2001

PRODUCTS	UK	OVERSEAS	Quantity	TOTAL
1. CONCENTRATED HERBAL PEPPER SAUCES (2oz / 56g)				
Mild	£3.75	£5.75		£
Hot	£3.75	£5.75		£
Extra-Hot	£3.75	£5.75		£
Super-Hot	£3.75	£5.75		£
2. GRAMMA'S HERBAL PEPPER SAUCE (x3) - Gift Set				
GIFT SET	£11.75	£17.75		£
3. CONCENTRATED HERBAL SEASONING (3oz / 85g)				
Original	£3.95	£5.95		£
Hot & Spicy	£3.95	£5.95		£
Curry	£3.95	£5.95		£
Creole	£3.95	£5.95		£
4. *CONCENTRATED HERBAL SEASONING (REFILL SACHETS)				
Original	£3.50	£5.00		£
Hot & Spicy	£3.50	£5.00		£
Curry	£3.50	£5.00		£
Creole	£3.50	£5.00		£
5. GRAMMA'S SEASONING (x2) / PEPPER SAUCE (x1) - Gift Set°				
GIFT SET	£11.95	£17.95		£
6. ZARA'S HERBAL TEA (4oz / 112g) - Sachet				
Zara's Herbal Tea	£14.00	£15.50		£
7. WILLOW TEA (4oz / 112g) - Sachet				
Willow Tea	£9.50	£11.00		£
8. COTTON MUSLIN TEA BAG - for brewing Zara's & Willow Herbal Tea.				
100% unbleached cotton	£1.50	£2.00		£
9. GRAMMA'S 'SEAWEED' (4oz / 112g) - powdered Irish Moss				
Seaweed	£4.95	£6.50		£
10. A MISSION OF LOVE (Book)				
Book	£19.99	£24.50		£
11. MISSION - 'THE CELEBRATION OF LIFE'				
Greeting Card + Badge	£2.50	£3.00		£
Badge only	£1.00	£1.50		£
12. LIVING FOOD FOR HEALTH - (Book); Dr Gillian McKeith				
Book	£ 7.25	£9.00		£
13. WRAPPERS DELIGHT (Headwrap Book); Dee McCalla				£
Book	£(available August 2001)			£

Please allow 5-7 days for the U.K. delivery
30 days for overseas delivery

TOTAL DUE | £ |

PLEASE DO NOT SEND CASH IN THE POST.

MAIL ORDER FORM.

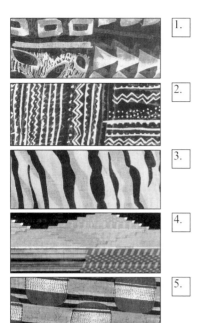

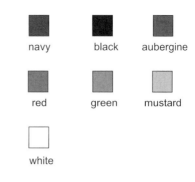

1.

2.

3.

4.

5.

navy   black   aubergine

red   green   mustard

white

Choose from our range of stunning African prints made from the finest quality cotton voile. Coordinate them with our vast range of plain colours to create your own unique styles.

(Material length approx. 3 metres).

ORDER FORM HEADWRAPS

PLAIN	U.K.	OVERSEAS	QTY	TOTAL
Red	**£12.95**	£14.95		£
Mustard	**£12.95**	£14.95		£
Aubergine	**£12.95**	£14.95		£
Green	**£12.95**	£14.95		£
Black	**£12.95**	£14.95		£
Navy	**£12.95**	£14.95		£
White	**£12.95**	£14.95		£

PATTERN	U.K.	OVERSEAS	QTY	TOTAL
1.	**£15.95**	£17.95		£
2.	**£15.95**	£17.95		£
3.	**£15.95**	£17.95		£
4.	**£15.95**	£17.95		£
5.	**£15.95**	£17.95		£

PLEASE DO NOT SEND CASH IN THE POST.

Please make cheques payable to: **Gramma's, P.O. Box 218, East Ham, London E6 4BG, ENGLAND.**

TOTAL DUE £

MAIL ORDER FORM.

(BLOCK CAPITALS PLEASE)

NAME: (Mr/Mrs/Ms) ··

ADDRESS: ···

···

POST CODE: ···

I enclose my cheque/postal order for £ ················· ,

made payable to:**Gramma's, P.O. Box 218, East Ham, London E6 4BG, ENGLAND.**

PLEASE DO NOT SEND CASH IN THE POST.

Signature: ······················ Date: ······················

* OVERSEAS PAYMENTS

must be made by **_bankers draft_**, issued from any of these four British international Banks: **HSBC, Lloyds, Barclays** or **National Westminster.**

INTRODUCE A FRIEND

'to the taste of Gramma's'

If you have a friend who may be interested in the products, simply complete their details below and I will send them a catalogue by return post. *Thank you.*

NAME (Mr/Mrs/Ms) ······································

ADDRESS ···

···

···

POST CODE ···

764.

The Final Word.

When I finally finished the book, God ended by saying;-

"There will be another edition of this book to come much later, which will contain a higher level of spiritual teachings.

   This is just the beginning of THE CIRCLE-OF-TRUTH"

It would be presumptuous of me to believe that I would be the one chosen to write the second book.

However, since '*life is eternal,'* what God calls 'much later' could mean a hundred, a thousand or even a million years time.

'In the Spirit' I wrote:-

"I'm now in absolute union with my Father, who visits me regularly. HE is fun, loving and spoils me but refuses to say what my future holds."

HIS reply:-

"It would spoil the wonderful exciting adventures of life, lessons and the beautiful surprises it holds and unfolds.

Just open your Soul to the universe and embrace all the love it offers.

Stretch your imagination and visualise your God-Self.

For I AM SPIRIT and so are YOU, created in MY image.

Hence, I AM GOD and so too are YOU... i.e. your authentic -self.

So strive to find your TRUE-SELF."

CHAPTER VIII.

Reference.

• USEFUL ADDRESSES AND INFORMATION.

REFERENCE

ESSENTIAL READING and INFORMATION.

USEFUL BOOKS 📖

BACK TO EDEN

The Jethro Klos Family
P.O.Box 1439
Loma Linda
CA 92354

An excellent factual book on ancient healing herbs & remedies.

THE WALLACE PRESS

4 Wallace Road
London N1 2PG
ENGLAND

Publishes a monthly journal called *'What the Doctors Don't Tell You.'* Factual case studies. Annual subscription £34.95 (U.K) and £42.95 (Overseas).

Their motto: *the informed consumer is a safer consumer.*

Tel No: 0207-354-4592

IN PURSUIT OF PURPOSE

Dr Myles Munroe
Bahamas Faith Minister

The Diplomat Centre
Carmichael Highway
P.O.Box N-9583
Nassau
Bahamas

A real understanding of life's purpose and how to pursue it.

THE BETRAYAL OF TRUST

Dr Vernon Coleman
C/o European Medical Journal

P.O.Box 30
Barnstable
Devon
EX32 9YU
England

Reveals the deadly dangers behind many prescribed drugs, unnecessary operations and animal experiments.

Price £9.95

ORGANISATIONS ✉

GREEN PEACE

Canonbury Villas
Islington
London N1 2PN

Tel No:- 0207-865-8100
International environmental organisation.

THE SOIL ASSOCIATION

86 Colston Street
Bristol
BS1 5BB

Tel No. 0117-929-0661
(promotes growing organic foods)

REFERENCE

ESSENTIAL READING and INFORMATION.

ORGANISATIONS ✉

(BAVA) - THE BRITISH ANTIVIVISECTION ASSC.

P.O.Box 73

Chesterfield

S41 0YZ

Tel No. 01246-230-474

A non-profit voluntary group whose purpose is to expose vivisection on moral, ethical, medical, scientific, environmental and economic grounds.

Donations welcome.

CANINE HEALTH CONCERN

P.O. Box 1

Longnor

Derbyshire SK17 OJD

ENGLAND

Tel No: 01382-320-467
Fax No: 01382-320-719
CODriscll@aol.com

Annual membership £12.00

A non-profit organisation promoting natural feeding and alternative health-care, who brought the issue of unnecessary and harmful annual pet vaccination to the attention of pet lovers, the media and the veterinary establishment.

CANCER TREATMENT
(*where to purchase*)

HYDRAZINE SULPHATE (60mg)

The Nutri Centre
7 Park Crescent
London
W1N 3HE
Tel No. 0207-436-5122

FRIENDS OF THE EARTH

26-28 Underwood Street
London
N1 7TQ
Tel No:- 0207-490-1555

International Environmental Group

.